ANTHROPOLOGY UNBOUND

A FIELD GUIDE TO THE TWENTY-FIRST CENTURY

THIRD EDITION

E. Paul Durrenberger and Suzan Erem

New York   Oxford

OXFORD UNIVERSITY PRESS

Oxford University Press is a department of the University of Oxford.
It furthers the University's objective of excellence in research,
scholarship, and education by publishing worldwide.

Oxford   New York
Auckland   Cape Town   Dar es Salaam   Hong Kong   Karachi
Kuala Lumpur   Madrid   Melbourne   Mexico City   Nairobi
New Delhi   Shanghai   Taipei   Toronto

With offices in
Argentina   Austria   Brazil   Chile   Czech Republic   France   Greece
Guatemala   Hungary   Italy   Japan   Poland   Portugal   Singapore
South Korea   Switzerland   Thailand   Turkey   Ukraine   Vietnam

Copyright © 2016 by Oxford University Press; © 2010 by Paradigm Publishers

For titles covered by Section 112 of the US Higher Education
Opportunity Act, please visit www.oup.com/us/he for the
latest information about pricing and alternate formats.

Published by Oxford University Press
198 Madison Avenue, New York, New York 10016
http://www.oup.com

Oxford is a registered trademark of Oxford University Press

Library of Congress Cataloging-in-Publication Data
Durrenberger, E. Paul, 1943-
   Anthropology unbound : a field guide to the 21st century / E. Paul Durrenberger
and Suzan Erem. -- Third edition.
      pages cm
   Includes bibliographical references and index.
   ISBN 978-0-19-026902-9 (pbk. : alk. paper) 1. Cultural relativism. 2. Anthropology--
Philosophy. 3. State, The. I. Erem, Suzan. II. Title.
   GN345.5.D87 2016
   301.01--dc23

                                                                    2015017546

Printing number: 9 8 7 6 5 4 3 2 1

Printed in the United States of America
on acid-free paper

Contents

ABOUT THE AUTHORS

Paul Durrenberger received a PhD in anthropology from the University of Illinois at Urbana in 1971. He has taught at Antioch College, Eastern New Mexico University, the University of South Alabama, the University of Iceland, and the University of Iowa and recently retired from Penn State University, where he was a professor. His many years of teaching introductory courses in anthropology are one foundation for this book. The other is his years of fieldwork among Lisu tribal people of the Thai highlands, Shan peasants in the lowlands of northwest Thailand, in Iceland, and in the United States. In the United States he has done ethnographic work with fishermen in Mississippi and Alabama, farmers in Iowa, and union members in Chicago and Pennsylvania. He has published numerous academic articles and books on these subjects. He collaborated with archaeologists John Steinberg and Doug Bolender in archaeological investigations of medieval Iceland. In 2014 he was awarded the Society for Applied Anthropology's Malinowski Award. He now lives in rural Iowa at Draco Hill (see http://Dracohill.org/) with his wife, Suzan Erem. With his longtime colleague, Gísli Pálsson, he edited a volume on the 2008 meltdown of the Icelandic economy, *Gambling Debt: Iceland's Rise and Fall in the Global Economy* (2014, University Press of Colorado). The memoir of his life as an anthropologist, *At the Foot of the Mountain: A Journey through Existentialism, Anthropology and Life* (2014, Draco Hill Press), is available at Amazon as the collection of his essays, *American Fieldnotes* (2014, Draco Hill Press). His webpage's address is http://www.personal.psu.edu/faculty/e/p/epd2/ and his e-mail address is epd2@psu.edu.

Suzan Erem earned her journalism and English degrees from the University of Iowa in 1985 and then spent more than a dozen years working in the labor movement before becoming a freelance writer. As an undergraduate, she was frustrated with anthropology that seemed confusing and irrelevant, but she saw its potential for making sense of the modern world. She is author of *Labor Pains: Inside America's New Union Movement* (2001, Monthly Review Press) and coauthor with Diana Dell of *Do I Want to Be a Mom? A Woman's Guide to the Decision of a Lifetime*. A long-time member of the National Writers Union, UAW Local 1981, Suzan's client list has included the American

Federation of State, County and Municipal Employees, International Brotherhood of Teamsters, Service Employees International Union, the American Federal Government Employees union, Leukemia & Lymphoma Society of Illinois, Infant Welfare Society, AIDSCare, and others. Suzan is the president of the Board and a co-founder of the Sustainable Iowa Land Trust (http://SILT.org/), organized a Slow Money branch in Iowa City, and is a member of the board of the Iowa Farmer's Union. She can be reached through her website: http://www.lastdraft.com/.

Paul and Suzan coauthored *Class Acts: An Anthropology of Service Workers and Their Union* (2005, Paradigm) and collaborated on a National Science Foundation study of unions in Chicago and Pennsylvania. They also coauthored a book on a 2000–2001 battle between Charleston longshoremen and the South Carolina attorney general called *On the Global Waterfront: The Fight to Free the Charleston 5* (2004, Monthly Review Press). They are married and live in Cedar County, Iowa, at Draco Hill (see http://Dracohill.org/).

Acknowledgments

We could start at Olduvai with the first of our ancestors who started to walk on two feet. But that's a long list. This isn't just a joke, it's also an important fact—none of us knows anything by ourselves. We are all in this together. We know our cultures the way we know our languages. And when we learn special parts of our cultures, like anthropology, the same still holds. So Paul thanks all of his teachers and all of his fellow students from undergraduate and graduate school—although it's a pretty long list.

There are some other anthropologists Paul needs to thank in addition. First are those who have written textbooks that he's read or used to teach, especially four who are now among the ancestors. He has used their ideas so much that they have come to seem like his own. These are the following:

Roger M. Keesing, *Cultural Anthropology: A Contemporary Perspective* (New York: CBS College, 1981). But that book was based on an earlier one, published in 1971 by Holt, Rinehart & Winston titled *New Perspectives in Cultural Anthropology*. That one was, in turn, based on a 1958 book by Roger M. Keesing's dad, Felix M. Keesing, titled *Cultural Anthropology: The Science of Custom*, also from Holt, Rinehart & Winston.

Charles F. Hockett, *Man's Place in Nature* (New York: McGraw–Hill, 1973).

Marvin Harris, *Culture, Man, and Nature: An Introduction to General Anthropology* (New York: Crowell, 1971).

Another is Walter Goldschmidt. His early work on industrial agriculture has been an inspiration, as has been his recent (2006) book on human evolution and the human condition, *The Bridge to Humanity: How Affect Hunger Trumps the Selfish Gene* (New York: Oxford University Press).

One of the things these books share is that they are sustained and coherent arguments, empirically supported theoretical statements. When you read them, you know what these anthropologists are saying and why they are saying it. They don't try to tell you everything there is to know about anthropology and they weren't put together by committees to try to make everyone happy.

We've returned to that tradition with this book, but many of our friends and colleagues shared their ideas about what such a textbook should be and do.

We especially thank Kendall M. Thu, Karaleah Reichart, and Josiah Heyman, who read earlier drafts of the first edition and helped us write a better book. We owe a special debt to Gísli Pálsson, who has contributed much to the substance of this book through his years of friendship and collaboration.

A number of other anthropologists read our proposal and outline and gave us their ideas and support early in the process, when we were just thinking about such a daunting undertaking as yet another introductory anthropology textbook. These include Edith Turner, Catherine Wanner, Myrdene Anderson, Sandy Smith-Nonini, Robert Muckle, Tom King, Lloyd Miller, Richard Feinberg, Alan Benjamin, Alan Sandstrom, Ann Hill, Barbara Dilly, Beverly Ann Davenport, Christian Zlolniski, Cynthia Miki Strathmann, David Griffith, Ana Pitchon, Garry Chick, Jim Acheson, John Steinberg, Joyce Lucke, Larry Kuzner, Lois Stanford, and Peter Richardson.

For the third edition, we can add our thanks to those colleagues who have used the book in their teaching and shared their students' reactions to it. They include Barbara Dilly, Lisa Gezon, Ana Pitchon, Karen Bankes, and Mark Levine. We have taken these student responses into account in preparing the third edition and thank the students and their professors for their help. We owe a special thanks to Robert Marshall, who corresponded with us to help us understand some subtle points in the book, Linda Jencson for her suggestions for the chapter on human variation, and James W. Carey of the Centers for Disease Control and Prevention for his help with the chapter on applied anthropology. We also thank those colleagues who provided sidebars for the third edition: Elizabeth Briody, Caroline Conzelman, Dimitra Doukas, Barbara Dilly, Erin Holland, Nina Jablonski, Kathi Kittner, Mark Nichter, John Postill, Kathleen Reedy, Ken Anderson, Bob Marshall, Patricia Clay, Grant McCracken, Charles McKelvey, a historian, and Robert Reich, an economist.

Suzan knows it's the anthropologists who make this book what it is and thanks all of those listed here and others she talked to about the project for their support and their enthusiasm for an affordable, accessible textbook. She also thanks Paul for his keen sense of when to fight over an edit and when to agree to one. Few spouses have the good fortune of the writing partnership we share.

We also thank the editor of Paradigm Publishers, Dean Birkenkamp, who encouraged us to take on this project when we complained to him about the lack of affordable comprehensive anthropology textbooks and who supported our approach to the topic, and Oxford University Press for taking it from there.

REVIEWERS

The authors also thank the reviewers OUP asked to review the previous edition and advise on this one: Beverly Bennett, Wilbur Wright College; William H. Fisher, College of William & Mary; Robert C. Marshall, Western Washington University; Paul Mullins, Indiana University–Purdue University Indianapolis; Riall W. Nolan, Purdue University; Bruce D. Roberts, Minnesota State University Moorhead; John P. Staeck, College of DuPage; and one anonymous reviewer.

Preface for Instructors

Colleagues:

There have been significant changes in our lives since the second edition was published. Paul has retired from Penn State. We have moved to our land in Iowa where we grow much of our own food and Suzan is working to organize a land trust that will help young people gain access to farm land to produce healthy food for local people. Finally, Oxford University Press purchased the book from Paradigm Publishers.

We're skeptical about the spate of new editions of the pricey introductory anthropology textbooks that keep coming off the assembly lines in response to surveys and focus groups. So why would we be complicit with our publisher to push a new edition of *Anthropology Unbound*? First, it's still as cheap or cheaper than any of the secondhand texts we're talking about, and we intend to keep it accessible to all students. We think this is important because we hold that all knowledge is collective property, not a commodity to enrich some or a weapon to impoverish others.

One change we're making in the third edition is to include a number of sidebars with more voices and topics. Some readers suggested the text was too continuous, unbroken. We therefore removed some material from the text to reorganize as sidebars as well. The Internet has changed the experience of reading. Instead of becoming immersed in the thoughts of a writer, readers are now accustomed to jump to short treatments of diverse topics as they jump from text to link and back or to another link. The sidebars provide something like that so that the text is less continuous, although the arguments remain so. The old-fashioned among you may ignore the sidebars and read continuously.

There are three kinds of sidebars. One is text that we wrote but thought would be better presented as asides or amplifications rather than as part of the argument. The second is illustrative texts from previously published works such as the excerpt from Malinowski's *Argonauts of the South Pacific* or Charles Frake's discussion of ecological anthropology. The third are sidebars we solicited specifically for this text.

We continue to emphasize those aspects of anthropology that make it unique. We have kept the long view of anthropology because we think it's important for us all to understand that we share common roots, that we are a single species, that racism is a feature of particular political and economic forms and not bred into us by our evolutionary history. But we have elimi-nated the chapter that described the process of our evolution as well as the prologue that told an Old Norse origin story. We included these in the first and second editions because creationism was on the rise during the admin-istration of George W. Bush, then in office in the United States, which favored rhetoric and policies that denied the value of science and of our understand-ings of evolutionary processes. The climate change denial movement spon-sored by energy corporations has kept this outlook alive in the United States, but the experience of the facts of climate change are so overwhelming that it has lost much of its salience. Evidence concerning the evolution of our spe-cies accrues so rapidly today that it requires separate treatment.

We've also dropped the chapter devoted to language. We included it in the first two editions because it is one of the traditional fields of anthropol-ogy, but chiefly because it provides an accessible understanding of the differ-ence between the facts we can observe (e.g. the sounds of a language) and the meanings that people attribute to them (e.g. how languages group the sounds into categories) or etics versus emics. This is an important distinction, but we think it is more effective to make it in other ways so that language does not distract from the main point.

We've added a chapter on applied anthropology that may offer some students ideas for jobs in anthropology beyond the academy.

We've kept some of the material from the second edition, including the following:

- Anthropological perspective on the global economic crisis;
- How the crisis is relevant for understanding class, government, labor, culture, and other dimensions of contemporary life;
- Analysis of the reasons for Iceland's recent economic collapse as an example;
- The discussion of Islamic and American fundamentalisms as reli-gious revitalization movements to provide context for discussing 9/11 and subsequent events; and
- The treatment of the concept of agency, including a critique of the individualism of conventional economic theory, seen as a projection of a class-based ideology onto nature.

We're also persuaded of the importance of feedback **loops,** as all of the dia-grams throughout the text emphasize. We've had some feedback from people who used the second edition about how they and their students responded. The text has been successful in drawing students' attention to current events and to what is going on outside their families, classrooms, colleges, and uni-versities and giving them the means to understand the mind-warping changes in our world and their relationships to those changes.

We thought we could amplify that dimension of the book and bring in important contemporary events, including the global financial crisis that the first edition accurately anticipated. Sociocultural anthropology differs from other social sciences because it is holistic, comparative, and ethnographic. But, as we pointed out in the first edition, it's hard to know how to ply our craft of ethnography to help us understand processes such as the World Bank or International Monetary Fund (IMF) policies and practices that aren't confined to any specific locale. That's where anthropology's practices of holism and comparativism help.

We have the impression that despite the feeling that events are moving at lightning speed all around us, a view from a little farther away suggests that maybe most of this has happened before one way or another, if we could stay still long enough to think about it or read enough to learn about it. As the American translation of the old French saying has it, "The more things change, the more they stay the same."

We show students how they can use the analytical perspectives of anthropology to understand the processes that produce the headlines—today's, tomorrow's, and yesterday's.

And we discuss places where there are no newspapers or headlines, the kinds of places where anthropologists have plied our trade for a couple of hundred years now until those places themselves have been swallowed up in larger processes. So that we don't lose track of the people of the planet that our discipline is all about, we've focused equally on the people those processes affect.

The first edition was published in the midst of the George W. Bush administration. Since that time, there have been political developments in the United States that few would have then predicted. That shows how inaccurate our media-derived political categories and questions can be. The news was that a woman and an African American vied for the Democratic nomination for president. The news was that the African American won.

These events achieved great symbolic salience as people could celebrate what appeared to be the triumph of social mobility over entrenched prejudices about race and gender. And Barack Obama has given the symbols substance as his administration made great changes within the limited range of acceptable American politics. Although we celebrate these changes such as a more accessible health-care system, we endeavor to keep our readers aware of the underlying causal factors at work—the immense power of corporations to shape our politics and our culture, the role of finance in capitalism, and the way economic systems work. For instance, health care and university tuition are not rights of citizens in the United States, as they are in most European countries. So, although small changes are significant, we should remember that they are small.

We do not want to be read as pro-Democratic or anti-Republican because we are neither. We are pro-human. That is the view we endeavor to communicate to our readers so that it can become a part of their moral, ethical, and political vocabularies alongside the more readily available American media representations of liberal/conservative and Republican/Democratic. We do that because in our minds that is the end point of a discipline devoted to the scientific study of humankind.

In the third edition we do not shrink from the ethical stance we developed in the first edition. We maintain the value of relativism; the ethical absolute that every person on the planet deserves no more or less than one share of the planet; the imperative that as students begin to understand more about the world and its people, it is their obligation to put those lessons into practice in their daily and work lives. We tell them what we believe . . . that acting together, we can change the world. And we urge them to act with us and other like-minded people.

Other changes include some new questions to provoke thought and discussion at the ends of chapters. We hope these will help spur instructors and students to come up with more questions, since today's events provide such fertile ground for that. Paul used to have his students come up with their own essay and discussion questions (with the ominous threat that if none of the questions is adequate, *he'll* come up with one for them) because that exercise alone requires a substantial understanding of the concepts he is relating. We hope you'll encourage your students to do that too. One of the things we emphasize is the importance of understanding the relationship between the question and the answer. Because questions largely determine answers, the questions deserve more attention than students customarily give them.

You can guide your students with the first principle that every person deserves one share of the planet and ask them to work out how each situation they find important diverges from that principle—and why. Who is benefiting more than others? Who gets hurt? Who has the power to make a difference? Could all of the people working together make a difference? And so on . . . they don't need answers so much as they need ways to think for themselves. That's what we were trying to inculcate with this book—more aware, conscious, and thoughtful citizens.

So here's a third edition, and these are our reasons for commending it to you and to your students. We hope the book helps you to help them. We know that a book isn't sufficient. It takes you, the teacher, to breathe life into anthropology, to make it real to students with your examples, your stories, and your passion.

We hope the new edition helps and we encourage you and your students to get hold of us and let us know how it's working out. Without feedback, there is no evolution.

EPD & SE
Draco Hill, Iowa

Introduction, or How to Read This Book

This is a book about anthropology—the study of people and their cultures. It will give you an idea of what anthropology has learned, how anthropologists think things through, the kinds of evidence we use, and the explanations we have worked out. It will give you a good tool for understanding the complexities of the world around you. As we prepared the second edition, our world was experiencing an economic crisis, but there's nothing mysterious about it, as you'll come to understand. The first edition accurately predicted that crisis. As we prepare the third edition, there is some hope for an economic recovery in the United States, but it is not at all a sure thing and the causal factors of that crisis are still in place and even stronger. Meanwhile the economic conditions of most Americans continue to decline. There is little reason to hope that we have developed a sustainable economic system. But this book will tell you what you can do about it personally and collectively, since that is a question we often get from students new to anthropology.

We're going to start that process here by explaining how to read this book. First, why should you read it?

The best reason is because you want to learn what anthropology can tell you, what it knows. If that's why you picked it up, great, read on. But lots of folks will probably be reading it because a professor assigned it for a class. That's fine, too. Professors assign some of the world's best books for students to read in classes.

You learned the drill for classes a long time before you got here. People have been teaching you since about the time you could walk about how to go to classes and take exams and sit still in a chair for an hour or two and how to pretend to be listening while your mind is off somewhere else or someone is texting you on your phone.

How much of those lectures contained information you could use for anything? Not much. Except you could use it for getting out of that class and moving on to the next one and so on until you got here. But what's the point of it all? Only a tiny part of all that knowledge teaches you how to fix computers, run a business, or help sick people in hospitals. What is all the rest of it for?

Let's see what an anthropologist would do with this question. We want to figure out what the role of schools is in our society and why we have them. To do that, we must be able to imagine something different—for instance, a society in which you learn everything you need to know just by growing up and people never see the inside of a school. That's the kind of vision anthropologists have; that's the kind of questions we ask.

So, why do we go to school? An anthropologist named Jean Lave observed that kids who don't do well in school could do complex computations to figure out a number of bowling scores at the same time. How could they do that and *not* do well in math in school? She also noted that people who *have* been to school don't use mathematics the way they were taught. When they are shopping and trying to figure out what jar of peanut butter to buy, people don't figure out the cost per ounce for the big jar and the little one and then select the best buy, although that's what we were all taught to do.

What we really do, she found out by observing lots of people, is compute by ratios. The big jar is about twice as much as the small one and costs less than twice as much. So it's the best buy.

Lave asked, if people aren't in school to learn the math they actually use, what are schools worth? In terms of the things we actually do, she came to the same conclusion you probably have come to. Not much.

So why do we have them? Why do we pay for them? Why do we hire teachers to teach if nobody is doing what they teach?

Lave's answer is that in the old days people knew their place. There were aristocrats and commoners. Everyone knew aristocrats were better than commoners, and everyone knew how to get along in that system. But in democracies nobody is supposed to be any better than anybody else. If that's so, how are we going to decide who gets the good jobs and who gets the bad ones? On the basis of merit.

Merit is something you earn. Nobody gives it to you. You aren't born with it. The problem was, how do you assign merit if everyone is going to be equal? One answer is to use school performance.

So, Lave argues, schools are the way of assigning merit to individuals in democratic systems. Many of you know exactly where you stood in your high school graduating class. You probably feel pretty good about that if you were somewhere toward the top. And if you were toward the bottom, chances are you didn't go to the next level of school. If you did, all the better for you. Why would we say that? Isn't that rewarding someone for underperforming? For being less than meritorious? It could be, if you think that how people do in school is really a measure of their worth. But Lave's point is that it is not. It isn't even a good measure of how good they are at math, something that's supposed to be the strong suit of schools, that's supposed to be something you can only learn in school.

Is this wrong? Is it good?

One of the things anthropology teaches, and one of the things we'll talk about a lot in this book, is that we don't make judgments like that. To understand, we cannot judge. Our job is to understand and explain, not to judge. More on that later.

We're not asking whether that's good or bad; we just want to understand it. If you understand what's going on, you may be able to do something about it. We'll come back to that one later, too.

Here's another thing about anthropology. We all agree that the world is complex. But instead of saying, "Let's simplify the world with an assumption such as 'All things being equal,'" anthropologists say, "Let's understand the complexity of it in real life."

Reality is complex; it's there in all of its horrible and beautiful complexity. Our challenge is to figure out how to get along with that. Our different cultures give us different ways of doing that so that we don't all have to start from scratch. We learn from watching our parents. It doesn't matter much what they tell us. It matters what they do.

If your parents tell you that they love each other but all you ever see them do is fight, you don't believe what they tell you. It isn't true to your experience. If they tell you that money isn't everything but spend all their time working and worrying about money, you don't believe it because it's not true to your experience. But you also learn what you're supposed to say.

The same goes for school. If your math teacher tells you to compare values by figuring out the per-unit price and comparing them, you can do it, but you also know that's not what you do when you're shopping. People are good at learning by doing. And we're good at learning what we're *supposed* to know and say. Walter Goldschmidt even says that's the most important and basic thing about being human. It's bred into us as a species by natural selection.

That's why you're going to read this book and learn how to use it to help you get a good grade in your anthropology course. But we're going to try to make it close to your experience, too, so that you don't have to make that same leap as you do when you say the "right answers" to questions about love, money, and math.

But that comes with a price. The price is that you're going to have to give up some cherished ideas or at least suspend them for a while. If you want to understand your experience, it is necessary to go beyond the easy answers your culture provides for you. That's what anthropology is all about.

In 2014 we went to visit a friend of Paul's. They'd been in graduate school together. He told us about how his daughter went to college and returned for her first visit and said she'd learned that everything about America was wrong. She didn't want to believe that. Neither did he. But they're Americans. If they were Icelandic or Bolivian or Vietnamese, they might well agree. You might get that from reading this book or from this course and maybe other courses. And if you're Icelandic, Bolivian, or Vietnamese, that might seem straightforward. But if you're American, you may not want to believe it.

The United States may have a strong military, and sometimes the economy is strong, but they don't translate into much for average citizens. Don't Americans own their own country? At least through retirement fund holdings of stock? No. Eighty percent of the value of stock is owned by the richest 10 percent and the 1 percent own 35 percent of the value of stocks. A ranking of livability ranks the United States in sixteenth place. The Social Progress Index puts the United States at twenty-third for cell phone and Internet access, seventieth for health, sixty-ninth for ecosystem sustainability, thirty-first for personal safety, thirty-fourth for access to water and sanitation, and thirty-ninth for basic education.

So who ranks high on the Social Progress Index? New Zealand is No. 1. Then come Switzerland, Iceland, and the Netherlands. Canada is seventh, Germany twelfth, Britain thirteenth, and Japan fourteenth. All of them meet the needs of their citizens better than the United States. Those are some of the things the United States is doing wrong. China is ninetieth and Mongolia is eighty-ninth. Ukraine is sixty-second and Russia is eightieth. In the United States the economy has done better than that of many other countries, but most people don't share in that success. For instance, the U.S. economy out-performed France's, but 99 percent of the French people enjoyed more gains than 99 percent of Americans. The average French person did better than the average American. Later in the book you will learn the reasons behind this.

The United States ranked No. 1 in one international Gallop poll in 2013, however: on the question of which country is the greatest threat to world peace, Pakistan was No. 2. The more concentrated economic power is, the more it controls legislation, and in the U.S. economic power is concentrated at the top while the government is one of, for and by corporations, as we will explain later.

So how can we go beyond the cheerleading and shouting? There's a method for doing that. It's scientific method. It's a method for bringing what we say closer and closer in line with what we experience. When we think we know what we're talking about, we are obliged to check it against experience. If we agree that other people are like us, then it follows that we're the smartest and most observant people on the planet and we are compelled to agree that anyone else could see the same things we see—that's what we call *reliability.* And we have to make sense to other people—that's what we call *validity.* Scientific method is a way of keeping what we say connected to what everyone can experience.

There are many connections going on here, but there's a way to keep track of these connections. Like all of the things we mentioned, it is a matter of putting simple things together until they seem complex or the other way around—breaking complex things down into simple relationships so that we can check them one by one. We can do this with words and with pictures. So far we've been doing it with words, talking about culture. Let's take something more concrete and develop some pictures to go with the words.

Eric Schlosser (2002) is not an anthropologist. He's a journalist who wrote a book called *Fast Food Nation.* It's not an **ethnography** (we're going to highlight every vocabulary word we think you'll need to understand to build the concepts that come later; you'll find the words in the back of the book in a glossary), which is what anthropologists call it when they live with a people and observe everything they do and say, but Schlosser compiled a lot of information about relationships that have gone into forming our culture. Paul's students have liked the book, so you might want to have a look at it some time.

Schlosser wants to understand all facets of fast food. He starts out talking about cars and the American love of our cars. What do cars have to do with fast food? Some restaurant owners in California made the first innovations in fast food to mass-produce hot meals for people in the same way that factories mass-produce cars, but they might have stayed in California if there wasn't more and more demand for fast food.

Automobile companies bought up the interurban and urban railroad systems and destroyed them so that people would have to either drive or ride the buses the car companies made. When mass transit was destroyed, people bought cars. Demand for fast food came as people drove more, and the interstate highway system intensified that trend. The interstate system started out as a defense project to link the United States after World War II, but it became a way for people to drive longer and longer distances. When more people had cars and there were more highways to drive on, people moved into suburbs, and developers built what we now call sprawl.

Why fast food? Because of cars. More interstate highways, more cars, and more sprawl. Cars make sprawl possible, and sprawl means people need cars because there's no alternative mass transit. We can make a map of these relationships (see Figure I-1). Figure I-1 means more cars, more fast food. But it's not that simple. More cars mean more sprawl and more interstate highways. At the same time, there are more interstate highways, more fast food, and more sprawl. Finally, there are more interstate highways, more cars, and so on. Each part reinforces the other parts and each part increases.

Take some time to study the diagram, because you'll see a lot more of them in this book, and they get hairier as we go along. Here are some things to look out for in these diagrams. How many boxes are there? Here there are four. What are the boxes? Here they are "fast food," "interstate highways," "sprawl," and "cars." Next, how many arrows are there? Here there are eight.

We expect that, like it or not, next time you get into a car, you will see things a little differently. Maybe you will start asking yourself and others questions. For instance, where is the mass transit system where you live? If there is one, how well does it work? Why is every place connected with

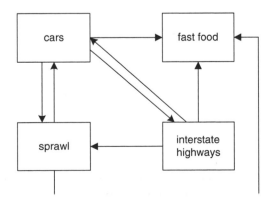

Figure I-1 U.S. fast food system.

highways? This book will help you figure out what some of those questions are and how to answer them.

We think this sort of thinking contributes to democracy by helping people be more aware of the conditions of their own lives. We've been driving down interstates when we got hungry. We've been in a hurry to get home after a long trip. We've pulled over at a fast food joint and got burgers and fries. We've both read Schlosser and lots of other things that tell us that fast food isn't the healthiest choice. We've read lots about different corporations, and we've experienced some of that. We know about congestion and sprawl and global warming, and there we were being part of the problem. We were eating unhealthy food, contributing to a corporation that treats its workers unjustly and to an agricultural system that's unsustainable, and spewing hydrocarbons into the atmosphere as we did it.

Pretty reprehensible folks, aren't we? That's why we're not going to try to preach to anyone. We felt like we didn't have much choice. And we like burgers and fries. We don't advocate taking it as far as Morgan Spurlock, the guy who made the movie *Super Size Me*. He wanted to find out what would happen if he ate nothing but McDonald's food for a month. It's not pretty. Part of his test was that he had to eat everything on the menu at least once. So he had lots of choices.

Sooner or later, anthropologists come to that question of choice. When do people have real choices and when do they not? We have a fancy word for that: **agency**. It's the idea that people act as agents on their own behalf, that they understand the resources available to them and use them in their own interests. It involves the choices you can make.

If you're an American, this may be a required course. You have no choice if you want your degree. You have to take it. But maybe it's required only for certain programs of study. Nursing. Once you decide to take nursing, you have to take anthropology. But you could have decided on business, and then it wouldn't be required. If you are in a business program, you're probably taking anthropology as an elective. You can choose it or not. It's your choice. Finally, nobody said you had to go to college. You could have gone to work full-time in a fast food joint instead of part-time as a student. But someone probably told you that if you went to college, you'd have a better job and make more money later, so it would be worth the investment of time, effort, money, and putting some other things in your life on hold. Some people you know from high school went straight into the military. Our military doesn't have a draft right now. It's voluntary. It's a choice. But if you talk to those high school pals, we bet quite a few will say that it didn't look like a choice to them. There were no other jobs, and the military was something they could do that promised a future. We hope they all make it back, and we sure don't blame them for going that way. Maybe you're a returning vet and you can help your classmates understand these things.

What if you lived in a society that said you don't have to go to college, or med school, or law school and you could be paid just as much as someone who did? What does that do to your choices? Or what if they said, "If you want to go to college, we'll pay the tuition and buy your books?" What if you could decide to join the military just because you want to experience the discipline, the world travel, and the skills the military has to offer?

If you're not an American, chances are you and all of your classmates think that education is a right, like the right to housing and health care. Then you need to understand just how alien these ideas are to Americans who believe in fundamental rights to freedom of speech, religion, assembly, and the right to bear arms, rights that are not even important in countries that grant their citizens what they need for secure lives as rights.

So agency—the resources you have and your knowledge of them—depends on your point of view, on where you are in a system and what choices that system offers you. It also depends on your past choices, like the choice to go to college. But the choices that are available depend on the choices other people have made, like the fact that somebody set up the college you're attending. In democratic societies, people are supposed to be able to make lots of choices about the significant things in their lives.

But now, let's go back to how to read the kinds of diagrams you are going to come across in this book. Here's some more vocabulary: we can call *fast food* in our diagram a **dependent variable**. Dependent variables hang on, or depend on, every other variable in the system. It is the thing we want to explain. Every other thing in the system is also a variable. A **variable** is something that can be more or less—it varies. So there can be more cars or fewer cars; more miles of highway or fewer; more or less sprawl. Each of these variables is an **independent variable** because each one causes or has something to do with the amount of fast food, the dependent variable.

Most real-world relationships aren't simple. For instance, more cars mean more highways, and more highways *also* mean more cars. These two are **interdependent variables**, like *cars* and *sprawl*. When an increase in one variable means an increase in another and *that* increase means an increase in the first one, we have a circle, or a loop, as we call it. The more of the first, the more of the second; the more of the second, the more of the first. This is what we call a **self-intensifying loop** or process. It keeps growing with nothing in the system to stop it.

All such processes grow or increase. Not only do they increase, but also the rate of increase increases, so they are exponential. Instead of being straight-line processes that grow at the same rate, they grow faster and faster.

Figure I-2 is an **exponential** curve of growth. You've probably noted that there's no limit here. That's one observation about exponential systems. But the other observation is that, unlike a mathematical equation, in real life there is always some limit. No such curve of growth is **sustainable**. That means that any time we see a system that contains self-intensifying loops, we are looking at a system that's more or less doomed to destroy itself.

The classic example is yeast. A few yeast cells multiply, and there are more. But each one multiplies at the same rate, so the rate of growth of the whole population is exponential. Yeast consumes sugar and produces alcohol as waste. Soon our liquid is teeming with reproducing yeast cells, each

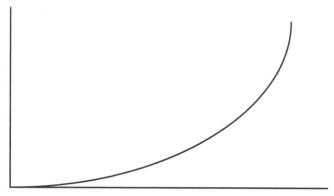

Figure I-2 Exponential curve.

one producing alcohol and consuming sugar, until the level of alcohol becomes toxic and they all die. Then we take over and drink what they left us. Good for us. Bad for the yeast.

To understand these diagrams, you'll need to remember the ideas of dependent variable—the thing we're trying to understand or explain; independent variables—the things in the system that influence the dependent variable; interdependent variables—variables that influence each other; self-intensifying loop—a circular relationship between two or more variables that keeps increasing each variable; and exponential curve of growth—a process whose rate of increase increases.

One more important idea about these systems is indirect relationships. *Sprawl* doesn't directly determine *highways*, but more sprawl means more cars, and more cars means more highways, so the relationship is indirect, through *cars*.

Schlosser goes on to show how sprawl means increased land prices around cities, and that means increased land taxes and inheritance taxes and how these contribute to the decline of farms; how the interstate highway system makes possible industrial food preparation far away from the places people eat it and how *that* contributes to industrial food production and the destruction of local markets and economic linkages. Nowadays, slaughterhouses don't depend on the pigs from an independent farmer. Family farmers are out of business, and corporations own the farmland, pigs, and slaughtering factories. The family farms that are left are contracted to big corporations that dictate everything they do and how they do it, so they're the same as employees, not really independent farmers at all.

At the other end, industrial food preparation means deskilling of jobs like cooking, and that means firms can use cheap and untrained labor; and that means low incomes, especially for teenagers who work in fast-food places; and low income contributes to people being depressed and dropping out of school; and that contributes to poverty and crime. Meanwhile, the cheap labor means more profits for the corporations and high pay for corporate officers. Those two things, the high profit rate and high pay for corporate officers, mean that corporations have money to contribute to political candidates who agree to support their view of the world and push legislation that favors the whole process, so the firms and their officers get involved in politics and use their influence to keep the minimum wage low and to pass anti-union laws so that the corporations will have access to cheap labor.

There are laws that are supposed to regulate job safety. The Occupational Safety and Health Administration (OSHA) is supposed to enforce the laws. It depends on Congress for funding. If it has no funds, it can't enforce the laws. Schlosser documents how corporate involvement in politics has made OSHA's job next to impossible.

Schlosser also shows how corporate politics gets firms subsidies and loans from the government, a kind of welfare for corporations. Auto manufacturers and banks in the United States went to the government for bailouts and the country was outraged at the millions of dollars in bonuses, from tax money given through those bailouts, that corporate bosses received, even as their companies and banks failed. Where else can you get a job that pays millions in bonuses for totally screwing up?

There are also effects on our culture. Many people think that corporations are business, that business is not involved in government, and that government is not involved in business. That's wrong, but it suits corporations and politicians if people think that, so they invest money in creating those ideas and pounding them into Americans from all directions, including in school.

Here anthropologists borrow an idea from political science. **Hegemony** means when one country rules or controls others. So, we could say the Soviet Union used to have hegemony over Ukraine and Kazakhstan. Anthropologists use the same word when one group has power over another, especially by controlling the way they think. So we can say that in the United States, corporations are hegemonic, meaning that they have a lot of power to control peoples' culture and everyday thinking patterns by telling us what's natural, normal, and just something we have to accept.

If you want to, you can put all of these relationships in a diagram, starting with the part that we provided earlier with cars, highways, sprawl, and fast food. If you read Schlosser's book, you can add in meat packing, costs to local governments, immigration, turnover rates, drug use, union busting, insurance rates, and insurance fraud as well as subsidies to households, cultural hegemony, and the spread of disease.

Does that make the fast food industry good or bad? It wasn't that good for Morgan Spurlock, the *Super Size Me* guy, but he could quit. Remember, it's not up to anthropologists to judge, just to understand. Maybe it wasn't that good for Spurlock, but it might have been good for some of the people who worked in McDonald's. When the anthropologist Katherine Newman did the ethnography of fast food workers in New York's Harlem, she found that the jobs were pretty good, given everything else going on around them. Fast food joints gave them an alternative to their family lives that weren't always that good, a group of people to be with, a constructive way to structure their time that didn't include joining a gang or breaking the law, some income, and these workers actually did better in school than kids without jobs.

Good for beer and wine drinkers is bad for yeast. Good for corporate officers may be bad for their workers; good for workers may be bad for corporate officers; good for politicians may be bad for their constituents. Schlosser documents a number of such relationships. From inside the system, we can say what's good for whom. Within a system, we can make judgments. We are citizens of democracies. We can ask what kinds of things make them more or less democratic. If we value democracy, the things that make our societies more democratic are good.

Aside from questions of good and bad, we can ask questions about sustainability. Spurlock's diet wasn't sustainable. His doctor said he would have died. Wherever there are self-intensifying loops, the system is not sustainable. At the same time, sustainable systems may look a lot like life in the Stone Age and that wasn't sustainable in the long run. We know that because nobody lives that way anymore. The remaining hunters and foragers who in some ways resemble it are parts of larger systems. The fierce hunters of the Amazon sell their game, buy shotguns and ammunition, and use factory-made machetes. The burning of forests to clear them for pasture for cattle even determines the kind and number of animals that live in the forests for them to hunt. These hunters are as much parts of the global system as anyone else.

So what can you do with the knowledge you get in this and other anthropology courses? Well, you could become an anthropologist, but given the job market these days, that might not be a good choice. Many anthropology instructors are adjunct staff. They're not on the old-fashioned tenure track when a professor could get tenure after six years or so of apprenticeship. Universities found that was costing them too much. They could contract out the teaching of courses to highly qualified people at much less expense. So they started replacing tenure-track faculty with adjunct staff.

Ask your instructor about this system. But there are a lot of other things a person can do with anthropology. About half of all anthropologists in the United States work outside universities. They work for Intel, Xerox, Motorola, and other large corporations. They work for government and international agencies like the National Marine Fisheries Service, the Park Service, the Centers for Disease Control, the World Bank, the Agency for International Development, and the military. They work for marketing firms and in product development. We've asked some of our colleagues to tell you about their work in some of these places. And for many of these jobs you don't need a PhD. You do need to be able to think like an anthropologist, and we hope this book will help with that.

SUMMARY—HOW TO USE THIS BOOK

Keep track of things like definitions and relationships. Work through all of the diagrams. Take the time to read the text and then study the diagrams.

You can test yourself by reproducing the diagram. If you can do that, you understand the process. If you can't, it's a good idea to go back and try again.

Note that when we talk about Trukese or Lisu or other people, we talk in the present tense, although we're referring to research that happened decades ago. That's called writing in the "ethnographic present." It's a way of talking about what anthropologists have learned from that culture in that time, even if it's changed a lot since then.

Rocket scientists aren't smarter than you; they just did the work to understand the systems and relationships that have to do with rockets. This isn't rocket science. It's a whole lot more complex than that. That doesn't mean you have to be a genius to understand it. You just have to keep your eyes and your mind open.

If you do that, you will come to see yourself and your society and your culture in a different way. You will start to ask hard questions when you read the newspaper or hear the news. And you will have a way of beginning to answer some of those questions.

Do this, and you become a better citizen. If lots of people do this, we will have better societies. In democracies, that's a good thing.

One author gets down and dirty! Paul Durrenberger is in over his head in this field-work in Iceland. *Photo by Rita Shepard. Used with permission.*

Science Basics

Anthropology asks how cultures and societies work and how they got the way they are. It asks about the history of our species from the beginning until now. It asks what kind of animals we are, how we got this way, in what ways that affects our cultures, and—the other way around—in what ways our cultures affected the kind of animals we are. To answer these questions, anthropologists specialize in one of four subfields.

Biological anthropology focuses on the history of our species, how we came to be the kinds of animals we are, and the role of culture in the process—questions about our biological nature and its relationship to culture. **Archaeology** concentrates on gathering and interpreting material evidence we can use to understand the histories of our cultures. **Linguistic anthropology** asks about the nature of language and how it is related to culture. **Sociocultural anthropology** is about how contemporary cultures and societies work and how they got the way they are. To these traditional four fields of anthropology, many add a fifth, **applied anthropology**: the use of anthropological insights and methods to solve practical problems.

Biological anthropology overlaps with anatomy and biology; archaeology can overlap with history and classics; linguistic anthropology overlaps with linguistics; and sociocultural anthropology can overlap with economics, political science, religious studies, history, comparative literature, and other social sciences and humanities. Being a sociocultural anthropologist is a lot like being a professional undecided major.

The focus of this book is on sociocultural anthropology. We're not so much concerned with what anthropology *is* as with what it *knows*—the results of the work of many anthropologists for the past hundred years and more. But to understand that, it is necessary to go into some basic assumptions.

Three things make sociocultural anthropology distinct from other social sciences or humanities:

- It is holistic.
- It is comparative.
- It is ethnographic.

Holism means seeing things as connected. Instead of looking at religion, literature, politics, economics, or history as separate spheres of life, anthropologists see them as connected. Anthropologists think in terms of systems.

3

A **system** is a set of elements that are connected such that if you change one of them, you also change the others. So we might ask how changes in an economic system affect the political system and how both of these affect religion, how all of these affect literature, and how literature and religion affect economics. Something about the religion may affect how people understand their history, and how people understand their history might affect their political system.

Everything may be connected to everything else, but some of the connections are stronger and more important than others. Although knowing that everything is connected may not help us understand the price of tea in China, as they say, knowing about systems of trade does.

Comparative means noticing and explaining similarities and differences among many different systems. For example, some social systems have institutional forms known as states, but others do not. Anthropologists ask what else goes along with states. To answer questions like this, we compare as many examples as we can to find out what other things always go with states and what things go with not having states.

Ethnographic means that we base our ideas of how any given system works on detailed local description. We don't rely on data sets from the Census Bureau or the Department of Planning. Ethnography means learning about the systems and people we want to understand by the closest observation we can manage. It often means living with the people, doing **fieldwork**. Bronisław Malinowski was one of the first to explicitly describe the process of ethnographic fieldwork in his 1922 book, *Argonauts of the Western Pacific*. His language is pretty old-fashioned, but his lessons remain true to this day.

There's a saying that to understand all is to forgive all. If you could really understand all the circumstances and reasons another person does things, it would all make sense to you, and you would see that you would do the same thing if you were that person. If you would do the same thing, you can't judge the other person. The flip side of this is that if you want to understand someone, you don't judge the person.

So understanding means getting into another person's skin. Ancient Aztec people took that idea farther than most of us would want to when they skinned their war captives and wore their skins in ceremonies. But we could understand the practice if we could get into their, well, systems of culture and society. To do that, we can't start off with the opinion that it's horrid to skin other people. That stops the questions and makes a conclusion before we start.

To do fieldwork means to suspend judgments and opinions and be open to understanding other ways of life. Anthropologists call this philosophical stance **cultural relativity**. We try to describe the points of view of the people we want to understand, and we do this by being there with the people in our fieldwork, doing ethnography.

The opposite of cultural relativity is **ethnocentrism**, thinking that your way of doing things is either the only way or the best way. All people think their way of seeing things is obvious and natural. For example, of course a person only marries one other person at a time. Or of course you pay money

SEEK AND YE SHALL FIND

Bronisław Mallinowski

Excerpt from *Argonauts of the Western Pacific*, pg. 24–25

O ur considerations thus indicate that the goal of ethnographic field work must be approached through three avenues:

1. *The organisation of the tribe, and the anatomy of its culture* must be recorded in firm, clear outline. The method of *concrete, statistical documentation* is the means through which such an outline has to be given.
2. Within this frame, the *imponderabilia of actual life*, and the *type of behavior* have to be filled in. They have to be collected through minute, detailed observations in the form of some sort of ethnographic diary, made possible by close contact with native life.
3. A collection of ethnographic statements, characteristic narratives, typical utterances, items of folklore and magical formula has to be given as a *corpus inscriptionum*, as documents of native mentality.

These three lines of approach lead to the final goal, of which an Ethnographer should never lose sight. This goal is, briefly, to grasp the native's point of view, his relation to life, to realise *his* vision of *his* world. We have to study man, and we must study what concerns him most intimately, that is, the hold which life has on him. In each culture, the values are slightly different; people aspire after different aims, follow different impulses, yearn after a different form of happiness. In each culture, we find different institutions in which man pursues his life-interest, different custom by which he satisfies his aspirations, different codes of law and morality which reward his virtues or punish his defections. To study the institutions, customs, and codes or to study the behavior and mentality without the subjective desire of feeling by what these people live, of realising the substance of their happiness—is, in my opinion, to miss the greatest reward which we can hope to obtain from the study of man.

These generalities the reader will find illustrated in the following chapters. We shall see there the savage striving to satisfy certain aspirations, to attain his type of value, to follow his line of social ambition. We shall see him led on to perilous and difficult enterprises by a tradition of magical and heroical exploits [Kula trading voyages], shall see him following the lure of his own romance. Perhaps as we read the account of these remote customs there may emerge a feeling of solidarity with the endeavours and ambitions of these natives. Perhaps man's mentality will be revealed to us, and brought near, along some lines which we never have followed before. Perhaps through realising human nature in a shape very distant and foreign to us, we shall have some light shed on our own. In this, and in this case only, we shall be justified in feeling that it has been worth our while to understand these natives, their institutions and customs, and that we have gathered some profit from the Kula.

for a product you get at the store. That's one of the features of culture—ethnocentrism is built into it. But once we understand that and we open our heads to the ways other people make sense of the world, we can try to be less ethnocentric and more relativistic in our thinking.

Melford Spiro, an anthropologist who studied people in Israel and Burma, defined three kinds of cultural relativism:

- Descriptive relativism;
- Ethical relativism; and
- Epistemological relativism.

Descriptive relativism means suspending your natural ethnocentrism so that you can describe another culture from the point of view of the people in it. It allows you to understand other cultures.

Ethical relativism is the idea that there are no absolute values of good and bad; ethical judgments depend on the culture. You judge an Aztec skinning a captive by Aztec standards, not by your own. This helps us understand other people because it teaches us not to judge them by different standards. That doesn't mean that we have to accept their standards, but it does mean we can't judge them.

There is a debate about where the line between accepting another system of values and not judging it should be. One subject of the debate is the female genital mutilation performed by some African and Mediterranean cultures. Some people say that calling it "mutilation" is already judging it, that we should be more descriptive and call it "female genital cutting" because it involves cutting the clitorises off girls. Some people say it's part of these cultures, and it's not ours to judge whether they should do it or not. Others say no matter what the culture, this practice is hurting women because the cuts get infected. The response is to suggest performing the procedure in sanitary clinics so that nobody gets hurt. The answer back is that women wouldn't choose to do this if the men didn't make them, so it's an issue of power. The answer back to *that* is that, in fact, older women make them do it because it's their tradition.

Look closer to home. Women are paid about $0.77 for every dollar a man makes. If a woman does the same work, is equally qualified, and does the work equally well as a man, she gets paid less. Is this just part of our culture that we must accept to understand the United States? Or is this something that we should change because we believe in equality? We could have the same discussion about apartheid in South Africa before it was changed or about racism in the United States.

Ethical relativity can be a problem if it neutralizes our sense of right and wrong. That may be a good thing insofar as it helps us suspend judgment; it may be a bad thing if it paralyzes us so that we can't make political judgments. We'll discuss that topic more later.

Epistemology means how we know things. Different cultures define different ways of knowing things. Some may value mysticism; some may value science. The idea of **epistemological relativity** is that all ways of knowing things are equally true. People who believe in this believe that no one way of knowing is any more true than any other. In this view, we can never really know reality; we can only know reality as our different cultures show it to us, and all those different ways are equally true.

Anthropology needs descriptive relativity and ethical relativity to describe and understand different cultures, but if we took epistemological relativity seriously, we couldn't really be descriptively or ethically relativistic. Epistemological relativity doesn't help scientists; it only helps tell a story from an ethnocentric point of view. All cultures have the assumption that they are natural, obvious, and true. If we pick just one, then we can only understand things from that one point of view and never question whether there are other ways of knowing the world. If we can't ask the question, we can't answer it. So, paradoxically epistemological relativity means no relativity at all.

Science provides an alternative. The idea of **science** is that we never accept anything as really true, just as what we *think* we know until we find out differently by checking it over and over again. The idea is to think of things we can check.

Science rests on two important principles: validity and reliability. **Validity** means that you're really measuring what you think you are measuring. Suppose you have an odometer for your bike. It's supposed to measure the distance you go. What it really counts is the number of times the front wheel turns around. If you put on a larger or smaller wheel, it will still count the number of revolutions, but it won't be a valid measure of distance.

Reliability means that everybody else who checks the same thing will get the same results. It doesn't matter how fast or how far you pedal, the odometer will measure the revolutions of the wheel and convert that to a measure of distance. That measurement will depend on the size of the wheel, not on the person pedaling.

Shall we just pick one story that is closest to our own beliefs and stick with it because we are ethnocentric? Or shall we decide not to commit to any belief, decide to try to get the story that best takes account of all of the evidence we can find, and then keep checking that story with every kind of evidence we can find?

Anthropologists take the second route because we want to be able to understand other cultures and times and not be trapped in our own, just going around in circles with our own stories.

Some people asked Nasrudin whether he knew where the exact center of the Earth was. "Yes," the wise man said.

"Then tell us."

"It's just under the left hind foot of my donkey."

"Are you sure?" they asked. "How can you be so sure?"

"If you doubt me," Nasrudin said, "measure it for yourselves."

Discussion Questions

- What makes science scientific?
- What makes science different from other epistemologies?

- What makes ethnography scientific?
- What is the difference between validity and reliability? Can you think of some other examples?
- Think of some reasons a statement might not be reliable or valid. For example, why is it difficult to get a reliable answer to why a particular piece of literature, poetry, or music is good? Why is it difficult to get a valid answer to which political party is best?

Suggested Reading

Appignanesi, Richard, Chris Garratt, Ziauddin Sardar, and Patrick Curry. *Introducing Postmodernism.* Cambridge, UK: Totem Books, 2005.

Kuznar, Lawrence A. *Reclaiming a Scientific Anthropology.* Walnut Creek, CA: AltaMira, 1997.

Salzman, Philip Carl. *Understanding Culture: An Introduction to Anthropological Theory.* Prospect Heights, IL: Waveland, 2001.

Sidky, H. *Perspectives on Culture: A Critical Introduction to Theory in Cultural Anthropology.* Upper Saddle River, NJ: Pearson, 2004.

We expect people to look different, and we celebrate these differences. But at the same time, differences among people have been the basis for discrimination and oppression. Yet, are we so different? Current science tells us we share a common ancestry and the differences among people we see are natural variations, the result of migration, marriage, and adaptation to different environments. The story of race is complex and may challenge how we think about race and human variation, about the differences and similarities among people. *Used with permission of the American Anthropological Association (TM).*

2

Human Variation
Race and Gender

RACE

If all people living today evolved from the same ancestors, why are we so physically different? There's a lot of talk about race and racism in America. What does race mean in terms of our evolutionary history?

It is true that the distribution of certain of our physical characteristics is not random—there are patterns. Think of these characteristics as being like elevation on a topographic map. If we connect all of the points of the same elevation, we define a cline. It's the same for weather maps—we can map barometric pressures by connecting all the pressures that are the same. If we do that for human physical characteristics, we see that they do not form into neat bundles that go together. One cline may go one direction and another a different direction.

For instance, skin darkness gradually increases from Mediterranean Europe south along the Nile or across the Sahara with no sharp breaks, so the "peak" would be in central Africa. Ancestors of all people came from Africa, and all were black before they went north. The frequency of the fold in the eye that many Europeans and Americans associate with Japanese and Chinese people, the *epicanthic fold*, gradually increases from west to east across Asia. Wavy hair increases in the opposite direction, toward Europe. You can see people from South Asia whose skin is very dark but who have sharp facial features and straight hair.

These distributions are the results of two processes: gene flow and natural selection. In biological terms, species and races are about who breeds with whom. Two populations that cannot interbreed are two different species. In biology, *race* is a large, geographically isolated population within a species that doesn't breed much with other populations of the same species. If there are different environments or some other differences in natural selection so that members of the different races can no longer interbreed, then each race may develop into a different species. So a race is a population on the way to being its own species.

A common idea of race is that there are a specific number of "types" of people that are all more or less the same but differ from other types. Americans typically think that they can tell the different types apart by skin color. Some

SKIN COLOR: A FUNCTION OF SUN

Nina Jablonski
Penn State University
Author of *Skin: A Natural History*. 2013, University of California Press. *Living Color: The Biological and Social Meaning of Skin Color*. 2012, University of California Press.

Human skin is unique among mammals because it comes in a range of colors which represent adaptations to different levels of solar ultraviolet radiation (UVR). Biological anthropologists estimate that our ancestors evolved mostly naked skin by about 1.5 million years ago (1.5 Ma), and that dark pigmentation provided essential sunscreen for humans living under high UVR in equatorial Africa, our homeland. The evidence for this comes from deductions about hair loss and pigmentation made on the basis of functional anatomy and exercise physiology combined with genetic evidence indicating that lack of variation in a gene that is critical to the production of melanin pigment, the melanocortin 1 receptor locus (or *MC1R*). Because UVR near the equator is strong year-round, the evolutionary pressure for protective melanin pigmentation was high, and natural selection on the *MC1R* gene was strong. The members of the genus *Homo* living in Africa around 1 Ma (1 million years ago) from which all modern humans evolved had naked and darkly pigmented skin.

Folate is essential for DNA replication and cell division, and these processes are essential for life, including the production of reproductive cells and the formation of organ systems in the rapidly differentiating embryo in a pregnant woman's body. UVR depletes B vitamin and causes folate deficiencies that result in various kinds of birth defects, such as spina bifida. Our ancestors who weren't sufficiently dark to prevent the breakdown of folates couldn't have normal babies, and wouldn't contribute their genes to the next generation. Maintaining sufficient levels of folate is one of the keys to successful reproduction of our species.

The darkness of pigmentation is related to the intensity of solar UVR. Thus, within Africa, people living near the equator or in very dry sunny areas have the darkest skin, while those living farther away from the equator or in generally more humid and cloudy places have lighter skin. When a small number of people walked out of Africa to Eurasia, they faced more seasonal and weaker UVR.

Although UVR is harmful, people require the vitamin D it produces when certain wave lengths, UVB, interact with the skin. At high latitudes, there is little UVB in sunlight so there is little potential for producing the vitamin D necessary for bone development. Because the sunscreen of the dark eumelanin skin pigmentation also blocked vitamin D production, people with pale skins who could produce vitamin D survived more and had more offspring. Genetic evidence gathered in the last decade indicates that depigmented skin evolved independently at least twice in human groups dispersing into high latitudes in Europe and Asia.

The evidence of strong natural selection operating at low latitudes to maintain dark pigmentation under high UVR conditions and at high latitudes to establish and maintain light pigmentation under low UVR conditions indicates that skin pigmentation is a Darwinian adaptation, which is the product of evolution by natural selection.

might add type of hair, nose and lip shape, and stature. There are the arche-types of Europeans with pale skins, straight or wavy hair, body hair, narrow noses, and medium to tall stature; versus central Africans with dark brown or black skin, wiry hair, medium body hair, thick noses and lips, and medium to tall stature; and Asians with pale to light brown skin, straight black hair, brown eyes, epicanthic folds, short to medium statures, and no body hair. Somewhere we can find a perfect representation of each type.

The Cunard Steamship Company has a building in Liverpool, England. Above the front door is a sculpture of Neptune, the Roman god of the sea. Evenly spaced around the building at the same level are wonderfully sculpted heads of archetypes of each race on the planet. The Cunard collec-tion of sculpture represents this idea of race.

Humans are a **polymorphic** species—*poly* means "many," and *morph* means "form." So we are a species of many forms, with many partially iso-lated breeding populations, but we kept moving and mixing, never stopping in any one place permanently enough to develop different species. That ex-plains the variation within groups and why it is greater than the variation among groups. We are a single species, a single breeding population.

Human characteristics don't fall into sufficiently neat packages to define races. Lots of people in Africa have thin lips and noses, wavy hair, and dark brown to black skin. Some South Africans have epicanthic folds, light brown to dark brown skin, and spiraled hair. So the actual distribution of people doesn't fit any of the archetypes of race.

In addition, archaeologists tell us that people have been in contact over very long distances since we started walking out of Africa. Where there's human contact, there's breeding. We're that kind of species and that's how we got here. In terms of our genetics, there is more variation within any cat-egory of people, or population, that you can think of than there is between them. So the differences between any two people from any single category of people are greater than the differences between individuals of any two dif-ferent categories. It has always been that way. There is no time in the past when races were pure but different and somehow got mixed later.

So, if race isn't a biological reality, where did the idea come from? Part of it is from ethnocentrism. Part of it is from the idea that other people are different from us. This doesn't always have to do with skin color, as it does in the United States. It can have to do with the way people speak. George Bernard Shaw wrote a play about that called *Pygmalion*. That play was later made into a movie with the same name and then into a musical called *My Fair Lady*. British people make the same kind of racist distinctions based on dialect or accent as Americans do based on skin color. In Britain, it has to do with class. We'll come back to that later.

The point is that people can emphasize any source of difference as a way to create categories of other people to treat well or badly. So where does this inclination to divide people into different categories come from?

This entire notion is pretty recent. It has to do with the culture of nation-states that developed in Europe in the sixteenth and seventeenth centuries and got consolidated into warring nations by the middle of the nineteenth century. When people tried to map languages across Europe, they couldn't find any clear lines of demarcation, so they described them as chains of dialects, each one intelligible to the next, but when you got several links away, they became unintelligible and thus different languages, and yet each was intelligible to its neighbors. The same thing happens in Southeast Asia and China.

So, you see, there aren't any real borders among people. Despite that, the rulers of European-style states like to define certain territories and fight over them. Their idea? That there is a homogeneous group of people all alike in their language and culture that gets along pretty well together. These people live inside the borders of the state and have a government that takes care of things for them and protects them from foreigners who may try to take over "our" country. Make people more afraid of foreigners than they are of their own rulers and they won't look too closely at who is really doing them harm. Every generation has a new leader who uses this to maximum effect. Adolf Hitler's slogan was "One people, one government, one leader."

If we believe that there is a single people with a single language, government, territory, history, culture, music, and literature, then each nation can claim to be the best one, because this ideology of nationalism is a powerful source of ethnocentrism. If we project that ideology onto the whole species and assume that people come in linguistically and physically defined groups, we get the idea of race. In fact, early writers used *race* and *nation* to mean the same thing. Another thing that nations do is keep track of people so they can draft them for armies and tax them to pay for wars. When they start counting people, they make categories—occupations, regions, religions, races.

So racism, along with nationalism, belongs to the cultures of states. In the United States, the idea of biological races and biological racism is also connected to the European conquest of the Americas and the slave trade. The Europeans and their American descendants could use color as a handy marker for who was fair game to capture and sell into slavery. Slavery was not legal in every state. In the "free" states, no one could be a slave. In 1841, a free black man from New York was kidnapped in Washington, D.C., and sold into slavery. The people depicted in the 2013 movie *Twelve Years a Slave*, based on the book by Solomon Northup, were real.

Back then, racism, the idea that people of one category are superior or inferior to people of a different category, could be used as a defense of slavery, as the film shows. After the U.S. Civil War, racism provided a rationale for political and economic repression. The history of that form of oppression is too complex to go into here, but if you haven't experienced some form of dominance because you're a woman instead of a man or because you're darker than someone else or because you have a different kind of name than someone else, then ask some people of a different gender, sexual preference, skin color, or surname system to tell you how that works.

A small but striking example comes from Florida in the late 1940s through the next decade, when a local sheriff and his deputies, along with the Ku Klux Klan, terrorized black people to keep them subservient to work for white citrus growers. This was not an isolated example, but was characteristic of many areas of the American South. That is why the Confederate flag causes the same response as the Nazi swastika does among many people. It's more than just a symbol of tradition; it reminds us of the terror that a racist group can cause when it controls government agencies.

The idea of race as a biological fact is itself a political weapon that some use to oppress others. Later, we'll explain how some people can control the culture of others. We mentioned hegemony in the Introduction and we'll come back to it later, but for now remember that if you're asking about the biology of race, you're asking the wrong question. The real question is about the politics of race. It's quite possible to ask about human variation and how that works biologically, but a precondition to doing that scientifically is to give up the assumptions of race, even the convenient assumptions of isolated human breeding populations. Otherwise, we're not doing science; we're justifying a pernicious political doctrine.

The Icelandic anthropologist Gísli Pálsson writes about an island mentality—that even anthropologists think about people as if they lived on little islands separated from other people. Biological anthropologists are trying to work out the history of our species by comparing the genetics of different groups. The problem is that if they assume such "islands" of population exist, they take their samples from the islands and guess what? They prove there really are islands. They wind up proving their own assumption. Another way to map genetic variation would be to divide the world according to a grid or some other method of random sampling instead of looking for islands of populations.

Pálsson points out that the people who share features such as dark skin and hair texture, Melanesians and Africans, are as genetically different as it is possible to be. In terms of molecular markers, white Europeans are closer to both black Africans and black Melanesians than Africans are to Melanesians.

The biological anthropologist Nina Jablonski suggests that the black people of South Asia used to be white until they went so far south. So what could a black race be? Some of the gene hunters, as Pálsson calls them, even try to define populations according to language. Most Americans are hyphenated Americans—Afro-Americans, Italian Americans, and so forth. And most of them speak English. This example isn't that strange. Language is one of the things that nationalist ideologies made into islands along with genes.

But aren't there differences in performance? A greater proportion of black people than white people in the United States are poor. Isn't that because they are not as intelligent or as industrious as white people? Racists say so.

There is a destructive and malicious form of unlogic that says if something negative happens to you such as poverty, losing a job or rape, it's your own fault. One label for this is blaming the victim. A woman wears a short dress, has a few drinks in a bar, and walks home alone. A man rapes her. It's her fault? Wasn't she "asking for it?" A National Guardsman gets killed in Iraq. He volunteered. He was dressed for it. He was in the wrong place at the wrong time wearing the wrong clothes and looking the wrong way. It's his fault? It's your fault if you lose your job because it moves to Mexico? It's your fault if the best job you can get can't keep you above the poverty line?

It doesn't make sense in any of these examples. Nor does it when it's applied to kids in school. Another label for this is **deficit theory**. That's the idea that if some group of kids doesn't do well in school, there's something wrong *with the kids in that group*. That there is some deficit. They may be stupid or lazy, but whatever it is, it's about them, not about the policies and the schools and the system they're in. Someone ought to teach these kids to be more energetic, to speak clearly, and educate them better so they're not so stupid. Black kids for instance.

Here's where it comes back to institutional racism. That is, the racism that's built into the institutions of the country. You may think a seminar can teach people how to tolerate other people they can't stand. You don't have to change the system of funding for schools that uses meager tax revenues from poor neighborhoods to try to keep open decaying schools in those neighborhoods. You can keep the tax system in place that lets rich neighborhoods buy computers and science labs and pay good wages to good teachers and even buy toilet paper and soap for the bathrooms. You can see plenty of good teachers who are white teaching in black schools, or black people who become doctors and lawyers so you see, the system is working if they exist. And there's no need to change that system if the problem is with the lazy and stupid kids.

But ability doesn't go with skin color; it goes with opportunity. Provide equal opportunity and there will be equal performance. The United States does not provide equal opportunity. Black people don't have the same chances of going to good high schools that get kids into college as white people, and so on. Continue to deny equal opportunity on the basis of skin color or any other difference, and there will not be equal performance.

Here we will shift gears for just a moment and mention that sometimes, as in this example, the racism is built into the system itself. It isn't a question of individuals being racist but of a whole system that's racist. We can have a black president and black Supreme Court justices and still have a racist system. To make a difference requires making a difference in the system, not in the people in it. You can change all of the people and keep the same system, and you'll get the same result.

Racism isn't just the prerogative of rulers. People who want to get along in the system can take up the practices and prejudices of the rulers. One example we recently came across is from Charleston, South Carolina, where we were working on the story of a union of black longshoremen. To understand what was going on, we had to understand about "race" relations in Charleston. We learned that people in the South aren't considered just white or black. There's a whole range in between. Historically, these people started out as the offspring of white slave owners and slaves. The white owners often helped their brown children by setting them up in business. A privileged brown elite thus grew up within the larger black community and acted as a link between the blacks and whites.

Although the brown people suffered the same kind of racism as the black people, they suffered less. They had many privileges in a system that ran on privilege. People in power give you privileges, so you must stay on their good side. Systems, when they're working in your favor at least, give you rights. You cannot move from privileges to rights unless you change the system, and that might annoy the people in power and the privileged. So the brown elite people helped to keep the system of racism going. They didn't want to change a system that was working well for them. They could deal with racism as long as they were getting along economically and had darker people to be superior to. During the civil rights movement of the 1960s, they advocated patience and reform rather than the big changes the civil rights movement promoted with its sit-ins and demonstrations. The brown elite wanted to avoid any kind of confrontation with the white establishment that might threaten their own privileges.

The point is that racism and prejudice can cut in any direction. Sometimes, when blacks are majorities and whites are minorities, black people can do unto others what has been done unto them—be racist toward whites in what some have called the oppression of the oppressed. Suzan saw some of this in her work with unions in Chicago. If racism and prejudice can cut in any direction, what is the solution? The solution is not to have any prejudice or any racism. Unfortunately, that's as easily done as having no more war.

We are a species on the move. Every homeland has always been just a stepping-stone on our journey to wherever we are now. So we've always been moving and mingling, mixing and matching, and above all, going on to the next place to do the next thing.

GENDER

We learn our gender roles from growing up in families where the older generations model them for us. Americans and Europeans tend to think of two genders, male and female, as biologically given by the nature of our genitals. But this is not a universal view. To learn about gender roles, we will stop and take a brief look at families. What is a family, anyway? Americans, like Europeans, tend to think in terms of a mom, a dad, and their kids living in a house with two cars and a dog and a cat. However, most of the people of the world for most of the time we've been on this planet don't think that way.

Why? Because most people form into larger groupings called **lineages**. Lineages come in two kinds—according to whether you can claim membership in them by virtue of the mom you have or the dad you have. Some are all the people descended from the same woman through their moms; some are all the people descended from the same man through their dads. Put that in Latin to make fancy academic words, and you have **matrilineal** (mother's line) and **patrilineal** (father's line).

These aren't mirror images of each other because the women's brothers often run the lineage, but it would be inaccurate to conclude that men are in some way naturally in charge everywhere just because they are in states and in global capitalism. In foraging societies and matrilineal cultures, men and women tend to share power. Here, archaeologists and ethnographers agree that women provide the bulk of the important food for the group although the men may hunt for meat. One of our chief points is that it is culture, not biology, that determines relations of gender. If men are often in charge of things, it's not because it's somehow bred into our species by evolution or it's somehow natural. Rather, it is a question of culture, and cultures change.

Usually, family values means valuing the people of your lineage, not just your household. An anthropologist we mentioned earlier, Bronisław Malinowski, wanted to find out about the relationships between fathers and sons in the Trobriand Islands, where he did fieldwork during World War I. He'd been reading Sigmund Freud, who was writing about the Oedipus complex: the idea that as boys grow up, they begin to compete with their own dads for the attention and then the control of their moms. Freud said as guys grow older, they want to kill their dads and possess their moms. That makes them feel guilty in all kinds of ways, and that guilt makes them give up any ideas of sex with their female relatives. The same sort of thing goes on with girls and their dads. Freud called that the Electra complex.

Malinowski wondered how that idea would work in a place with a different kind of family structure than Freud observed in Vienna. The Trobriand Islanders have matrilineal lineages. The most important adult male in any kid's life is his mom's brother, what Americans would call an uncle. Kids belong to their mom's family, not their dad's. The dad is just a sperm donor for the mom. The men of the mom's lineage, the mom's brothers, are responsible for raising the kids and for their family values. So, all of the closeness is between the children and their mother's side, and the uncles raise the sons and model maleness for them. The uncles are in the roles of Viennese dads.

What about the Trobriand dads? They're involved with their sister's kids, the kids that belong to their families, their lineages, but to their "own" kids they are indulgent, like uncles in Europe. With a whole different kind of family structure, there wouldn't be any struggle between the dad and the son for the mom. It's not about moms and dads but about who has authority over the kids (Trobriand uncles and European dads) and who can be indulgent to them (Trobriand dads and European uncles).

So what does any of this have to do with gender roles? One of the things that all people share is some kind of prohibition on having sex with certain relatives. We call that an **incest prohibition**. What's interesting is that different groups define the incest prohibition with respect to different relatives. Breeders who want to breed livestock or pets for certain characteristics look for males and females that share the thing the breeders are looking for, which are likely to be closely related individuals. So breeders encourage incest to bring out the traits they are looking for. The incest prohibition doesn't have anything to do with genetics or fear of inbreeding. Cleopatra, for instance, was the result of several generations of brother–sister matings. The Inca kings of Peru were so godly that no ordinary woman was good enough for them, so they had to mate with their sisters. The French anthropologist Claude Lévi-Strauss's answer to the puzzle was that the incest prohibition forced groups to have social relations with other groups so that they could help each other out when they needed it. That was the advantage of the incest prohibition.

Here's the point: the kind of kinship groups and the definitions of family are variable, and one of the things that goes along with those differences is differences in gender roles.

In the mid-1930s, the anthropologist Margaret Mead set out to explore the varieties of gender relations in her work in New Guinea. She found that Tchambuli women were dominant and the men were dependent; women were impersonal and managerial and the men were irresponsible—the women seemed more like American males than American females in their behavior. Among the Arapesh, nobody was masculine by American judgments, and everyone was fairly equivalent in their cooperation and gentleness. Mead found Mundugumor of both genders to be aggressive even in making love. Her conclusion was that there is a wide variety of gender roles.

Some later anthropologists have criticized Mead's methods, but many others have found her conclusions sound. Whatever one's opinion of Mead's work, anthropologists agree that there is no necessary connection between biological characteristics and gender roles.

Nor is there any necessary single definition of marriage. Several men may be married to one woman at the same time. Several women may be married to one man at the same time; women and men may marry ghosts or trees or spirits; men may marry other men; women may marry other women.

Different kinds of lineages define different roles and statuses for women. In matrilineal lineages, women's influence may be very public. For instance, Annette Weiner's ethnography in the Trobriand Islands confirms much of what Malinowski found, but also describes much that he did not. For instance, women derive status from their participation in a separate trade network from the men's famous kula that Malinowski described. Among the matrilineal Iroquois of the Northeastern United States, women controlled land, farming, homes, and farm produce, whereas men controlled meat, trade in luxuries, and war tribute. Iroquois women enjoyed such high status that early European observers described them as a matriarchy.

Even in examples of extreme male dominance such as that noted in patrilineal Middle Eastern social orders, women may have great influence that is not publically visible. Elizabeth Fernea described her experience as the young wife of an anthropologist in a village in Iraq in the mid 1950s before Saddam Hussein came to power. She found that women had a profound influence in their households although it was not visible from the outside. Lucien Hanks described a similarly powerful role for women in Thai households despite the Buddhist ideology that subordinates women to men.

Forms of marriage are as varied as forms of gender practices. Anthropologists may disagree about *why* this is so, but most would not disagree about *whether* it is so. Comparative studies of sexual practices challenge our own ideas about what is sexual, let alone what is normal.

Europeans from the first Spanish and French explorers on the American plains describe an anomalous gender category they called *berdache,* a word

---

Marriage as partnership

Tibetan herders, at least before the Chinese took over, used all of these forms of marriage. The particular form depended on the livestock situation of the tent. Each child of the parents owned an equal share of the livestock, but the parents have two shares. So if there is a family with two sons and two daughters, each son and each daughter owns one-eighth of the herd. The father and mother each own one-fourth of the herd. Everything else hinges on the facts of herd ownership.

Two brothers might decide that they could do better by keeping their herds together. They know there cannot be two women in one tent unless the women are sisters or mother and daughter. So the older brother might offer to share his wife with the younger brother. So there's one woman and two husbands. The arrangement can be fragile because the woman may favor one husband over the other and kick one of them out with his herd, or the younger brother may want his own wife.

A family may have only one daughter, or maybe all the daughters except one have already married. The parents may bring in a son-in-law as a son. The only difference is that he is married to the daughter and he can't set up a tent apart from the wife's parents' tent. If the father dies, the mother and daughter may share the same husband.

A wealthy married man may take a new wife and set her up with half of his share of the herd, but the two tents will stay together, even if the two wives are in separate tents. A man may marry several sisters, or a father and son may share a single wife, and so on. Robert Ekvall, who lived with these herders, says that the economic conditions of the herds determine the patterns of marriage in particular tents.

This can happen because people don't equate sex with marriage, so there's a lot of sexual activity between people who aren't married to each other. The birthrate is also low, so there aren't many children, and people value them highly. People don't have to be married to be sure that any children they have will be taken care of. The important thing is the management of the herd. That does require the stability of marriage.

The management of herds requires a partnership of men and women working together. Women take care of newborn and young animals and do all of the milking. This gives them the right to veto any livestock decisions any of the men might make, which, Ekvall says, "she can press with emotional intensity."

The important thing here is that the particular form of marriage depends on what is going on with the herds. As situations change, so does the marriage form.

---

derived from Persian meaning a slave boy that is suggestive of male prostitution in European languages. The practices varied considerably but share the characteristic that they did not fit the Euro-American categories of male and female genders. Some refer to them as a "third gender" and others as male homosexuals.

Euro-American observers from the early explorers to anthropologists remarked on the acceptance of these individuals, who might be males dressing and acting as females or females dressing and acting as males and some combinations and mixtures of male and female roles, and the fact that they might

STATEMENT ON MARRIAGE AND THE FAMILY
American Anthropological Association (2004)

The American Anthropological Association's executive board issued this statement in 2004 when there was discussion of a constitutional amendment to limit marriage in the United States to one man and one woman:

> *The results of more than a century of anthropological research on households, kinship relationships, and families, across cultures and through time, provide no support whatsoever for the view that either civilization or viable social orders depend upon marriage as an exclusively heterosexual institution. Rather, anthropological research supports the conclusion that a vast array of family types, including families built upon same-sex partnerships, can contribute to stable and humane societies.*

be honored rather than despised by others and were freely allowed to develop the gender identities their spiritual development dictated. In other words, although it was an alternative gender role, it was not deviant, nor was it a matter of personal choice. The anthropologist Donald J. Blakeshee reviews anthropologist's treatments of berdache and concludes that the confusion and puzzlement of Euro-American observers is a consequence of transposing cultural categories to behaviors that did not fit them, that is, ethnocentrism.

A more contemporary term among First Nations is "two-spirit people" because they exhibit more than a single gender spirit, although each group has its own terms. An accurate appreciation can only be gained by developing locally relevant descriptions. In the next chapter we discuss how this practice of projecting our own cultural categories onto others, ethnocentrism, leads to confusion and how we can avoid it. For now, it may suffice to suggest that gender is a cultural construction and is therefore variable across different cultures.

Some New Guinea people believe that girls don't need any help developing; they naturally become women because women raise them. However, because women also raise boys, they hold back the development of the boys' masculinity. Initiation rituals separate boys from women. In the rituals, fully developed men instill men's values in the boys and give them the strength of warriors. Boys get this strength by consuming the semen of older unmarried men in oral sex. The men believe that they control everything through their control of semen. Only the men can drink the sap of a special tree that restores their semen. Their semen creates babies and feeds them because it causes breast milk to flow. It turns boys into men; it turns girls into wives; it keeps the whole society going. Women say they create milk by themselves and don't need any help from men.

In another New Guinea group, the boys get the semen they need to grow into men from older bachelors their fathers select to have anal sex with the boys when they are about ten or eleven. But, according to these people, virgin boys make the best hunters because animals won't appear to men who are having sex with women.

We've called these practices oral or anal sex, but it isn't clear that the New Guineans think of it as sex at all. Just because our culture thinks of these actions as sexual doesn't mean that New Guineans do. These practices are parts of larger systems of exchanges between age-defined groups of men that also involve food, meat, and sometimes painful acts of inducing vomiting and bleeding. So it is misleading to think of these acts as sexual in the same sense they might be to us. Anthropologists have analyzed such actions in terms of Freudian ideas that are centered on ideas of sex and the erotic but that are not appropriate in this cultural context of exchanges of substances.

Furthermore, the whole idea of seeing these acts as sexual is connected to the Western idea of sexual desire as something deeply personal and individualistic. We will return to the idea of individualism later, but for now, know that even acts that look to us like sex may be part of a different system of meaning than we are accustomed to, part of a different cultural world. The anthropologist Deborah Elliston says that to think of these acts in the same cultural terms we use instead of their own New Guinean terms of exchanges of substances is to be ethnocentric.

One test for cultural relativism is the practice of female circumcision or genital cutting, the removal of all or part of the clitoris and sometimes a more extreme form of sewing the vagina together called *infibulation*. These practices are common in parts of Africa.

Some argue, in accordance with relativism, that such practices are aspects of those cultures and that it's not up to us to judge them. Others argue that the practices are dangerous because of the risks of infection and that they are misogynistic or antiwoman because they deprive women of an important part of their bodies. Kirsten Bell wondered why her American anthropology students found female genital cutting abhorrent but thought male genital cutting or circumcision was normal. Some international health organizations think of male circumcision as a "medical" procedure but oppose female circumcision altogether.

Male circumcision became popular in Victorian times as a way to control masturbation to ensure physical and moral "hygiene." Some people advocated clitoridectomies to keep girls from masturbating as well.

Freud taught that mature women had orgasms from their vaginas because when girls reached puberty, sexual excitability transferred from the clitoris to the vagina. In this view, the clitoris didn't have anything to do with sex. During Victorian times, doctors would cure a woman of hysteria by massaging her clitoris until she had "hysterical paroxysms," but the Victorians did not think of that as anything sexual. What Americans today think of as a sex toy, the vibrator, was invented in the nineteenth century to mechanize the process of "pelvic massage," as the Victorians called it.

Culture defines what is and what is not sexual, whether it's oral or anal intercourse in New Guinea or clitoral massages in Victorian England. By the late 1940s, clitorises became so unimportant to the mostly male medical establishment that anatomy textbooks didn't even include them.

In the mid-1970s, *The Hite Report* showed that most women's orgasms come from clitoral rather than vaginal stimulation, and people started wondering why clitoral stimulation wasn't a normal part of sex. Westerners returned to an earlier idea of understanding the clitoris as a female penis—understanding women's bodies in reference to men's.

In fact, although circumcision may reduce the sensitivity of the penis, it doesn't prevent masturbation, and cutting a woman's clitoris off doesn't prevent her from having orgasms.

Today, lots of books and other media suggest that women get sexually warmed up by talking and cuddling, whereas men are mindlessly attracted to body parts. The twenty-first-century view is that men are always ready and willing, testosterone-driven creatures who can't control their penises, but women are delicate and passive. In this view, even cutting off part of a guy's penis doesn't slow down his powerful sex drive. It's even a good thing to reduce the sensitivity of a guy's penis because he can perform longer and better for the woman. But whacking off any part of a delicate and passive woman's sexual anatomy would cripple her.

Bell says that these kinds of cultural assumptions are behind all of the discussions about genital cutting—thinking that it's bad for women but OK for men. She doesn't say that physiology has nothing to do with sexuality, but she does say they aren't the same thing.

Doctors and policy makers are ready to condemn female circumcision and approve of male circumcision because of what they think are the *natural* effects. But that tells more about the culture of the doctors and policy makers than it does about physiology. Like gender, sexuality is cultural. And cultures change through time and across space. So even something as "natural" as sexual intercourse becomes part of culture, and people understand it differently in different times and places.

CONCLUSION

Race and gender are two of the big categories for classifying people as similar or different. Some say our experience is determined by race and gender. We said there wasn't such a thing as race. How can it determine experience if it doesn't exist? Just because something doesn't exist doesn't mean some culture won't make a big deal of it. Most Americans don't think witches and spirits exist, but they are a big deal for the Lisu tribal people in northern Thailand, with whom Paul lived, as they were for Medieval Icelanders and many other people.

Sometimes there really are things that our cultures don't recognize. For instance, Victorian doctors could massage a woman's clitoris until she had an orgasm, but they didn't think of that as any kind of sexual experience. So, in America there is a rigid class system, but it's almost as evil to talk about class as it is to talk about masturbation or money.

So just because Americans make a big deal out of race doesn't mean that it's real. And just because Americans don't make a big deal of class doesn't mean it doesn't exist. Race isn't real biologically. But it is real politically, and people experience it because the United States has a racist system that discriminates against people based on the color of their skin or their surname.

If you're a black American, your experience teaches you that you're the one who is different. Every black person can tell a story about when he or she first figured out that not everyone was black and that being black made a difference. It's usually painful. If you're from a Spanish-speaking family in the United States, you probably remember the first time someone told you you'd better speak English or that you speak with a strange accent. You may remember relatives from Spanish-speaking countries telling you that you had a strange accent. So no matter what language you speak, someone's going to be annoyed, unless it's another person from the same barrio or region of the United States.

If you're a white female, you may wonder why some things are harder for you than for males. You may have noticed it in sports or in math or somewhere else along the way. If you haven't noticed it, you will when you learn that you will probably be paid less than a guy for the same work.

If you're a white male, you probably won't understand this stuff. You'll be inclined to think that everything is fair and equal because it seems that way to you. You may wonder why people of color and women talk about a racist and sexist system. You are the minority, but it is the minority that runs the country. You are the one for whom the system operates best, so you never need to think about either being white or being male.

Race and gender do affect us, often in ways we never think about. It's the job of anthropology to make those ways more visible. But in addition to race and gender, there is one other thing that is more powerful than either, one thing that in America today is more invisible than either race or gender. That is class. If we ignore class, we ignore all of the causal forces that make race and gender work the way they do. So, yes, we categorize and label each other, and that very practice, along with the ideologies of nation-states, provides the basis for racism and sexism.

That practice of categorizing and labeling is part of our ability to use language.

Nasrudin was in the Land of Fools. Every day, for days on end, he stood in the square and preached, "People, sin and evil are everywhere. Sin and evil are hateful." One day he was about to start up with his usual sermon when he saw some of the Fools standing around with their arms folded. "What are you doing?" he asked. "We've just decided what to do about all this sin and evil you've been talking about," they answered. "You've decided to avoid it? To steer clear of it? To shun it?" "No," they answered, "we've decided to shun you."

Discussion Questions

- Have a debate where one side argues that race and gender differences are real, defined by present-day understandings, and one side argues that there is no basis for them. Keep track of the arguments each side makes. Where do those arguments come from? How did you learn them? How can they be tested?

- How does your current understanding of race conflict with what you've read in this chapter? If everyone accepted the anthropological explanation of race, how would our country be different? How would our world operate differently?
- Apply these same questions to gender differences.
- Discuss how racism has reinforced or not reinforced nationalism in the past. How does it affect nationalism today?
- What are some of the ways we treat men and women differently in the United States? Why do you think we maintain these differences?
- Are there any scientific reasons to prohibit same-sex marriages? Are there political reasons? If so, what are they?
- Discuss how you feel about the ideas that anal and oral sex and massaging a woman's clitoris aren't really sexual. Why do you think you feel that way? What cultural assumptions are involved?

Suggested Reading

Blakeslee, Donald J. Who Were the Plains Indian Berdaches? *Lambda Alpha Journal of Man*, Vol. 11, No. 1 (1979): 41–65. (Also available at Witchita State University's Open Access Repository, http://soar.wichita.edu/handle/10057/1747/.)

Hanks, Lucien M. *Rice and Man: Agricultural Ecology in Southeast Asia.* New York. Aldine–Atherton, 1972.

Herdt, Gilbert. *The Sambia: Ritual, Sexuality, and Change in Papua New Guinea.* Belmont, CA: Thomson/Wadsworth, 2006.

Jablonski, Nina G. *Skin: A Natural History.* Berkeley: University of California Press, 2008.

King, Gilbert. *Devil in the Grove: Thurgood Marshall, the Groveland Boys, and the Dawn of a New America.* New York. HarperCollins, 2012.

Stack, Carol. *All Our Kin: Strategies for Survival in a Black Community.* New York: Harper, 1974.

Stack, Carol. *Call to Home: African Americans Reclaim the Rural South.* New York: Basic Books, 1996.

Warnock Fernea, Elizabeth. *A Street in Marrakech: A Personal View of Women in Morocco.* Prospect Heights, IL: Waveland Press, 1988.

Weiner, Annette. *Women of Value, Men of Renown: New Perspectives in Trobriand Exchange.* Austin: University of Texas Press, 1983.

Ideas about kinship vary over time and place. There was a time in many parts of America when this family was considered illegal. *Photo used with permission.*

3

From Inside and Out

One of the most basic tenets of anthropology is understanding the difference between what people say and think they do and what they actually do. You might say it's the difference between seeing things from the inside and from the outside. Marvin Harris (1981) has a description that may make sense:

> Anthropologists regard it as their solemn duty to represent the hopes and fears, values and goals, beliefs and rituals of different groups and communities as seen from within, the way people who belong to these groups and communities perceive them to be, the way they want them to be seen by others. But that can only be half the job. The other half is to describe and explain what people are actually saying and doing from the standpoint of the objective study of culture and history. (p. 15)

So here's a way you can learn how to do this, right in the palm of your hand. Linguists discuss the difference between the sounds we really make (phonetics—or from the outside) and the sounds we hear (phonemics—or from the inside). For example, some of the sounds we hear as the "same" are really different. Americans, for instance, hear the "t" of "tip" as the same as the "t" of "pit." If you hold your hand in front of your mouth and say each word, you'll feel a puff of breath after the "t" of "tip" but not after the "p." But if you try it with "pit," the puff is after the "p" but not after the "t." That breath is called aspiration. The aspirated and unaspirated "p," with and without the puff, are different sounds. So are the aspirated and unaspirated "t." Some alphabets have separate letters for these different sounds, but in American English, we hear them as the same. They may really be different, but we don't hear that. So from the American perspective, there's no difference. From the anthropologist's outsider perspective, there is an observable difference.

Sociocultural anthropologists extend the idea from language to the rest of culture with the ideas of emic—how we define or describe something from the inside—and etic—what's observable from the outside. In this chapter, we're going to explain how these ideas help us understand how people know which relatives they can marry or have sex with and which ones they will avoid sexually, although they may be close in other ways. Yes, that's what we said—which *relatives* they can marry or have sex with. Already we've gone outside of what most Americans think is a normal falling-in-love scenario.

Stay tuned: this will provide us with some hints about how to understand other relationships between the realities we live in and the various ways we understand them.

KINSHIP

Everyone has relatives, and we can make a genealogy of any person that goes as far back as memory can take us, if not all the way back to our first ancestors. We use triangles to represent males, circles to represent females, an equal sign to mean marriage, and vertical lines to indicate descent—whose son or daughter a person is. As you go up the diagram, we say you *ascend*—Latin for "go up"—and as you go down the diagram, we say you *descend*—Latin for "go down." Every genealogy has a reference point, an "I" that defines all of the relationships. We call that I by the Latin word for I, *ego*.

Here's a hint on how to read this next part. Make a copy of Figure 3-1 so you can keep it close to the book and don't have to keep turning back to see it. And don't be afraid to use your finger to point to things as you work through them.

Figure 3-1 defines what most Americans think of as a family: a mom, a dad, a brother, and a sister who are kids of the mom and dad. We can link such relationships to make larger genealogical diagrams as Figure 3-2 shows.

This diagram shows an ego, her brother, mom, dad, aunts, uncles, and cousins. (We'll get to the superscript X's, Y's, and ?'s in a minute.) At least that's how most Americans would see it. But not everyone on the planet would agree. For instance, many folks would say that it's weird to lump all of those people in ego's generation, A, B, C, D, E, F, G, and H, into the same category and call them the same thing because they are obviously so different. What makes them different, from many points of view, is that they belong to different lineages. Remember, a lineage is a group of people who trace descent from a common ancestor. As we said in Chapter 2, they can be patrilineal if people trace descent in the male line or matrilineal if people stress only the female links.

Think in terms of a matrilineal lineage like the people of the Pacific Island of Truk do. They get their lineage affiliation from their mothers, which means ego and her brother belong to the lineage of their mother. Mother's brother and sister also belong to that same lineage. We'll call that "Lineage X."

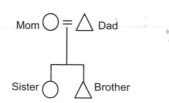

Figure 3-1 Elements of genealogy.

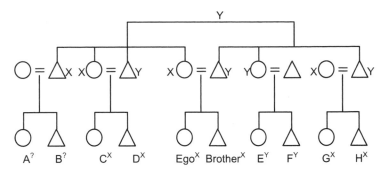

Figure 3-2 Matrilineal lineage.

Because they only stress the female links, C and D also belong to the same lineage. A and B belong to the lineage of *their* mom. That will be a different lineage because of the incest prohibition on Truk that prohibits people from marrying other people of the same lineage, because an X man cannot marry an X woman. Ego will call her brother "brother." But she will also call D "brother" and C "sister" because they are in her lineage and in the same generation as she is. B is a guy she can think about for a husband.

Lineages are the important units when people think about "family." A person's family is not just her mom, dad, and siblings; it is all of her lineage mates that are brothers and sisters as well as the women of her mother's generation who are the same as her mother. Ego's dad belongs to a different lineage (Y) from her mom or else it would be a brother marrying a sister—if they were in the same lineage. He gets his lineage affiliation from his mother, so he is in the same lineage with his brothers and sisters—all of them are Y's.

Because it is lineages that are families, it is lineages that have relationships with other lineages. If ego's dad married her mom, that is a relationship between those two lineages—X and Y. Suppose Dad's lineage is supposed to marry women from Mom's lineage. Then all Y men marry X women, as in Figure 3-3.

Then Dad's brother, the father of G and H, would also marry a woman from Mom's lineage. So G and H would be in lineage X and therefore be brothers and sisters of ego, and their mom would be ego's mother's sister.

So, ego would call C, D, G, and H her siblings, and she can't marry them or even fool around with them. E and F are of lineage Y because their mom is Y. Because Y men marry X women, the father of C and D is also from lineage Y, but because his wife, mother of C and D, is from lineage Y, they also belong to lineage Y.

That means ego is likely to fall madly in love with F and F will fall madly in love with ego, and they are going to be married. Why? Because X women marry Y men and Y men marry X women, and ego has known and experienced this all of ego's life. Ego could also marry B because he is from another lineage, and he's not a brother, but that would break the pattern of exchange. It wouldn't be consistent with family values.

Figure 3-3 Women of lineage X marry men of lineage Y. Men of lineage Y marry women of lineage X.

So what Americans call cousins the Trukese people think of as either brothers and sisters or potential spouses, but surely different from each other and not at all the same kind of thing. Anthropologists call the ones that Trukese think of as potential spouses **cross cousins**. (Now is a good time to pull out the copy of Figure 3-2.) Here's the formula. Cross cousins are the children of ego's parent's siblings of the opposite sexes. That's Dad's sister's kids and mother's brother's kids. Anthropologists call what Trukese think of as brothers and sisters **parallel cousins**. They are all of the children of the parent's siblings of the same sex—father's brother's and mother's sister's kids.

The only reason this is a little confusing to Americans is that we don't think in terms of lineages and because we think of all cousins being the same kind of relationship and probably nobody you'd marry.

We can break all genealogies down into "mother," "father," "brother" and "sister," "son," and "daughter." Anthropologists call these M, F, B, Z (for sister), S (for son), and D. So cross cousins are ego's MBD, MBS, FZD, and FZS. Parallel cousins are MZS, MZD, FBD, and FBS. What we are doing is using genealogies to represent lineage relationships.

What kind of lineages do Americans have? We don't. Our last names work somewhat like patrilineal lineages, but they don't define groups. Americans and most Europeans have what we call **kindreds**—that's the group of all relatives within a certain genealogical distance that are related by any link at all, all the cousins, for instance. Only siblings have exactly the same kindreds. Americans share exactly the same cousins only with brothers and sisters. Kindreds were important to the medieval Icelanders for vengeance. If someone hurt one of "us," then we would get our kindred together and hurt them back.

The genealogical diagrams define an *etic grid*—that is, an outside view or a universal system of kin relationships. Just as each language has its own phonemic system, the sounds and meanings that matter to only that group of people, different people have different ways of organizing genealogical relationships into emic patterns that are meaningful to them.

Remember the problems with Freud in our discussion of gender? That was the problem of assuming that everyone's culture defines sex in the same way Victorian Viennese people did, that their cultures defined the erotic and the sexual in the same way Freud did. So Freud was assuming there was an etic grid for this stuff, but in fact, he was being ethnocentric because he was thinking that *his* way of thinking about things was the natural way, the only way to do it. It is necessary to be careful not to be **ethnocentric** when we talk about emics and etics. Ethnocentrism is thinking that your own emic system is a universal etic system.

For instance, whenever people get married one of the first things they have to decide is where to live. If there is some pattern to it, we call it a **residence rule**. If the newlyweds usually live with the husband's people, we say they are **patrilocal**. If they live with the wife's people, we say they are **matrilocal**. If they live in a different place from the family (remember, this is usually a lineage) of either mate, then we say they are **neolocal**.

What difference could any of this make? Anthropologists have tried to figure out whether the kind of residence is necessarily connected to anything else, like the kind of lineage (it's not) or the way they get their food—from gardens, from plowing farms, from foraging.

An anthropologist named Ward Goodenough was working in Truk in 1947. He did a census of all the households on the island and figured out which people followed which residence rule. When he finished, he compared his results with those of another anthropologist, J. L. Fischer, who had done another census of the same people just three years earlier. Goodenough found that the same people were in the same households, but he and Fischer had counted differently, so their results didn't agree. For instance, in one household lived an old man and his second wife, his three sons by his first wife, and the wife of his oldest son. This looks like it is a patrilocal extended family—a patrilocal family of more than one generation, since the son's wife as well as the father's had joined the men's household. Both of the wives had moved to the same household when they married men from the household.

But it wasn't that simple. Remember that family in Truk means matrilineal lineage. Land belongs to lineages, not to individuals. The father had married a woman and moved to her lineage place to live in a house that her lineage owned. The first wife's lineage sister lived nearby with her husband and their kids. The pattern was that the women stayed put with their lineage and their husbands joined them. Now it looks like matrilocal residence. In Truk, family values means being with brothers and sisters. Nobody would want their kids to grow up separated from their siblings. So when the father's first wife died, her lineage allowed him to stay on with his children so they could be with their brothers and sisters. For the same reason, they let him stay there when he remarried.

It's important for newlyweds to think about how to make a living in Truk just as it is anywhere else. They need access to some land because gardening is the only way to provide for people. Lineages own land. If they want their kids to grow up with their siblings, they look for some land in the woman's lineage place. If the wife's lineage doesn't have any land for them to use, then the couple can look in the husband's place. If neither of those places has any land, they can check her dad's lineage or his dad's lineage place.

Matrilineal lineages aren't mirror images of patrilineal ones because the men have formal authority in both. In Truk, that means that men stay close to their own lineages so that they can take care of their responsibilities to their own brothers and sisters.

If the new husband's lineage can give the couple more or better land than the wife's lineage can give them and the wife's lineage is far away from the husband's place, then they might live with the husband's lineage and give up on raising the kids with their siblings.

Their choice is not between living with the wife's parents or the husband's parents. Goodenough concluded that the whole etic grid for residence rules was ethnocentric. The rules that anthropologists used for residence rules weren't the same as the Trukese rules.

Goodenough's conclusion was that anthropologists shouldn't use their own ideas as universal ones; we should find out how people make sense of their own worlds and not assume that they think about things the same way we do. We discover the emic categories that are important to the people themselves, just as we discover the sounds that are important to their languages or what relatives count as brothers and sisters.

CULTURAL CODES

Genealogical diagrams are etic. They tell us actual relationships. But don't confuse genealogy with biology. Goodenough found that the people Trukese listed as fathers in their genealogies weren't necessarily their mothers' sperm donors. You wouldn't want to assume that genealogies accurately represent biological relationships.

Kinship systems are emic. They tell us how different groups of people think about those relationships. For instance, one culture's cousin can be another's brother or sister. Incest prohibitions prohibit marriage to brothers and sisters. But a different kind of cousin may be a preferred marriage partner. We can broaden the idea of emics and etics beyond language and kinship and think in terms of **cultural codes**: not only the emic categories people use to make sense of their worlds, but also how they use them, for instance, to figure out where to live after they get married.

To understand this inside point of view for the people of Truk, we should know about matrilineal lineages, who controls land, who makes decisions in lineages, family values, and the alternatives that are available to people. Cultural codes are the assumptions people use in everyday life, ideas about reality, meaning, how to divide things into categories (cousins, cross cousins), and how things are related to one another (a person marries a cross cousin).

The biological approach to curing in many industrial lands is more or less mechanical. According to this view, all of us are mechanisms that can malfunction. When our body mechanisms malfunction, we are sick. Doctors are supposed to identify the malfunction and fix it by giving us a drug to change our body chemistry, by surgery or physical therapy to rearrange some component of the mechanism, or by some combination of these. Even physicians like Dean Ornish, who are way out on the margins with ideas like meditation to reduce stress, operate in terms of effects on the mechanism.

In the late 1960s and early 1970s, Paul lived with Lisu people in the mountains of northern Thailand. They thought that if some malfunction causes a person to be sick, then medicines and physical therapies can fix it. They even have specialists in herbal medicines to treat these cases. They think of hospitals and doctors as doing the same kinds of things their medicine women do.

But they think that no amount of medicines will help a person if a spirit is causing the sickness. Then the only effective thing to do is to find out what spirit is responsible and what the human victim did to offend the spirit and then make good the offense. There were twenty-three households and about 105 people in the Lisu village where Paul lived. He recorded that people sacrificed 311 chickens and 100 pigs in 411 ceremonies during a single year. During the same year, they made seven visits to lowland hospitals—four for cuts, two by the same man for a shotgun wound, and one for an intractable disease of a shaman's wife. A total of 101 people came to Paul for help—some from different villages—and he did the best he could with his limited skills and supplies to help people with tropical ulcers, cuts, and whatever else aspirin, tetracycline, and disinfectants could treat.

There were also "injection doctors," usually former Thai Army medics who had learned a little about treating sickness in the army and decided to do it for a living for part of the year or full-time. Village people got 43 injections from these traveling medics. That came to 411 cures that involved spirits somehow and 151 that did not, a total of 562. So, approximately 73 percent of the curing efforts were about spirits and approximately 27 percent were about mechanics.

Here we want to pause and insert a note for future reference. Note that whatever else is going on, people are killing chickens and pigs, spending time and money on medicine as well as ceremonies, and all of their actions have consequences for their households and their village. We will come back to these points later, but for the moment, think about how any time people do anything, we leave traces for future archaeologists to find. Our actions have consequences.

Industrial folks have a theory of disease that says it's mechanical. It is elaborate and has many branches to deal with cells, cell reproduction, genetics, bones, kids, moms, women, men, microorganisms, infections, populations, hearts, lungs, and a lot of other things people can go to medical school to study. Sometimes it makes one wonder if they got all the specialties together to make a person what kind of creature they would come up with.

Lisu have a different theory of disease. According to their cultural code, causes may be mechanical but may involve spirits. If they are mechanical, they respond to medical treatment; and if they are not, they do not (see Figure 3-4).

Somebody is sick. Lisu interpret the symptoms they see according to their theory of disease to figure out what to do about it. Since they know that spirits can cause people to be sick, they need information about whether a spirit

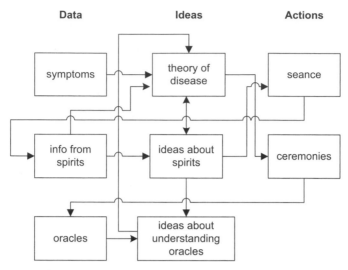

Figure 3-4 How the Lisu use their cultural code to heal sick people.

is behind this instance and what might be going on. To get this information, they ask a **shaman**, a person whom spirits can possess, to call down his spirits so that they can ask them directly. Two shamans lived in the village where Paul lived. Someone would ask one of the shamans to help, and the shaman would come to the person's house and stand in front of the altar.

On the back walls of most houses hangs a plank or two. On these planks are Chinese teacups, the same small, handleless cups you can find in Chinese restaurants in the United States and other countries. Each of these cups represents a spirit. Facing the altars, the cups represent, from left to right, the household head's mother, father, father's mother, and father's father. If you guessed that these folks have patrilineal lineages, you are right.

Next come the spirits of the lineage. The first, right after grandfather, is the third-generation great-grandfather, the first of the ancestors who can be a lineage spirit. He is the most junior of the lineage spirits. Each lineage then has a series of spirits, each with its own name, that are ranked from least to most powerful.

The shaman stands in front of the altar and invokes his third-generation great-grandfather spirit, the most junior of the lineage spirits, by saying, "The people have called me to help them. Someone here is sick. I am asking you to help me. Please come down." The shaman bends from the waist and holds a handful of lit joss sticks as he sways back and forth, whistling, until the first spirit comes to ride his horse. Then the shaman begins his "spirit singing," as Lisu call it. He speaks with the voice of the spirit who talks to the people.

"Why have you called me?"

Now several people are gathered in the house, and someone answers that this person is sick and the people need some help.

"I am just a minor spirit. I don't know much. If the spirits help you, you will have to use your pigs, use your chickens, use liquor, use joss sticks."

"We have pigs to offer; we have chickens to offer; we have liquor to offer; we have joss sticks to offer."

The people explain the problem, and this most junior spirit calls on more powerful lineage spirits, who come down one by one to see whether they can help. These spirits get in touch with other spirits and ask who is causing this person to be sick in this way. They usually find an answer—it may be the spirit of the stream, the stone spirit, the hill spirit, or one of a number of others that the person has inadvertently offended, perhaps by stepping on it on the way to work. In any case, the person must make recompense.

People then use their theory of disease to interpret this information and conclude that they will offer a chicken or pig to a certain spirit. The next morning, the household may offer a chicken to the spirit. After the ceremony is done, the people eat the chicken. Or the spirit may demand a pig. Then a lot more people come to the feast that follows the offering. A male relative builds an altar like a small table of bamboo outside, near the place where the offense happened, and offers the animal alive. Then he kills the animal. If they sacrifice a pig, someone expert in interpreting omens looks at the pig's liver to see whether the spirit has accepted the offering, whether it was directed to the correct spirit, or whether it is the correct spirit but too small an offering. Then people would cook the animal, and the officiant would offer it again, cooked. If people offered a chicken, people would cook and eat the chicken and then check the thigh bones for oracles by tapping splints of bamboo about the size of toothpicks into the holes in the bones and reading them for information.

There are standard ways of reading oracles. They aren't random or personal opinions; they follow a definite system. People then use their theory of disease to interpret this information and decide whether more ceremonies are necessary. People use their cultural code—ideas—to understand the world (or data about it), they base their actions on these understandings, and their actions have consequences for the world.

This keeps on going until the symptoms go away, until the people have some reason to think that spirits aren't involved, or until the person dies, whichever happens first. Usually the symptoms abate after a while.

When Paul discussed this with a physician, the doctor said that it was a good thing that most human ailments don't last more than about ten days or his profession would be in trouble.

So, if we see a Lisu person get sick, ask a shaman to call down his spirits, and then offer a chicken or a pig and we want to make sense of it, we would ask, first, How does it make sense to the people doing it? What is their cultural code?

The logic of this system is that you can do things that annoy other people. When you come to know about something like that, it's up to you to do something to make it right with the other person. If you don't, they have the right to hurt you, so it's in your interest to do something quickly. Spirits are like people, except that we can't see them, and they are more powerful than we are. Because we can't see them, it's easy to annoy them. Like people, they then hurt the person who offended them. That's the indication that the person must do something to make it right with the spirit. The person must find out who is offended and what it would take to make it right and then do whatever it is.

We can generalize this approach to understanding people. There are realities that people understand in terms of cultural codes. People base their actions on their cultural understandings, and those actions have consequences for the realities (see Figure 3-5).

Suppose that one of the central assumptions of your culture is that individuals are important and that their choices determine everything that happens to them. Some kids decide to drop out of high school. That's their choice, and they live with it. Some go to college. That's their choice, and they have better chances in life than the kids who finished high school but didn't go to college. Or someone who works a minimum-wage job doesn't have any health insurance. Why? Because she chose not to buy it. Everything is a matter of individual choices.

Now we look at a city or region and see that some folks aren't doing as well as others. What do we do? We teach them to make better choices. We educate them. Teenage girls are getting pregnant? Teach them not to mess around. Kids are doing drugs? Teach them to just say no. People have good hearts and want to help folks do better, so they start teaching kids these things. That's the "action" part. The culture tells us that we can fix any problem by educating people, so we start up programs to do that. That has consequences, too—now kids have to sit through boring, stupid discussions and classes about how to just say no and why they shouldn't be having any fun. But someone gets paid for those programs. And that means those resources aren't going somewhere else. So there's no soap or toilet paper in the bathrooms, and the school building is falling down.

We look back at the same system after our programs are operating and say, "Oh, the school is falling down. We should teach these people to keep up their schools," and so on. That's the way cultures work. We try to understand what we see in terms of the ideas we have, then we base our actions on those ideas, and our actions make a difference in the real world, and so on. Sometimes we see a problem, but instead of finding out about it, we just understand it in terms of our culture, and we try to fix it, and things get worse than they were before. That's how we can have people with good hearts working in systems of institutional racism. People don't think what they are doing is racist, but racism continues.

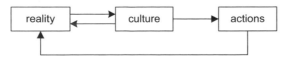

Figure 3-5 Our cultures tell us how to act and our actions change things.

Maybe you're tired of hearing about racism. So, you need to get to work and to school. There's no good bus system or trains. You earn some money and buy a car. Now you can get where you need to be when you need to be there. And you have a car, and that feels good. You're in control. You can manage your schedule.

You've heard of greenhouse gases? Every time you turn the key in your car, you're adding to them. You've figured out things according to your culture; you've solved problems according to the ways that your culture makes available. And you make a bad situation worse. Is this because you just make bad decisions? No. Is it because you really want to screw up the planet? No.

For one thing, it's because car companies made it impossible for you to ride a train or a bus when they purchased the public transportation systems and destroyed them in the early decades of the past century. Why? So they could create a market for their product. In late February 2009, when Barack Obama delivered his first address to a joint session of Congress, he said he believed that "the nation that invented the automobile cannot walk away from it." The press was all over him because they say it was actually a German who invented the automobile. We *can* walk away from the automobile and we should—as fast as we can. One thing we could have done is kick the automobile industry while it was down and reintroduce mass-transit systems from buses to interurbans to high-speed trains between cities. We should be making the world safe for bikes and trains, not cars. But that didn't happen in the United States because the corporations are strong enough to affect political decisions.

So what do we do? Educate people? Teach them they're doing something bad whenever they get in their cars? Will that make any difference except to make good people like yourselves feel guilty when they drive? Does that accomplish anything? Does educating people about drugs, sex, and gun violence make any difference? No.

We say we must get outside our cultures and understand systems for what they are. To do that, however, we must give up some ideas that we think are natural, just "the way things are." One of those is the idea of individualism.

Figure 3-5 on the previous page defines the research program for anthropology, one that someone pursuing anthropology could take up. We must understand not only how others understand their worlds and their cultures, but also how their cultures inform their actions and how those actions affect the realities in which the people live.

Think about the situation facing Nasrudin when the king announced that he would hang anyone who lied from a gallows in front of the city gate. Nasrudin was the first one at the gate. The king's officer asked him where he was going. "I'm going to be hanged," Nasrudin said. "But," said the officer, "if I hang you, you were telling the truth, and I'm only supposed to hang people who lie. But if I don't hang you, then you were lying."

Sometimes it's tough to be a bureaucrat.

Discussion Questions

- A student from a tiny Lisu village just got off the airplane. You meet the student and you both go to the downtown of a big city. Pick three things that you would have to explain to the student and explain how you would do it. How do the concepts of emic and etic apply to these explanations?
- Discuss where the American prohibition against marrying cousins comes from. What purpose does this belief serve? (Remember, avoidance of bad genetic traits from inbreeding is not the answer.)
- How have our own cultural codes determined our medical practices? Consider discussing childbirth, acupuncture, herbs, and psychotherapy as they relate to Americans' understanding of acceptable medical procedures. Try to develop an etic understanding of some of these—what would it look like?
- Remember the last time your family got together for a holiday. How did that go? What would have been different if your neighbors, employers, and the grocery store clerks—all cousins of one kind or another—had been there?

Suggested Reading

Ekvall, Robert. *Fields on the Hoof: Nexus of Tibetan Nomadic Pastoralism.* New York: Holt, Rinehart & Winston, 1968.

Harris, Marvin. *America Now.* New York: Simon & Schuster, 1981.

Malinowski, Bronisław. *Argonauts of the Western Pacific.* Long Grove, IL: Waveland, 1922 (reprinted 1984).

Weiner, Annette B. *Women of Value, Men of Renown: New Perspectives in Trobriand Exchange.* Austin: University of Texas Press, 1976.

The Lisu village Paul lived in during his fieldwork in the late 1960s. *Photo by E. Paul Durrenberger.*

4

Ecological Systems

Cultural codes are mental, things in our heads. But the logic of our cultural codes is the only way we have to think things through. So we base our actions on the conclusions we can draw from the evidence we have and the logic of our cultural codes. Our actions have consequences, many of which we never notice or necessarily want to happen. Whether we understand the consequences or not, it is necessary to deal with them. As people, the only way we have to deal with our environments is the cultural codes that define our understandings of reality. For instance, every time you put the keys in a car and turn on the engine, you contribute to global warming. It doesn't matter what you think about it. You may be "for the environment" and you may be driving a load of stuff to the recycling center or on your way to buy organic food or to camp in the wilderness. Your actions have exactly the same consequences as if you'd set out to pollute the environment.

All industrial processes are polluting. It doesn't matter whether they are in Poland or China or the United States or Brazil. There may be different laws about how much of the pollution the process can allow into the water and air, but all industrial processes are inherently polluting. You can't make a car without polluting the environment. You can't drive a car without polluting the environment.

Some kinds of agriculture in some places may be sustainable, but not all forms are. Industrial agriculture like people use in the United States, for instance, is not. We know that because it takes more energy to produce the food than the food has in it. That's why growing corn to make ethanol to burn in cars isn't the answer to oil dependency. It takes more energy to grow the corn than the ethanol has in it.

Another corn-growing culture was the Maya, and their civilization collapsed. The descendants of the people are still there, but their kings and wars and temples—the whole complex of their civilization—are gone. Some people say the Maya rulers didn't understand that they were in trouble and didn't do anything about it. In other words, what they were doing had some negative consequences, but the people didn't notice until it was too late. Others say that the Maya knew they had some problems with corn production and tried to solve them by increasing production. According to their cultural code, the way to increase corn production would be to make the gods happy. To make the gods happy, they built temples and made sacrifices. But when they took labor away from corn production to build temples, there was less corn, and the problem got worse. So they built more temples, and so on.

The question for us is whether Americans are like the Maya in either of these interpretations. Do we just not notice pollution and global warming? Or do we know what's going on and not do anything about it? Or is there something in the way we respond—with our political or religious or any other cultural system—that is making it worse instead of better? It's hard to know the answers to these questions from inside the system and until the story is finished, when we can look back on it with the benefit of time. Even then, not everyone agrees, as with the Maya.

Sometimes people do things that work well without even knowing it. How can they solve problems without knowing what they are? Over the course of years, they have tried things that turn out to work for them and continue to work for them, so they don't need to know how the system works; it just does. People's understandings of what they are doing, their cultural codes, may differ from ours, but what counts ecologically is the results of their actions.

There are ecological consequences whenever Tsembaga people of New Guinea kill pigs. They kill pigs to pay their debts to their ancestors. They are in debt to ancestors because the ancestors helped them in a war with nearby groups, so they kill their pigs and sponsor a great feast to pay back the ancestors for their help and to treat their allies. But they still owe the ancestors, so they promise to pay the ancestors when they have enough pigs and start with the pigs that remain to rebuild their stocks of pigs. Tsembaga cannot go to war again until they pay the debt because the ancestors won't help them. All of this stuff about ancestors and debts is part of their cultural code. But it informs their actions, and their actions have ecological consequences.

Pigs eat the same food people do—sweet potatoes—and women do most of the work to grow the sweet potatoes in their gardens. At the end of a war, they have only a few pigs. Since they only have to feed the people and a few pigs, the women make fewer gardens, and the land that they aren't using can lie fallow and recover its fertility. First, people pen their pigs up on the old garden spots to root around and soften the ground. The pigs act as bionic plows. Then wild plants take over the garden spot. The longer the land recuperates, the more fertile it is, and the women can use the most productive gardens. The longer they use the gardens, however, the less productive they become until they aren't worth cultivating and cannot be used for gardens until they lie fallow again.

Figure 4-1 shows the relationships among these elements as a system. This diagram indicates that the number of gardens fluctuates up or down with the number of pigs; the length of fallow changes opposite the number of gardens, so the more gardens, the shorter the fallow periods; the fertility varies in the same direction as the length of fallow; and the fertility goes in the opposite direction from the number of gardens. More pigs, more gardens, shorter fallow, less fertility, more gardens. Fewer pigs, fewer gardens, longer fallow, more fertility, fewer gardens.

As there are more and more pigs, the women make more gardens, the fallow decreases, and they need more food for more pigs but work harder for each sweet potato as the fertility declines. Pigs aren't docile. They get into neighbors' gardens and root around and destroy other people's crops. When this happens, the other people complain and take legal action against the pig's owner. So more pigs also means more disputes and more complaints of overwork from the women. Figure 4-2 shows how this works.

The elders hear all of the disputes and decide how to resolve them. The same guys (yes, all guys) deal with the women increasingly complaining about too much work. When these negative aspects of having so many pigs become intolerable to the elders, they conclude that there are enough pigs to pay off the debt to the ancestors and sponsor another big feast and kill off most of the pigs. Then they are free to go to war again because the ancestors will help them.

There's one other variable in this system—how healthy the people are. That's not so much because their health determines how hard they can work but because when someone is sick, like Lisu, they sacrifice a pig as part of the curing ritual. So if everyone is in good health, the population of pigs grows faster than if they kill off some of the pigs for curing ceremonies.

Roy Rappaport, who studied Tsembaga and wrote the book *Pigs for the Ancestors*, concluded that Tsembaga ritual was a regulating mechanism in this system. A regulating mechanism is a part of the system that keeps the values of variables within certain limits. The classic example is a thermostat. When

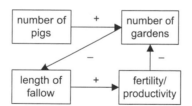

Figure 4-1 How pigs affect the fertility of gardens.

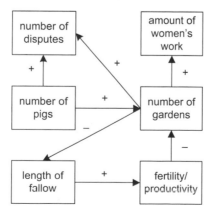

Figure 4-2 How pigs affect social relations.

the temperature in a room gets hot enough, the heat trips a heat-sensitive switch that turns off the furnace. As the room cools down, the switch turns on the furnace, and it begins to heat up the air again until the switch turns it off. The heat-sensitive switch is the regulating mechanism that keeps the air temperature within certain limits. The Tsembaga cultural code keeps the number of pigs within certain limits because it provides a way to turn on or off the sacrifice that regulates the number of pigs. So there are always some pigs, but they don't get out of hand and eat the people out of house and home. The critical question in the system is what is "enough pigs?" Enough pigs is the number that makes the complaints and disputes too annoying for the elders, so they are willing to flip the switch and repay the ancestors the pigs they owe them from the last war. After they do that, they can go to war again until they have enough pigs to pay the debt they got into from starting the war, and so on, as Figure 4-3 shows.

In terms of the model we developed at the end of the previous chapter, we can understand this part of Tsembaga cultural ecology according to Table 4-1.

This ritual cycle assures local groups a supply of good protein, especially when they need it most—when they are sick. It distributes local surpluses of pork throughout the region by the feasts so that those who have extra pigs feed those with less than enough. It facilitates trade because the allies people invite to their feasts bring gifts. It keeps the number of people adjusted to the area of land. It limits the fighting to frequencies that don't endanger any of the groups. Finally, but most important, it maintains the environment in good condition for gardening by guaranteeing that the fallow periods don't get too short or the fertility too low.

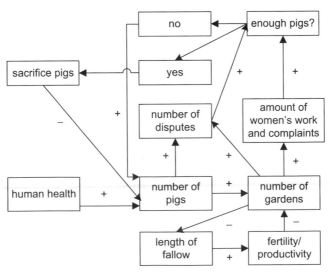

Figure 4-3 When are there enough pigs?

Table 4–1

Reality	Cultural code	Action
Number of pigs	Ideas of debt	Kill pigs
Productivity of gardens	Ideas about ancestors	Raise pigs
Length of fallow periods	Debts to ancestors payable in pigs	Make gardens
Number of disputes		
Amount of work for women		
Number of complaints from women		

Tsembaga warfare is not like American wars. First, they can't fight another war until they are out of debt for the previous one. Then, they don't use napalm, drones, machine guns, fragmentation grenades, Humvees, tanks, and airplanes. They use spears and bows and arrows. Their warfare is more like American football—long meetings with short periods of violence. People get hurt, and some die, but not all that many.

Although our agriculture isn't like theirs, there are some similarities. The more livestock we feed, the more of our land and agricultural effort goes to growing feed for the animals. If you drive across the vast expanses from Illinois through Iowa early in the fall, you see the beauty of an endless sea of corn waving gently in the breeze as thunderheads gather on the horizon. This corn goes to pigs and cattle as well as to factories.

Giant factories in the Midwest convert corn into ethanol as an additive for gasoline. Corporations seem to have the fix in with politicians from the area to support tax breaks for ethanol and promote this fuel additive as environmentally safe. Just outside Cedar Rapids, Iowa, is a plant that fills the sky with plumes of fragrant white vapors. At the plant they convert corn into endless tank-car-loads of corn sweetener destined for soda and bakery goods. The biggest single "food" in the United States diet is soda. It accounts for one of every five calories that Americans consume. Some researchers think that such sweet drinks are a major cause of obesity in the United States.

Check the contents of almost any industrially produced food or drink product and you'll see "corn sweeteners" or "corn syrup," most likely from ADM, the giant agricultural corporation, Archer Daniels, Midland. That's why it supports an army of lobbyists in Washington, D.C., to retain a high tariff on imported sugar and work with the right-wing sugar magnates who fled from Cuba to Florida and drained the wetlands of that state to reestablish their sugar plantations in the United States. Together, ADM and the Cubans form a strong political block to keep Cuban sugar expensive relative to their products.

As with Tsembaga, the political decisions (How many disputes are there in the group? Can we go to war with other groups?) are connected to the economic ones (How many gardens, how fertile, and how many women work in gardens?) and the economic actions (killing pigs) have consequences for the environment (longer fallow periods, more fertile gardens).

Much of the rest of the corn from the Midwest that doesn't go for sweeteners or ethanol is destined to feed livestock in industrial animal production facilities close by or to feed livestock in Russia, China, and other lands. One thing that's different from Tsembaga or Lisu is that it's hard to find any regulating mechanism that puts limits on anything in this system.

We'll get to the similarities between the system in the United States and others in more detail later, but here we'll just mention that the signals that go through the system determine how it will act. For instance, Tsembaga women complain of overwork. That's a signal. There are too many disputes. That's another signal. When the signals all align, the elders trip the regulating mechanism and the feasting begins. Like Tsembaga, the American system responds to signals—some of them about pigs and their feed.

Julian Steward is the anthropologist who did a lot to develop cultural ecology in the mid-1950s with his book, *Theory of Culture Change*. Roy Rappaport's work on Tsembaga is an example of cultural ecology. This is an approach in anthropology that emphasizes that although all of the elements of a culture are interrelated, the parts that have most to do with the way people make their livings are the most important and determine the rest.

Steward called the social, political, and religious patterns most closely connected to the way people get their livings the **culture core**, or central aspects of the culture. Different emic systems define different cultures. Steward wanted to understand the reasons these differences came to be. He ruled out the environment itself because people with different cultures live in the same environments. It could just be the history of the people, but that doesn't answer the "why?" question—it just leads to another question: why do different cultures have different histories?

Steward borrowed the idea of ecology—the total web of relationships among life forms in an area—from biology. Just as ecology understands a population in terms of its relations with the web of life in an area, cultural ecology describes the interactions of physical, biological, and cultural factors in an area to explain why different cultures take different forms. Steward suggested that anthropologists analyze the interrelationships of the productive technology with the environment—for instance, how Tsembaga men make gardens with digging sticks and how the women tend the gardens and keep them up after that; how women keep pigs, what they feed them, and where they get the food. We already see a division of labor between men and women, and we go on to see how people organize themselves for production and what the consequences are.

People solve problems, and the solutions create other problems. For instance, Tsembaga feed their pigs sweet potatoes, but the more gardens they make and the more pigs they have, the more the pigs invade other people's gardens and cause disputes. Steward suggested that after we describe the interactions of the technology and the environment, we check how the patterns of behavior involved in making a living affect other areas of behavior. For instance, Tsembaga ritual regulates the frequency of warfare, the number of pigs, the amount of land people cultivate, and the fertility of the land.

TO EACH HIS OWN

Charles O. Frake

"Cultural Ecology and Ethnography," 1962, *American Anthropologist*,
Vol. 64, pp. 53–59

The necessity of coming to terms with one's informants' concepts is well recognized in some ethnographic endeavors, kinship studies providing the most notable example. No ethnographer describes social relations in an alien society by referring to the doings of "uncles," "aunts," and "cousins." Many ethnographers do, however, describe the pots and pans, the trees and shrubs, the soils and rocks of a culture's environment solely in terms of categories projected from the investigator's culture. In comparison with studying religious conceptions or kinship relations, the description of the tangible objects of a culture's ecosystem is usually regarded as one of the ethnographer's simpler tasks. If he does not know a word for a specimen of fauna, flora, or soil, he can always ship it off to a specialist for "identification." However, if one insists that no specimen has been described ethnographically until one has stated the rules for its identification in the culture being studied, then the problem of describing a tangible object such as a plant may become rather more complex than the relatively simple task of defining contrasts between categories of kinsmen. Consider, for example, the problem of identifying plants according to the Hanunóo system of folk botany (Conklin 1954, 1957). The Hanunóo, tropical-forest agriculturists of the central Philippines, exhaustively partition their plant world into more than 1,600 categories, whereas systematic botanists classify the same flora into less than 1,200 species. To place correctly, by Hanunóo standards, a newly encountered plant specimen in the appropriate one of the 1,600 categories requires rather fine discriminations among plants, and these discriminations rely on features generally remote from the botanist's count of stamens and carpels. By discovering what one must know in order to classify plants and other ecological components in Hanunóo fashion, one learns what the Hanunóo consider worth attending to when making decisions or how to behave within their ecosystem.

An ethnographer, then, cannot be satisfied with a mere cataloging of the components of a cultural ecosystem according to the categories of Western science. He must also describe the environment as the people themselves construe it according to the categories of their ethnoscience. From a presentation of the rules by which people decide upon the category membership of objects in their experience, an ethnographic ecology can proceed to rules for more complex kinds of behavior: killing game, clearing fields, building houses, etc. Determining the requisite knowledge for such behavior shows the ethnographer the extent to which ecological considerations, in contrast, say, to sociological ones, enter into a person's decision of what to do. The ethnographer learns, in a rather meaningful and precise sense, what role the environment in fact plays in the cultural behavior of the members of a particular society.

The kinds of factors that are important to cultural ecology are interrelations of land use, land tenure, kinship, residence rules—all of the emic or cultural code stuff that has consequences for how people produce things. But Steward also wanted to understand consequences of actions. For instance, he would want to understand the consequences of the Tsembaga ritual system or of the United States' love affair with cars and soda. So cultural ecology also studies the results of people's actions, such as obesity, global warming, and environmental pollution, whether or not the people have the same understanding of these things as we do. Our understandings may differ because we develop etic understandings based on different assumptions and procedures than the ones in the cultural codes of the people in the systems. This gets tricky when we're talking about our own culture. And we're going to show you later that it's no mistake that it's so tricky because there is a good reason for some people to try to confuse everyone else.

Each kind of technology poses different problems with different solutions. People are constrained to do some things a certain way or not at all; other things they can do any number of ways. Steward's idea was that people solve similar problems in similar ways everywhere and at every time. That's what explains cultural similarities. And the different problems of using their various technologies in dissimilar environments cause the cultural differences. These ideas started a lot of research that's still going on.

From the point of view of cultural ecology, the environment is much broader than people's physical surroundings. It involves other social groups as well. For instance, we cannot understand Tsembaga, unless we understand how they trade and make war with their neighbors.

Solving problems—**adaptive** responses—can have disadvantageous side effects. Marshall Sahlins (1968) wrote, "To adapt . . . is to do as well as possible under the circumstances—which may not turn out very well at all" (p. 369). It is not to achieve a perfect fit but to find reasonable solutions to the problems that face people.

Regarding **cultural adaptation**, Sahlins wrote, "Lots of things people do are truly stupid, if understandable." Archaeologists recover their remains and try to figure out what went wrong, as with the Maya. Remember that there is no necessity in evolution. Just because a system needs something doesn't mean it's going to happen. Was it stupid for Mayans to continue to build temples when they were running short of corn? Maybe—from our perspective. But what would you do if you knew that the gods gave you corn and to get the gods to cooperate, you had to build temples? What would you do if you knew about global warming? What would you do if you knew about the connection between politics and corn sweeteners?

Sahlins wrote about how in Fiji, people fish for food and make dried coconut, called *copra*, to sell for money. Many cosmetic products and some food products use coconut oil from this copra. Fijians use boats for fishing, but it costs money to buy and maintain a boat. Since they use boats for fishing and fishing is a subsistence activity, all kinsmen can use the boat because there is an ethic of mutuality and share and share alike for anything that has to do with subsistence. On the other hand, people can put their money into houses with tin roofs to gain prestige. Then their kinsmen can't use the product of their work. So the question Fijians face is how to allocate their money—to houses or to boats? They put it into houses so that they can reserve the benefits to themselves in line with the individualistic market ethic of coconut production. If they use it for boats, they help themselves, but they help their kinsmen just as much, and the kinsmen do nothing for it.

Everyone continues to have relatives, but they put their resources into houses and have fewer and fewer boats. Because there are fewer boats, they fish less, and their diet has less protein. Thus, the quality of their diet decreases, and they live in hot and unhealthy houses. But it is their way of adapting to the factors they face in their daily lives. Is it smart? Maybe not. Is it adaptive? Yes. Is it sustainable? No.

Cultural ecology directs our attention to those aspects of the culture most related to making a living, that is, economic systems. We need a framework that allows us to compare all economic systems such as Tsembaga and the American one in the same terms.

Although it is important to understand systems from the inside, to understand their emic meanings, anthropologists step outside them to develop frameworks that do not depend on the ideas of any single culture so we can compare cultures. and. In the next chapter, we'll explain how we can understand all economic systems in the same terms. We'll develop an etic system for studying economics whether in the United States or in New Guinea.

There's a story about an accomplished dervish who was walking beside a lake thinking about absolute truth when he heard someone on an island chanting. He noticed that the chant wasn't quite right. It wasn't the way the dervish had learned it. The scholar got a boat and rowed to the island, where he found another dervish chanting.

The scholar taught the other dervish the correct chant and got back in his boat to return to shore, satisfied that he had helped someone toward truth because his books said that this chant was so powerful that, if people did it correctly, they could walk on water. The scholar had never seen anyone walking on water, but he knew the difference between correct and incorrect chants.

As he rowed, the scholar heard the island dervish starting to chant again. But the scholar heard the wrong sounds again. As the annoyingly inaccurate syllables became louder and louder, the scholar looked over his shoulder to see the island dervish walking on the water toward his boat. "How does that chant go again?" he asked. "I've already forgotten the correct way to do it."

Remember this story when we tell you about how economists always know the right chants and go around our planet screwing up people's economies.

Discussion Questions
- Check the label on a container of soda or a bakery product. What does the label tell you about the cultural ecology of your country?

- What are some of the elements that make up your cultural ecology? Think about cars, fast food, grocery stores, corn sweeteners, and what's going on in Washington and your state capital.
- Among Tsembaga, the women complaining is an important ecological signal. What happens to complaints in your university? What is the ecological impact of not paying attention to signals like this? Are people who raise grievances called whiners to silence them? How do the signals flow through your university's system?
- Can some people send more powerful signals than others? For instance, compare the impact of a complaint you make versus one of a rich alum who donates lots of money to your university.
- What things do these signals regulate in the system? How does that happen?
- What are some of the similarities and differences between biological and cultural evolution? Does natural selection work the same way in both? What's being changed in each?
- Explain how some of the aspects of our cultural ecology work against one another, as in the example of Fiji.
- What's the point of the story about the dervish? Has anyone ever corrected you? Were you wrong to think or do what you were thinking or doing? Does the point of view make a difference?
- Why do you think we have such different perceptions (emic view) about our country than the statistics (etic view) show? For instance, the U.S. health-care system is the worst and most expensive of any developed country. Our life expectancy is lower and infant mortality higher than in most developed countries. More people live in poverty in the United States than in most developed countries. The gap between the rich and most of us is greater in the United States than in most other developed countries.

Suggested Reading

Evans-Pritchard, E. E. *The Nuer: A Description of the Modes of Livelihood and Political Institutions of a Nilotic People.* London: Clarendon Press, 1967.

Hanks, Lucien. *Rice and Man: Agricultural Ecology in Southeast Asia.* Honolulu: University of Hawaii Press, 1992.

Mintz, Sidney W. *Sweetness and Power: The Place of Sugar in Modern History.* New York: Penguin, 1995.

Rappaport, Roy. *Pigs for the Ancestors: Ritual in the Ecology of a New Guinea People.* New Haven, CT: Yale University Press, 1967 (reprint: Prospect Heights, IL: Waveland, 2000).

Shan village in Maehnogson Province, Thailand, where Paul did fieldwork in the mid-1970s. Note the irrigated rice fields. *Photo by E. Paul Durrenberger.*

5

An Anthropological Approach to Economics

There's a story about an economist, an anthropologist, and a historian who are walking together and fall into a deep, dark hole.

"We'll never get out of here," said the historian. "This is precisely what happened to Ethelred the Unready in the thirteenth century, and he died in the hole." The economist smiled.

"I think you're right," answered the anthropologist, "because on the island of Bongo Bongo where I've done extensive fieldwork, whenever people fall into a trap like this, they die." The economist smiled again.

The economist said that he wasn't a bit anxious. "Don't worry," he said. "We'll get out of here."

"How?" asked his two colleagues.

"Well," he said in a cheerfully optimistic voice, "first of all, assume a ladder."

The economic framework that anthropologists have developed does not share much with what you learn from economists in a department of economics or business administration.

For starters, the wisdom of ethnography is "Assume nothing." Any assumptions we bring with us are likely to be based on our own cultural codes and experience and thus could mislead us in understanding the people we want to understand. We'd be understanding them in our own emic terms instead of either their emic terms or etic terms. Here we are going to develop an etic economics.

First, we know that all societies provide themselves with the things people use. Second, we know that all useful things are products of someone's labor. Third, we see that people exchange some things for others. These three observations define three dimensions of economic life: consumption, production, and exchange.

Everyone consumes things. We do this by direct consumption such as eating and by using things to produce other things. The classic example is seed. People can eat it or plant it to grow more food and seed. Either way, they consume it.

For production, we'll just repeat the statement, because it's important, that all useful things are the product of someone's labor.

Exchange means that people trade things for other things. Anthropologists have distinguished three forms of exchange. **Reciprocity** means giving as much as you get—at least in the long run. There's usually a time delay between the giving and the getting. If I have a car and you need a ride, I give you a ride. Sometime when I need a ride, I know that someone will give me a ride. Or we may make an explicit deal: I'll take care of your kids tonight, and you take care of mine tomorrow night. Or it might just be sharing as people do when they have joint bank accounts and both put in whatever they have and take out whatever they need.

Christmas presents, birthday presents, and wedding and graduation presents in the United States are examples of reciprocity with different time delays. Someone gives you a birthday present, and you give that person a present when his birthday comes along. People often compare Christmas presents to be sure they're not giving too big or small a present, considering what the other person gave them the year before.

Redistribution is based on the idea of reciprocity—give something and get something equal—but it works differently. Instead of giving something directly back to the person or group that gave it to us, we give things to some central person, who then redistributes them to the people who need them. Systems of taxation are examples. We all pay taxes to various governments. When we lived in Pennsylvania, we had to pay taxes to the borough, to the township, and to the state as well as to the U.S. government. These government agencies then use the revenues for things that everyone needs, like water, sewer systems, and roads. The U.S. government uses a lot of our taxes to support a war machine. Some people who disagree with this redistribution become "war tax resisters" and don't pay their taxes in protest at the risk of being fined or jailed.

The third form of exchange is the one that's most familiar to us: the market. In **market exchange**, people exchange things for money. One of the things that people exchange for money is their labor. A **commodity** is something that people can buy and sell on a market. Most of us don't think that everything is a commodity—for instance, justice is not supposed to be a commodity that people can buy or sell. But there's that saying that in the United States you are entitled to as much justice as you can afford. But there's no doubt that labor is something we can buy and sell. You can hire someone to fix a broken electric switch. Or someone can hire Paul to teach anthropology courses or Suzan to write a newsletter or a speech.

What determines the price of things in markets? Things are valuable because of their uses, the needs they fill. This is **use value**, and it's qualitative, not something we can count or quantify. If we want to rake leaves, a rake is useful for that. It may be useful for batting a ball or swatting a groundhog, but other things are more useful than a rake for those tasks. And rakes aren't useful for driving nails or digging holes. A broom is useful for sweeping. A rake might help, but it's not very good. A coat is useful to keep us warm. We can't really compare the use values of rakes, brooms, and coats except to say that they are different. We can't say one is more useful than the other except in terms of what we use it for. For keeping warm, a rake is no good. For digging a hole, a coat won't help.

People exchange things with one use value for things of different use values. So, people might trade a rake for a coat. If people can do this, the ratio of exchange—how many rakes per coat or coats per rake—is the **exchange value** of the two things. This is **quantitative**, something we can count. People may have to trade five rakes for one coat. Or people can use money to keep track of these relationships. If the value of a rake is $1, then the value of a coat is $5. So our question is, where does the exchange value of things come from?

The one thing that all useful things have in common is that they are the product of someone's labor. The amount of labor that it takes to make things is their exchange value and sets the ratio of their exchange in markets. So, if it takes the same amount of labor to produce one pig, twelve bushels of rice, two hoes, five rakes, and one coat, people would exchange them at those ratios, either directly or indirectly using money as an intermediary.

To repeat, the exchange value of things comes from the amount of labor it takes to produce them. We distinguish between price on the one hand, what you pay for something, and value, the labor it contains. Here, we think in terms of long-term averages. Furry boots may come into fashion when a movie star wears them. So lots of people want to buy furry boots, and they are expensive. Soon every company is making the boots, and the price comes down. And finally the boots are out of fashion, and you only see them at thrift stores. The **price** of things can differ from their value because of these kinds of processes. But the exchange value of things is determined by the amount of labor they contain.

What is useful depends on what people need and want beyond food. This sets the needs people have for production. Consumption, production, and exchange are related in such a way that if one changes, the others also change; they form an **economic system**. How the things are produced is the cultural core, the most important dimension of the system, since it conditions how people can exchange and consume. The task of anthropology is to figure out the systematic relationships.

We can look once more at Lisu, with whom Paul lived. The feasts that go with curing ceremonies provide a way for people to enter into reciprocal exchanges. If I invite you to a feast today, then I expect that you will invite me to your feast when you sponsor one.

People grow rice, opium poppies, and corn on slash-and-burn or **swidden** fields. They cut the trees, let them dry, burn them, and then plant rice, corn, or opium poppies in the field. The people of the household provide the labor, but sometimes they need to have a lot of labor in a short time. When they need to concentrate labor at one time such as harvests, they ask neighbors to help and promise to help them with their harvests. These are reciprocal exchanges, too. But people also hire some help, especially from opium addicts who live in nearby villages of other groups. Everyone produces more than just enough to eat. To be able to sponsor feasts for curing ceremonies, people keep pigs. And, as with Tsembaga, someone grows the food to feed the pigs—or at least enough of it to keep the pigs coming home for supper every evening.

The pigs stay in pens near the houses, but people let them forage freely in the forest during the day so that people don't have to feed them so much. To get them to return to the pens, people feed them corn, and, like U.S. farmers, they grow the corn to feed their pigs. If they are going to sponsor feasts, they also need enough money to buy home-distilled liquor from whoever may have recently run off a batch at the village still.

Figure 5-1 shows how people allocate their labor to grow different crops and what happens to the product of their labor. Figure 5-1 shows that 62 percent of the labor went into opium production, 9 percent into corn production, and 28 percent into rice production. The rice went for subsistence and was 41 percent of the total value produced. Corn went to pigs that people used for subsistence—eating—and reciprocity through feasts. Five percent of the total value that people produced was pigs for subsistence. People used cash to buy liquor and bamboo shoots for feasts, and together the liquor, food, and pigs for feasts accounted for 18 percent of the value produced. Twenty-eight percent of the value produced went for consumption goods such as cloth for clothes, needles, thread, kerosene, lamps, soap, and other things people bought in the lowlands. Finally, 8 percent of the total value they produced went to purchase the labor of neighboring opium smokers to help, especially with the tedious harvest of the opium from the poppies.

Like Tsembaga, Lisu have a cultural code that makes it reasonable to sacrifice pigs to make sick people well. But sacrificing a pig sends another message, too. It lets people know that the household is keeping up with its responsibilities to other households, that it is keeping its place in the reciprocal relationships. When someone in a household falls ill, the householders think about when they last sponsored a feast and who has sponsored feasts lately. If the household is falling behind, they will sacrifice a pig. If they are

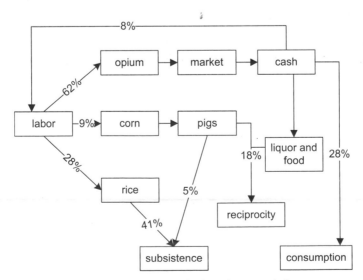

Figure 5-1 What Lisu labor produces and what they use it for.

already even or a little ahead, they will sacrifice a chicken. So the curing ceremonies also have a political dimension. They are the way everyone keeps up with everyone else in this egalitarian society. This provides the motive to produce pigs, rice, and opium. "You can't be a poor Lisu," one person told Paul. "You have to have pigs to sacrifice." And you need good clothes and silver to wear to festivals. To stay equal, everyone produces rice and pigs and opium so that they can sponsor feasts.

In this system, we see market transactions and reciprocity but no redistribution. Note that because the land is freely available to anyone who wants to clear and use it and because people rely mostly on household members for labor, there are no categories of capital, rent, and wages. This can sometimes be confusing to people who grew up with the emic system of markets and economics, as people in the United States do. Thinking of kinship in terms of kindreds, all of our cousins on both sides, makes it difficult for us to understand lineages based on the father's or the mother's side, but anthropology helps us move beyond this kind of ethnocentrism so that we can understand other cultures.

There are two ways to study economic systems. One is as a business tool. To anthropologists this seems like Ptolemaic astronomy that puts the earth at the center of the solar system. It works well for navigation on our planet, so there's no need to challenge it if that's its use, but it won't work for going to the moon or keeping a calendar so that religious celebrations like Christmas and Easter always fall in the winter and in the spring. And it may not be the best scientific knowledge. Just because some system of knowledge is not scientific doesn't mean it's not useful or that it doesn't work. But just because it's useful doesn't mean that it's scientific. We'll explain later why economics is more like a religion than a science and how it got to be that way.

Economics may be sufficient as a tool for business calculations, but that doesn't make it adequate to describe real economic systems or useful as a framework for comparing economic systems. Anthropologists have developed other ways of seeing economies as cultural systems, as parts of cultures, so we can compare them with others. It's this etic system we're explaining here.

In some systems, market exchange is the main way of organizing production. This doesn't mean everything is done by market principles, but it does mean that the market organizes most production. For instance, someone in every household washes dishes, cooks food, and does the laundry. A married couple may share these tasks. That's not a market exchange. Or the husband or the wife may do most of it. That's not a market exchange, either. Or they may hire someone to come in and clean and cook for them. That is a market exchange.

Someone must take care of the kids. The mom or the dad may stay home and do that. That's not a market exchange. If the parents pay to put the kids in day care or preschools, that is a market exchange (in some countries the government provides this service because they value families). So some of these tasks may be more or less organized by the market. But in this example, if we look at the whole economy—all of the houses and cars and food production and everything else—it's fair to say that the market is the major way of organizing production. There is money, and people buy and sell commodities, including most raw materials, tools, machines, labor, and almost everything else.

If there is market exchange and people buy everything for production, then labor is a commodity just like coal, sand, and steel. People use labor, tools, and raw materials to produce commodities with different use values and sell them. In this kind of system, they use money to buy commodities (labor, machines, raw materials) to make commodities (products) to sell for money. But the reason people do this is not just to get the same amount of money but some extra that we call **profit**.

Where does profit come from?

Remember that the exchange value of commodities comes from the amount of labor they contain. If you buy all of the inputs, even the labor, where does the value of labor come from? This is a bit like a riddle. The value of labor comes from the same place as the value of any other commodity— the labor it contains. How can labor contain labor? People must consume to work. The amount of things others produced that we consume so we can work is the value of our subsistence. That is what determines the value of labor for a period of time—the amount of labor it takes to produce all of the things someone needs to work for that period of time and to reproduce labor for the next generation to keep the system going.

Think back to the household where the worker lives. The house, the food, the water, the fuel, the car—almost everything in the household is a commodity. The domestic partner is probably not a commodity, but a commodity worker—a maid—may do the domestic jobs. Most of us aren't that rich, but even if we're talking about ordinary people who do their own work, the point is that they could have been working for money, so that household work has value, too.

If we buy labor at its value, we pay for all of the necessary subsistence goods for the time we use the labor. Necessary subsistence goods may include the value of a house, a car, television, food, cooking, cleaning, child care, and education for kids. Part of the value of labor is the amount of value it takes to produce the next generation of workers to keep the system going—that is, to reproduce the system. The total amount of what it takes to keep people working and reproduce workers is what we call necessary value. This total value is what people get paid as wages.

Put the other way around, wages is the value that a worker needs to keep working and to keep the system going. That's where the value the employer pays to the worker comes from—the value of labor is the labor it contains, like any other commodity. But where do profits come from? We're getting there.

When we hire workers, we ask them to produce the amount of value of their wages and some more. Remember, if we're just producing the same amount that we put into the process, there's no point to it. So we ask people to put in enough work to equal the amount of their wages and some more on top. That "more on top" is the profit.

It works like this: we call the amount of value to pay for wages necessary value and the amount of work to produce it **necessary labor**. It's necessary in the sense that, without it, there couldn't be any labor at all. The extra value the labor produces beyond that is the source of profit. We call that work **surplus labor** and the value it produces **surplus value**. We call it "surplus" because it is above and beyond the amount of value that is necessary to pay for the value of the labor.

Some people figure out how long they work before they have enough to pay their income taxes. Suppose you pay 25 percent of your income as taxes. Then the first three months of any year you're working for your government. Only after you pay off the government can you start working for yourself. You can think of dividing the working day in the same way. Think of necessary value as the amount of value the workers you hire produce just to pay their wages, to produce the amount of value they need for the day of work. After they are done with that, the rest is yours. That's the surplus value; that labor is surplus labor, and that's where the profit comes from. Figure 5-2 shows how this works.

Most of us aren't bosses who hire other people to work for us. So let's turn it around and think of it from the worker's point of view. If it takes me half a day to produce the value of my wages, then I'm working for myself that half of the day. The rest of the day's work the boss gets to keep in return for letting me come to work and get any wages at all. In the old days, this was clear. You could see how much coal you dug, you knew how much it cost to buy, because you had to heat your own house and cook, so you could know when you started working for profit for the boss instead of for yourself. But what about the mine's clerk? Or the railroad engineer who drove the train to take the coal to where someone needed it? That gets more complex. It's the same set of relationships, but it's more difficult to see because it involves lots of steps. Here we're just working on the basic ideas.

If two firms are both producing the same thing using the same machines and raw materials, they will offer their products on the market at the same price. If one of them invests in a process that produces the same things with less labor, it can sell the products for less. Then the first firm can either imitate the second or improve the process of production even more or go out of

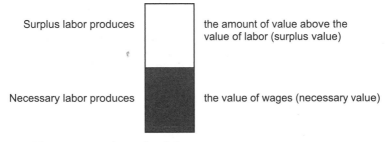

Surplus labor produces — the amount of value above the value of labor (surplus value)

Necessary labor produces — the value of wages (necessary value)

Figure 5-2 Necessary and surplus labor.

business. The same amount of labor produces more of the product—the productivity has increased, just as when Tsembaga have longer fallow periods in their gardens. Now the amount of labor in each thing is less and the value is less, so the firm can sell it for less.

Through this process of competition, the production processes come to use less and less labor. Anything that consumes less labor has less exchange value and is less expensive. As this happens throughout the whole society, the value of the things necessary to support workers decreases and the value of labor decreases. As the value of labor decreases, the surplus value increases. This is the Wal-Mart phenomenon: low wages, high profits.

Think about the first automobiles that people built by hand, piece by piece. Then came Mr. Ford. He may not have invented the automobile, but he did invent a way to produce lots of them with his assembly lines. That radically improved productivity and lowered the value of cars until Americans could imagine everyone owning a car. Then came the Japanese, with their robot factories that could build cars with just a couple of folks to watch the computers. But people had to build Mr. Ford's factory and the Japanese robots. More on that later.

Think about farms mechanizing at the same time that automobile production was mechanizing. First people were using horses to plow and pull implements. In those days there were lots of farmers for everyone who wasn't. In 1900, 39.2 percent of the U.S. population lived on farms, and 38.8 percent of the labor was employed on farms. Then they got tractors and could do the jobs faster, with less labor, because they didn't need to grow oats for horses or take care of them. Productivity increased. By 1990, 1.8 percent of the population was living on farms, and 1.8 percent of labor was employed on farms. As the machines got bigger and more powerful, the productivity increased to such an extent that there are just a few farmers now. Some people talk about replacing people with technology. In what's called the *industrialization of agriculture*, productivity increased as people invested more and more in technology.

It's important to keep basic relationships in mind. One is that labor creates all value. As we've explained, profit comes from people's labor. We'll explain later why some people are confused about this and think that profit comes from money. But money can't produce things. Only labor does that. That's why it's important to keep the basics in mind. So where do the machines, factories, and robots come from? People can use profits to invest in research and development to increase productivity. But it's the labor of the working people that created the profits that bought the machines.

We call the money that goes into production capital, and we call any system organized in this way a capitalist system. Among the many advantages of such a system are greater specialization, productivity of labor, and efficiency. A capitalist system is a precondition for this dynamic to take hold. The preconditions for capitalism include:

Market exchange;
Labor that is available to hire;

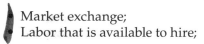

- The possibility to expand labor time beyond necessary labor to create surplus value; and
- No interference with the process.

Karl Marx put together the ideas of use value, exchange value, necessary value, surplus value, and how all of those relate to wages and the development of the capitalist system in his 1867 book *Capital*.

As this process continues through time, production develops from handcraft, making carriages, for instance, to mass production like Ford's assembly lines and increasing automation and reduction of necessary labor. As necessary labor decreases, surplus labor increases and the rate of profits increases. Marx called this the increasing increase of relative surplus value—that is, surplus value increases over time relative to necessary value. Thus, the rates of profit increase over time and the value of labor decreases.

The increase of the production of value in the economy is called the growth rate of the economy. In 2014, the French economist Thomas Piketty published a book called *Capital in the Twenty-First Century*. In the United States, it became a best seller. He used mainly tax data from many countries to compare the rates of growth of the whole economy and the rate of growth in financial return to investments, the rate of return on capital. His finding that surprised many was that over several hundred years the rate of return to capital exceeds the rate of growth of the whole economy. Marx was way ahead of his time. Piketty finds that the returns to labor, wages, do not keep up with returns to capital or the growth of the economy. Thus, an inherent part of capitalism as a system is increasing inequality.

As we will see in our discussion of class, Americans do not like to admit to inequality or class differences of wealth. Thus, the reception of Piketty's book in the United States was not totally enthusiastic. Piketty asks why American corporate officers receive so much more income than their workers. Why so much more than their counterparts in other countries? It has no relationship to productivity, he suggests, but the differential is only because they assign their own remuneration. A political fact.

Recognizing the importance of political relations in economics, Piketty seems to offer a different view of economics, but in the end, as the anthropologist Chris Gregory points out, his understanding is based on the same assumptions as that of classical economists and his understanding of the dynamics of the distribution of wealth between the owners of capital and the owners of labor is that it is the result of the tidy operation of quantitative relationships among several variables in a political vacuum. The book was widely discussed in part because it was a rare example of an economist developing empirical data and asking political questions, even if his approach and answers were conventional.

The American economist Paul Krugman suggests that much of the discussion of the book in the United States revolved around the fact that conservatives do not like Piketty's demolition of their cherished myth that we live in a meritocracy, in which the wealthy earn and deserve their wealth because they create jobs for others. However, Krugman is doubtful of the political impact of the book in the United States, where money exerts a powerful influence on the political process. He goes on to call those conservative critics who claim either that inequality is not increasing or, if it is, that it's a good thing, "inequality deniers" and puts them in the same category as climate-change deniers, as members of powerful groups interested in rejecting facts or creating a fog of doubt. In short, it is politically motivated mind control.

Joseph Stiglitz, another American economist, points out that Picketty's finding of a concentration of wealth and income at the top is correct, but returns us to issues of political economy. Stiglitz suggests that the stagnation of wages and increases of inequality in the United States are a consequence of our political system, not a necessary feature of capitalism. They are the result of political processes that favor the wealthy. Stiglitz points out, as we have, that markets are not natural; they are established through a political process that lays down and enforces rules of the market. He concludes, "The main question confronting us today is not really about capital in the twenty-first century. It is about democracy in the twenty-first century."

Firms that produce things to sell—exchange values—produce most things in capitalist systems, but there is also a previous kind of production that we call **household production**. Households don't produce exchange values, only use values; if they produce things to sell—like Lisu producing opium—it's so they can buy commodities they need. The usefulness of the things households produce is relative to the needs of the people. What's the value of washing the dishes after supper? Of cooking supper? Of shopping? Of taking care of the kids or picking them up from day care? Their value is the use to the people in the household. People don't sell these things. They aren't exchange values.

How can we compare the usefulness of a bushel of rice when there is no rice in the household versus the same bushel of rice when the granaries are full of rice? The usefulness of goods declines as you have more of the goods. The more of something you have, the less you need the next one. This is what economists call **marginal utility**, or the usefulness of the next thing compared with the one before. Accountants used to keep track of such differences by putting the difference in the margin of the account book; hence, the idea of marginal utility, the usefulness of the next thing.

If a person has a beer on a Friday night, it might go down well and feel good. The second beer is less urgent and the third even less. Depending on the person's tolerance for alcohol poisoning, each beer is less useful than the one before it, until some point where the next beer is worse than useless; it has the person hugging the toilet and puking. That's what economists, in their optimistic way, call **negative utility** but what ordinary folks might call damaging.

Figure 5-3 is a graph of that process. The horizontal axis is the amount of value people have produced. At the left, they haven't produced anything, and they have great needs. The more they produce, as we go along the horizontal axis toward the right, the less they need to produce any more.

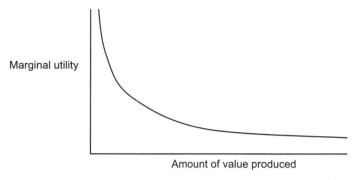

Figure 5-3 How much do you need the next one?

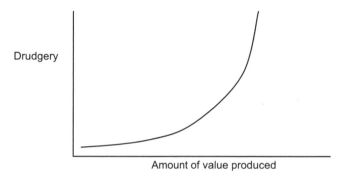

Figure 5-4 How much you don't want to do the work to get the next one.

Peoples' valuation of the amount of work they want to do runs in the opposite direction. The more people work, the less they want to work anymore. Figure 5-4 shows this exponential curve of increasing **drudgery** of work. At the left, when people haven't produced anything, they haven't done any work. The more they produce, the more work it takes, and the less they want to work anymore.

Figure 5-5 puts the two curves together to show the point at which it is no longer worth a person's while to produce any more—when the marginal utility of the next unit of value produced is equal to the drudgery of the work it takes to produce it. That's when people in households stop working.

In Figure 5-6, you see that drudgery of labor is inversely related to productivity. If the same amount of effort produces twice as much value, then the drudgery of labor is cut in half.

Here, each value of drudgery in the dotted line is half the value of that in the solid line for each unit of value because the people have some way to double productivity. Perhaps they have access to an irrigation system or a harvesting machine—something that doubles the amount they produce in the same time. Note that although people increase production with the new technology from point A to point B, they do not double it. So the increase in

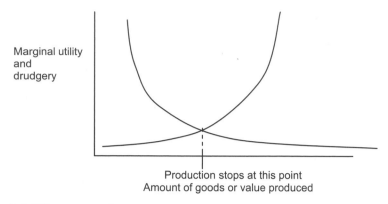

Figure 5-5 When you quit.

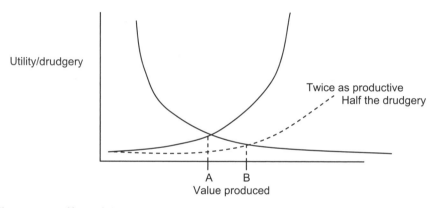

Figure 5-6 Effect of doubling productivity.

production is not doubled even if productivity is—the relationship between productivity and amount produced is indirect.

Marginal utility is relative to needs: the greater the need, the higher the curve of marginal utility.

In Figure 5-7 the dotted line shows an increase in the marginal utility of the value produced; that is, these people need the product more than the people with the solid line. This could be because they have more mouths to feed, or it could be because they must pay taxes for the irrigation system or pay off a loan for a harvesting machine. The source of the need doesn't matter. Any increase in need acts the same way as adding mouths to the number of consumers in the household. Again, the production increases from A to B.

When we put the two curves together in Figure 5-8, we see that the overall level of drudgery with the new technology—the drudgery (on the vertical axis) to produce up to the level of B—is higher than without it—the old system where they only produce up to the level of A. B would be the new amount they would produce considering both the increase in productivity

That's what you get

The agricultural economist A. V. Chayanov is the person who put the observations noted here together on the basis of his empirical studies of Russian peasants in the early decades of the twentieth century. After the revolution of 1918, there was a great food shortage in the new Soviet Union. The country was being invaded by England and the United States. The supporters of the czar started a civil war, and the peasants stopped producing much of anything beyond what they needed for their families. That contributed to a shortage of food for everyone who wasn't a peasant. Stalin wanted to start large industrial farms that would operate like factories and be done with the reactionary peasants once and for all. Chayanov thought that peasants would respond to the needs of city people better if they could organize into cooperatives and sell their food, but Stalin disagreed. Stalin solved the Chayanov problem in his typical way, by having him shot in 1931.

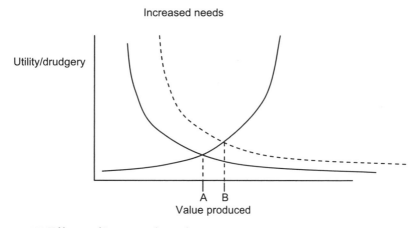

Figure 5-7 Effects of increased need.

and the increase in need that the new method of production creates in the household. So in this example, given a choice, people wouldn't accept that alternative; they'd keep doing things the old way.

Paul and other anthropologists have done lots of ethnographic work around the world to check out these ideas to be sure this is the way household production units actually work. So this isn't just theory.

The preconditions for capitalism include market exchange and people who are willing and able to sell their labor. This wouldn't work in prerevolutionary Russia because the serfs were not free to sell their labor. In fact, capitalism would rarely work if people were given the choice. We can understand this from the point of view of people working in terms of the logic of household economies.

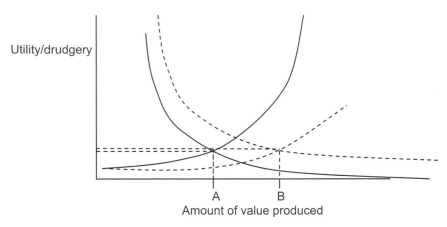

Figure 5-8 Costs and benefits of new technology.

Someone sets up a factory with the most advanced technology there is, something like the water-powered textile mills of Lowell, Massachusetts. The owner offers to pay a worker maybe the amount of necessary labor, but it takes twelve hours of labor to produce that. If the owner is only paying the value of necessary labor, there is no profit in the system, so it's not worth the owner's while. If the owner can get people to work one extra hour, however, there's some surplus in the system. But why would anyone trade what they had in their household economy for the monotonous and dreary work of a factory?

They wouldn't. The best the factory owners could do is to hire the daughters of farmers. From the point of view of the farmers, the daughters could earn a little extra income without hurting the household economy too much. From the point of view of the girls, they could set aside something toward getting married and maybe get out of the house. From the point of view of the factory owner, he could start extracting surplus value. And they could control the value of necessary value by providing dorm rooms and food for the girls, so the owners knew just how much their necessary value was.

But it wasn't always so nice an arrangement. In most places, people simply refused to work in factories until the government gave them no alternative. Governments drove people off their land with policies that kept them from being able to produce their own subsistence so they would have no choice but to work in factories. We will see some of these policies at work later. When people were denied access to their land to make a living, they had no other way to make a living except to sell their labor. These developments were no less draconian than Stalin's measures, but they were necessary for the capitalist system to get started, and once it did get started, there could be fast progress through the technological developments that came with the process of competition that we explained before.

The point is that labor is not naturally a commodity that people can buy and sell on markets. Some government policy makes that happen, that changes the structures of choice so that most people can no longer satisfy their subsistence needs through their household economies. Such policies are likely to anger the people who get thrown off their land, so policies like this require force—armies and police and a government that is willing to use force to make all of this work together.

So when people say, "Isn't it better for an Indonesian peasant girl to work for a couple of bucks a day than to have no job at all?" we know that's the wrong question. The question we need to ask, and to answer, is, "Why can't the Indonesian peasant girl work on her own family's farm?" Maybe her dad is a tyrant, and it's no better on the farm than in the factory. Or maybe there's no farm left. We cannot know until we do the ethnography and find the facts of these cases. That's what anthropology is about—finding facts, not making assumptions.

One of the consequences of these political and economic developments was ideologies and institutions to make the new system of production possible and to make it seem reasonable. One of these ideas was the idea of freedom. Free people are people who are not bound to lords or landowning farmers or lineages or tyrannical dads or anyone else. They are free to sell their labor. Thus, one reason to oppose slavery was that it stood in the way of free labor, in this case meaning available labor that producers could hire, a critical commodity for capitalism to develop.

In capitalist systems of production, there are people who sell labor and people who buy it. Where is the middle class? The middle class is in our imaginations. It's one of those ideological myths that was made up to make the system seem reasonable. We'll come to that in a bit.

Discussion Questions

- Draw your own diagram that describes your definition of drudgery. Explain how much you would work, for how much, and when you would quit. Do you think that is the same for either of your parents? Your grandparents? Why or why not?
- Iceland's constitution does not include the right to freedom of expression, or religion, or even the freedom to own a gun. But it does include the rights of health, education, a job, a place to live, and security in old age. Discuss the difference between these rights and the freedoms that the U.S. Constitution provides. What are the benefits of each? What are the costs? What does the economy have to do with any of this?
- If the reasons for the difference are economic, why can a small country like Iceland grant such rights, whereas a large, rich one like the United States does not?
- Check the local or international business news this week and find a story about wages, stock prices, productivity, and/or profits. Apply what you learned about economics in this chapter to any part of that news story or stories and discuss.
- Can you think of an example of household production from your family? How is that different from earning a wage? Describe the

lifestyle, the level of work, the quality of work and lifestyle, and any other comparisons you can make.

Suggested Reading

Browne, Katherine E. *Creole Economics: Caribbean Cunning under the French Flag.* Austin: University of Texas Press, 2004.

Gregory, Chris. "The Three Faces of Thomas Piketty: Reflections on a #1 Best-Seller." *Anthropology of This Century.* Issue 11, October 2014. http://aotcpress.com/.

Krugman, Paul. "On Inequality Denial." *The New York Times.* June 1, 2014, A21.

Krugman, Paul. "The Piketty Panic." *The New York Times,* April 24, 2014, A25.

Newman, Katherine S. *Declining Fortunes: The Withering of the American Dream.* New York: Basic Books, 1993.

Stiglitz, Joseph E. "Democracy in the Twenty-First Century." September 1, 2014. Commentaries. http://www.project-syndicate.org/commentary/joseph-e--stiglitz/.

Wells, Miriam J. *Strawberry Fields: Politics, Class and Work in California Agriculture.* Ithaca, NY: Cornell University Press, 1996.

White, Jenny B. *Money Makes Us Relatives: Women's Labor in Urban Turkey.* Austin: University of Texas Press, 1994.

Yates, Michael D. *Naming the System: Inequality and Work in the Global Economy.* New York: Monthly Review Press, 2003.

The 2004 "Rally for Women's Lives," held in Washington, D.C., is an example of how people in the United States voice their political views and how the state maintains control through its police force. *Photo by Suzan Erem.*

6

Political Systems

One key to capitalism is the availability of people who are willing to work for a wage—or who have no choice except to work for a wage. Such people are called **free labor** because they are not tied to the land or to lineages and are not slaves. They are free to be hired.

As we saw in the previous chapter, surplus labor is the source of the profits that drives the whole capitalist system and creates the dynamic of growth. Households stop production when they reach a definite level of well-being, so they produce no surplus value unless a government or someone else forces them to. Then the amount they are forced to produce is, as Chinese peasants say of their government, "another mouth at the table." Household systems are static unless something changes their needs. Having children is one way this happens. Taxes and the demands of government are another. Being in debt is a third.

Despite its dynamism and potential for progress, capitalism can never compete with households for labor. Households never benefit from sending people to work for wages as a major means of subsistence unless they have no access to resources to use for their own production. Think about it in terms of the logic of household production from the previous chapter. A person's wages is what the person produces. It's always more advantageous in terms of the curves of productivity and drudgery to work for yourself than to work for someone else because you keep everything you produce except what you must pay in taxes, tribute, or debts. If you work for someone else, they take most of what you produce and you still must pay taxes, tribute, and debts.

The places where capitalism can get people to work are those where the conditions of work are so bad that working for wages looks good. That's what happened in nineteenth-century Iceland when if you didn't have land, the law said you had to work for someone who did. All you got was enough to get you barely through the year. The landowners did everything they could to keep commercial fishing from getting started; they knew people would go work in the fishing industry for wages because anything was better than working on a farm. That would deprive the landowners of their inexpensive supply of labor. Landowners were in the Parliament and made the laws. But people finally just disobeyed the laws and went to the fishing villages to work. Life was hard, but it was better than life on the farms if you didn't own any land.

GOVERNMENT AND CAPITALISM

In the mid-1970s, Paul lived in a village of people called Shan in northwest Thailand. He first visited the area for a summer in 1967 before he began his work with Lisu. Back then, people leveled rice fields in the floors of the valleys, dug irrigation ditches, and built small dams across streams and rivers to irrigate their rice. In the 1960s, they were able to get two crops of rice from these fields, but later, when a bridge across a major river and roads made the provincial capital of Maehongson accessible, people began to grow garlic and soybeans to sell at the market in town. When pickup trucks could drive to the villages from the capital to buy crops, the villagers could do better selling these crops than growing a second crop of rice during the off season, so the agricultural system changed.

There weren't enough irrigated fields for everyone to make a living, so people who didn't own land made swiddens—land cleared by slashing and burning—like Lisu, in the hills nearby. In Thailand, all forests belong to the government. The government can grant the right to use trees for timber and, if it has the power to enforce it, can dictate everything that happens in the forested hills. Not long after the new roads connected villages to the capital, a new airport with long cement runways replaced the grass field where, in the 1960s and 1970s, World War II–vintage twin-engine DC-3s had landed.

When Paul was there in the 1960s, villagers sold rice to the rebel army in Burma by the elephant load, and members of the Shan States Army came to visit relatives or settled down in border villages. In the 1970s, the occasional thumping beat of helicopters announced that the Thai Army was in the area, watching.

In the capital's open morning market, representatives of a dozen or more rebel groups and warlords shopped, and after a coup d'état in Bangkok, a Thai Border Patrol Police guy showed up to drink and gamble with the young men in the village where Paul lived. The government tried with little success to organize a border guard from the village men. The headman was appropriately enthusiastic, but there was not a military bone in the body of any of the village farmers, although one kid was drafted and went on to make a career in the army.

Now we come to the punch line. In the 1970s, a few people owned much more land than they needed, and some people owned none. But the people with extra land could not hire people to work it. People could do better working for themselves on swiddens than they could working for others for wages. Remember, a hired worker gets necessary value as a wage but, in return for that produces surplus value. A worker in a household system only produces necessary value without the demand for surplus value. So although there was a market and other preconditions of capitalism, it wouldn't work because people had the alternative of making swiddens instead of working for wages. In the 1980s, with more control, the government was able to assert its power over the forests and prohibit swiddening. Then, those people who did not have enough irrigated rice land to feed their families had no choice

The Burmese border

Since 1961, there has been a revolutionary war—or, depending on how you look at it, several of them—in Burma. Burma's name is not really Myanmar, like you see on some maps these days. Myanmar is the name the military dictatorship made up for propaganda to make it seem like things were better than they are. The people call it Pama Myo. *Myo* means "country"; *Pama* means "Burma." To the English who colonized it as part of their Indian Empire, that sounded like "Burma," and it's not too far off. Some of the revolutionary armies in Burma are made up of Shan from the Shan States in the northeastern part of Burma. They and others financed their revolutions with opium. This is similar to Afghanistan during the American occupation in the twenty-first century.

The revolutionary groups and several opium-trading warlords, as well as remnants of Chiang Kai-shek's U.S.-supported Nationalist Kuomintang who fled China after Mao Zedong's victory in 1949 to trade opium and guns in northern Thailand and Burma, occupied the border areas along with the peaceful rice-growing peasants who sold them rice. One motive for the bridge, roads, and airport in Maehongson was so the Thai government could exercise greater control of the area and ensure that the Shan people living there didn't get any ideas about joining with the Shan in Burma to make their own separate country.

The Thai government improved health services and provided schools so that the Shan people would learn to speak, read, and understand the related Thai language with its different alphabet but familiar sounds. The Thai Army radio station broadcasted its version of news and other programs in the area, whereas Burmese radio broadcasted propaganda in Shan.

In the 1960s and through the 1970s, Shan could make swidden fields to supplement their irrigated rice crops or, if they owned no irrigated fields, as their only source of rice. Slowly, the Thai state asserted its authority over this remote and formerly independent Shan state.

but to work for the people with more land than they needed. When some people are directly or indirectly forced to sell their labor rather than use it for their own households, we see the beginnings of a system of classes in which some people buy labor and some sell it.

THE TRANSITION FROM FEUDALISM TO CAPITALISM

In this small corner of the world in the late 1900s we see the same drama that unfolded across Europe in the 1700s. After the collapse of the Roman Empire, the rise of Islam reoriented commerce toward the Islamic world. Local lords, not that different from the warlords of northwest Thailand, dominated Europe with their system of feudalism and incessant warfare until some could make good their claim to being God's chosen kings.

These aristocrats required exotic goods beyond those that ordinary peasants produced and used. Merchants began to supply them with these goods from the East, and new **markets** developed. Money began to circulate, and banks developed to help merchants handle it. Then began a process we now call **import substitution**, making the things for yourself instead of importing them. Not that aristocrats worked, but they had their peasants do it for them. Crafts developed and then workshops; this was the beginning of the factory system.

Royalty controlled the economic and political system. The sources of wealth were taxes, skimming from traders, and warfare, not production of surplus value. Aristocrats did not control production, but they wanted to control wealth. So, as people experimented with new ways of producing things and found better ways, the political system was increasingly at loggerheads with the cultural core.

It wasn't the kings and aristocrats who grouped craftsmen together into workshops where they experimented with new and more productive technologies. The rulers just wanted the products—they didn't care how they were produced. But the people who were producing things were developing new technologies and new ways of organizing production and beginning a factory system. They were on the verge of capitalism but had to play by the old rules of the aristocracy.

Throughout the eighteenth century in Germany, France, and the English colonies in America, there were revolutions to break the power of the aristocracy and change the rules of the game to allow the people who were organizing the production of wealth to control it.

But these would-be capitalists faced the same problem the Shan landowners in northwest Thailand faced. As long as people were either tied to the land as serfs or peasants or had access to land for their own household production, they wouldn't work for wages. If people had access to land, they would not sell their labor, and there would be no commodity labor. The solution was to deprive people of access to land. That's what the enclosure acts throughout the nineteenth century in England were about. They enclosed the land people had been using for their own subsistence and gave the land to large landowners for their sheep herds. The people who had been farming were left with no alternative but to go to the towns to look for work. There were similar policies throughout Europe.

By one means or another, governments across Europe made policies that made cheap labor available. They changed the structure of choice. If people could work for themselves in household production, they would never work for wages. The new governments systematically prevented that option. They drove people from farms to cities.

AMERICAN EXCEPTIONALISM

Some argue that what makes America different from any other place is that we had vast amounts of land available on our western frontiers. That's why a lot of people went to America in the first place. There was so much land that this policy wouldn't work at first. For labor, industry had to rely on new immigrants coming to the cities. But by a hundred years ago, most of those lands were no longer available. The land grabs of railroads, coal mining companies, and other corporate interests caused the almost immediate imposition of a system of taxes, permits, and deeds, all designed to limit access to land, on pioneers heading west.

Hollywood's Wild West was short lived compared with the capitalism that quickly followed. There had been the great Civil War to decide whether slavery would continue or whether people would be available to sell their labor as a commodity—the only two choices for the majority of people living in the South—and it's not quite right to call either one a choice. Even if America was the exception, as these "exceptionalists" claimed, it hasn't been for quite a while.

There's a thumbnail sketch of European and American history from the fall of Rome until now. A historian would have a stroke over this abridged version, but the point is that because of the attractions of household production, capitalism can only be established by government policies. That's why there were revolutions in the eighteenth century to establish new governments friendly to capitalism. Those governments made household production impossible for most people and provided the labor the new capitalists needed for their factories.

After capitalism develops government policies such as antitrust laws, labor laws, banking and contract laws, laws against lying, and other rules of the game maintain it. Those rules are enforced by a police force and a judicial system. Americans grow up knowing these rules from being exposed to mass media that tell what happens when people break them. And Americans found out that a lot of people they had trusted were breaking the rules when the economy began to collapse in 2008 because of their lying, cheating, and stealing.

It seems as natural to Americans to separate politics, religion, and economics as it seemed to Aztecs to sacrifice human beings to their gods. But the lesson of comparative anthropology is that economic, political, and religious systems are closely linked. Cultures are systems.

So, we cannot understand how economic systems work unless we understand how political systems work. To anthropologists, that means putting them in comparative perspective so we can talk about the whole species.

EGALITARIAN SYSTEMS

We're not sure it ever bothered Americans, but one of the things that really puzzled British anthropologists was how people could get along without kings and aristocrats and governments. They called such folks **acephalous**, which is a Latin word that means "headless."

The answer is that as long as everyone depends on everyone else, as long as everyone needs everyone else, they will find ways of getting along with each other and don't need judges, cops, courts, and armies to make them behave. It's called reciprocity. Do unto others as you would have them do unto you, and the converse—others do unto you as you do unto them. If everyone follows that rule, people don't need all of the apparatus of governments. It's beautiful. It's simple. It works. It's true.

Shan have a word for it: *joi kan*. The *kan* part means "each other," and they explain the *joi* part as being something like "help," but the two words together mean "You help me when I need it, and I help you when you need it." Someone is repairing the roof on a house and needs help. Fellow villagers show up and help out because when they need to repair their roofs (and sooner or later, everyone does), other people will come help them out. And if you don't, then nobody will help you when you need it.

We've already talked about reciprocity as a kind of exchange. This is the same thing, and where reciprocity is the main mode of exchange, there is a political form that we call **egalitarian**. The word means that everyone is equal, but that's not quite what anthropologists mean.

We understand that in every society there are differences among people. There are men and women; kids, grown-ups, and old people; married people, newlyweds, and people who aren't yet married. So we modify it a bit and say that there's equality within each age and sex category. What do we mean by equality? One of the cultural ecologists, Morton Fried, gave it this definition: as many positions of prestige as there are people capable of filling them. That means that talent and effort pay off in prestige. Nobody can fake anything when everyone knows all about you from the time you were born. There's no way you can fake your résumé if you don't usually bring home the game or the vegetables or if you have no pigs.

Why doesn't the strongest person just take over and rule with an iron hand? The answer is that people wouldn't put up with it. They can leave. They have relatives and in-laws all over the place who would be glad to see them and have them in their own groups. People depend on each other, so if people leave one person alone, that person won't be able to make it. When the people who leave join other groups, they won't have anything good to say about the guy they left, and none of the other groups will help him out.

Lisu say, "Whenever you keep two cups together, they will rattle." That's something elders say to people in one of their several marriage ceremonies. It means that couples don't always get along. So how can egalitarian people deal with conflict? If everyone depends on everyone else, nobody wants to split up the group. Relatives will back you up, but they will also pressure you into getting along so that you don't split up the group. They don't want your problem to become theirs, so they pressure you to solve your problems with other people. They also help you solve them in any way they can so they don't spread. (If you grew up in a small town or a close-knit neighborhood, some of this may sound familiar.)

There may be someone who acts as a headman, but this person has no power over anyone. He summarizes public opinion, but he listens more than he talks. Finally, many people have an idea like witchcraft or the evil eye. It's the notion that some people make bad things happen to others. Many people think the only way to deal with these people is to either ostracize or kill them. The people most likely to be labeled and treated as witches are what we would call malcontents who can't get along with others. So, for many reasons, everybody has an interest in getting along with everybody else. Another Lisu saying is "You can't eat with one chopstick."

The most important thing about egalitarian societies is that everyone has equal access to all resources. Like Lisu, land is theirs to use while they use it, and when they stop using it, they have no claim on it. If there are fish to catch, anyone can catch them. If there is water, everyone can use it.

Reciprocity relies on a sense of obligation. If someone gives you something, you owe them something of equal value. You owe a day's labor for every day other people give you. Here we run into another contradiction because in systems of household production, not all households are equally able to produce. Imagine a household with a young couple, a five-year-old daughter and a one-year-old son, and an aging grandfather. The couple feed themselves, as well as the kids and the grandfather. Now suppose one of the adults gets injured or sick. Then there is only one person to do all of the work. If there are many consumers and few workers, then each worker works harder.

Another household may be lucky enough to avoid sickness and injury, and their children may be old enough to help. Suppose we have a similar household with teenaged kids. Then there are four workers supporting five people rather than one worker supporting five people. Health is a matter of luck.

Lisu control household production. They set their production at just the amount the least able can produce to keep up with the obligations for feasts. That means that the households with more workers per consumer can slack off, and they do. They don't try to overproduce because that would be ostentatious. It's good to be equal; it's not good to get too far ahead or behind.

Luck comes in other ways. Take a look at a poppy seed bagel. Each one of the seeds on it is the same size as the seed for an opium poppy. (Don't get your urine tested for drugs after you eat a poppy seed bagel, by the way.) Lisu broadcast the seeds into their swidden fields just before the monsoon rains begin. How can you tell when the monsoon will begin? Everyone has a pretty good idea of the general time when the weather begins to change, but if someone plants too early, there isn't enough rain, and the sun scorches the plants as they come up. It's just as unlucky to plant right before a gully-washing rainstorm carries all of the seeds down the hillside so that all the poppies come up in a bunch at the bottom of the field and crowd each other out. It's just luck.

HIERARCHY

Unless there are strong inhibitions on ostentation like those the Lisu have, a lucky household can get a little bit ahead. If they give more than they receive, the less lucky households become obliged to them. Everyone owes them, and the goods begin to concentrate with them. But they are obliged to give away what they receive. Thus, they can move into the center of a **redistributive system** of exchange. In highland Southeast Asia, everyone knows about this dynamic. Lisu don't let it happen, but some folks do.

Redistribution comes with its own political form. The central person in a redistributive system of exchange has more prestige than others. He may have titles and fancy headdresses, and people may show him deference. In these **rank** systems, there are fewer positions of prestige than people capable of filling them. There may be more than one person equally able to be at the center. Except for these differences, rank-organized societies are similar to egalitarian ones. Everyone has equal access to resources, and the center person doesn't have any power over others except persuasion.

The cultural ecological anthropologist Marshall Sahlins studied the political systems of the Pacific islands. He found that where there are diverse ecological situations, there are advantages to redistribution. People can specialize to increase the productivity or efficiency of their work. If some people grow sweet potatoes inland and others fish on the shore, everyone can enjoy both seafood and sweet potatoes. The diet can be more diverse. Food may become available at different times of the year in different areas. Distributions of food may come just when people need them, so they don't have to worry about lean periods of the year. In short, everyone benefits, and they can achieve a higher degree of well-being with less labor.

In rank systems, the center person, often with a title like chieftain, has no more power than others. But in redistributive systems of exchange, there may be another development. The center person may not distribute everything that comes in—he may keep some for his own family or kinsmen and start producing less than others.

When you get exactly as much as you give, as in a barter relationship, we call it **balanced reciprocity**. When there is no exact equivalence, or people don't keep track of it as Shan *joi kan* or family sharing, we call it **general reciprocity**. Some things are in between, like Christmas presents. Some people keep track of them and try to make it a balanced relationship, but others do not, and it's a relationship of general reciprocity. When there's an exact exchange such as days of labor among Shan, then we call it **balanced reciprocity**. Some relationships aren't balanced at all. In these, you give and you receive, but you don't receive as much as you give. That defines a relationship that's not symmetrical, and we call it **asymmetrical redistribution**. Egalitarian relationships are symmetrical. Reciprocity is symmetrical. But redistribution is not necessarily symmetrical. The central person may hold back some of the goods for his family.

An example of asymmetrical redistribution is the people of the Trobriand Islands where Bronisław Malinowski lived during World War I. They had matrilineal lineages, like the people of Truk, and a patrilocal system of postmarital residence, so the women joined their husbands on the men's lineage land, unlike Truk. But the land and the product of the land belonged to lineages. The men stayed on the lineage's land where their wives, members of different lineages, joined them and worked to produce yams. Then, following their sense of family values, the men gave most of the yams to their sisters because the yams were the product of their sisters' land, the place the sisters had left when they got married to live with their husbands on their husbands' lineage land. So the yams that the men ate did not come from their own gardens but from the gardens of their wives' lineages as presents from the men's brothers-in-law (the wives' brothers) who owed the yams to their sisters (the men's wives). So I grow yams and give them to my sister, and I eat the yams my wife's brothers give to her. That makes a great insurance policy.

If I'm a man who belongs to the Smith lineage and my sister marries a Jones and goes to live with him on Jones lineage land, I owe her the yams from my garden. My wife is a Brown, and her brothers owe her yams. So I give my yams to my sister and eat the ones my wife gets from her brothers. This is a way to even out some of those differences in luck.

There's another wrinkle. The Trobriand lineages are ranked so that some are higher than others according to how close they are to the original ancestor. One of the men of the highest-ranking lineage is the chieftain, and he is at the center of a redistributive system that also distributes yams. But because of the prestige of his lineage and his titles, he had up to sixty wives from other lineages that wanted to make alliances with him. So he got yams from many brothers-in-law and had so many that he could let them rot in a display of wealth.

More important, he could support some of his kinsmen and didn't have to work as much as others. Some of the people he supported knew the magic that could help or harm others. So there was a sense that if you didn't go along with the system, the chieftain could hurt you. But he didn't have an army or a police force.

STRATIFICATION

When central figures take that step and start supporting kinsmen to make an aristocracy and start providing some people with weapons so they can have more force than others do—when that happens—they can deprive other people of access to resources. **Stratification** means that people don't all have equal access to resources. An example is the Shan village where Paul lived, where some people owned irrigated land and others did not.

Throughout history, most stratified systems have been like an extra consumer in households or that extra person at the table. People must produce a little extra to pay taxes or tribute. People are still involved in household production, but they produce more to support the rulers.

Stratified systems are based on **classes**. Some people have more access to resources than others. That defines two classes of people: takers and givers or haves and have-nots. The only way to keep stratified systems going is by force.

Stratification is inherently unfair because some people have the ability to deprive others of their livelihood, something that never happens in egalitarian or rank systems because there aren't the structures that make it possible

---

Love it or leave it

In highland Southeast Asia, chieftains may try to make the shift from rank systems to stratified ones. Trobriand brothers give their sisters yams because of their family values, and it's a good insurance system to protect against bad luck. When Southeast Asian chieftains say that they want to change the system from one based on family values to one based on land ownership, one of two things can happen, according to Edmund Leach, the British anthropologist who lived in the Kachin Hills of Burma during World War II while he was organizing Kachin guerillas to fight against the Japanese who had invaded Burma. (These same Kachin revolted against the Burmese government in 1961.)

In Leach's time, Kachin people could either go along with the chieftain, who tried to get them to level and irrigate land and become Shan under his leadership, or refuse and be egalitarian like Lisu. There were advantages to either response.

---

and because everyone relies on everybody else. Because they are unfair, stratified systems are fragile unless there is some means for controlling access to resources—for being sure the haves have what they want and the have-nots give the product of their labor to the haves.

The Shan Paul lived with cultivated both irrigated and swidden rice. The same amount of work on an irrigated field gave people three times more rice than that same amount of work on a swidden field. In other words, labor on irrigated fields was three times more productive than swidden labor. In terms of the logic of household production, that's a good deal. If you have irrigated fields, you can give away half of your harvest from the irrigated land and you still come out ahead of where you would be cultivating swiddens. But if it wasn't that way, there was no advantage to going along with a chieftain who just wanted to aggrandize himself and his family, and, because he didn't have any force, people could just refuse and not accept the idea that some lineages have more prestige than others—they could repudiate the principle of rank. Without any force, there was nothing the chieftain could do about it if people decided to go that way.

The seeds of stratification are in the system of asymmetrical redistribution. The chieftain can hold back some of the goods he collects instead of giving them away immediately. He can make the collection period last longer to get more goods. He can do things that increase production and outputs by increasing productivity or without increasing productivity just get people to work longer hours to produce more, for instance, for the glory of the kinship group. Then the chieftain can hold back some of this increased production to support himself and his family.

If the chieftain can convert his control of the redistributive system into control over resources, he has created a stratified system. Sometimes people go along with this because it benefits them. For instance, it would be a good deal to go along if you can triple your productivity by getting access to irrigated fields, even if you have to pay half your crop in rent or taxes.

If the chieftain doesn't have any force, no cops or army to call, then people don't have to go along with such a shift. Kachin, for example, often didn't. If people don't agree to it, there's nothing a chieftain can do, unless he can control or get some force to use against his own people. That's what defines stratification—the ability to control access to resources by force.

When people go along with such a shift, the chieftain can quickly gain the resources he needs to control access to resources by force. Then people have little choice. They can leave and go somewhere else if they can find a way to make a living, or they can stay and work on the chieftain's terms.

In a stratified system, the chieftain is the ultimate giver because he gives wealth to his subordinates. He is the ultimate receiver because everyone owes him a share of what they produce. A hierarchy of chieftains may develop so people give the product of their work to one chieftain, who passes it up the line to a king. The kings and chieftains use some of the wealth to support armies, palace guards, and warfare and to build forts and palaces. They may use wealth to build churches, temples, pyramids, and cathedrals. The reason they do these things is to create or support a cultural code that makes the system seem reasonable and natural. These systems are like the feudal system of Europe and developed at different times in Africa, China, Japan, and Southeast Asia.

The Inca Empire in Peru divided village lands into three parts—one each for the church, the government, and subsistence. They drafted forced labor from villagers to build roads, great monuments, and buildings. In the center of the whole system was a god-king. The Inca had force if they needed it, but they also had religion working for them, telling the people that without this god-king running the show, the whole cosmos would fall apart.

Any stratified system has a **ruling class** that has access to resources and **subordinate classes** that do not. The ruling class takes away some of the product of the labor of the subordinate classes. This isn't always a bad deal for subordinate classes, especially if there's some increase in productivity for them, but once these systems get established, they can't be undone. So far, this has proven to be an irreversible one-way process.

The unfairness of stratified systems makes them fragile unless their ruling classes develop some means to ensure their privileged access to resources. They can use two means for this. Force is one. The other is what the American anthropologist Marvin Harris called **mind control**, or directing how people think by controlling the culture, such as Inca having a religion that persuaded everyone that things had to be that way or nature would fall apart. Mind control is a lot cheaper than force, so rulers like it better than force. The ruling classes of all stratified systems develop institutional ways of keeping control of resources.

As we've said, hegemony is from a Greek word meaning "authority" or "rule." It usually means the predominant power of one country over others such as American hegemony or, in past centuries, British, French, Spanish, Roman, Ottoman, Mongol, or Chinese hegemony. Anthropologists have borrowed this word to mean the predominant power of one class—especially the power to control the content of the cultural code.

Some argue that nobody can really fool people, even by controlling their culture. People can see what's going on around them. Hegemony only works because it has force behind it, and people know if they resist too much, they'll be on the receiving end of that force. If the ruling class cannot or do not develop control by force or cultural hegemony, they cease being the ruling class, and the system of stratification collapses when ordinary people repudiate it because it is unfair.

In the next chapters, we will discuss how ruling classes control stratified societies because that's central to understanding our own modern systems of most contemporary societies. Anthropologists call the institutional means for controlling stratified societies **states**. We will give a more thorough description of what states are and how they operate later. Here it's enough to remember that states are the ways that ruling classes manage force and hegemony to control their people and their cultures and make it all seem reasonable. Stratified systems without states don't last long because they are inherently unfair, and people will refuse to cooperate with them unless compelled by force, hegemony, or both.

Edmund Leach saw rank systems become egalitarian, but in our ethnographic work, anthropologists haven't seen a stratified system without a state to maintain it. We do have historical examples, however. One of the most vivid is medieval Iceland, where there was a highly stratified system, but the chieftains couldn't get together to create institutions that worked for them as a class. That system lasted about four hundred years, from the first settlement in 870 until Iceland became part of the Norwegian Kingdom in 1262. In the next chapter we tell that story.

Discussion Questions

- Think of some present-day rules and regulations in American society that limit access to resources, including land, food, and fuel. What purpose do those rules serve? Who benefits most? Who is most deprived? Why?
- Why do people steal? Is it possible to create a political or economic system in which stealing would not be necessary? Who defines what is "theft"? What if you had a different definition? Can you think of examples of institutional or corporate theft?
- The French philosopher Pierre-Joseph Proudhon said that property is theft. What do you think he meant?
- Develop examples of redistributive systems you have seen or read about. What do they have in common? Where do you see them, and where do you never see them?
- What are some examples of reciprocity? How do they work? What would an American economic system built on reciprocity instead of money look like?
- We assert that stratified systems are fragile. Do you agree? Why or why not? If so, what are some of the mechanisms stratified systems use to

maintain themselves? How do those manifest themselves in today's society? If not, why not?

- You are probably going to college so you can get a better job. Why do you have to get a job at all?
- What class are you a member of? OK, you're in the anthropology class, but in the system of stratification, where do you fit? Ruling class or working class? How did that happen?

Suggested Reading

D'Altroy, Terrance. *The Incas*. Boston: Blackwell, 2003.

Fried, Morton. *The Evolution of Political Society: An Essay in Political Anthropology*. New York: McGraw-Hill, 1967.

Weiner, Annette. *The Trobrianders of Papua New Guinea*. Belmont, CA: Thomson/Wadsworth, 1988.

Archaeologists excavating a Viking-era settlement in Iceland. *Photo by Suzan Erem.*

7

Stratification without a State
Medieval Iceland

In the previous chapter, we saw that stratification means differential access to resources. If a society is going to be stratified, it needs some institutional way to enforce that differential access so that some have more than others. Anthropologists call such arrangements of institutions *states*. Here we are going to see what happens to a stratified society that does not have a state. That kind of organization is rare because it is so fragile. Usually either such societies develop states quickly or the people don't put up with the stratification and become egalitarian. Understanding an example like this helps us understand exactly what it is that states do, how stratification works, and how societies change over time.

In medieval Iceland, we see a stratified stateless society collapse because the ruling class refuses to have a state. It is an excellent example of how the ruling class needs a state to maintain the stratification from which it benefits.

The story of the naming of Iceland comes from a Norwegian who went there before the first permanent settlers in 870. According to the story, he was so taken by the hunting and fishing that he didn't bother to make hay, so when the winter came, his livestock all died. When he looked out over the land, all he could see was snow and ice and no way to make it to spring, so he said something like "This place is an ice land." The name stuck.

In the ninth century, Norway had a lot of small chieftains with asymmetrical redistribution, somewhat like the Trobriand system, except that they didn't have matrilineal lineages—they had kindreds, as Europeans do to this day. Remember, a kindred is all of the cousins out to a certain distance. And they didn't grow yams but relied on wheat, cattle, and sheep. On the west coast of Norway, there was a lot of fishing as well.

One of these chieftains was named Harald Finehair. He invited other chieftains to join him to form an aristocracy with him as king. Some did, but others did not see that they would gain anything for their household economies by paying taxes to a king who could do nothing to improve their productivity and wanted to impose taxes that would mean extra costs to households. Check Chapter 5 on household production to see how this would affect them. It was not a favorable equation for households.

With the power he gained from his coalition, Harald fought the chieftains who would not join him and in a battle in 885 beat them and became the king. The remaining chieftains had three choices: they could join Harald, fight him, or leave.

Some fought and died; some fought and then left; some just left. Those who left loaded their livestock, families, slaves, and followers onto their Viking ships and went to the British Isles or Iceland. Some of the chieftains who went to the British Isles later came to Iceland to settle. The first thing they did when they reached the uninhabited Iceland was to claim land and define the borders of their areas. Then they parceled the land out to their followers.

They brought with them from Norway a firm concept of land ownership as well as an institution of slavery. Both of these things show that there was a system of differential access to resources, stratification. But there was no one king over all of the chieftains. Some of the slaves rose up and killed their masters and took off for the Westman Islands off the east coast of Iceland. The kinsmen of the dead masters hunted down the slaves and killed them all. These chieftains were not going to let their slaves change anything in the new land.

People hunted and fished for subsistence, but they relied mostly on their livestock—sheep and cows. To bring their stock through the winter, they had to cut and store hay before it got too cold. Iceland was too cold and the growing season too short for grain, so they traded wool for grain from Norway.

The more hay a person could get in and store, the more livestock he could bring through the winter. People had to figure out the balance among horses, cows, and sheep. Horses could fend for themselves pretty well during the winter, but they did better with hay. People needed to keep cows and sheep inside during the winter and feed them. The more sheep a farmer kept, the less cattle he could feed with the winter's supply of hay.

The cattle and sheep as well as horses provided provisions for people. Icelanders ate horses then as they do now. Landowners used their provisions to support their slaves and followers. The slaves provided labor for haying, for managing the livestock, and for hunting and fishing.

In the early 900s, there were about thirty-six chieftains. The sagas tell us that some of the chieftains were more cunning than others, some more ruthless, some better at law, some braver, but they were about equal in their power. A chieftain had to be generous to his followers and protect their interests or the followers would have no reason to stay with him. Chieftains also made alliances with other chieftains, especially through marriages.

If we diagram their economic system as we did the Lisu one, it would look like Figure 7-1. We can read the diagram as saying the more slaves, the more labor; the more labor, the more livestock; the more livestock, the more provisions; the more provisions, the more slaves and followers; the more livestock, the less hunting and fishing; the more hunting and fishing, the more provisions.

In this system, where the chieftains were about equally powerful, the limiting factor was access to labor. More slaves meant more labor and so on. With needs limited by the logic of household economies and plenty of land, labor was the limiting factor.

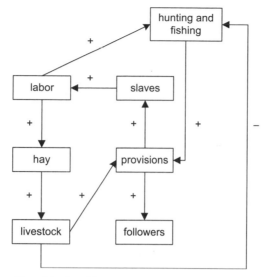

Figure 7-1 The medieval Icelandic economy.

Within sixty years, by the year 930, people had claimed all the land, and the chieftains agreed to establish a general assembly where everyone would meet once a year to settle disputes and to make what they called law. Their idea of law was not like the modern one. It was a blend of tradition, custom, religion, ethics, and law. In those days, before they had writing, they sent one man to Norway to memorize and bring back the system of law from an assembly with which many of the chieftains were familiar. That man was the first law speaker, responsible for knowing the law and reciting one-third of it from memory each year at the assembly. Others listened and learned the law, and then they could be law speakers for three years.

Still, there was no authority above the chieftains. There was the general assembly, but it had no authority. People could take disputes to the assembly, but winning a dispute gave the winner the right to enforce the verdict himself—if he could. If someone killed your brother, you could make a case against him and win. If you won, you could claim half his property and get him banished, but you had to go collect the property yourself, and you had to enforce the banishment yourself. If you weren't stronger than your opponent, there was nothing you could do. Almost every saga has stories of people trying to get enough force together to enforce such decisions.

So the system rested on force. The people who could maintain large followings and strong alliances could focus the most force and were therefore the most powerful. In addition to the three dozen chieftains, there were a number of independent farmers who were their followers.

Some people had settled in the highlands, and some had stayed close to the inlets and rivers where they landed. As more livestock grazed in the highlands, the grass cover diminished, and the soils literally blew away in the high winds. The loss for the highlands was a gain for the lowlands, where those soils settled and made the fields more productive. But highland people had no way to make a living.

The people from these households began to offer to work for other farmers in return for the part of their subsistence that they couldn't provide for themselves. For the first time, wage labor was available. This changed the whole system.

Slave owners had to support their slaves through the year to be able to benefit from their labor at peak times, such as the sheep roundup in the fall, sheering, and hay making. The slaves could produce enough to support themselves, necessary value, but not much more. It was better for landowners to hire people for part of the year when they needed lots of labor and not have to support them for the rest of the year. That way, the landowners could benefit from the surplus value the workers produced because landowners did not have to feed them through the rest of the year just to get the labor when they needed it.

When hired labor was available, there was no advantage to keeping slaves, so landowners began to free them. These freed slaves began looking for land, but there was none they could claim except the small plots that landowners offered them on the edges of their holdings. There, the former slaves could make part of their living and fill in the rest by working for the landowner, their former owner, for wages. Sometimes, instead of hiring labor, landowners rented out their land. It came to the same thing: extracting surplus value from the people who produced it.

Large landowners and chieftains began to buy or take over smaller farms. If a farm was too small to support a household, it wasn't of much use, so a person might sell it and then rent land from the landowner. More and more people had less and less land. The few people who owned land owned more and more of it. There were fewer landowners, each with larger farms.

Now, access to labor was no longer the limiting factor. With plentiful labor, land was the limiting factor. But all the land was already claimed. However, there was no overarching authority; there was no state to prevent a powerful person from taking land from a less powerful one. Figure 7-2 shows these relationships.

This system has several self-intensifying loops. More followers, more land; more land, more hay; more hay, more livestock; more livestock, more provisions; more provisions, more followers. This system depends on the availability of people for wage labor and a chieftain's ability to gain enough followers to secure and enlarge his claim to land.

The supply of labor came from the same process. The smaller the land claim, the less hay, the less the livestock, provisions, and security of the land claim until one didn't have enough land to support a household and had to sell the labor of the household.

Figure 7-3 shows another way to envision the process. Because it was possible to extract surplus value from wage workers, there was no limit on the amount of land a person could use. More land meant more surplus value and more power. So chieftains started taking land from others, and everyone

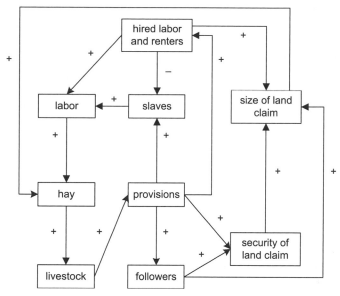

Figure 7-2 Land and labor in the medieval Icelandic economy.

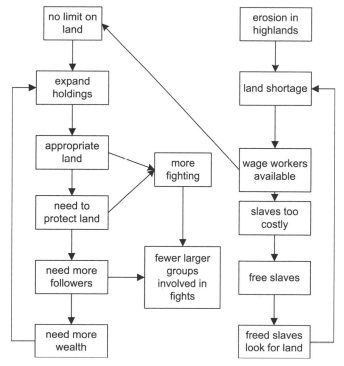

Figure 7-3 Effects of free labor in medieval Iceland.

who claimed land had to defend it because they couldn't call a cop if someone tried to take away their land. The process became exaggerated at each turn until there were a few large groups fighting frequently.

As more and more farmers were drawn into fights to support their chieftains and their own land claims, they had less and less of a stake in this unstable system. A typical farmer thought, "Why should I risk my life for some ostentatious chieftain except that he will whack me if I don't?" It would have served the farmers better to have a state to protect their land rights rather than to have to fight to defend their land or to support their chieftain in his quest for more lands.

Note that a state wouldn't have done anything for the workers, just the farmers. In fact, that's the way it turned out and the way it was for about the next six hundred years. We'll tell that story later.

The chieftains had two sources of income: rents and the products of wage labor. Everything in this system rested on the control of land. A person who didn't control land gained sustenance for his household from wages in kind and the trifling crops from working on property he rented. The control of land depended on the force a person could muster, and that depended on the size of his following. The way to secure a following was to be generous and "chieftainly"—to support followers in their causes and be as generous to them as one was ruthless to enemies. The importance of the followings and the trappings of chieftaincy led to an exaggerated sense of chieftaincy and more grandiose displays of wealth and of power.

The whole system rested on land ownership, but there was no institutional structure to support laws about ownership. It was every person for himself—and yes, all chieftains were "he's," although there were some remarkable women. Each person had to defend land claims on his own. Chieftains or powerful landowners took land from others by force whenever they could get away with it. At the assemblies, the most powerful usually won. Everyone was competing for land and power because the biggest and most powerful had the best chance of winning. Everyone wanted to expand, but there was no place to expand to except other people's land.

By 1220, 350 years after the first settlement, there were five big chieftains' families in Iceland fighting among themselves. Just to put the time framework into perspective, not until 2126 will it have been 350 years since the American Revolution in 1776.

By 1262, one guy, Gissur, won and turned the whole bunch over to the king of Norway and became his earl. He might have become king of Iceland, but Icelanders might have resented it, and Icelanders agreed that Norway was the place where there was a real civilization. Icelanders had a long history of ambivalent relationships with Norwegian kings. They hated them, but they also loved the pomp and poetry of the court and all of its finery.

When Gissur became the king's earl, Iceland became part of a state, but it was not an Icelandic state. It was ruled by a foreign king as a colony, and Norway could enforce its power by controlling or even withholding trade with Iceland. Then, in 1380, Norway became part of Denmark, and Iceland went along and became a Danish colony until 1944, when it gained independence after more than six hundred years of colonial rule.

That six hundred years of colonial rule wasn't such a bad deal for farmers; at least they didn't have to worry about the chieftains anymore. They became the power on the island and once again began to defy the king, this time of Denmark. In the eighteenth and nineteenth centuries, the king told the Icelandic ruling class that they shouldn't treat their own people so badly, but the farmers did not wish to change a system that benefited them so much. After all, they were getting virtually free labor. That was the law. The landowners controlled Parliament and made the laws.

The medieval chieftains wanted to keep the system of stratification because they were at the top. Each chieftain thought he could win in the competition for total control. Finally, they all lost because they could not agree to form a state. They wore themselves out fighting with each other, and when the Norwegian king took over, there was the first peace in a long time, and a lot of people were relieved.

Figure 7-4 summarizes these historical events. These are the lessons we learn from this story:

- Stratification without a state is messy and unstable, but it can last for a long time—four hundred years in Iceland.
- Stratified systems either develop states or stop being stratified. We don't see stratification without states today.
- States hold stratified societies together. Cooperation and reciprocity hold egalitarian and rank societies together.

In this system, we see there is wage labor but no market, so capitalism did not develop. It remained a system of asymmetrical redistribution, but it came to be oriented around the king of Norway rather than around the chieftains.

Acting on the logic of household production and their cultural code, these Icelanders created a system that did not serve anyone's long-term interests, a system that not only was not sustainable but also was self-destructive. The only people who could have changed it were the ones who got the most out of it, the chieftains. Later it was farmers.

In medieval times, just because a state system would have served the landowning farmers well did not mean it would have served the chieftains well. And we ask how well any system served slaves and renters and wage workers who had to scrape by from one year to the next in this marginal ecosystem in a political system run by arrogant and self-serving goons. Another fact about stratified systems: adaptations of the system do not serve all interests equally. Once there are class systems, we ask whose interests are served by what structures and developments. There is no longer any sense in which everyone's interests are served.

In 1000, two other things happened in Iceland. One was the introduction of Christianity at the general assembly. Some of the chieftains were pagans and some were Christians. The king of Norway was pushing for the Icelanders to

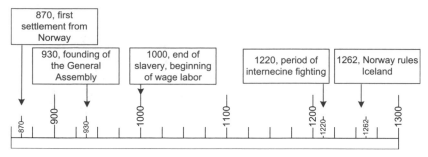

Figure 7-4 Time line for medieval Iceland.

convert, and he could use his clout as their major trading partner for grain and timber. At the meeting of the assembly in Iceland, people were restive and agreed that they could not live with two laws—two sets of customs, cultural codes—one for the pagans and one for the Christians. They agreed to let one person arbitrate. The arbitrator was a pagan himself, but after a long period of seclusion and thought, he decided that everyone should be Christian. At that point, all of the pagans went to a hot spring to be baptized.

Another event of that time was the outlawing of Erik the Red. When a person was outlawed, it meant that someone had won a case against him at the assembly. The person then had the choice of defending himself against the winner, leaving the island, or hiding out. If a person could remain in Iceland without being killed for twenty years, the sentence was lifted. Two people almost made it. One hid out for twenty years before he was whacked. The other made it for eighteen years.

Erik left and went to Greenland to start a new settlement. His son was Leif Eriksson, who continued the westward exploration to Newfoundland, now part of Canada. Archaeologists have located and excavated the site of this settlement at what is now called L'Anse aux Meadows. Icelanders spent several winters there, and one woman had a child in America, but they finally returned to Greenland and Iceland rather than settle the new continent. In the summers of 2005 and 2007, we worked with a group of archaeologists to locate and map her house in Iceland and to piece together this story by locating the early settlement farms and then the later ones where renters lived.

Why did Icelanders turn down the opportunity of settling in America? The Icelandic system depended on captive labor—either as slaves or as desperately poor people who offered their labor for sale. In the new world, slaves could escape. Iceland is large, but there are not that many places to make a living and it's not so large that someone could hide out for as much as twenty years. The interior is all volcanic rock. There are some places to disappear, but not many and not for long. The coastal areas are the only ones suitable for fishing and growing grass. There was no place for runaway slaves to go, as the ones who got to the Westman Islands found. But in America, there was an indefinitely large frontier. The land was so full of fish and game that anyone could make a living without having to be dependent on a landowner. The Icelandic system of land owning and extracting surplus value would not work in the New World.

So, how do we know these stories? If the early settlers had to send a person back to Norway to memorize the law because they couldn't write, then how could they write their sagas? They didn't write them right away. Part of the measure of a chieftain was his reputation. A chieftain's reputation was made or broken in the stories people told. These stories were as important a part of the political economy as the sheep and hay. They were as good as a credit rating.

With Christianity, some people began to learn how to write. One of the first things they wrote was a grammar book about the Icelandic language. Another was the book of settlements that recorded the stories about the first settlers and their land claims. The sagas are stories from the ninth through twelfth centuries that weren't written down until the thirteenth century, in the middle of all of the strife as the system collapsed onto itself.

The saga writers wrote down the old stories, but they also wrote about current events. That's why we have almost ethnographic accounts of the collapse of the system. One of these writers was Snorri Sturlason, the next-to-last chieftain standing.

The end of the world for Snorri, the scholar-chieftain, came in the basement of a priest's house in 1241. Snorri left Norway without the king's permission. That offended the king, who wrote to another powerful Icelandic chieftain, Gissur, to tell him to either get Snorri back to Norway or kill him. Gissur knew Snorri didn't want to go back to Norway, so with seventy followers and more in reserve, Gissur rode to Snorri's establishment and broke into his house where he was sleeping.

Snorri ran to the priest's house to hide. Gissur followed him. The priest said that Snorri wasn't there until Gissur told the priest he had come to make peace with Snorri. Then the priest admitted that Snorri was in the basement, and Gissur sent five men downstairs to murder him.

Because they could not develop institutions to keep order in their stratified society, the Icelandic chieftains became absorbed into a state that could maintain order. Reciprocity and mutuality maintain order in egalitarian and rank societies; states maintain order in stratified societies but in stratified societies without states, there is no assurance of order. In the next chapter, we explore how states maintain order, but, first, a story from another time and place.

Every Friday, Nasrudin sold a donkey in the market for next to nothing. In the same marketplace, there was a rich merchant who couldn't compete with Nasrudin's prices.

"My thugs force farmers to give me the food for my donkeys," the merchant explained, "and I pay no wages to my slaves to take care of the donkeys, and I still can't sell them for as low a price as you." Finally, the merchant asked how Nasrudin could sell his donkeys for such a low price.

Nasrudin said, "You steal the food and labor. I steal the donkeys."

Discussion Questions

- In the United States throughout most of the twentieth century, people like Emma Goldman, who called herself an anarchist who supported the notion of a stateless society based on reciprocity and cooperation, were branded, brought up on charges, imprisoned, and in other ways punished. Can you think of reasons why there was such a strong response to these ideas?
- It took Iceland four hundred years to go from being stratified without a state to a state. Imagine the United States four hundred years from now. What might our society look like? If we don't manage to make our planet completely uninhabitable by then, will our government still be in place? Will it look as it does now?
- The sagas were written centuries after the events they tell of actually happened. They reflect the times in which they were written, as well as the times they tell about. Can you think of other stories that were written down long after the events? Does that color your understanding of texts like the Bible, the Torah, or the Koran?
- Why is it that stratified societies have cops and courts and egalitarian societies do not?

Suggested Reading

Durrenberger, E. Paul. *The Dynamics of Medieval Iceland: Political Economy and Literature.* Iowa City: University of Iowa Press, 1992.
Smiley, Jane. *The Sagas of Icelanders.* New York: Penguin, 2001.

Mustafa Kemal "Ataturk" is considered the father of modern Turkey. His image was widely displayed throughout Turkey until the rise of the Islamist AK Party in the early 2000s. Like most contemporary societies, Turkey is an example of a stratified society. *Photo by E. Paul Durrenberger.*

8

How States Work

The American anthropologist Charles Hockett (1973) summed up states this way:

> *The Mafia, General Motors, the Roman Catholic Church, and the governments of the United States and of the Soviet Union, however greatly they differ, are all cultural cousins, all specialized descendants of the arrangements worked out by the earliest successful as-yet-undifferentiated racketeer-capitalist-bishop-laborboss-governors. (p. 549)*

The Soviet Union has been dismantled, GM was heading the same way until the government bailed it out in 2009, unions in the United States are on the skids, and the scandal-ridden Roman Catholic Church is much poorer than it was then, but the essence of what Hockett said remains true.

Stratified societies are formed of classes with differential access to resources. This creates tensions because the majority of the people would benefit from the equal access to resources enjoyed by people of rank, the equal access that egalitarian societies enjoy. The ruling minority benefits most in a stratified society.

The fundamental predicament of stratified societies is this inequality of distribution. The solution is a set of institutions we call states. The institutions of states solve the problem by two means, as we mentioned earlier: **thought control** and force.

THOUGHT CONTROL

Any university has at least one office dedicated to the task of public relations that enjoys as many resources as just about any department of anthropology. When Paul taught at the University of Iowa, he served on the faculty committee that was supposed to advise the Office of Public Information. (It's usually called something like that rather than "department of propaganda" or something more accurate.)

Whenever anything came up, he always suggested telling the truth as far as people could figure it out. The director, a professional information manager, could never understand that. The job of these offices is to manipulate people's ideas about the university or, as they might say, "to promote the university's interests." Penn State and other universities have several such offices—one dedicated to the sciences; one for alumni; one for athletics; one that deals with research—and others as well.

Americans are so accustomed to spin doctors and advertising assaulting our every sense that we are like antibiotic-resistant microorganisms; a lot of it rolls right off us. But at least some of it sinks in and works. Maybe you've seen a magician who directs your attention to the left hand while performing the trick with the right. That's what this kind of media manipulation is all about. Think celebrity news.

George Orwell had seen a lot of the world before he wrote his novel *1984*. He had worked with the British suppressing Burmese villagers and had been with the anarchists when Franco's fascists invaded Spain in 1936. Orwell knew about the machinations of states. He set his novel in a future that is now decades in the past, and we've seen a lot of what he wrote about—for instance, what he called "double-speak," or reversing the meanings of words to disguise things. The "Office of Public Information" is where you won't get straight talk. The "Department of Defense" is a "Department of War." The Reagan administration named a certain kind of missile "peacekeepers." The slogan for the Cold War U.S. Strategic Air Command, armed with atomic weapons, was "Peace Is Our Profession." And just think about the whole notion of "friendly fire." How friendly is it to get killed by your own side? The examples are so numerous that they have entered our language, and we no longer think about them. That's why they're so insidious, like computer viruses in our brains, misdirecting our thinking.

Think about the rhetoric of any American political campaign. How can everyone be for "freedom," "hope," "America's future," and "family values" and stand for anything that means anything to anyone?

Or the messages of television commercials. "You are the ugliest, foulest-smelling, hairiest, most unfashionable, undesirable worm on the planet. But our product can fix that." The media reach into every corner of our lives with their messages of insignificance and powerlessness. The rulers of preindustrial states weren't that lucky.

They used what Marvin Harris called "magico-religious" specialists, such as the Inca priests who treated the ruler as the "son of the sun." Imagine how important it would have been to the people who farmed for a living to produce enough extra food to support the son of the sun as well as his priests. The Inca priests spread the doctrine that the order of nature depends on commoners subordinating themselves to aristocrats. If you can get people to think that way, you don't have to use force to keep them in line; they do it themselves.

These rulers used collective wealth instead of the media to spread the word through monumental structures such as the pyramids of Egypt and Mexico, cathedrals, and other great edifices designed to make ordinary people feel powerless and insignificant.

Part of the purpose of the doublespeak of today is to convince people that "we are all in the same boat," our enemies are somewhere else, some other state, some other people. In the United States they used to be Soviets; now they're Islamic terrorists. True or not, this reinforces a sense of nationalism—in other words, the state and the status quo.

Maybe you've heard about the Romans offering their citizens "bread and circuses" to distract them. What they could have done with television and the Internet! With modern media, people can get the feeling of participating in something larger than themselves without ever leaving their living rooms. We can participate in the Superbowl, the World Series or March Madness, gut-clenching crime stories and light-hearted romantic comedies, serious documentaries or silly cartoons. Through video games, we can save the earth from aliens, bash heads, enjoy our own private wars, race cars, create make-believe communities, or travel in space. We can get lost for hours online in games and social media. What we don't do is get in the streets.

But thought control comes through in more ways than the media. If some-one asks why we shake hands when we meet someone, we would probably say something like, "How else would you greet someone? It's obvious." We only come to see our cultural codes when we contrast them with others that are different. People think spirits cause them to be sick? The king is not a god that controls the sun and the rain?

Where do these assumptions come from?

When Thai people greet each other, they put their hands together in front of their chins in something like an attitude of prayer. They aren't praying, but they are making statements about their relative prestige. If their hands are in front of their noses, they are saying they are subordinate. If they are at chest height, they are saying they are superordinate. And they have to figure out which pronoun to use. They don't just say "I" and "you" but have special pronouns for higher-ups and lower-downs. They use a term of address that at least shows the speaker's gender. This already indicates something about prestige and status because males are higher than females. The term of ad-dress also indicates something about the relative status of the two people. The tone of voice, the hands, the pronouns, and the terms of address all say where the two are relative to each other in a cosmic karmic hierarchy of beings. No Thai person has to even think about this. It's just natural. "How else would you do it?"

But it wasn't so natural to the poor and rural Shan village where Paul lived. There, people greeted each other by saying, "Where are you going?" "Where are you coming from?" or "What did you eat?" and didn't do anything special with their hands. But then again, they weren't Thai; they were Shan.

When Shan kids go to Thai-run school, the teachers coach them on how to greet people in the properly polite Thai fashion. The postures of respect come along with the language. It's part of being Thai. Shan kids learn it in school because they have their own Shan customs at home, but the Thai run the country. Thai kids learn it by the time they can walk because their parents show them. So by the time they can talk, they've got the whole system of hierarchy down pat and would never think that people could be created equal.

Are all men created equal?

One of Paul's most difficult moments as an anthropologist came in 1976 when he was living with Shan. A presidential election was going on in the United States, and villagers had been hearing a lot about it on Thai radio. One evening after supper, Paul was drinking tea on the veranda of the house where he lived when the headman of the village and a group of villagers came into the compound. The headman asked whether it was true that American people really believed that "all people are created equal."

"How could that be?" he and others asked. "You can see that some are clever and others are slow; some are strong and others are weak; some are rich and others are poor." This doctrine flew directly in the face of a fundamental assumption of the villagers' Buddhist worldview—that people's lives are determined by the balance of their good and bad deeds in all of their past lives, their karma. That explains why the king is the king and a farmer is a farmer and a beggar is a beggar. What could be clearer?

But these folks had heard from an authoritative source that some other people actually thought that the law of karma did not operate, that all people were created equal. They had come to Paul to see whether this could possibly be correct. How could anyone think such a thing?

Paul struggled to find the Shan words. He didn't know how to say "distributive justice," "equality under the law," or "equal rights for all." He didn't know how to explain how it is that black people go to jail more frequently than white ones, how to elucidate the imbalance of gender and inequality of pay for men and women, how to explain the concept that you can get as much justice as you can afford.

Finally, he said something like, "It has to do with law. We say we use the same law for everyone. We say that, but we don't do that."

In American schools, we have similar examples. One day our daughter came home with a middle school class assignment to imagine a colony on Mars fifteen years from now. She had to answer questions like "What form of government will this colony have?" and "Which religion will the people follow?" We suggested she ask different questions, like "What if there were no government?" and "What if there were no religion?" But the assumptions that there is some government and some religion were built into the assignment. By the time most of her fellow students were done with school, they could never think there could be a society without a state or without religion, yet there have been.

When you think about it, the really interesting question is why anyone ever thought that Americans think that people *are* created equal. The fact that we say that at all is testament to our ability to learn to replace our own experience with what we know we're supposed to say.

Lisu are different. It never occurs to them to think about whether people are equal. It never comes up because everyone has access to the same resources. They know they're as good as anybody else. They learn that by growing up in an egalitarian society.

Let's look at one more American example. How many times do kids say, "It's not fair!" Every grown-up knows the answer to that one: "Nobody said it's a fair world," meaning "Don't expect fairness." People who grow up not expecting a fair world are willing to accept an unfair world. It is a powerful form of mind control to tell kids not to expect a fair world. What kind of world would it be if we all tried our best to *make* it fair? What if whenever we had anything to say about it, we did the fair thing? What if our teachers and parents taught us that we should fight for fairness every chance we get?

So we learn a lot of these assumptions just by growing up. Schools and religions polish and shape these assumptions. It never seems like propaganda because nobody questions it—unless the people or the assumptions come from a different system of thought and practice. These assumptions guide people through the complexities of social life.

In industrial societies, people also need to learn skills such as reading, writing, and math. But as we've noted, schools teach a lot of other stuff as well. In the United States, schools teach how to say the Pledge of Allegiance to the flag, how to sing patriotic songs, and how to do other rituals of patriotism. We don't mean to single out American schools from Peruvian, Mexican, Chinese, Turkish, or Thai schools. Schools are part of state systems. People without states don't have schools, and they don't need them.

In 1963, the American anthropologist Jules Henry wrote a book about life in St. Louis, Missouri. He pointed out the distance between our cultures as tried and true solutions to problems and creativity with all of its risks. To ensure continuity, people teach their kids certain things. But the cost of continuity is creativity.

In her ethnographic work in central New York, the American anthropologist Dimitra Doukas found that the working people she was trying to understand did not agree with the supposedly American cultural values of individualism, optimism, competitive consumerism, and upward mobility. They shun conspicuous consumption, are suspicious of upward mobility, respect hard work, are reasonably pessimistic about the larger world, and value community integrity. She argues that the culture of the people is rooted in an old economic system based on locally controlled, craft-based rural industries integrated with farming that was dominant in the United States until the turn of the twentieth century. Then corporations sponsored a great cultural revolution to make the corporations seem natural and expected rather than rapacious and pathological as the older values judged them to be. Doukas locates the cultural tensions of America in the differences and contradictions between these two conflicting cultural codes.

Doukas (2003) says, "The two sides do not know each other. If they could meet, it is possible to imagine that the perpetrators of corporate abuses would face an irresistible democratic challenge in the land of their headquarters" (p. 8). She also says that the consolidation of corporate capitalism in the

IS THAT A GUN IN YOUR POCKET OR . . . ?

Dimitra Doukas
Independent scholar

Whether or not you want to own a gun, you may want to consider the wider impli-cations of gun control. I did. People I studied forced me to. I study the U.S. work-ing class in beat-up former factory towns. One of them was Ilion, New York, home of Remington Arms, a gun manufacturer since the 1820s.

At the time of my fieldwork in the 1990s, Ilion was a scene of deep social division, with local activists charging government corruption and mounting protests in the streets. Harassed relentlessly by agents of local government, the activists cried "tyr-anny!" and quoted Thomas Jefferson on the sovereignty of the people. They saw the power of the state being used to crush the people.

Firearms came up in activists' discussions as the people's last resort in case of tyr-anny. It was not a threat to use firearms. The region's many gun owners generally keep their prizes polished up and locked away. One activist said that he pointed his hunting rifle at an aggressive land surveyor but only to make a point. He would never have pulled the trigger. It was symbolic. The surveyor was trespassing on his property.

It was as if these activists turned around an old National Rifle Association slogan—from "if guns are illegal, only criminals will have guns," to "if guns are illegal, only *police* will have guns." Across the working-class U.S., the symbolic force of firearms goes beyond style and self-defense. Guns symbolize the ability of "ordinary" people to resist the tyranny of the state.

> Let them take arms. . . . The tree of liberty must be refreshed from time to time with the blood of patriots and tyrants. It is its natural manure.
> —*Thomas Jefferson (to W. S. Smith, 11/13/1787)*

There was little debate over the right of "free men" to bear arms in the early United States. Arms were the mark of a free man. Explicit in the Bill of Rights, among the other things that the United States may *not* do, was disarm the citizens.

What got enough people on the side of gun-control legislation? In a word, fear-mongering. The earliest targets were indigenous people and free African Americans. The disarming of African Americans intensified under "Jim Crow" segregation laws. Im-migrant "foreigners" were added to the gun-control fear list in the early twentieth cen-tury, while new taxes raised the cost of legal firearms, limiting poor people's access to them. Since then, federal gun-control laws have expanded to include a variety of pro-hibitions, more taxes, and increasingly complicated regulation schemes.

I argued in the journal *Anthropology Now* that the new target of U.S. gun-control fear-mongering is working-class conservatives, especially veterans ("Targeting the Gun Question," 10/26/2010). Meanwhile, as citizens scare each other with the new bogey-man, the U.S. is becoming a "security" state.

The classic gun-rights argument has an anchor in the reality of how states work. Guns do not have to be brandished to deter tyranny. Those guns in U.S. citizens' closets have done well enough so far. Consider the implications of gun control. A state in which only the police have guns is a police state.

United States "produced a decades-long cultural war of titanic proportions, played out on local battlefields across the United States" (p. 7).

That is the battle that we witnessed in our ethnographic work with unions. We sat at the bargaining table and saw a management that embodied corporate capitalism not understanding its own American workers because both sides share so few assumptions about what is natural, right, fair, and just. It became obvious that management and workers were from different worlds. We will return to this later. Doukas documents the workings of the older system and its culture based on the gospel of work, the idea anthropologists base our comparative economic analysis on, that labor is the source of all value. The gospel of wealth, that capital is "the wellspring of national prosperity . . . was at the center of the cultural revolution that the trusts [corporations] were trying to orchestrate" (Doukas, 2003, p. 100). This gospel is embodied in the discipline of economics parading its religion as science. What makes it religion? It requires belief in the gospel of wealth. Why is it not science? It does not test its hypotheses against observable realities. This is what the Nobel Prize–winning economist Joseph Stiglitz argues in his book *Globalization and Its Discontents*. Why do so many believe in economics? Because it benefits them to do so, and it provides a bulwark to an ideology that makes these ideas seem as natural and inevitable as the god-kings of the Inca were.

Doukas documents how the trusts, emergent corporations, orchestrated a campaign to reshape American culture—what she calls a cultural revolution. They knew that for their religion to seem natural, it had to have the imprimatur of scholarship. They endowed the professorships and university chairs to make their ideology respectable.

To see how modern corporations continue to do the same thing today, take a look at a film called *The Corporation* or the book that it's based on, *The Corporation: The Pathological Pursuit of Profit and Power*, by the University of British Columbia law professor Joel Bakan.

Now we close the loop and remind you of your own college's or university's propaganda machine. We don't know about your school. Look for yourself. Penn State has a Schwab Hall, a Carnegie Hall, an ethics center named for a Texas oilman who funds it, an honors college named for a beneficent donor, and a college of science named after another such donor, a career center named after the Bank of America, and many others. Every university has a whole bureaucratic mechanism devoted to courting such donors. It makes strategic plans that call for transforming our land grant university into the research and development branch for agribusiness corporations.

When graduate assistants tried to organize a union at Penn State in 2002 and 2003, the administration was adamantly opposed and initiated an antiunion campaign worthy of any corporation. Whom does the administration represent? Who provides the money? The universities provide the respectability for the ideologies that support those people; universities endow those ideas with the aura of being as natural and inevitable as the rising of the sun in the morning.

Meanwhile, people learn from growing up in their own families that there really should be something like fairness, that we really do care for our neighbors, that we really do need to pull together and help each other out and can't really grasp the supply and demand stuff our schools expect us to believe. And so the older American culture lives on despite its retreat from the public view. But it doesn't always feel comfortable, especially when you're looking into the steely eyes of management's lawyers across the negotiating table when they tell you about "reality."

When the economist John Kenneth Galbraith (1992) turned to similar matters in his book *The Culture of Contentment*, he said he would "use the method of the anthropologist" to examine the "tribal rites of strange and different peoples," because "they are to be observed but not censured" (p. 11). This is cultural relativity again. Galbraith argues that because the two dominant American political parties are so similar, reasonable people do not think they have a choice, so most do not vote. The minority of adult people who do vote are those the system serves and who thus feel part of it because they think they might benefit from something the system does. But that's never a majority.

THE ILLUSION OF CHOICE

This is wrapped up in our American illusion of choice. We all take great pains with our decisions. Suzan has seen Paul paralyzed in front of a case of dairy products trying to find some reasonable basis for selecting one container of milk over another. He's even worse with peanut butter. When Paul was a graduate student, he knew a guy who worked in a shortening factory who explained how they used the same machines and ingredients to make every brand of shortening; they only changed the labels. Later Paul saw the same process in factories in Chicago. That defines the range of choice. Same product, different label. Same thing with the two American political parties.

But wasn't Obama really different from McCain/Bush? It's a question of more or less, not a question of whether or not. The common question as Obama arrived at the White House was: Will Obama change Washington or will Washington change Obama?

Obama pushed through the Affordable Care Act over heavy resistance from conservatives, but Americans still do not enjoy access to health care as a right of citizenship, as most Europeans do. American insurance companies continue to treat health care as a commodity for them to make a profit from, now codified in federal health-care "reform," an outlook alien to most industrial societies. Obama managed to reduce the debt that his predecessor had piled up, and he did restore the economy that was at a historic low point when he came into office, but he appointed the same men who drove the policy that created the Great Recession to preside over the U.S. recovery. As of this printing, not one person has been criminally charged for the actions on Wall Street that crippled the U.S. economy for years and displaced hundreds of thousands if not millions of people from their jobs, their homes, and their communities. He ended our involvement in some wars, but began or continued it in others. His election never changed the balance of power in

American politics or in the workplace. His election never created systems that would build toward a more egalitarian America. Yet his election allowed many people to say, "See? Racism is over in America. We elected a black president." It allowed many to justify the status quo while white police officers continued to use excessive force against unarmed black men in the streets without repercussions.

Let's look at U.S. foreign policy under Obama, the Nobel Peace Prize–winning "change" president. Even before U.S. troops pulled out of Iraq and Afghanistan, contractors from corporations such as Blackwater moved in and worked as trainers and guards and in other military roles. The global war on terror took on a life of its own and became a self-perpetuating industry with foundations, journalists, book writers, generals, and warriors. It may have replaced the nuclear weapons industry of the Cold War. Obama did not stop it. A Republican administration launched the war on terror, but a Democratic one legitimized and expanded it. Obama strengthened the powers of the executive branch of government and streamlined the process for assassinating "enemies." He initiated or continued shadow wars in Afghanistan, Pakistan, Yemen, and Somalia without the scrutiny of either the legislative or the judicial branch.

As large-scale military deployments wound down, the United States escalated its use of drones, cruise missiles, and Special Operations raids such as the one that killed Osama Bin Laden in 2011. The journalist Jeremy Scahill documents this process in his book, *Dirty Wars: The World Is a Battlefield* and explains why the United States could support Arab Spring rebels against dictators in Tunisia and Libya but not Yemen. Yemen's dictators were so enmeshed in U.S. foreign policy that the United States could not turn on them and support the people of that land when they tried to overthrow them.

But it's hard to predict what the historical judgment will be. Many people now believe that Ronald Reagan was one of our best presidents, when by any measure of achievement he was one of the worst. That is because the conservatives who put him in power and benefitted from his presidency developed a powerful propaganda machine to make him a secular saint. It remains to be seen whose version of history will win out when it comes to Obama.

Where do we get the illusion of consequential life choices? This is one of those things that's inculcated in us from the time we are children at home, school, and church. Many of the choices we agonize over, like which peanut butter to buy or which candidate to vote for or which church to go to, are not really choices. But the idea of choice is so necessary for a consumer economy and so heavily promoted by all media that it becomes a tenet of our culture. So, we are supposed to believe that the differences between Democrats and Republicans are significant. That's what political campaigns are about.

Yet health insurance is a great example of how little choice we have. Anyone who has tried to purchase health insurance in the United States knows how mind-bending the options can be—deductibles, copays, out-of-pocket expenses. But anyone who has done the math has figured out how little difference there is.

Keeping a lid on it

One thesis about American political parties is that when populists offered a real alternative toward the turn of the century when the corporate cultural revolution was under way, they showed signs of success. Grassroots organizations like the Grange and the cooperative movement were successful. They organized into the Farmer-Labor Party, the People's Party, and other populist parties. They carried some governors' offices and elected some legislators. When they became a threat to corporate America, the two dominant parties had an interest in working together to maintain their monopoly on the machinery of the American state to serve the corporations.

The premise of this argument is that both parties attempt to keep the level of well-being just high enough to prevent a majority of people from being attracted to populist alternatives. Democrats would pull it up just a bit, and Republicans would let it slip a bit. And both serve the same corporations. Take a look sometime at the big donors to each party and to each presidential candidate and you'll see what we mean. The Reagan–Bush years were a downswing, Clinton stopped the downswing, helped by the emergence of the Internet, then George W. Bush presided over a crash, and maybe Obama brought a bit of an upswing to restore the balance a little, yet wealth become more concentrated than ever under Obama.

Did anything change in the composition or roles of the parties? How about the economy? Did everyone get a good-paying, 40-hour-per-week job or did Wall Street disappear? Were CEOs imprisoned and their companies shut down or taken over by the government for the public good? Did the foreclosed-on homes become the property of towns and cities so they could rent them out cheaply to the unemployed? These are the kinds of things populists call, and when their call is effective and tenacious, the two ruling parties find a way to throw the populists, and the public, a bone to maintain order.

But here's a real choice, a real difference. Rational democracies have single-payer insurance; the government pays for medical care because people in those countries don't believe anyone should profit from someone with cancer or a broken leg or diabetes. These systems work much better than the American one. They deliver better health care at lower cost. That's a well-documented fact. But in the United States health care is a valuable commodity from which corporations make lots of money. That's not natural; it's policy.

What if American leaders allowed "the market"—we'll discuss that more later—to decide between government health care and the private sector? That was much of the debate over the Affordable Care Act, yet conservatives labeled it as "unfair" and "government-sponsored" and "socialist." That's how health insurance companies got to stay in the health-care loop and how states were allowed to opt out of federal exchanges. To date, no major American political party has had the courage to say that health care is too important for corporations to make money off of, but when health insurance became such an onerous burden on people's budgets, the government did just enough to keep people from getting radicalized over it.

America has a radical history, one in which small groups of dedicated people have threatened the status quo. In 1930, eastern Iowa was under martial law. The National Guard manned machine guns at rural crossroads to quell a growing rebellion of farmers. But when Paul began to study this populist movement, he asked students and colleagues whether they had ever heard of the main organizer, Milo Reno, president of the Farmer's Union, or whether they knew of the Farmer's Educational and Cooperative Society. None had except one colleague who was a descendant of Reno's crew. No one was aware that Iowa had been under martial law. That is how effectively our schools and our media eradicate the events of our history so that they don't become threatening models for the future.

We have countermoves in books such as Howard Zinn's (2003) *People's History of the United States* or in movies like *Matewan* and *Norma Rae* and Michael Moore's documentaries and books, but they are few and far between. And the Internet has allowed more such work to get dispersed more widely than ever. As long as you're on the Internet, you're not in the streets. So we're not saying that the state or corporations control your brain from the time you're born. They try, for sure. Sometimes it takes some real effort to bust out, but that's what you're doing here.

Corporations have their countermoves as well. One countermove to populism was to organize a "safe" alternative for farmers. The Sears, Roebuck Company and several railroad companies joined together to form the Farm Bureau. They gave their ideological organization more clout by getting it grafted onto the agricultural extension service of the land grant universities. These universities—such as Penn State, the University of Illinois, Texas A&M, and Washington State University, just to name the ones Paul is indebted to for his job or his education—were supposed to be the bastions of the yeoman farmers who were supposed to be the backbone of our country. Congress gave these universities federal lands to support them and gave them the mission of research and development to support small farmers.

But to get the newest research speedily into the hands of farmers, they organized the extension program with the U.S. Department of Agriculture. And the extension program worked through the Farm Bureau. If a farmer wanted the latest developments, he had to belong to the Farm Bureau. Even today, many think this right-wing ideology mill (and insurance company) is speaking for farmers. As a historical footnote: in their championing of corporate agriculture, both the Farm Bureau and the land grant colleges have done more to destroy small farmers than to preserve them. We'll pick up that story later.

These are not things of long ago. The same cultural mechanics are operating today. Lewis Lapham, for instance, documents the successes of the ultra-conservative millionaires in orchestrating a massive propaganda program from endowing foundations and think tanks, sponsoring publications, books, briefings, and mass media campaigns to make *liberal* a bad word. He attributes the successive dumbing down of our public discourse to this extension of the cultural revolution that Doukas describes. He concludes by pointing out that both candidates in the 2004 presidential election presented themselves as embodiments of "values" rather than proponents of any ideas. Critical thought wilts under such a barrage. Intelligent political discussion dies. And of such machinations are the cultures of states made. Of these machinations are our cultures made. In the United States, the Koch Brothers are but one example in their targeting of any "liberal" candidate and support of ultraconservative candidates in all states.

Industrial and preindustrial states alike use mind control. Schools and media are one avenue, but states also sponsor religions that preach that if you tolerate poverty and misery in this life, everything will be better in the next life, that people deserve whatever hardships happen to them and not to question it, or that you should feel guilty if something good happens. When we look at the topic of religion later, we will see that there are two major types of religions: state religions and nonstate religions. All of the state religions share one thing in common: they demand that their followers believe something.

This is one of those elements of cultural codes. You may be thinking, "That's what religion *is* after all, belief in something." For now we'll just say this: what state religions ask people to believe isn't as important as that they ask people to believe *something*. That is because all state religions ask people to accept ideas that are contrary to what they experience in everyday life. Belief is based on faith, not experience. The only way people can accept such counterexperiential things as their state religions teach them is if there is some way to *disconnect* those teachings from experience. Belief and faith do that. Some state religions have or had institutions to enforce compliance, such as the Inquisition. Others are more subtle. Why do all U.S. presidents end their speeches and talks with invocations of God? It's normal in the United States, but when the Icelandic president did that just before the economy there crashed in 2008, a sense of dread fell over the entire country. Everyone realized the news was horrible when an elected official resorted to calling on a god for wisdom or strength!

This is what makes science different from religion. Science teaches us to believe nothing, to be skeptical of everything, to check whether everything anyone says is true against our own experience to see whether it matches what we observe.

So, media from inscribed stones to Internet, families, and churches are all forms of mind control that states have used since ancient times. Schools are a more recent secular addition to the machinery.

Seeing the world this way can make a person feel pretty hopeless sometimes. If we are all controlled by these kinds of mind control, what's the point? All of us have deep-down feelings about fairness, and we know that even if we don't experience a fair world, we want it to be fair. Cooperation is one of the things that made us the kind of species we are. We can't just deny that because our experience runs against it. Everyone who has been treated unfairly or has seen others treated unfairly knows those feelings. A lot of times there is nothing we can do. But sometimes there is.

What we can all do is to first try to understand how our own societies work and why they work that way so that we can understand better what we can do to make the world more fair. The more aware you become, the more you can move these feelings and thoughts from the back of your mind to the front, the more you can move them from being unquestioned assumptions of our culture to being questions you ask, the better able you are to see alternatives and to give yourself some choices and to make a difference.

We know it's hard to see these things "from the inside." But it's not impossible if you keep your mind open to it. That's why so many anthropologists over the years have gone to exotic places to study people—it gave them that automatic outsider's view that also made it easier to see their own culture in a new way when they came back. When you see that outside view, you can help others. We're just showing you how to make those nagging doubts into questions that you can answer and that you can act on the answers you develop. It's that knowledge that states try to suppress when they rewrite history or only ask you "which" instead of "whether." They don't want kids growing up challenging the system the way Milo Reno did.

Want to read something really radical? Get a copy of the American Declaration of Independence sometime. Those guys went way out on a limb. But, if you don't like the tree, out on a limb is a good place to be. For an experiment some time, see whether you can get anyone you know to sign it today.

FORCE

All stratified societies also make use of coercion. Force. The political scientist James Scott found that Indonesian peasants aren't fooled by state propaganda. They see through it and understand their situations quite well. And to the extent they can, they resist. But, he points out, they know that they don't have much space to act because the state will use force on them to keep them in line.

The state wants to draft young men for an army or work detail? Send the youths away when the government agents come. The government wants to tax your land? Lie about how much of it you have. Be too stupid to understand what the government agents are telling you. In the Icelandic sagas, there's an archetype of the stupid slave. To believe the sagas, these guys were just barely aware that they were alive, much less able to follow the instructions of their owners. This is what Scott calls resistance. But take it too far, and they kill you. Force.

We see this in its starkest forms when societies are in transition. Remember Stalin and Chayanov? Stalin had millions killed to gain compliance with government programs. The emperors of China were as nasty as any when it came to using force against anyone who disagreed with them. Their Communist successors were no better. The English used force to ensure compliance to the enclosure acts that drove people from their land into the cities to sell their labor. When they couldn't make a living selling their labor, people started stealing, which the English punished by banishment, imprisonment, and hanging. And of course the United States was founded on force, starting with the genocide of hundreds of thousands of Native Americans who were here first.

Then came the corporate cultural revolution in America. It wasn't just a matter of talk. The corporations used guns as well, hired guns like the Pinkertons. They killed innumerable working people who tried to organize unions. Not until 1935, in the throes of the Great Depression with Roosevelt's New Deal being enacted, did the Wagner Act give American working people the right to organize. After World War II, in 1947, the Taft–Hartley amendments to that act pulled the teeth from the Wagner Act, and there has been a concerted war on the labor movement ever since. And it *has* been a war. Just ask workers who go out on strike only to be confronted by militarized police as they try to march through their own town or stop strikebreakers from crossing their picket line. So, in the use of force, archaic empires, revolutionary states, and parliamentary democracies are pretty much the same.

How does this apply to kinship? States use coercive political and economic powers to control stratified social orders, so kinship is not an important organizing principle. Trobrianders and Kachin have ranked lineages and ranking within lineages. When the highest-ranking people of all lineages share more in common with each other than they do with their lower-ranking lineage mates, when they can think of making kinsmen into renters rather than relatives, then kin groups fall apart. Then the important groups aren't lineages but classes—aristocrats and commoners. This is the move that Harald Finehair accomplished in Norway in a system based on kindreds. When he got all of the high-ranking people together, they formed an aristocracy of a kingdom. The kindreds ceased to be important because the high-ranking kinsmen had no interests in common with low-ranking ones.

We can understand these developments in systems in terms as self-intensifying loops similar to the ones we've discussed before. Because stratification defines different interests between people with privileged access to resources and those without, kin ties become less important, and order is less based on kinship, mutuality, or cooperation. That makes kin ties even less important and differentiates the classes even more. The differential interests contribute to an increasing division of labor that erodes kin relations in favor of occupational ones. As kinship ties become less important for maintaining order, formal systems of law develop and these begin to replace the role of kinship and cooperation in maintaining order. This is more or less what was happening in ninth-century Norway but not in Iceland. Iceland, with no state, had no mechanism for the universal application of law.

States maintain order in stratified societies by upholding three principles by mind control and by force:

- Hierarchy is natural and just. Some people naturally and justly have more power, prestige, authority, and access to resources than others.
- Property is natural. Some people have the *right* to use certain things, and others don't.
- The power of law is for the good of everyone. There are universal rules to govern property and social relations. They are not personal,

they don't depend on who you are, and they are for every one of the same group—all commoners or all aristocrats.

There are many ways to legitimate hierarchy. One is the idea of closeness to an ancestor to define hierarchies within and among lineages. This is an integral part of redistributive systems of exchange. But with the development of states and the waning importance of kinship groups in stratified societies, religious ideas can support hierarchy with concepts such as god-kings or the idea that some gods or god gives the kings the right to rule and makes aristocrats better than ordinary people. State religions often communicate ideas, such as if common people interfere with the operation of the state—by resistance, for example—or don't do proper rituals, pay taxes, and obey their rulers, the gods will be unhappy and punish everyone.

Revolutionary ideologies can enshrine hierarchy as well. In Mexico, the Soviet Union, and China, the rulers ruled in the name of the revolution, and if you disagreed, you were counterrevolutionary and had to be shot. We see examples from Tiananmen Square to Stalin.

The American form is "democratic." Americans are supposed to all believe that our rulers represent the will of the people. They were elected in one-person, one-vote elections that give them the authority to rule by "majority rule" even when less than 50 percent of the eligible population ever votes or when the president can lose the popular vote and still win the election thanks to the Electoral College, which was supposed to be something like a parliamentary system but has now ceased to have any real function. Or when a Supreme Court decision can steal an election, as many believe it did in 2000. Yet the

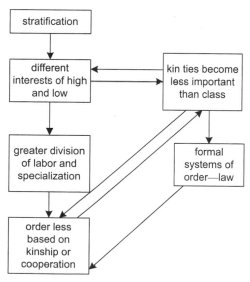

Figure 8-1 How states work.

message of the Occupy movement and its "99 percent" captured the imaginations and hearts of millions of Americans and people around the world. People do know the difference between equal and unequal, fair and unfair, democratic and undemocratic, but it is not the state's job to give them those choices.

Not everyone has a concept of property. Remember Lisu, who have free access to agricultural land if they clear it for their own use. Property is the idea that some people have the right to use something and others don't. Here we aren't considering small things like arrows or clothes, but basic resources like land. If someone can use the land and someone else cannot, if there is privileged access, then there is property. Icelandic chieftains, for instance, established this principle when they first landed and claimed land.

In medieval Iceland, law was not universally applied. If a person had sufficient force of arms to impose a penalty, he could justify it by appeal to a decision of the assembly and law. *Universal application* means that the same law applies to everyone of the same class equally. When that happens, people don't settle disputes by feud, as they did in medieval Iceland, or by consensus and public opinion, as among Tsembaga, but by law and the officials who decide how to apply it on behalf of the state. Feud is against the law because it is disorder. To control people, the ruling classes concentrate force and monopolize force and maintain order through law enforcement. Everyone must follow the same rules.

To maintain order is to keep a stratified society working. No longer is it sufficient just to cooperate, as in nonstratified social orders. States are the institutions that the ruling classes devise to accomplish the tasks of maintaining order by ideas and practices of hierarchy, property, and the rule of law.

STATES AND LABOR

Here's how it all comes together: The ruling class uses the labor of a subordinate class to benefit them. The subordinate class provides labor for the ruling class. Another way of saying this is that the ruling class appropriates surplus value from the subordinate class. The state provides institutions that govern the subordinate class, and the subordinate class supports the state. For this to seem reasonable to people, they must accept the legitimating ideology of the state whether it be religious, revolutionary, or democratic.

The state promotes this ideology via its schools, churches, and media, and the ideology justifies the state and makes it seem natural and inevitable to the subordinate class. Meanwhile, the state protects the interests of the ruling class, and the ruling class controls the institutions of the state. The legitimating ideology justifies the ruling class and makes them seem natural, inevitable, ordained by god, or justified by a vote or the revolution, and the ruling class promotes the legitimating ideology via media, schools, and other forms of thought control. Is this some grand conspiracy? You might think so, but it's more like an interest-assisted evolution, with the ones who benefit the most doing the assisting.

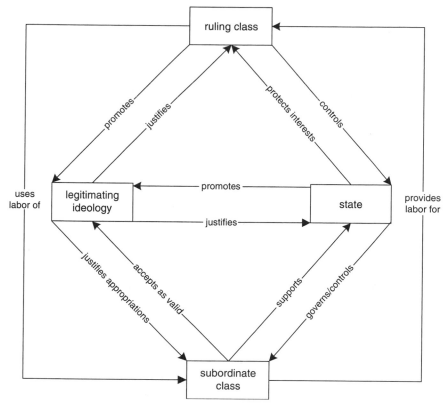

Figure 8-2 How stratification makes kinship less important.

Here is the natural, inevitable, and if not God-given, at least author-provided, diagram that shows how these parts all form a system and how if one of them changes, the others change, too (Figure 8-2). As Hockett suggested in the opening quote to this chapter, all states do not operate in the same way, but this much they all have in common.

Discussion Questions
- Remember when you were a kid or watch parents with their kids when you can. What rules do parents enforce (aside from those that keep their children safe)? Why? What would happen if they didn't enforce those rules?
- Whether or not you believe in a religion, you are probably familiar with some of the basic tenets of some major religions. List them and discuss what makes those tenets so valuable to a state society. How do you think people would behave without those tenets given them by formal religion?
- What are some ways that college students "resist" certain laws? (Consider speeding, underage drinking, and other common infractions.) Can you

think of any ways Americans work collectively to resist the rules? Is there a difference between individual resistance and collective resistance? If so, describe it. If you can't think of any examples of collective resistance, why do you think that's so?

- Seek out one event in history that you weren't taught in school. Talk to your parents and grandparents, or look in Howard Zinn's *People's History*. It should be an event that affected a large number of people or an entire community—a strike, a fight over environmental damage, a racially charged incident. Research it and then discuss why you believe that event didn't make it into the standard history textbooks.
- If you have classmates who are from the North and from the South, have a conversation about the basic facts surrounding the Civil War, or the War between the States. Or use events from elsewhere in the world such as the division of India and Pakistan or the Palestinian intifada and the founding and expansion of Israel. Identify the differences in different peoples' understandings of that historic event. Why do those differences exist? What do they have in common?

Suggested Reading

Berdan, Frances. *Aztecs of Central Mexico: An Imperial Society*. Belmont, CA: Thomson/Wadsworth, 2004.

Bonanno, Alessandro, and Douglas Constance. *Caught in the Net: The Global Tuna Industry, Environmentalism and the State*. Lawrence: University Press of Kansas, 1996.

Chomsky, Noam. *Necessary Illusions: Thought Control in Democratic Societies*. Cambridge, MA: South End Press, 1989.

Doukas, Dimitra. *Worked Over: The Corporate Sabotage of an American Community*. Ithaca, NY: Cornell University Press, 2003.

Scahill, Jeremy. *Dirty Wars: The World Is a Battlefield*. New York. Nation Books, 2013.

White, Curtis. *The Middle Mind: Why Americans Don't Think for Themselves*. San Francisco: Harper, 2003.

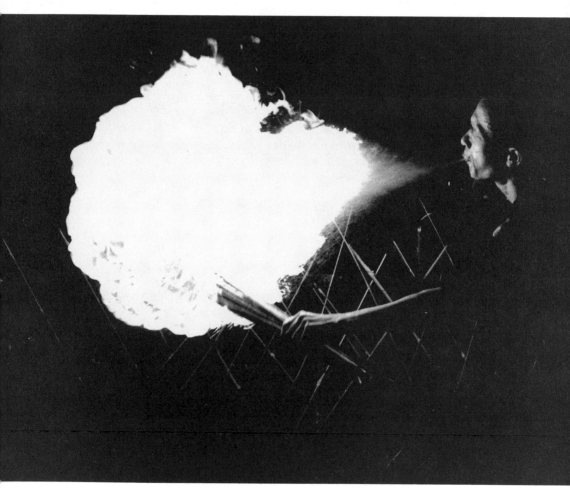

A Lisu shaman chases bad spirits. *Photo by E. Paul Durrenberger.*

9

The Anthropology of Religion

STATES AND REVITALIZATION MOVEMENTS

The anthropologist Anthony F. C. Wallace was interested in understanding how the Seneca religious leader Handsome Lake developed a new religion in 1799 that helped his people adapt to reservation life after a losing fight first against the British and then against the Americans. After a struggle with alcoholism, Handsome Lake had three visions that guided him in instructing his people. Because the events of their own lifetimes had left many Seneca people as disoriented as Handsome Lake, a number of them followed his new teachings.

Wallace found that there were many similar movements, including the Ghost Dance movement in the West at the end of the nineteenth century. There in 1889 the prophet Wovoka had visions of the return of the buffalo and the ancestors and the restoration of the old ways of the plains Indians. The anthropologist James Mooney arrived three years later to interview Wovoka and do what anthropologists do—participant observation. In 1896 he published his book on the subject, *The Ghost Dance Religion and Wounded Knee*. There have been many other such movements.

In 1956 Wallace wrote a paper about **revitalization movements** that has been reprinted so many times that it has become the standard reference. Revitalization movements, he observed, reorient cultural codes overnight when people's expectations no longer match their experiences. In the previous chapter we said that religions of states require belief because they ask people to accept things that don't agree with their everyday experience. One of the problems that state religions face is that if their teachings are too far off from people's experiences and if the people find themselves in dire straits, the people are likely to change their religion and then change realities to match the new religious ideas of a better world. Handsome Lake was able to facilitate this process. Of course, the Ghost Dance wound up at the Little Big Horn and then Wounded Knee.

Wallace found that revitalization movements often happen when a colonial power has moved in on a people. Marvin Harris argued that in its beginnings, Christianity was one example of such a radical change of religion that was also a revolutionary movement to change realities for a colonized people.

Islam revitalized

Here's just a little history to offer some context about Islam.

In 622 the Prophet and his followers left Mecca and went to Medina, where he established the first Islamic state system. Eight years later, they returned to Mecca. Thus, Islam gained adherents and followers and became more and more powerful until it had covered the civilized world of that time. Within a hundred years it had spread to all of the Near East and entered Spain, where it persisted for almost eight hundred years. Empires rose, spread, and fell across India and Asia but most relevant here is the Ottoman Empire, which was founded in 1299 and in 1453 conquered Constantinople, along with the Byzantine Empire of the Greeks. They renamed the capital Istanbul. By the mid-1500s the Ottomans were well into Europe and controlled most of Hungary.

The Europeans began to push back and in 1699 they defeated the Turks and re-claimed Hungary. Then, with the help of the British, the Greeks waged a war of inde-pendence in 1832. In 1830, on the western edge of the empire, the French conquered Algeria, and in 1882 the British occupied another part of the empire, Egypt. Greece, Algeria, and Egypt were parts of the Ottoman Empire. The French and the British left in the 1950s, after more than a hundred years, but with the end of the colonial phase came a kind of disguised colonialism. One way or another these areas have been oc-cupied, conquered, and ruled by foreigners ever since the Romans. Just as Handsome Lake and the Ghost Dance were responses to American colonialism and Christianity was a response to Roman colonialism, the Islamic revitalization movements of the past hundred years or so have been responses to Ottoman and then European and American colonialism and occupation.

Another such movement was Islam. Eric Wolf suggested that when the kinship system of the Middle East failed to function well for the complex necessities of trade at the juncture of all the trade routes in Mecca, the Prophet Muhammad provided a vision that reoriented the society so that it could transcend the limitations of the kinship system. His first vision was in 610. Islam allowed the wealthy of all lineages to share interests with each other as opposed to those of their poor kinsmen—it made the transformation of Figure 8-2 of the previous chapter happen all at once.

The media images of giant passenger planes crashing into the World Trade Center towers in New York on September 11, 2001, are branded into the eyes and imaginations of all who saw them repeated over and over again in the following days and months. We heard a lot about Islamic militants who, the Bush administration said, wanted to destroy the United States because they irrationally hated America and freedom.

We can understand these events better with the help of an anthropologist and several journalists. The anthropologist is E. E. Evans-Pritchard, who was posted as a political officer with the British Military Administration in 1942 during World War II to what would later become a province of Libya. He was already well known to anthropologists for his studies of Nuer and Azande in sub-Saharan eastern Africa. He never got along with Malinowski, who ruled the academic roost in Britain in those days, so he couldn't get a job in England. He had been teaching in Egypt (which was under English control), where he learned Arabic. When World War II started, he was too old to serve in the armed forces, but he volunteered for service and was sent to Syria for a while and then to Cyrenaica in Libya. From his time in Egypt and Syria, he already knew about an Islamic religious movement of Sufi mystics like Nasrudin, about whom we keep telling stories. They were called the Sanusi brotherhood. Evans-Pritchard describes the order in contrast to another that had grown up in Saudi Arabia, the Wahhabi.

Both movements, Evans-Pritchard tells us, created states, the Wahhabi in Arabia and the Sanusi in Libya. These movements were dangerous to the states where they grew. At that time the powers were the English who occupied Egypt and to the west, the French who ruled Algeria. In between was Libya, with a couple of port towns on the coast, some arable land inland, and a lot of desert, where Bedouin herded camels, goats, and sheep. To be left in peace, the Sanusi brotherhood went to Libya and began to set up sedentary centers of agriculture, trading, and teaching around oases in the desert.

Why did the Bedouin allow this intrusion? First, the Sanusi were holy men, men of the book, and Bedouin respected that. The Bedouin were also Muslims, if not very devout by urban measures. But there was a more important reason. The Bedouin were organized into patrilineages, as we discussed in Chapter 3. But there was a twist to the lineage pattern. These were what Evans-Pritchard called segmentary systems.

In a segmentary system each part of the lineage is its own organization. So one camp might be one lineage. The next camp would be another. But the lineages also claimed agricultural land, grazing lands, and water resources for their own. The lineages that were closest in space were also closest in kinship. And the important point is that there were no other means of organizing or governing.

That meant that people could get into feuds. If one of your guys hurts one of ours, we try to hurt you in reprisal. That kind of thing can escalate as both sides get more allies until the point that people are equally allied to both sides. Then they try to make both sides resolve the dispute. But that may not work, especially when it's a dispute about access to land or water. The tribesmen so respected the Sanusi that the Bedouin called on the brothers to arbitrate their many disputes. The brotherhood thus provided an important service for the Bedouin, who in return helped to support them.

Until 1923 all of the Middle East was part of the Ottoman Empire centered in today's Turkey. The French, British, and Russians had been busily trying to disassemble this empire by arming rebel groups along the borders, including Greeks and Armenians. Meanwhile, the English wanted the Suez Canal to connect them to their empire in India and controlled Egypt to control the canal.

Italy wanted to join the British and the French as a colonial power. What more natural place than the ancient breadbasket of the Roman Empire, just across the Mediterranean in Libya? The Italians first invaded in 1911 and fought until 1917. They invaded again in 1923 and finally took Libya in 1932. Their main opposition were the Bedouin under the leadership of the Sanusi brothers. The Italians ruled until 1942, when the British took Libya during World War II. Evans-Pritchard's summary of the situation is especially important so we're going to quote it for you here:

> *Throughout the Near East in particular, but also everywhere in the world where coloured peoples were articulate, the struggle was seen to have a deeper significance than a mere transfer of territories from Turkey to Italy, or the mere acquisition of another bit, one of the few remaining bits, of Africa by a European Power. Like a great octopus, Europe had stretched out its tentacles to seize and exploit the whole of Africa and Asia. The tentacle which now held Tripolitania and Cyrenaica [the two provinces of Libya] in its grip belonged to the same beast which held half the world in its clutches. It was not the future of a handful of Bedouin being decided, but the future of Europe.* (Evans-Pritchard, 1949, p. 116)

The rest of the Muslim world contributed funds and volunteers to support the *mujahidin*, holy warriors, fighting in Libya against the Italians. And the Italians had expected that the Bedouin would welcome them as liberators from the Ottoman Empire! In the same vein, almost a hundred years later, some Americans expected Iraqis to support their invasion as a liberation from Saddam Hussein.

Evans-Pritchard's book, published in 1949, was way ahead of its time. Instead of focusing on a small and supposedly isolated group of people, he described all of the complexities of the religious order, their relationships with the Bedouin tribes, the Turkish administration, the reasons the Italians wanted the place, their invasions, and the Bedouin resistance. The Italians, he says, were not fighting an army, they were fighting a people, "and a people can only be defeated by total imprisonment or extermination" (Evans-Pritchard, 1949, p. 171).

So in 1931 the Italians resorted to bombing, mechanized raids, fencing off whole areas of the country with barbed wire, and concentration camps. So with mass extermination and imprisonment they won—until the British showed up in World War II.

In the eighteenth century, Abdul Wahhab led a revitalization movement in Arabia to purify Islam, especially of heresies like the Sufi practiced. He banned all holidays, and his followers destroyed graves and other holy sites that they considered idols. He gave his followers permission to rape and plunder anyone who didn't follow his form of Islam.

Other Muslims thought he was a dangerous heretic and in 1744 they drove him out of the central part of Arabia. But he sought protection from the first founder of a Saudi state. The Ottomans put down both the new state and the religious movements, but a strong link between the religious Abdul Wahhab and the political Mohammed bin Saud had been formed and was handed down from one generation to the next. From that time, the Wahhab doctrines became the official religion of the Saudis. In the nineteenth century, there was another attempt to form a Saudi state, but it collapsed because of family infighting.

In the 1930s there was another movement in Arabia led by the Ikhwan, who wanted to purify Islam by holy struggle or jihad. In the name of jihad they massacred thousands of villagers in Arabia. The Ikhwan were especially disgusted with the king's alliance with Britain, his lavish lifestyle, and his polygamy. The king could not tolerate this kind of alternative political power, especially since it was directed against him in the name of religious purification. But the king couldn't declare war on clerics without the permission of other clerics. The Wahhabi clerics gave the king the sole right to declare jihad and thus the power to obliterate his opposition and to claim that they were wrong to talk about jihad. In return, the king made the Wahhabi the religious establishment of the kingdom. Then the British used their air power and armored cars to help the king chase down and deal with the Ikhwan. These events strengthened even more the connection between the Wahhabi and the royal family.

When oil money began to flow in, the Wahhabi got a share of it and invested it in religious schools to perpetuate their view of Islam—especially in Sudan, Afghanistan, and the tribal areas of Pakistan that border Afghanistan, where their students, or Taliban, also fought against invading foreigners.

In 1978 there was a Communist revolution in Afghanistan and Islamic students and mullahs took up arms in the border areas of Pakistan. Saudi Arabia's World Muslim League and the Pakistani and Saudi intelligence agencies built new religious schools, madrasses, and introduced new texts based on Wahhabi teachings. In his book, *Ghost Wars: The Secret History of the CIA, Afghanistan, and bin Laden from the Soviet Invasion to September 10, 2001*, the journalist Steve Coll describes the close connections of Saudi Arabia, Pakistan, the United Arab Emirates, the Central Intelligence Agency, and the Taliban and how sometimes Pakistan's intelligence agency bypassed the civilian government. The Central Intelligence Agency and the White House became prisoners of alliances with Saudi Arabia and the Pakistani intelligence agencies. If the United States wanted their help to fight the Taliban, then the United States would have to tolerate their other political moves it might not approve of.

All of this was in the context of Pakistan's ongoing war with India in Kashmir and its nuclear weapons. The Taliban in Kashmir tied down a dozen Indian divisions. This led the Pakistanis to turn a blind eye to Taliban terrorism in Pakistan itself. U.S. support of corrupt regimes made Al Qaeda's work easier and Pakistan and Saudi Arabia were penetrated by Al Qaeda.

So, Saudi Arabia and Pakistan supported the Taliban and hence Al Qaeda in Afghanistan; the United States supported Saudi Arabia and Pakistan as allies despite their support of the Taliban and Al Qaeda.

In his Pulitzer Prize–winning book, *The Looming Tower: Al-Qaeda and the Road to 9/11*, the journalist Lawrence Wright chronicles the development of the modern Islamist movements from this part of the world and how they have attacked the governments of Egypt, Algeria, and Saudi Arabia and how the governments have responded with imprisonment and torture. The events at Abu Ghraib, no matter how reprehensible to Americans, were nothing new in the area. That does not excuse the people in the Bush administration for their use of torture, but one lesson was that torture produces more members, and also more extreme members, of the movement.

Likewise, the use of force against terrorists has resulted in more people joining them. A tribal Sheik in Yemen told the journalist Jeremy Scahill that the government provides no basic services such as schools, hospitals, roads, electricity, and water. Al Qaeda, he said, is a terrorist group; it wants to attack the United States, but that's not *his* problem. His problem is his people. In his area Al Qaeda provided security against looting and theft and the government did not. What he saw as terrorism was drone attacks that killed his people randomly. As the U.S. war on terror gained its own momentum, as we discussed in the previous chapter, there were drone, missile, and Special Operations strikes in Afghanistan, Pakistan, Yemen, Somalia, and other countries that might have eliminated key terrorist individuals, but did not address the political and economic causes and in the process alienated a lot of other people and drove them into the arms of the terrorists. Thus, the war on terrorism became its own self-fulfilling prophecy.

In trying to understand T. E. Lawrence's (Lawrence of Arabia) role in the early twentieth century Middle East, the journalist Scott Anderson discusses German attempts to bring down the British Empire by conspiring with Ottomans. Their idea was to incite a pan-Arabian jihadist movement against the British. His book, *Lawrence in Arabia*, is interesting because he documents British dominance in the Middle East and a long-standing international jihadist inclination long before American involvement in the area.

Many call these movements fundamentalist because they seem to fit the pattern of other religious movements that strive to return to a more pure form, a more fundamental form of the religion. The religious scholar and former nun Karen Armstrong argues that because the religious truths of the past are no longer reliable guides to action in the new global world, fundamentalist religious movements of Jews, Muslims, Christians, and others have arisen around the world. They all share a number of characteristics. They fear colonization, experts, uncertainty, foreign influence, science, and sex. Nor is it a coincidence that women are subservient in these religions.

She argues that changing gender roles and assertive women threaten the masculinity of the men. Feeling castrated, the men insist on dominating the women with a virile, gun- or sword-toting masculinity. This insecurity underlies their hatred of feminists, gays, and, in the United States, gun control.

We have seen how these movements developed in the Middle East, but that is not the only place they play out.

In the United States far-right politicos have played to these insecurities by opposing gun control and women's choice about abortion. Especially in the South, the American version of colonization is federal power, so they opposed "big government," too.

The ancient truths were not powerful enough in the world of science, business, and the market. Since science was valued above all else, American fundamentalists claimed scientific status for their faith in a doctrine of inerrancy, the idea that religious texts are correct representations of realities.[1] One example of this is attempts to replace Darwinian evolution with "intelligent design" or "creation science," especially in our secondary schools. The other big anti-Darwinians, by the way, are fundamentalist Muslims.

Armstrong argues that making science and religion equivalent confuses both. She suggests that religious rituals speak to deeply rooted psychological questions such as the meaning of life and fears of obliteration. When people have no way to deal with these subconscious fears, they seek comfort wherever they can find it. These deeply personal matters moved many ordinary working people in the United States to support fundamentalism, and that resonated with the political message of the extreme right. The television evangelism of the 1970s and 1980s would lead to the megachurch phenomenon of the 1990s and early 2000s, which drew middle-class, suburban, economically insecure and socially uprooted people by the tens of thousands in the United States.

But Armstrong isn't the only one to document this. A number of journalists, sociologists, and anthropologists have researched the methodical pairing of religion and politics in the United States over the past few decades. Wearing the mask of religion, the conservative political right disguised its corporate agenda as morality, a much more appealing campaign slogan than corporate greed. With the ear of high-powered politicians, fundamentalists had a new avenue for their agenda. The fundamentalists, corporations, and politicians rewarded each other handsomely.

In the United States the insecurities that brought people to religious fundamentalism fueled the radical right's single-issue political campaigns. The right could offer hope of restoring men's virility by ensuring that women were subservient and denied the control of their own bodies, that gays were outlawed or at least not allowed to marry each other, that there would be limits on government power, and that nobody could interfere with a person's right to carry a gun.

Dominionism is a new militant Christian political movement, a hybrid of Pentecostals, Southern Baptists, conservative Catholics, Charismatics, and evangelicals who believe that America is destined to become a Christian nation led by Christian men who are directed by God. They believe that Jesus has directed them to build the kingdom of God here and now. America is an agent of God and all opponents are agents of Satan. Dominionists will return the United States to a legal system based on the Ten Commandments and base education on creationism. The federal government will proselytize and protect property rights and the security of the homeland.

The religious right and its powerful corporate underwriters developed one of the most formidable political machines in the world with an agenda not that different from that of the Taliban, Al Qaeda, or other fundamentalist Islamic groups. So while an Iranian woman is sentenced to one hundred lashes for committing adultery, we have Americans who believe our law should reflect scripture (Numbers 5:11–31) and say that a woman charged with the same crime will go to her priest, drink a potion of dirty water, and expect her thigh to rot if the charge is true.

We should note that one of the by-products of the Obama campaign in the early twenty-first century United States was the rise of a new kind of evangelism that focused on environmental and social justice. It's too early to tell whether these new evangelists will be able to uncouple from the corporate agenda that has been woven into their movement, but it is yet another sign that no change is permanent.

Our comparative method gives us the general idea of revitalization and fundamentalist movements as responses to situations in which our cultural codes no longer work for us because of changed circumstances, often because some foreigners have taken control of our societies. At that point someone has a vision and many people follow the new prophet. This may result in a peaceful religion or a militant revolutionary movement, but both leave behind new religions.

Not all religions are revitalization movements. When we get away from the "religions of the book" as Judaism, Islam, and Christianity are often called because of the shared parts of their traditions in the Bible, the comparative method shows us that the religions of people like the Tsembaga and Lisu who have no states are similar to each other in many respects, whereas those of Shan and other people of states share many features with the religions of the book.

RELIGIONS OF PEOPLE WITHOUT STATES

The Lisu world is populated with spirits, as it is with people. The spirits are about the same as people, except they are more powerful and people can't see them. Paul never saw Lisu being reverent about spirits. True, they kneel and bow and say amen when they are supposed to at the end of a prayer to make offerings to spirits, but Paul never noticed anything that looked like reverence as distinct from the respect that people owe to those who are more powerful, like Thai officials. Nor did Paul notice anything like awe, fear, dread, or trepidation with respect to spirits.

If you do something to offend a person and you want to make it right, you take a bottle of liquor to the person and offer to sit down, have a drink, and talk about how to resolve the matter. That's the responsibility of the person who commits the offense. If the person who is offended has to wait too long for an apology and a settlement, that adds to the injury and makes it worse.

Remember that Lisu are egalitarian people. They don't have any cops, courts, judges, or juries. The last recourse you have, if someone has done you harm, is to harm that person back. Anthropologists call it **self-help**. And that can lead to **feuds** that get ugly for everyone. So everyone has an interest in seeing to it that people settle things short of self-help and try to help people come to terms with each other. But people can't do that for spirits. The only way you know you've offended a spirit is when the spirit attacks you by making you sick.

So, people can offend spirits, but we never know what might have offended them. When Paul asked the abstract question, someone told him that just about anything could offend a spirit, that to avoid offending spirits a person would have to stay in bed all day long—and *that* would probably be offensive to some spirit. To be alive and moving around in the world is to risk offending spirits.

What can anthropology say about this that could have anything at all to do with Christianity or Islam or any other religion? What do all religious traditions have in common?

We have the same problem with religions that we have with economic and political systems. To understand religion in comparative terms and from the point of view of the people we want to understand, it is necessary to guard against imposing our own categories on other cultures. By now you know that we do not all believe in one god any more than that we all have one spouse at a time or buy all our food in markets with money.

"The supernatural" is one way to answer the question of what religion is about. This assumes that everyone thinks in terms of a distinction between nature on the one hand and something else, "supernature," on the other hand—something beyond nature. For the Lisu villagers that Paul lived with, there was no such contrast. Spirits are just a normal, everyday part of life and just as natural as other people, plants, and animals. The anthropologist Robert Lowie wrote a book about the anthropology of religion in the 1940s. He said that to understand religion, we should study a number of different religions to see what they all have in common. But then he had to figure out what to study in different cultures. He suggested that feelings of awe and mystery were central. But Paul didn't see any awe or mystery with Lisu.

Some have suggested that religion has to do with the ultimate. The anthropologist Melford Spiro pointed out that if baseball is your ultimate, that makes it a religion. Others say religion makes us feel safe and explains things we can't understand. But religion raises more questions than it answers—what do you do with issues like Job, the Trinity, and Immaculate Conception or shamanistic séances nobody can understand? Some say religion makes people feel safe. In the words of the country-and-western song, "I don't care if it rains or freezes long as I got my plastic Jesus riding on the dashboard in front of me." The problem is that religion may make people afraid in other situations. It may offer guilt instead of security.

So defining religion in terms of what it does doesn't really give us much to go on. Religion may do a lot of things, but other institutions do at least some of the same things, and we can't point to one thing that religion does that no other institution does.

Spiro suggested that religion is "an institution consisting of culturally patterned interactions with culturally postulated superhuman beings." An institution is something people learn by growing up when and where they do, like their language or lineages or kindreds or schools. Spiro talked about two different kinds of interactions: one is doing what superhuman beings want or like, and the other is doing things to influence these beings. For instance, Tsembaga don't go to war until they pay off their debt to their ancestors. It would make the ancestors angry if they started a war before they paid off their debt, and the ancestors wouldn't help them: a sure way to lose. Tsembaga also sacrifice pigs to the ancestors to please them so that they will help cure sick people.

The interactions are culturally patterned. That means that what people think their superhuman beings like and don't like and what they think influences them are all matters of their cultural codes. The ideas that ancestors can help you in a war and that giving them pigs gets them to help you are both parts of the Tsembaga cultural code. Lisu think that they can offend spirits and spirits can hurt them. They think that people can give spirits liquor and animals to make them stop. This is part of their cultural code.

Superhuman beings are beings that people think have more power than they do. Because people get their ideas of superhuman beings from growing up in groups, these ideas of superhuman beings are something that is reasonable in that cultural code.

BELIEF

We often explain what people do in terms of what they believe. People cheer at football games because they believe it will help their team score. As anthropologists, we ask how we know the people believe that. We have two ways of knowing—either they say so or they are doing it and we can't think of any other reason they might be doing it. They *must* believe it helps. That is, we assume they believe it. But this violates our first principle of ethnography—assume nothing.

Many people have ideas and practices similar to Lisu ones about spirits. Some also participate in one of the major religions such as Islam, Buddhism, or Christianity. One of the things that puzzled Spiro when he was studying religion in Burma was how Burmese villagers could at the same time believe in the doctrines of Buddhism and believe in spirits. This seemed to him such a contradiction that he concluded that there are two different religions, each answering to a different part of people's emotional needs. Buddhism provides explanations for long-term and abstract things like life and death and why some people are rich and some are poor. Belief in spirits helps people deal with concrete problems such as sickness in the here and now. What puzzled Spiro was how people would express skepticism with regard to spirits but act as though they believed in them.

Lisu expressed the same kind of skepticism. One man told Paul that he disbelieved in spirits so much that when he died, he would not return to the ancestor altar at all. But he did the same ceremonies as other people did. How can people kill a pig and make an offering to a spirit they don't believe in?

This happens in the same sense that many of us would take an antibiotic although we don't especially believe in it. Nobody asks us to believe in an antibiotic. The doctor doesn't check to see whether you believe in a certain antibiotic before prescribing it. It just doesn't matter whether we believe in it. Another example: you don't have to believe in gravity for it to work. Even if you stop believing in gravity, you're not going to float away. Whoever asked you to believe in wireless Internet? You might be able to point to evidence of it, much like believers point to Jesus in a grilled cheese sandwich or the awesomeness of the cosmos, but can you see it? Touch it? Feel it? Smell it? No, but you don't have to believe in the technology for it to work.

The point about antibiotics is that we have some reason to suppose that they might help us. It's not a question of belief. In the United States it might be a question of finances if you don't have health insurance that covers drugs. You might not be able to afford the expensive antibiotic that the doctor prescribes. You may not even be able to afford the doctor. But it's not a question of belief.

A belief is something that's beyond evidence. It doesn't depend on experience or arguments or facts. It only depends on your opinion about something. For instance, some people hold deep religious convictions about the creation of the earth and all of its inhabitants. They don't rely on scientific evidence but on their religious opinions. And no amount of arguing or proof will change their minds. That's what belief is—something that's beyond any evidence.

Sometimes people say they don't believe something but act as though they really do. Folks in Burma are Buddhists, but they also make offerings to spirits—something that's not in Buddhist doctrines. They act as though they believe in spirits.

In fact, some anthropologists discuss religion as a belief system. Often, we can't show that anyone believes anything in particular. Do people really believe that cheering helps their team score? Burmans said they didn't believe in spirits, but they made offerings to them. Lisu don't believe in spirits either, but they make offerings to them and talk about them.

When Paul asked Lisu about these things, they said they believe what they can see. They can't see spirits, so they don't believe in them. Lisu aren't Buddhists, so they don't have to worry about doing things that don't match up with some standards of religious practice.

Lisu do say that their shamans can see spirits and ghosts. One time, after a guy was accidentally shot and killed, Ngwa Pa, a shaman, came into Paul's house and said he'd seen the ghost of the dead person behind the house. Paul asked Ngwa Pa to show him the place. The other Lisu sitting around in the house laughed and said Paul wouldn't be able to see the ghost because only dogs, horses, and shamans could see ghosts. But Paul went with the shaman anyway. The shaman pointed at a place behind the house and said, "Right there, see?" Paul said, "No." Just then all of the horses started stamping and neighing, and all the dogs started barking. There may have been a ghost, but Paul couldn't see it.

A test of faith

One time a Thai guy came up to the Lisu village where Paul lived and said he had a very powerful talisman that would protect people from gunshot wounds. Lisu asked him to put it on and let them shoot at him to test it. If their bullets couldn't hit him, they'd know the talisman worked. The guy didn't want to risk it. So the Lisu folks said he could put it on a pig instead and they'd shoot at the pig. If the pig wasn't hurt, they'd know the talisman would work for them, too. The Thai guy was grossed out at the idea of putting a powerful religious thing on a pig. That was just too disgusting to think about. So he didn't sell any talismans.

In the same way, most Lisu never see spirits and have no reason to believe in them. "So why do you do these ceremonies?" Paul asked. "What else can we do?" they would ask back. "This is what we do."

If nobody believes religious ideas, how can we explain religious actions like sacrifices?

One way is by their ecological consequences. For instance, Tsembaga have ancestors in their cultural code, so they will participate in a ritual cycle that regulates their ecosystem for them and keeps them from destroying the land by farming it too much. Nobody invented it; nobody thought it up. But because they do it, and because it works, they continue to do it.

The second kind of explanation is in terms of social consequences. People believe in witches so that they can kill malcontents and others who can't get along. This lets them maintain order without courts and cops and states.

Both of these are etic ideas. They rest on some ideas that don't belong to the cultural codes of the people we are trying to understand. We can put this in terms of the system we developed earlier when we were discussing cultural ecology (Table 9-1).

The ecological consequence is that Lisu keep pigs so they can offer them. They're like health insurance. The social consequence is that everyone can stay even with everyone else and nobody gets ahead of anyone else in feasting and obligation, so no redistributive system can develop, and hence no rank or stratification can develop.

Anthropologists try to understand what people are doing from their own point of view, in terms of their emic systems, in terms of their cultural code and worldview. Lisu act as though there are spirits because according to their understandings of social life, it is reasonable to think that there might be spirits, whether they know it or not. It doesn't matter to anyone whether someone believes in spirits, whether anyone does a certain ceremony. Because of certain other ideas, ideas about how people get along together, it is reasonable to think that there might be spirits. And people act in terms of that idea. Nobody asks you whether you believe in gravity when you get on an airplane.

We can ask why Lisu have that kind of cultural code. Lisu spirits can cause people to suffer, and offerings can make the spirits stop bothering people.

Table 9-1 Feedback.

Reality	Cultural code	Action
Sickness	Spirits make people sick	Call shaman
Spirits speak	People have offended a spirit	Make a sacrifice

These ideas follow from ideas about how people are. It's obvious to Lisu that a person's productivity is related to wealth. The more you work, the better off you are. Americans say that, but it's obviously not true because the richest among us work the least, and the ones who work the most are not the richest. But it's different when everyone has access to all of the same resources, as Lisu do.

People use their wealth to sponsor feasts, as we discussed earlier. When you sponsor feasts, other people eat your food, and their sense of obligation gives you power. It's that power that gets hurt if someone offends you. They take away some of your power if you let them get away with it. So it's up to them to restore your power by apologizing—bringing a bottle of liquor to your house and talking about it—and then by compensating you to make it right again. If my pig roots up your opium plants, I apologize, we talk until we agree on the amount of damage, and I make it up to you by giving you a pig or two or maybe some opium or money.

Remember what happens if I don't do this. You can try to hurt me. Self-help. Just like a spirit.

The productive part of a person is the soul. If your soul goes away, you don't want to work. If you don't work, you don't have wealth; and without wealth, you have no power. If your soul stays away, you die. You can't see souls, but you can tell when they're gone because people have bad dreams, don't sleep well, and don't want to work. It's similar to what Americans call depression. You fix it by getting the soul to come back. Maybe a spirit has captured the soul; maybe it has just left because, as Lisu say, "Sometimes you wake up in the morning, and all you can see is pig shit."

You can make a small ceremony and tell the person's soul, "Come back, come back from wherever you are. Come look at your beautiful family, your rice in the baskets. Come look at your pigs and your wealth. Come and be with your family. We all want you to be with us." That's just got to make a person feel appreciated.

Or you can do it up grand, if you need to sponsor a feast, by killing a couple of pigs and having everyone in the village make a similar prayer.

So, by this logic, anything that's productive has a soul. Like a soul, you can offend it; and if you do, it will hurt you. Nobody has to believe anything. It's the same logic for people and for spirits. People take the logic of social relations for granted—it's just the way we are—and assume it is true, but they don't believe it or not believe it. It's no big deal. It's the same kind of thing as being patrilineal. You don't have to believe anything to be patrilineal; it's just one way of doing things. Lisu are patrilineal, but they also know about matrilineal systems and can explain them to you.

So, a couple of points. First, if we want to understand other religions, we can't be ethnocentric and let our categories guide our understanding. For instance, belief may be important for some kinds of religions, but it isn't for all of them. This is the same as Goodenough's conclusion about residence rules. Rather than assuming that a set of rules works everywhere, we should find out how the people we want to understand actually think about things.

Second, remember systems? The economic, political, and social are really all one thing. They aren't separate. When Lisu sacrifice a pig, it's a medical event, a religious event, a political act, and an economic phenomenon all at the same time.

Third, we cannot understand what people do and why they do those things, unless we understand their cultural code from their point of view.

But remember Julian Steward? His idea of the cultural core is that the way people make a living is the most important part of their cultural system. So why are we even talking about religion? Because shamans' séances, monks' sermons, offerings, and other kinds of ceremonies all offer anthropologists a rich field of symbols to understand. These symbols are good places to start understanding people's cultural codes. If we understand Lisu spirits, for instance, we understand a lot about Lisu politics and economics and the important points about being Lisu—things like wealth and productivity and honor.

The central part of this system of symbols is productivity. Remember our discussion of household economies? There, one of the central ideas was also productivity because people's judgments of drudgery depend on the productivity of their labor, and the amount they produce depends on the intersection of the curves of their need—or marginal utility—and the drudgery of the work to produce that amount of value, whether it be rice or money.

People symbolize things that are important but that they can't articulate well, like the relationships among marginal utility, drudgery, and production that are at the center of household production. One way they symbolize these things is the way Lisu do, with the idea of some kind of power that people and spirits share. Shan do the same thing, and their ceremonies to spirits aren't very different from Lisu's. In fact, wherever people are involved in household production, they have some kind of religion based on spirits or something like them. It might be jinn in Islamic societies or saints in Christian ones.

Why make such a big deal out of belief? Because we want to understand the difference between religions like Lisu that demand no belief and those like Buddhism that do.

BELIEF AND STATES

What kinds of religions do demand belief? The one thing all of these religions have in common is that they support state systems, as we explained in the previous chapter. Is it natural for some people to have more and others less? No. But to support systems of stratification, the ruling classes of states support religions that say it is natural and necessary. Listen to the teaching of a Buddhist monk as he delivers a sermon to Shan people in a temple:

> *If you live in the village, you follow the ways of the village; if you are a housewife, you keep the place of the housewife; if you are a house husband, you must keep the place of the house husband; if you are the children of parents, you must keep the place of the children; if you are the headman of the village, you must keep the place of the headman; if you are village elders, you must keep the place of the elders. If you know the appropriate place, you can stay together peacefully as the Buddha taught. If people cannot live together, it is because they do not keep the appropriate places; the young act like elders; the old people act like young ones; men act like women; women act like men; common people act like kings; kings act like common people. All are opposite. They do not know their places. We do not respect or believe each other. If we do not keep our places, we cannot live together. We would be like animals.*

The lesson is clear. Know your place and keep it. If you're a king, act like one; if you're a common person, keep your place. Or else you'd be like an animal.

State religions demand belief because they teach their people things that do not match their experience. If your husband beats you or is a drunk, you're still supposed to stay in your obedient wifely place. If your government is getting into wars and drafting your kids or brothers, you're supposed to keep your place as a commoner and not question it. Buddhism promises justice in the end. The laws of karma work the same for everyone. Everyone is rewarded for good deeds and charity. Everyone is rewarded for bad deeds. It's automatic. Do we see such justice around us? Neither do Shan. But Buddhism assures them that everyone gets what they deserve in the long run. And for Buddhists, that's a lot more than just one lifetime because you get reincarnated many times.

Shan even told Paul not to worry about government corruption. It wasn't his problem. It's a problem only for the officials involved. Why? Because it's their karma that's at stake, not Paul's. If they do bad things, it's bad for their karma, but it's not our business. And what do Christians say? You've got two choices: heaven or hell. Be a good person, behave, don't make any waves, render unto Caesar that which is Caesar's, honor your mother and your father, be meek, and it's pie in the sky when you die, right? Don't, and you'll get yours in the afterlife.

Remember that if there is commercial production where everything that goes in and everything that comes out is a commodity, then there must be markets. If there are markets, there is ownership. If there is ownership, there is stratification. If there is stratification, there are states. If there are states, there are ideologies to support them. One of these is religion.

Most people these days live in some kind of state society. Remember that capitalism takes surplus value from those who produce it, but household economies do not. That's the reason capitalism can't compete with households for labor. So there are usually household production units even in state societies. Shan are an example. That's the reason they have both forms—state religion and one based on the logic of household production. The Buddhist part is the state religion, and the spirit part comes from symbolizing household production.

The British anthropologist I. M. Lewis's descriptions of spirit cults in Islamic cultures are similar to Spiro's for Buddhist Burma. In Christian cultures there are often cults of saints that are similar. So, wherever we find state religions, people are likely to also have some form of religion based on household production. People don't see any contradictions between the two forms of religion.

This chapter has several lessons. One is that we cannot understand other religions in our own terms. We must use the peoples' own emic terms. Another is that we can understand why they have such cultural codes if we connect the cultural codes to other dimensions of the people's lives such as their social and political organization. We can understand the cultural codes also from the point of view of their ecological consequences—the results of the actions people do because of the way they understand their worlds. This takes us back to the diagram (Figure 9-1) of the relationships of reality, cultural codes, and actions that then have consequences for the reality, a feedback loop.

We see that spirit-based religions are symbolizations of the relationships of household production and that people who are involved in household production have similar cultural codes that center on power. We also see that those religions that demand belief are the ones that teach things that run against people's everyday experience, things like "If you keep your place, everything will be good" and "There's justice in the long run." These religions are the parts of state systems that make them seem reasonable, inevitable, and just, although they are not any of those things.

Finally, the lesson about anthropology is that the answers we get depend on the questions we ask. If we ask "What do people believe?" rather than "Do people believe anything at all?" we don't see the relationships among states, belief, and stratification.

Time to lighten up a little before the next chapter.

The author Pierre Delattre tells a story about the current Dalai Lama. When he was a boy, before the Chinese came, he had to answer a riddle each year. All of the scholars and monks of Tibet would gather at the Potala, the central monastery in Lhasa, to hear the god-king's answer to the riddle and learn from it. A tutor would always clue the incarnation of past lamas in to the riddle and the answer. He had the riddle and the answer, but he didn't

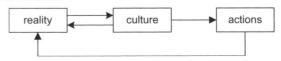

Figure 9-1 Our cultures tell us how to act and our actions change things.

want to do this again. He worried so much that he looked much older than his years. He told the regent that this year he wanted a better question, a question about something real that would make him more aware of the conditions of life here on earth, not a stupid riddle that nobody could understand.

Then, he appeared in front of all of the monks and scholars and waited for a new question, for a question about something real.

Nobody dared to say a thing. It got later and later and nobody said a thing. The sun went down. It started to get cold. Finally, a young monk said, "Aren't you cold? Shouldn't we go inside?"

"Yes," said the Dalai Lama, "I'm cold. Aren't we all?"

Everyone agreed.

Then the Dalai Lama said, "Let's go inside."

When everyone was inside and drinking tea, the Dalai Lama had returned to his young self, smiling, and said, "That's the kind of question we should ask each other, and that's the kind of answer we should give."

That's an important lesson we need to remember in anthropology.

Note

1. Malise Ruthven. *Fundamentalism: The Search for Meaning.* Oxford; New York: Oxford University Press, 2004.

Discussion Questions

- List the ways an anthropologist's approach to religion challenges your own belief system. What basic assumptions have you made about religion and the supernatural? How would an anthropologist describe the emic cultural code of your religion?
- How would an anthropologist describe how your religion fits the rest of your culture as part of a system? What would the etic description of your religion look like?
- Religion and politics often intersect in American public discourse these days. Offer some examples of how one amplifies and supports the other. Discuss the contradiction between those examples and the fact that our Constitution requires a separation between church and state.
- In these examples, substitute Islam for Christianity, and discuss how a government that intersects or overlaps with Islam as much as ours does with Christianity would look and act. Discuss the similarities and differences between the two.
- Attend a church, synagogue, or mosque this weekend and compare and contrast the service with one of the two quoted events in this chapter (the Lisu shaman or the Buddhist sermon).
- Look in a Bible and find descriptions of women's rights or treatment that would apply to today if Dominionists won control of our government. Now compare it to examples from countries where fundamentalist Islamists are in control. How is religion used to protect or promote the government?

Suggested Reading

Anderson, Scott. *Lawrence in Arabia: War, Deceit, Imperial Folly and the Making of the Modern Middle East*. New York. Doubleday, 2013.

Coll, Steve. *Ghost Wars: The Secret History of the CIA, Afghanistan, and bin Laden from the Soviet Invasion to September 19, 2001*. New York: Penguin, 2004.

Ekvall, Robert. *The Lama Knows*. Novato, CA: Chandler & Sharp, 1981.

Evans-Pritchard, E. E. *Nuer Religion*. New York: Oxford University Press, 1971.

Evans-Pritchard, E. E. *The Sanusi of Cyrenaica*. ACLS E-Book Project. Ann Arbor: University of Michigan Scholarly Publishing Office, 1999.

Evans-Pritchard, E. E. *Witchcraft, Oracles and Magic among the Azande*. New York: Oxford University Press, 1976.

Gottlieb, Alma, and Philip Graham. *Parallel Worlds: An Anthropologist and a Writer Encounter Africa*. New York: Crown, 1993.

Lewis, I. M. *Ecstatic Religion: A Study of Shamanism and Spirit Possession*. 3rd ed. New York: Routledge, 2003.

Sandstrom, Alan. *Corn Is Our Blood: Culture and Ethnic Identity in a Contemporary Aztec Indian Village*. Norman: University of Oklahoma Press, 1992.

Scahill, Jeremy. *Dirty Wars: The World Is a Battlefield*. New York. Nation Books, 2013.

Tannenbaum, Nicola. *Who Can Compete against the World?: Power-Protection and Buddhism in Shan Worldview*. Ann Arbor, MI: Association for Asian Studies, 2001.

Wolf, Eric. "The Social Organization of Mecca and the Origins of Islam." *Journal of Anthropological Research* Vol. 7, No. 4 (1951): 329–356.

Wright, Lawrence. *The Looming Tower: Al-Qaeda and the Road to 9/11*. New York: Vintage Books, 2006.

Some of the union workers Paul and Suzan worked with in the mid-1990s. The dynamics between unionized workers and management help provide for protections such as the ones these workers enjoy. *Photo by E. Paul Durrenberger.*

10

Political Economy

What does it say about the choices people make if cultural ecologists are right and the most important part of any culture is the way people make their livings, as we suggested in the previous chapter? Is everything we do and think determined by something outside us—larger political, economic, or historical **structures** that we don't have any say about? Or do we have some choice in what we think and do?

Choice is a big deal to middle-class Americans because we have an ideology that the anthropologist Katherine Newman calls **meritocratic individualism**. That means that we like to think we are separate individuals who think for ourselves, make significant choices, determine what happens to us, and get rewarded according to our individual merit. **Agency** is the idea that people act as agents on their own behalf, that they understand the resources available to them and use them in their own interests. It's the flip side of the economists' assumption of maximizing individuals, from the point of view of the person rather than the system.

Newman also suggests that working-class people think more in terms of structures than choices because they've experienced layoffs and plant closings that they know had nothing to do with the effort or quality of their work. Whereas working-class people blame systems for bad things, middle-class people tend to blame themselves. "You get what you deserve" also means "You deserve what you get." We'll come back to this issue when we discuss class explicitly, but it is enough for now to hint that it is something about our culture that makes the question of agency even relevant. That means that when we talk about agency, we're likely to be projecting one of our own emic categories, part of our own cultural code onto other systems.

Economists base their understanding of the world on the idea of individual choices. Each person does what is rationally best for that person without any regard for anyone else. If everyone does that, economists argue, then everything turns out for the best for everyone. This may make a nice religion, but it makes poor science because people don't act that way.

To economists, then, markets are the solution to all problems. In Chapter 16, we're going to see how well this worked out recently in Iceland. Or you can ask yourself how that's working out for you. But for now, suppose the police nab you and your friend and slap you in jail because they think you robbed a bank. Whether you really did doesn't matter, but they have no evidence on you. You and your pal were just hanging around looking like bank robbers. The attorney general is on the cops; she wants to appear to be hard on crime because an election is coming up.

The cops put you in separate cells. One comes to you and says that if you rat out your friend, you'll go free and, if your friend says nothing, she'll get ten years in jail. On the other hand, if she rats you out too, you both get five years in jail. But if neither one of you rats on the other, you both get six months. That'll teach you to go around looking suspicious!

What is in your best interest here? Economists assume that both of you want to go free, and who gives a damn about a friend, right? Easy come, easy go. So do what's in your own best interest and the devil take your friend. So you confess that you and your friend did rob the bank and expect that you'll get off free. But your friend thinks just the same way. So both of you rat on the other—you both act in your own interests with no concern for the other and you both get a rotten deal, five years in stir. That'll teach you to be a snitch.

Wait a minute! You both acted in your best interest, but it wasn't the best outcome. The best outcome is for both to go free, but that can't happen unless only one person confesses. The next best is the six-month sentence if neither of you confesses. What happened here? Both people got five years. That's why some economists started looking into game theory where they could explore such issues.

They knew about what they called the tragedy of the commons, which is similar. You and I own a pasture together, in common. I put a sheep on it. You see that my sheep is eating our grass and put your own sheep on it so you can use some of the grass before my sheep eats it all. I see that and figure if you are going to let your sheep eat our grass, I might as well put a whole herd of sheep on it. You see that and do the same and before long there's no grass for anyone. If each of us owned half the field, it would be in our interests to keep it up and not overgraze it. The only way out of this dilemma, economists say, is not to allow common ownership of anything—grass, air, water, anything. Everything must be private property and subject to the market.

But guess what? People don't act that way. A lot of ethnographic work shows that people figure out ways to manage their resources whether they be pasture, water, or fish in the sea. Economists have built up a whole line of reasoning on the prisoners' dilemma we described above, but if you set this up as a real experiment instead of a thought experiment, people won't rat each other out. People aren't as dumb as economists. In experiments, people favor loyalty to their friend over going free for themselves, since they know they will meet again. After all, they're friends. People build up relationships they can rely on and that let them reap the benefits of cooperation. They can work out how many sheep to put in their pasture and happily raise sheep there forever. They aren't the selfish antisocial people that economists assume them to be. For economists, the solution to anything is the market and private property. That's one reason we're facing so many problems today—following the religion of economics is like the Maya making more sacrifices to their gods.

Here's the important point for understanding agency: what happens to you doesn't just depend just on what you do; it also depends on what your friend does. And you can't know what that is going to be. In the prisoners' dilemma, your friend may confess or remain silent, but you can't guess which. You can either write off your friend or trust her, but there's no way you can know for sure what she's going to do. Agency is our ability to use relationships with other people to get what we want and need. Being human is figuring out how to use our relationships with other people to get our own needs met.

Some anthropologists who can't break away from their own cultural codes follow their middle-class ideology to focus on what individuals do and talk a lot about agency and about identity. Yes, people do things for their own reasons, and yes, their actions have consequences, and yes, those consequences can change the nature of systems. When we get in a car and turn on the ignition, even if it's a hybrid or an electric car, we're contributing to global warming. The hybrid still burns some hydrocarbon fuel and it's likely the electricity that charged the electric car came from a coal- or gas-powered power plant. So our actions have consequences, often consequences we don't expect, intend, or know about.

But in all this, if we focus on the individual struggles, how it feels to be an American who thinks she's in the middle class when she's actually in the working class, if we focus on how it feels really good to her to own the car and drive it because it means she's really in the middle class and she's afraid of falling into what she sees as the helplessness of the working class, and focus on where she's going and why—we lose track of the whole political and economic system of which she, her car, and its emissions are parts. Those personal struggles are a deep part of the human experience from which we can learn a lot. They are often the focus of storytellers, myths, novels, plays, and art. They are the stuff of drama, and drama is everywhere in the world of humans. But it is the larger systems that we live in that determine the dimensions of our individual struggles. We do not and cannot determine those dimensions by ourselves.

We want to focus on those systems because the problems of the system aren't the fault of any individual in it, but of the way the system is put together. If we don't understand that, we can't understand why systems falter and fail and we can't understand how we could change systems that are not working well. If we cannot get outside our cultural systems' emic systems, we can't develop that kind of understanding.

Before, we asked questions about cultural codes and why they are the way they are. Cultural codes provide us with ways to think. We may be able to expand those cultural codes a bit, but we can't just make them up for ourselves any more than we can make up our own languages. Well, people can do that, and some do, but the very fact that they are making them up and that nobody else agrees with them makes them crazy one way or another.

We can understand the reasons cultural codes are the way they are in terms of the cultural core, the basic shape of the economic system. The important question is not about how individuals make their way through the system, but how the system comes to be the way it is in the first place. Here's an example.

Paul first went to Iceland in 1981 because he was interested in shamanism. Some anthropologists have written about what happens when spirits speak through shamans. Claude Lévi-Strauss, for instance, suggested that the shaman's séance gives people a story that they can tell to make sense of things and that makes them feel better about whatever it is that's bothering them. With the story, they can understand things they couldn't understand before.

When he was living with Lisu, Paul couldn't figure out a way to find out whether people felt better after a shaman was possessed. A lot of times the story people could put together from what the spirits said didn't make much sense to them. If you feel sick and see a doctor who tells you a story full of big Latin words about what's wrong, do you understand it? If she says what drug she thinks might help, do you feel better? Probably not, at least not right away. But then, most things that ail us get better all by themselves if we don't do anything.

So what does Iceland have to do with any of this? A sociology graduate student at the University of Iowa kept telling Paul about how Icelandic skippers got drunk and dreamed about where to find fish. Here was something like a shamanic séance—at least something that doesn't involve rational calculation. But in Iceland, it's not connected with something subjective like feeling better; it's connected with something that's easy to measure: tons of fish. It should be possible to find out whether the skippers who dream about fish catch more than others.

So Paul went to Iceland in the summer of 1981 to see what he could find out. The student introduced Paul to Gísli Pálsson, an anthropologist who had been doing ethnographic work in a fishing village. Paul and Gísli worked out a program for studying the "skipper effect," the difference in catch that the skipper makes.

First, they listed and measured all the mundane things that would affect a skipper's success: the size of the boat and the number of nets, crewmembers, and fishing trips. They decided whatever was left would be the amount of difference that the skipper made. So Paul put all of Gísli's numbers into a computer and did some statistical modeling.

He found out that there was virtually no skipper effect. If you took into account the size of the boat and the number of times they went fishing, the skippers didn't make any difference at all.

Paul and Gísli had just done themselves out of an interesting question, and they were pretty depressed about it for a while—until they figured out an even more interesting question: Why did Icelanders ever *think* there was a skipper effect if there really wasn't one?

Although fishing has always been important to Icelanders, there weren't always skippers. In the nineteenth century, the guys in charge of fishing boats were called foremen. They fished in the North Atlantic from rowboats. Catching a lot of fish didn't make a foreman a good foreman. But his seamanship—his ability to get a crew out to sea and home again without losing anyone—did make him a good foreman.

At that time, there was no market for fish. People were fishing as part of their household economies, so there was a ceiling on production as we discussed in the chapter on economics (Chapter 5). In 1920 came the first motorboat.

At about the same time, Iceland was becoming more independent from Denmark and controlling more of its own economy. Instead of a Danish trade monopoly, there were Icelandic merchants, and some of them started trading in fish. Thus developed an international market for fish. With the motor boats, fishermen could go farther out and catch more fish. With this technology and the developing markets, commercial production was possible.

But they had the same problem that faced a lot of entrepreneurs when they wanted to become commercial producers: there was no free labor, no people to hire to produce surplus value. Everybody was busy working on farms. There was even a law that if you didn't own land, you had to have a contract with someone who did own land to work for that person either as a laborer or as a renter of some kind. That meant very cheap labor for landowners, which they didn't want to give up, but no labor for fishing.

Poor people started voting with their feet. They left the farms and went to the coast to work in the fishing industry. They didn't care if it was against the law. There was no way the government could enforce it. Were they going to throw everyone in jail? The people worked as crew for fishing boats, for processors to cut and salt fish, and for all of the other jobs that keep the boats going back out to catch more fish. Since they didn't have their own means of production, it was better for them to work for wages than to work for landowners for virtually nothing—just enough to scrape by for the year. If you have to sell your labor, you should be able to sell it to the highest bidder.

People first started talking about the skipper effect during the expansive phase when commercial fishing took off and there was no ceiling on production. Suddenly there were international markets and whole industries of processing fish and outfitting fishing ships. Skippers were racing for bank loans, for the backing of processors, and for fish.

Processors were important because if you could get your boat in and unloaded ahead of others, you could get back out fishing and fish more than they could. Some skippers owned their own boats, but many others worked as skippers for the owner or owners of the boat. If a skipper wanted to buy a modern boat, he had to get a loan from a bank—in other words, ask a bank to bet on him. So the reputation of the skipper was important for getting access to a boat, either through loans to buy one or by getting a position as a skipper on someone else's boat, and for loading supplies and unloading fish. That meant lots of competition among skippers, and anything that would enhance their reputation would contribute to this "star" system.

The whole idea of mystical processes fit well with other themes in the Icelandic cultural code, such as elves and other worlds, that are common, if not dominant, in Iceland to this day. When Alcoa wanted to put up a big new aluminum plant in 2004, they had to hire an expert to certify that there were no elves on the site that the plant would disturb. Put the star system together with the preexisting cultural code and the idea of the skipper effect becomes reasonable and credible—it makes sense—in terms of the Icelandic cultural code.

But that doesn't mean there really is a skipper effect. The statistics showed that there wasn't one—that given the same size boat and the same days fishing, every skipper would catch the same amount of fish whether he was a dreamer or not. So here there was an idea of a skipper effect but no real skipper effect.

As a result of the expansive phase of fishing in Iceland when fishers caught all the fish they could, the populations of different species of fish were diminished to the point that the government started to use quotas to regulate fishing. The first quota said that after so many tons of each kind of fish were caught, everyone had to stop fishing because the stock couldn't survive if they took any more. Then they changed the system so that each boat got a quota based on the history of its catch in the past. Boat owners could sell or buy quotas under this system, which is called **individual transferable quotas,** or **ITQs** in government talk. You could also get a loan on the basis of your quota. Overnight, what had been common property became private property because of the ideology of the neoliberal free-marketeers. More of this later when we discuss the collapse of the Icelandic economy in Chapter 14.

Under this system, the whole concept of the skipper effect diminished in Iceland, so that now people don't think that it is strange to say that there really isn't a skipper effect. "Of course," they say. "How else could it be? Your catch depends on your quota." But before that system was in place, people got offended if you'd suggest that there wasn't really a skipper effect. It was something like telling Americans that the United States isn't really a democracy. Anything that challenges a cultural construct makes people feel uneasy.

The idea here is that if we understand the economic system and the cultural code that were already in place, we can explain why there was a cultural construct of the skipper effect in Iceland during one period of its history. As the economic and political system, the **political economy,** changed from household production to industrial fishing, the cultural code changed. As the political economy changed again, the system of quotas was put into place; the cultural code changed again as well, and that change led to the downfall of the whole economy, as we will tell in Chapter 16.

The general point is that if we want to explain why cultures are the way they are, we ask what the connections between the political economy and the culture are. Then we ask how the political economy developed to be the way it is. Once we've done that, we have answered our big questions of what is the nature of the culture and how did it get that way.

Culture is all of the ideas we learn by growing up when and where we do. It includes lots of assumptions about the way the world is from what is a cousin, a sibling, or a parent to what's just and fair. People do what they do because of the way they think. Understand how people think and you understand why they do what they do. Culture is what gives people ways to think. So understand culture and you understand what people do.

Now, we've just said that we can understand cultures if we understand how political economies got the way they are. So which one is right? Do we use culture to understand what people do, or do we use what people do to understand culture? The answer is both. This is one of those mutual determination loops we talked about at the beginning of the book. Each determines the other.

People think and act in the terms their cultures give them, and their actions determine what other people can do, and so on. We'll explain this interaction in some detail as we go along. Just remember that the loop goes both ways—from political economy to culture and from culture to political economy. People change the systems they live in, but not always in ways that they understand or that they intend. For instance, a lot of changes happen even if we don't understand them or mean for them to happen.

Here we will stop for a moment to look at the idea of political economy a little more. The basic idea goes back to the concept of systems and holism, the idea that an economic system never exists by itself apart from the rest of the institutions and culture. For instance, in medieval Iceland people had an idea of property that was important, but there was no institution of a state that could enforce property law. That was one of the reasons the system collapsed into warfare among the people who were powerful enough to even claim to own property. The political institutions limited the economy. But the cultural code played a role because the landowners had the idea of ownership, one of the pillars of states. Even so, they were not able to come together as a class to create the institutions of a state. That's why their system finally collapsed. Realities, cultural codes, and political economies never line up perfectly. That's why our social and cultural systems keep changing.

We've seen the same thing in our discussion of capitalism. If the political institutions don't support some necessary part of capitalism, it can't develop. So, when there wasn't enough free labor for capitalists to hire, the system couldn't develop, as in the example of the Shan village where Paul lived or Europe before the revolutions of the eighteenth century. Those revolutions established new political orders that made capitalism possible.

For capitalism to work, everything must be available as a commodity on a market—labor, raw materials, manufactured goods. There is a whole institutional structure that guarantees the operation of markets. As economists found after the collapse of the Soviet system, markets don't just come into being wherever there are people; governments create the institutions that make them possible. Americans have lived in such a system for all of our lives, so we're likely to take markets for granted or even suppose, like economists, that they are somehow natural.

Reciprocity as a system of exchange requires an institutional structure to make it work. Reciprocity also requires a cultural code that says if people do something for you, you do something for them. All people have some idea of reciprocity, but if their cultural codes about it don't match, they will be disappointed or angry at the behavior of others. It won't make sense to them.

Redistribution is related to a different institutional structure and to a different cultural code. Redistribution also requires the notion of reciprocity, but it adds the idea that some people are different from others, higher than others, or more central. So if a big man says he's going to organize a feast, you pitch in and help. You know the big man will help out when you need it, but you also know that there's something different about the big man and you. He's the guy with the feathers or the title or whatever. So there are never just economic systems or even economic actions but always political economies that are built on economic actions, cultural codes, and institutional structures.

We live our lives in terms of the political economies of the times and places in which we live. We usually think of the realities we experience as just the way things are. These experiences are so powerful that they shape the ways we think. It is the political economies that define our choices.

For example, you can't just decide what courses to take—you must select among the ones that are available any given quarter or semester. You can choose among the available ones, but you can't choose which ones will be available. The courses available depend on who is available to teach what and what the administration has decided is important to teach. So your range of choice is highly constrained by the structures in place. In the same way, political economies constrain people's choices and define the terms in which they can make them. Just as you come to think of the requirements you must fulfill for your degree as just what you have to do, so people come to think of their choices and the terms of their choices as just natural.

In their study of the skipper effect in Iceland, Gísli and Paul were comparing the etic statistics with the emic cultural code of the skipper effect. When we discussed kinship in Chapter 3, we showed that there is an etic grid in terms of which we can think about all of the different systems of kinship. The etic grid represents all possible kinship relationships although different cultural codes may classify these relationships in different ways.

Paul studied shrimpers in Mississippi and found that they don't have any idea of a skipper effect, and they are right—there really isn't one. Why would there be a cultural concept of skipper effect in Iceland but not Mississippi? Fishing is a commercial enterprise in both places. In Mississippi, there was always more ability to process shrimp than there has been supply of shrimp. In Iceland's expansive phase of fishing, there was more supply of fish than ability to process them so there was competition among skippers. In Mississippi, because of the greater capacity for shrimp processing, this kind of competition never existed among shrimp skippers. So a difference in the political economy explains a difference in the cultural code.

When we wanted to learn how American union members think about their unions, we found that there is an etic grid in terms of which we could match people's ideas. Law and practice both define the etic grid. There is a management side with people who supervise the work, supervisors. Supervisors answer to managers. Usually there is also a vice president for human relations who handles all personnel issues.

On the union side, there are the members who voted to have a union in their workplace. There are also stewards, usually people whom the members elect to help them with any problems they might have at work. If a steward can't handle the problem, she can call a union representative. The union uses members' dues money to pay representatives, who are a bit like lawyers, to come in and help the stewards whenever they need it. The stewards can deal with supervisors and managers. The reps can deal with managers and vice presidents.

"Independent" shrimpers

If you talk to shrimpers on the Gulf Coast today, they'll tell you how independent they are, how they can't get together on anything. That's part of their cultural code. But it hasn't always been that way. In 1932, Mississippi shrimpers organized a union that lasted for twenty-three years—until 1955, when processors sued them under antitrust laws to bust their union. The processors argued that each shrimper owned his own gear and boat, and that meant shrimpers didn't work for processors but for themselves. Each shrimp boat was its own corporation, like General Motors. Therefore, for all of these corporations to get together to set the price for shrimp was against antitrust laws. The court agreed and disbanded the union.

That meant it was against the law to have a shrimpers union. So it's just not true that shrimpers are too independent to cooperate or organize. Why would shrimpers believe it if it's not true? First, it's consistent with their experience because they experience themselves and other shrimpers as stubbornly independent rather than as working together. But there are a number of reasons for that. One is that this cultural code works well for processors who benefit from keeping shrimpers from organizing, and it benefits bureaucrats who have to regulate them. Processors want to bring in cheap imports of pond-raised shrimp from all over the world. That undercuts the price shrimpers can get for the shrimp they catch. But as long as shrimpers aren't organized, they can't do anything about it. Bureaucrats must enforce regulations about shrimping. That would be a lot more difficult if shrimpers were organized to resist the regulations.

So it benefits processors and bureaucrats if shrimpers think of themselves as independent. The only way it benefits shrimpers is that they can think of themselves as somehow set apart, elite, or more independent than other people. They pay dearly for that feeling, but with the law, the processors, and the bureaucrats aligned against them, they're not strong enough to change the law or the institutional structures. So once again, we see that the political economy causes the cultural code to have the form it does, and the cultural code informs what people do. What people do then reinforces the institutional structures and so on.

So there are two sides to this: union and management. In each side there is also a hierarchy. On the union side, the hierarchy is from member to steward to rep. On the management side, the hierarchy is from worker to supervisor to manager to vice president.

On the basis of this etic grid, we devised a way to find out how people think about their union. Despite the etic grid, people can think in any number of different ways. Americans can put their mother's brother's kids right in with their mother's sister's kids and call them all the same thing, cousins. Lisu and Navajo do it differently.

To find out how people think about their unions, we used a method that can show how people think about similarities. It's called a *triads test*. You ask people which of three things is the most different. For instance, if you asked which of these is most different—blue, purple, green—people might say "blue" because although purple and green have blue in them, blue is the only one that's a primary color. It might be harder if we asked, "Purple, green, or orange?" because green and purple both contain blue, purple and orange both contain red, and orange and green both contain yellow, so any answer is equally correct.

We took all of the terms of the etic grid except vice president—steward, other worker, rep, supervisor, and manager—and put them into every possible combination of three and asked people which is the most different. As with the color examples, there is some similarity between the two things that someone does not select.

We did this with the staffs of three union locals in Chicago and one in Pennsylvania and found that they all agree with the etic grid. We checked to see how much all the people agreed with each other. If there isn't much agreement, then all you can say is that you aren't looking at anything that's cultural—different people think about it differently, and it's based on something individual, but you can't see any cultural code at work here. But if most folks agree, then you can say it's cultural.

Although staff agree with the etic grid, as we might expect because of the work they do, we got different pictures from members at different worksites. Members at industrial worksites for one local saw themselves as low on the hierarchy scale relative to both union and management folks and equally different from both. So they didn't see themselves as having anything in common with either management or the union.

Some health-care workers at hospitals fit the staff–etic pattern closely and others did not. When we compared the different conceptual schemes with what we knew about the worksites, we concluded that it was the relative power of management and the union at the different worksites that made the difference. Where the union was powerful, members saw themselves as part of it. Where the union lacked power in the worksite, members didn't identify with it so much.

At one hospital, there was one interesting difference between what the members thought and the etic pattern. They put their steward above their rep in the hierarchy. That was reasonable because the rep was new, and the steward had been there for more than two decades and ruled that place like a grandmother ruling her lineage. When management informed her that the women in her kitchen should wash the pots, for example, she answered, "My girls don't do pots." That was the end of that.

But she had carpal tunnel syndrome from a lifetime of hard work. When she retired, another long-term steward joined her, and the workers were left with no leadership. The hospital management was building a new wing, and, in the meantime, they weren't full of patients. They said that because they didn't have enough work for everyone, they'd lay off some folks. The union countered that if they would let everyone continue working, each person would work fewer hours until the construction was finished and the rooms filled again. Management agreed. When the new wing was finished and all the rooms were full, management did not return all of the workers to their full hours as they had initially agreed. Instead, they started hiring temporary workers, workers who were not eligible to be in the union.

Just at that time, the bargaining team was negotiating a new contract for the union members. When the bargaining was finished and the members were voting on the contract, we did another triads test and found that since the first one two years before, the members had shifted from seeing themselves as close to the union to seeing themselves as closer to management.

Because we had seen the same relationship between power and union consciousness in the other bargaining units, we knew that this shift in cultural code was because of the shift in power from the union toward management that happened when the two long-term stewards retired and the rep could not find any experienced and knowledgeable replacements for them.

So, as with the skipper effect, here with the unions in Chicago, we see that the cultural code depends on the political economy. If the political economy of a worksite changes, so does the cultural code.

This tells us that it isn't what people think or decide that makes a difference—it's their daily lives that determines how they think—their cultural codes. If we zoom the lens out a little and take a more wide-angle view, we see that the hospital is a nonprofit corporation. Here it's the "corporation" part that's important. All corporations have some things in common. One is their concern for their bottom line. That's part of our cultural code. It's also part of our law. Later we'll show how corporations shape both our cultural code and our law. The point here is that one group's cultural code sets the actual realities for another group.

Here class is important because the range of choices you have depends on your position in the system of political economy as well as your awareness. So, if we change laws or change cultural codes that define how corporations work, the realities for workers would change as well. If you can't do that, you can try to change the realities at work by showing workers that they can always accomplish something if they stick together. They can use that solidarity to make changes in the workplace that then affect others' cultural codes and so on. That's the job that union organizers and representatives have.

Now we're going to zoom out from the microscopic focus on bargaining units at particular worksites and look at the whole labor movement in the United States to develop a more widescreen view, something like the reach of the view we developed for Iceland and the skipper effect.

When we were doing these studies in the late 1990s, there were two different views from inside the union movement of what unions should be like. One view said they should be like insurance companies. You're a worker. You pay your dues. In return for your dues, you get a rep to help you out if you get unfairly fired or disciplined for something you didn't do. You also get someone to come in and bargain with management to get you a little bit better deal, or at least not a worse deal, with every new contract. Maybe you get a small pay raise. Maybe the union can get management to back off a little bit on their demand that you pay more of your health insurance so that you only pay 20 percent of it instead of 60 percent. Members pay dues and get services. This is called the "servicing model" of unions.

In the old days, unions were much stronger than they are now. More than a third of all American working people belonged to unions instead of 10 percent and the New Deal government of Roosevelt actively supported unions. In the 1930s, when workers at a worksite had a problem with management, they could strike until management figured out how to solve the problem. A problem for workers quickly became a problem for management. The union members didn't call a union rep. Their worksite leaders could call them out on strike over one person's grievance with management. They could do that for two reasons. The first is that they were well organized inside every worksite. We'll come back to the second reason in just a minute because it's even more important to our story here.

Today, this is called the "organizing model." That means that the union puts its effort into being sure that each unit is so well organized that it can take care of itself. Then the union can let its reps spend their time and effort organizing places that don't yet have unions. As workers at more and more places join unions, union strength grows.

Then unions can mobilize their members politically—to vote in elections and keep friendly politicians in power. The politicians who owe their positions to unions can then see to it that there is legislation that helps rather than hurts unions.

But in the 1990s, unions weren't that strong. They had declined in strength ever since 1947, when they were at their strongest ever. The original laws that allowed unions to organize, that made union representation a right of any workers where a majority voted for a union, were passed in 1935 as part of the effort to combat the Great Depression. The law is called the Wagner Act.

After World War II, the leaders of industry got together and pushed through some changes in this basic law. It was 1947 and Harry Truman was president. He vetoed the legislation, but Congress passed it over his veto. This was called the Taft–Hartley amendments to the Wagner Act.

Understanding key policy changes in history is important for developing that widescreen view of unions we were talking about when we looked up from the worm's-eye view of the ethnography of each individual shop to try to see what is going on in the whole country.

The Taft–Hartley amendments caused many labor leaders to become complacent. They were no longer radicals trying to change the balance of power in the workplace and give workers a voice. Instead, they were moving with the big boys, smoking the fancy cigars, driving the fancy cars, living in the fancy suburbs, and sending their kids to prep schools with the bosses' kids. You couldn't tell the difference between a labor leader and a boss by smelling the cigar or looking at the suit or the car.

And the unions changed from being centered on organizing and developing power in workplaces to big bureaucracies for dealing with the problems of their members and negotiating new contracts for them every few years. As long as they had enough power to negotiate a contract with a raise and some

What a difference a law makes

The Taft-Hartley amendments said that unions couldn't strike during the term of a contract. As soon as the members at a worksite agreed to the contract, they couldn't strike about anything. This took away the major source of unions' ability to influence management and the ruling class in their worksites. If there was some problem that the steward couldn't handle to the satisfaction of the members, then they could call a rep from the union. This law changed the union reps from organizers into dispute handlers and insurance people. Their role changed from organizing to servicing. Under the new law of 1947, if there was some dispute or issue that the reps couldn't handle with management, they could take it to arbitration. Both sides had to pay for half of the costs of an arbitrator, who would hear both sides of the case and then make a judgment. Neither side could appeal the judgment of an arbitrator. The arbitrator's word was final.

If management's pockets were deep, they didn't mind taking lots of cases to arbitration because it would cost the union as much as it cost them. As a result, unions had to be careful about what cases they took to arbitration. The law also set up boards of people to decide about charges of unfair labor practices. For instance, if the management fires someone because the person is active in the union, it's against the law. The union can file an unfair labor practice charge. The problem is that the members of these boards are political appointees. So they can be more or less friendly to management or labor depending on who won the last election and appointed them.

Grievances were no longer a matter of right or wrong, fair or unfair—ideals that workers would strike over. They were now a matter of legal skill—how well each side could negotiate an agreement or how persuasively someone could argue the interpretation of the contract language, perhaps the evidence of the case, and sometimes the relative influence of management and the union.

---

decent benefits each time around, members were happy. As long as it was cheaper or easier for the boss to give the raises instead of deal with labor unrest or a strike and still make a profit, management agreed to the increases.

Every year the management bosses gained strength and the union lost strength. The labor bosses weren't paying that much attention. Everything was fine for them. But then several things happened in the 1980s.

First corporations moved manufacturing into third-world countries with cheap labor and many union jobs left the United States. Then, in 1981, the air traffic controllers got fed up with the conditions of their work and decided to strike. They had complained for years that poor scheduling and understaffing were causing exhaustion that would lead to disasters in the air. Harry Truman and FDR were long dead. Ronald Reagan, the candidate these air traffic controllers had endorsed during the election, was president. He decided that these government employees weren't going to get away with a strike. He fired them all, replaced them, and the air traffic controllers' union was busted. Others in the labor movement, thinking those workers got what they deserved for endorsing a Republican, sat back and chuckled, never realizing the cannons were turning toward every other union in America. Sort of like Wyle E. Coyote in the cartoons right after he runs off the cliff and before he looks down.

That year, 1981, was a turning point. From then on, unions were on the defensive against management. The new policy that Reagan started was that if the union went out on strike after a contract expired and before they negotiated a new one—the only time it was legal to strike—management could bring in other workers to replace the strikers permanently. Let's put that another way: the law says you have the right to temporarily withhold your labor—to strike—but it now said, according to Reagan, that you could permanently lose your job if you exercised that right.

That left unions with little power.

Then in 1985 there was a big strike of packinghouse workers at the Hormel plant in Austin, Minnesota. About the same time, a whole new way of processing meat was coming on line. A company called Iowa Beef Processing, or IBP for short, was opening a new kind of meat-processing plant. It was automated. The plant didn't need the skilled work of butchers. It could hire anyone off the street and in an hour or two show them how to do a couple of simple things and have them doing one little part of taking apart a continual stream of steers or pigs and putting meat in boxes to send to stores.

The old-style plants sent sides of beef to stores where butchers cut off exactly the part a customer ordered. The new factories sent boxes of meat to stores. The stores didn't need butchers anymore, and neither did the plants. Instead, IBP could now hire unskilled workers at a much lower rate, undercutting everyone else in the industry. Hormel couldn't compete with IBP, and the workers went back to work after a long strike with a worse contract than before they went out. It was the beginning of the end of the success of that union.

This is the competitive process we described in Chapter 5 on economics. Productivity increased, and IBP didn't need as much labor or any skilled labor.

It was worse at other plants. In Waterloo, Iowa, and other plants in the Midwest, Rath Packing went out of business completely, leaving tens of thousands of people out of work. More than a decade later, with the local industrial economies in tatters, IBP moved into those towns, started up their own plants, and hired workers at a fraction of the wages their uncles, mothers, and fathers had made fifteen years earlier. Safety conditions were so bad they caused high turnover, which in turn created a shortage of labor (but no shortage of amputations, carpal tunnel syndrome, and other disabilities) in local communities. Then IBP began importing workers from Mexico and other parts of the world.

Here's the point. Their power came from the law and the way the government enforced it—the policies in place. Unions lost their power as Republican politicians and others friendly to management changed the law, interpreted old laws in new ways, or enforced them differently according to different policies. That's why we can't just speak of an economic system. It's a political economy.

Now cut to the 1990s when we're working in Chicago. By then, some new union leaders were in place, and they were trying to get the unions to pull their head out of the sand enough to make an effective resistance while there was still something to work with. The ones we studied argued that unions should change their way of doing things—they should change from the servicing model to the organizing model. Unions should organize. This meant there were three things they had to do:

- Organize more workers and more places and get stronger;
- Organize to support friendly politicians to change the laws and labor boards; and
- Organize in worksites so that the stewards could help members take care of their problems without calling on reps all the time.

That meant that it couldn't be business as usual anymore for these locals. They had to change and change fast. Every local would have to be involved. So the message went out (maybe *down* is a better preposition) to the locals.

The presidents of the locals got the message loud and clear. Some liked it and some did not. The presidents passed it on to the reps, and the reps told the stewards.

Here's where ethnography comes in handy. Suzan was working for a union local in Chicago at the time, so she had a close-up inside view of what was going on. She wrote about that in her 2001 book, *Labor Pains: Inside America's New Labor Movement*. We wrote a book together about that part of our work in 2005 called *Class Acts: An Anthropology of Urban Service Workers and Their Union*.

To understand what was going on, we had to understand the social and political relationships inside locals. The presidents of locals are elected. The members get to vote for their president, unless the president does something wrong, something that violates the union's own rules or the law. If that happens, the international union can replace the president with a trustee—someone the leaders trust to be honest and get the local back on the right track. There was a lot of that going on in Chicago in the 1990s. But a trustee in the unions we studied could only serve up to eighteen months. Then an election had to be held, and the members could decide whether they wanted to keep the same leader.

But in one union, it was so difficult to get on the ballot that you had to already be in charge before you could get your name on a ballot so that people could vote for you. As a result, there wasn't a lot of opposition. It was sort of like those old elections in the Soviet Union with one guy running, and that one guy always won.

But there had to be an election because that's what we Americans mean when we say "democracy." One-person, one-vote elections. That means the members have to actually more or less vote. And that means someone has to get them to vote. Someone has to let them know there's an election and get them to vote for the president. Otherwise, it would be against the union's own rules, and the law and the local could be trusteed.

Presidents relied on reps to deliver the votes for them. The reps depended on stewards to deliver the votes for *them*. So there was a kind of pyramid scheme. Stewards deliver votes to reps, and reps deliver votes to presidents. If people didn't play their assigned roles, the whole thing would fall apart.

How could reps be sure that stewards would deliver the votes? How could they be sure that members would vote the way they should? The best way was by having the stewards and members obliged to the reps. Remember reciprocity? Reps did that by their servicing. If there was a problem, the rep would fix it. Then the member and the steward owed the rep. Folks in Chicago talk that way. When they say, "I owe you one," they mean it. And you can actually collect.

This is much like medieval Iceland. There, if someone hurt you, you organized enough goons to go hurt that person back. In just the same way, "I owe you one" can cut both ways in Chicago, so reps had to be sure it was cutting their way and not against them.

If the reps delivered the votes, the president would like them and help them gain access to the resources they needed to keep their members and stewards happy—maybe an arbitration, maybe some fried chicken to help get members to a meeting. The rep might even get promoted or the president could ask her to run for office on his slate.

When the word came down about the organizing model, the reps weren't too anxious to do any of it. To do those things would mean that they would not serve their members as much, that they would lose touch with them and lose their own base of power. In Chicago, they call it their base. Different folks have different power bases.

But create a system where reps are irrelevant to anything going on at the worksite, because now stewards solve all the problems, and from the rep's point of view, it looks like she's doing herself out of her job. It's like training all the passengers on airplanes to fly, so nobody needs a pilot. Are pilots going to support that? Are they going to train us to fly?

So the reps all said, "Yeah, sure," and got on with what they'd always been doing. The program hit a stump. Paul was in a rep's office when a sociologist did a phone survey of reps to see whether they were with the program. The sociologist asked some clever question like "Are you with the program?" and the rep said, "Sure," and the sociologist was convinced. Later, the sociologist published a paper in which he proved that the reps really liked the organizing program. It was another three years before Suzan left that local, and the program wasn't even up to a crawl by then.

In the meantime, we did some surveys of our own—with stewards. We didn't ask whether they liked the program. We did what's called a *paired comparison*. That's where you ask people which of two things is more of something. For instance, we might ask people, "Which thing is bigger?" and then give them several combinations:

- Elephant/goat
- Elephant/mouse
- Goat/mouse

These are all possible combinations of two. The people would probably select "elephant" in the first and second ones and "goat" in the third. We give each thing one point every time someone selects it. So if we talked to one hundred people and they all agreed, "elephant" would have two hundred points (a hundred from "elephant/goat" and a hundred from "elephant/mouse"); "goat" would have one hundred points (from "goat/ mouse"), and "mouse" would have zero. So the ranking would be

Elephant	200
Goat	100
Mouse	0

And we'd conclude that these folks think that elephants are bigger than goats and that goats are bigger than mice.

This lets people tell us what the scales are and whether there are any scales at all. Maybe nobody agrees with anybody else. Remember, if that happens, then there's no cultural code about that; it's just a matter of individual opinion. And maybe there's no scale. People may like apples better than oranges and oranges better than bananas, but they like bananas better than apples to make a circle instead of a scale or line. Anthropologists don't tell people they're crazy or what they *should* think; we try to figure what they *do* think.

We did that with stewards and found out that the least important things for them were anything political, like helping to elect friendly politicians. The next least important thing for them was organizing other workplaces. The top things were negotiating contracts and dealing with grievances—servicing their members. So the program wasn't percolating down to the stewards.

But look at it from the stewards' point of view. Every day their job is to try to keep the peace in their workplaces. They must know and enforce the contract. Management won't help. Management will violate the contract any time they can get away with it. So the daily life of stewards is centered on these things right in their own workplaces. After all, that's a steward's job for the members (and this is almost always an unpaid volunteer job). The other parts of the program, organizing other workplaces and electing friendly politicians, are just something they heard in a speech or read about in a pamphlet or newsletter. They're not even real.

Same thing for reps. They know their jobs and do them. But what's important to them is keeping the structure of reciprocity and obligation in place with their members and stewards so they can help get their president reelected.

Here again we come to the conclusion that the political economy determines the culture. But we're down in the wormhole of ethnography again. That's where anthropologists feel most comfortable. So we'll try to get out and finish developing that big picture we promised a few pages ago.

The law changed in 1947 to make unions lumbering bureaucracies instead of organizing machines. The unions go along with that and work in terms of the servicing model. The political balance shifts from labor-friendly Democrats to management-friendly Republicans. The policy changes again in 1981 to make permanent replacement workers acceptable. That sets off a whole rampage of union busting across the country. The ruling class declared war on the working class. There really is a class war. We'll get to that later, but for right now the thing to know is that all of these legal things set the stage for the way things happen at the worksites.

The law determines what goes on in worksites, and that determines how people think—what seems reasonable to them—their cultural codes. So now we have all the links between political economy and cultural codes for working-class Americans.

What's the answer to the question we started this chapter with? The question was about personal choices and structure. Americans like to think that everything is a matter of our own choices. That's part of our cultural code. Thomas Frank, the author of *What's the Matter with Kansas? How Conservatives Won the Heart of America*, says that conservative propagandists believe that thinking in terms of hierarchy is just plain Marxist and therefore wrong. The Soviet Union collapsed, after all. So we're all in this together, one big middle class. According to conservative ideologists, the model is a high school cafeteria, segmented into self-chosen taste clusters like "nerds, jocks, punks, bikers, techies, druggies, God Squadders," and so on. "The jocks [he's quoting one of the ideologues] knew there would always be nerds and the nerds knew there would always be jocks . . . that's just the way life is." We choose where we want to sit and whom we want to mimic and what class we want to belong to the same way we choose hairstyles or TV shows or extracurricular activities. We're all free agents in this noncoercive class system (Frank, 2004, p. 26).

Frank continues, "As a description of the way society works, this is preposterous. Even by high school, most of us know that we won't be able to choose our station in life the way we choose a soda pop or even the way we choose our friends" (2004, pp. 26–27).

He's right. There's precious little choice. Our cultural codes are given by our political economies and those are given by the histories of political economies—how all of the parts of the system interact with the other parts and change each other. Remember the system diagram that went like Figure 10-1. The actions impact the realities; the cultural codes give us ways to think about realities and help us decide what to do, our actions. And where you are in the class system makes a big difference in the effects of your actions and the cultural code you have.

So does this mean that we can never change anything? That we just cycle through this? No. First, this is from an actor's point of view, not from the

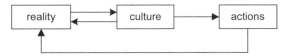

Figure 10-1 Our cultures tell us how to act and our actions change things.

system's point of view. We can see change and the possibilities for change better from the perspective of the system than from the perspectives of people in it. But even from the individual point of view, we can see that although we are limited by our cultural codes, we can try different things. If a lot of people go in the same direction, they can have an impact on the reality. That's what happened in Iceland when the people who worked for farmers for free just quit and went to the coast to work in the fishing industry for wages.

That's one kind of *collective action*. That's what the civil rights movement was. That's where greenhouse gases and unions come from—a lot of people acting in the same direction. Sometimes they don't especially mean to have that effect—greenhouse gases are a by-product of driving cars and industry. Sometimes they do—we get unions only when lots of people act together and mean it.

But then some people oppose both greenhouse gases and unions. How effective they are depends on how powerful they are. The more powerful, the more effective. If the ruling class of the United States were as against greenhouse gases as they are against unions, we'd sign the Kyoto agreements and reduce our air pollution. All of this structure stuff makes us feel uncomfortable. We are used to thinking in terms of choices. But that's our culture. That's our emic system. That's our economic system based on consumption and the idea of consumer choice. Sometimes we're like Paul looking at milk or peanut butter in the grocery store—faced with lots of apparent choices but no real ones. Democrat or Republican? Half a pound or eight ounces?

The culture of choice and the illusion of choice doesn't make it real any more than the skipper effect is real because some folks think it is. But anything that goes against our cultural code makes us feel uncomfortable. That's why Icelanders didn't much like it when Gísli and Paul said there was no skipper effect.

It's OK to feel uncomfortable about things that challenge our cultural constructs. We're built that way so that we don't easily give up on things that work for us. But sometimes we find it difficult to give up on things that don't work for us, like shrimpers giving up on the idea of individuality long enough to get organized. That's especially so if there's a class dimension, as there usually is. For instance, all the powerful processors and well-educated managers continually tell shrimpers they are right to think that they're too individualistic to organize.

That's where science comes in—to help us sort out the cultural illusions from the political economic realities. That's why we think it's good practice to be scientific in our anthropology. We can tell you, "This is what we found," and we can show you why we think it is valid and reliable. Then you can check it for yourself.

That doesn't mean that we don't have any choices. But it does caution us to understand what the choices are and to base them on reality as best we can know it. We showed that the realities of daily life shape the awareness of workers. But we also showed that those realities were dependent on the strength of the union in the hospital. And that's something that can change with some effort.

When Nasrudin Hodja was teaching school, one of the students asked which was the greatest achievement: to conquer an empire, to be able to conquer an empire but choose not to do it, or to prevent someone else from conquering an empire. Nasrudin said, "I don't know about empires and conquests and the greatness of achievements, but I know something that's even more difficult than any of those things."

"What's that?" the student asked.

"To teach you to see things as they really are."

That Nasrudin Hodja—he knew about emics and etics and the differences between them.

Discussion Questions

- Go to a newspaper or online news source and find a news story that focuses on politics. Show how that story is related to something economic. Now find a story in the business section and show how it's related to something political.
- What are some of the things you considered in deciding which college to attend? If you had no constraints, what college would you have chosen?
- One thing that 2004 presidential candidates George W. Bush and John Kerry had in common was that they both went to Yale and both belonged to the same elite society, Skull and Bones. Was Yale one of your choices? Why not? If it was one of your choices, explain. Move the discussion up four years. John McCain graduated from the U.S. Naval Academy and Barack Obama graduated from Harvard Law. Ask yourself the same questions.
- If your parents went to college, where did they go? If Yale was one of your choices, explain what that had to do with your mom or dad being a Yalie.
- Can you think of something in your life that is like the skipper effect, where people get credit for a skill they don't really have? Explain it in emic terms and etic terms.
- In America, some people say that hard work leads to financial security and success. In your family, do you see the relationship between hard work and financial success? Do you think that all successful people have worked hard for their money? Why or why not?
- Make a systems diagram with boxes and arrows to show the relationships among the variables involved in the Icelandic skipper effect.

Suggested Reading

Durrenberger, E. Paul. *Gulf Coast Soundings: People and Policy in the Mississippi Shrimp Industry.* Lawrence: University Press of Kansas, 1996.

Durrenberger, E. Paul. *It's All Politics: South Alabama's Seafood Industry.* Urbana: University of Illinois Press, 1992.

Durrenberger, E. Paul, and Suzan Erem. *Class Acts: An Anthropology of Service Workers and Their Union.* Boulder, CO: Paradigm, 2005.

Erem, Suzan. *Labor Pains: Inside America's New Union Movement.* New York: Monthly Review Press, 2001.

Lewis, Michael. "Wall Street on the Tundra." *Vanity Fair* (April 2009): 140–147.

Pálsson, Gísli. *Coastal Economies, Cultural Accounts: Human Ecology and Icelandic Discourse.* Manchester, UK: Manchester University Press, 1991.

There are two classes: the capitalist class and the working class. These members of the working class have organized into a union to protect their interests. *Photo by Suzan Erem.*

11

Class

L .A. detective Captain Gregory is talking to hard-boiled detective
Phillip Marlowe:

> *"I'm a copper," he said. "Just a plain ordinary copper. Reasonably honest.
> As honest as you could expect a man to be in a world where it's out of style.
> That's mainly why I asked you to come in this morning. I'd like you to believe
> that. Being a copper, I like to see the law win. I'd like to see the flashy well-
> dressed mugs like Eddie Mars spoiling their manicures in the rock quarry at
> Folsom, alongside of the poor little slum-bred hard guys that got knocked over
> on their first caper and never had a break since. That's what I'd like. You and
> me both lived too long to think I'm likely to see it happen. Not in this town,
> not in any town half this size, in any part of this wide, green and beautiful
> U.S.A. We just don't run our country that way."*

It's in Chapter 30 of Raymond Chandler's book *The Big Sleep*. It was published
in 1939, shortly after the Wagner Act but before the United States got into
World War II. We use these kinds of examples not because they're old timey
but because they are timeless.

That was way before Enron or Martha Stewart, Tyco or AIG, or any of the
other corporate or political crimes or shenanigans of the later twentieth and
early twenty-first centuries. "We just don't run our country that way."
Nobody runs any country that way. The kind of justice Captain Gregory was
thinking about doesn't happen.

Before we go any further, we want you to know that we understand the
anger that wells up in people when someone else tells them their myths are
myths or that what they've believed all their lives isn't true. And if we were
studying Lisu in 1970 or medieval Iceland, the people we studied might
never learn that we walked away with that information. Most Lisu in 1970
didn't speak the language that anthropological journals are written in, and
the saga Icelanders are dead. But more and more, thanks to technology, the
people anthropologists study learn about the results, and invariably the emic
and the etic run into each other somewhere.

When American anthropologists study the present-day United States, that
collision happens faster, and it tends to happen with more force. In this chapter, you will probably experience it. Talking about class does two things: it
ratifies the feelings of working people who have struggled for years with the

contradictions America offers ("Anyone willing to work hard can get ahead") and it infuriates people who either refuse to admit they are members of the working class ("We're middle class") or really are in the ruling class, because anthropology bares the truth in an undeniable way.

Conservatives believe that the government is bad. They say it fails whenever it tries to do something, like manage a health-care system. But governments of other countries manage health care well. They have better health-care systems than the United States does and operate them at lower cost. It is necessary to understand objectively what governments can do well and what they can't do well. We can do that by comparative studies of other countries. In the United States, the idea that governments do everything badly is part of a political philosophy of conservatives who believe that everything should be done by markets because that's where businesses are supreme and government should stay out. Corporations promote this ideology through their think tanks like the Heritage Foundation and the Cato Institute. Their mission is to manufacture **ideologies** to make corporations seem natural, inevitable, and good. We've used the word *ideology* loosely, as almost a synonym for *cultural code*. When ideologies are political—conservatism, liberalism—the people select parts of their cultural code to support one political position. That's what ideologies are.

Why would think tanks do that? Because these ideologies promote profits for the corporations that back them. They play to the elements of the American cultural code they can identify and locate. One is that people in the United States don't like negative things. If you can't say something good, don't say anything at all. There's no room for negativity. That's whining. So any reports of corporate bad behavior are just negative whining, and the people making them should just shut up.

But to see negative consequences such as global warming and pollution and increasing poverty as negative is being controlled by this ideology. What we need to do is see and assess facts. We don't have room for opinions. We don't want to trade opinions and come to the conclusion that everyone's opinion is equal. First, it's not true. Second, this is the kind of cultural relativism that stifles the search for ethnographic reality. Questions of good or bad judgments aren't relevant. Those are the wrong questions. Science asks questions of validity and reliability.

It's easy to see why people don't want to think about this stuff. We're surrounded by messages that manipulate us, and part of the American cultural code is to think for yourself. The easiest way is to think for yourself and reject all messages. But if we do that, we have no evidence, no ideas, no logic to work with. We have only our opinions. It's good to be open to ideas; we should test them rigorously. If we do that, we can build understanding. The discussions and debates we should have are not about trading opinions; they're about assessing logical and empirical adequacy.

All around us we see corporations. They are a major institutional form. Some say they treat people badly. Our question should be whether that view is true, not whether it's good or bad or positive or negative. Those questions only matter in opinion slugfests, not in ethnographic work. The problem is that corporations manufacture culture and try to get us to accept it.

Are governments or corporations more efficient at delivering health care? We know from comparative studies with European countries that governments do a better job of delivering better health care at less cost. Americans get worse and more expensive health care because we rely on corporations. Can governments be inefficient? Of course they can, especially if they're staffed by corrupt political appointees and cronies. Witness the U.S. government's response to Hurricane Katrina in 2005. Especially if they don't do their job of regulating things—witness the 2008 meltdown of the Icelandic economy and the crisis of the American economy. But that doesn't mean corporate solutions are the only alternative. But corporations want us to think that, so they try to bend our culture to that image.

Now we're going to discuss class. That doesn't depend on culture or opinions. It depends on realities. So here we go.

All stratified societies have classes and unequal access to resources. That much is true by definition. We've seen that states are the institutional arrangements to keep stratified societies working by making sure in one way or another that the subordinate class accepts the unequal allocation of resources. People are not in the same boat. What works well for the ruling class may not work at all well for the subordinate class.

This was clear in medieval Iceland when the chieftains landed and claimed land for themselves and began to work it with their slaves. The chieftains were as antigovernment as any of our twenty-first-century American **neoconservatives**, so they didn't want to set up a state to maintain their system of stratification. But they didn't want to give up the stratification, either. We've seen what happened to them. They were able to keep the subordinate class in its position, but their real problems were with each other.

We have classes here in the United States, but we don't like to talk about it. In fact, we spend a lot of energy denying that we have any classes. We like to think that we're all one big middle class. We don't like to believe that a very few of us run the show and the rest of us serve them. Class warfare became visible in the United States in 2011 with the Occupy Movement when people started talking about the 1 percent and the 99 percent. The press picked up on it and it was no longer impolite to mention class.

At the end of the twentieth century and the beginning of the twenty-first, with Halliburton's Dick Cheney as vice president of the United States and the oil companies' George W. Bush as president, there was no doubt that the ruling class was in charge in the United States. These were the people Bush jokingly but accurately referred to as his base in the Michael Moore movie, *Fahrenheit 9/11*. What some find curious is that they were elected, at least for their second term, although they may have gotten in for the first term by less than honest means. In *What's the Matter with Kansas? How Conservatives Won the Heart of America*, Thomas Frank (2004) suggests that for some reason the Democrats stopped thinking of economics as a political issue.

We suggest that the reason they didn't make economics a big issue is because their candidate was as much a member of the ruling class—and certainly as beholden to it—as the incumbent. Because the Democrats were standing in that glass house, they couldn't throw too many stones. So, as more and more manufacturing jobs go to the cheap labor markets in the global system (in a process that we discuss in the next chapter), people are working more for lower wages and for fewer benefits such as health insurance and pensions, and our presidential candidates are often completely disconnected from that experience, although Barack Obama may have been more connected than most.

People who once had jobs in steel mills or automobile factories or making television sets have been looking for what economists politely call "service sector jobs": flipping burgers, working cash registers, cleaning buildings, taking care of sick people. Many of those jobs are being automated. "Pumping gas" is no longer a service sector job as it was when Paul was a kid. ATMs replaced bank workers. Lots of travel agents are out of work thanks to the Internet. Airport clerks have been replaced by ticket kiosks. Even flipping burgers has become automated. So in the twenty-first century more people have no work or, if they do have jobs, they are in the "service sector" and don't pay enough to support a single person, much less a family. Their experience teaches them that they're in the 99 percent.

The folks who used to make union wages with union benefits notice the difference, and they're angry. People who work all the time know they are working class. So do people who've been thrown out of work.

And they know there are snotty liberals around flapping their sandals and sipping lattes and jabbering in Latin about everything that's wrong with America. So when the angry workers get a chance, they vote against those liberals and put straight-talking neocons in office. The neocons cut taxes, usually a little at the bottom of the scale and a lot at the top. The workers notice a little difference. The rich notice a whopping difference. And those snotty liberals go on blithering about "the disappearance of the middle class," refusing to admit that they too are members of the working class, yet wondering why workers won't vote for "their candidates" anymore.

Under the guise of protecting democracy and freedom, the neocons increase military spending to give their client corporations like Halliburton, KBR, and Blackwater big contracts. Tax cuts mean less tax revenue, but spending for the military–industrial complex means less money for programs to help people, so then, in the name of "fiscal responsibility," the government cuts budgets to agencies like Occupational Safety and Health, Medicaid, Medicare, and the Environmental Protection Agency and it tries to get completely out of Social Security, one of the most successful government programs in American history. A neocon government refuses to consider nationalized health care like every other advanced country has because the insurance companies are making outrageous profits from health care and invest a lot of money in politics and politicians. So instead it's labeled "socialist" and dismissed. Neocons refuse to regulate pharmaceutical companies for similar reasons.

With less tax money, the government cuts programs that workers and their families need, and that makes life that much worse—for workers. The neoconservatives put the power of the government behind union busting, and that makes it even worse. Neocons advocate a global market policed and controlled by American arms for American corporations. This translates into unlimited spending on arms, the support of Israel, and preemptive strikes against any opposition.

So working people get madder and vote out more liberals and vote in more neocons. This is one of those self-intensifying systems that we discussed earlier in the book. Worse conditions—more anger—more votes for neocons—worse conditions.

Let's take a look at the U.S. system in our systems terms (see Figure 11-1).

Thomas Frank is a journalist, not an anthropologist. But journalists are doing a lot of the same kind of work that anthropologists do. He thinks the corporate-backed neocons have successfully manipulated America's cultural codes to turn them against working people; for instance, "Liberals think they're better than you," "Liberals are pussies," "Neocons are as mad about it as you are," "Everybody has to look out for themselves—so if you get a cut in your taxes, it doesn't matter if someone else gets a bigger cut; you should be mad at the liberals who think it does matter." We'll come back to the American cultural code and explain where it came from later.

The economist Robert Reich suggests this process continues because there's no opposition, and there's opposition for three reasons. First, because there are no unions to protect working people any more, members of

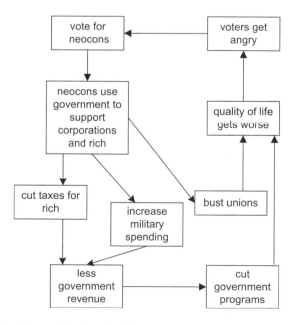

Figure 11-1 What the matter is with Kansas.

the working class fear they will lose their jobs. Second, students don't raise their voices because they are up to their eyeballs in debt in the United States, where education is a commodity rather than a right. Finally, he suggests that the American public has become cynical and don't think any change is possible because the government is totally co-opted. That's the reason, Naomi Klein suggests, that it's not possible to meaningfully address the dangers of global warming.

The American historian and writer Michael Lind suggests that it is not moronic yokels who are responsible for the increasing move to the right in America. This idea comes from attempts to understand the rise of Nazism in Germany, which saw it as a populist movement. Rather, Lind indicates, Germans of all classes, including elites and corporations, supported German National Socialism. Lind analyzes election results to suggest that it is not angry, white, working-class people who support the American Tea Party, a right-wing branch of the Republican Party, but the well-off, because the agenda of the right supports them. He cites polling data to indicate that white, working-class Americans believe their economic system unfairly favors the wealthy, that one of the biggest problems in the United States is that it doesn't give everyone an equal chance in life. Working-class people favor raising the tax rate on Americans with household incomes greater than $1 million per year and think that corporations moving jobs out of the country is responsible for America's economic problems. So, it's not working people who support the right, but the privileged.

What's wrong with corporations? Anthropologists from Walter Goldschmidt in the 1940s to Dimitra Doukas in the opening years of the twenty-first century have argued that corporations destroy communities; break up the ties that bind people into local economic, social, and political systems; and in the process annihilate any hope of democratic self-determination. For example, no amount of Wal-Mart's feel-good advertising can change the fact that people are so badly off that neighbors fight each other for the low-wage jobs the richest retailer in the world offers in local communities. No marketing slogan can lighten the heavy load Wal-Mart places on local social services because, first, most of its workers don't have health insurance and often make so little that they are eligible for food stamps, and, second, it often gets massive tax breaks to move into a town, lowering the available tax revenue that funds those services.

Or think of the IBP factories we discussed in the previous chapter. Anthropologists have shown just how the importation of lots of low-wage workers damages the communities that are so anxious for "growth" that they invite IBP to come in. The schools are stretched to the limit with education in several languages, the local clinics are overwhelmed with people injured at work who have no health insurance, there is more drug use and theft because of the poverty, and the police departments are stretched beyond their limits. Life isn't good for the workers the company brings in, either.

So, as corporations tear up the ties that bind communities, the power to make decisions is taken from people who know each other and their areas

Witnessing class war

A fall evening in 1997 found Paul sitting at a folding table at the back of a large audi-torium in Teamster City, close to Chicago's Medical Center stop on the blue line train. Next to him was the political scientist Adolph Reed, then at the University of Illi-nois, Chicago. He knew about anthropologists because he was once married to one. He's not the usual political scientist. You wouldn't find a usual political scientist at the installation of union officers that was taking place on the stage in front of us.

The president of a Service Employees Union local had just won his second uncon-tested election after taking over a local that had been trusteed, or taken over by the international union. This was cause for celebration and for some preaching to the choir.

Well, not *exactly* the choir. All in that hall were not unanimous in their opinions about all things, even in their daily understandings of all things, as the ethnographic work Paul had been doing with Suzan was beginning to reveal. From the stage he heard about new directions, about organizing and other moves that would bring unions to control ever-larger segments of the labor market. They all heard about po-litical action that would bring labor-friendly politicians into office, politicians who knew where their support was, politicians who would help, or at least not hurt as much as some of the neocons. From the floor they heard a lot of chatter about work and family, some good-natured ribbing, and, every once in a while, a question about a grievance posed to union staffers sitting at the tables, chowing down with workers they knew.

Adolph was there because he had become convinced that the only viable political future for working people in America was the Labor Party. That's why he kept in touch with labor leaders in Chicago. His writings were more familiar to readers of *The Village Voice* and *The Nation* than to those of arcane academic journals that are the literary hangouts of most political scientists. That evening, Adolph and Paul spoke of labor, class, anthropology, and the Labor Party.

Adolph collected some of his writings into a book called *Class Notes* that warns in no uncertain terms of the political dangers of identity politics that distract from the more fundamental relationships of class and make that divide less visible or less salient. If you grow up black, you experience race and racism. If you're a woman, you know all about sexism. If you're gay, you know all about homophobia. But somehow we are all supposed to be in one big middle class, so we don't talk about class or classism. We don't experience that in the same way that we experience race or gender bias. These kinds of politics have blinded us to class politics.

Paul walked through the auditorium and greeted people he had met during the two years he worked with this local. There was the slim figure of the Filipina organizer dis-playing her femininity in her high-heeled shoes and low-cut gown. There were the more substantial African American matrons of hospital kitchens who had shown him that corner of working America. There were the organizers and reps with whom he had ridden through the farther reaches of Chicago listening to story after story in his search for patterns. The pattern he found didn't have anything to do with the differences between blacks, Latinos, or whites or men and women. The patterns Suzan and

Witnessing class war *continued*

Paul found were based on where in the system people were looking up or down or across from; it didn't matter their race or gender.

Two years later, Paul sat in the designated smoking area behind a local hospital in the coal-mining region of Pennsylvania. Miners built this hospital for their fellow miners and their families a hundred years ago. Recently, the hospital's management had received loans from the Department of Agriculture to build a modern medical facility with the name of the old one. Now the management was in bankruptcy, and the members of the union were negotiating a new contract for a future they could not predict.

Members of these locals elected teams of fellow employees to work with their union representative to negotiate contracts. They sat in the plastic lean-to that resembled a bus stop and waited for management and the union organizer to complete a sidebar, an off-the-record negotiation designed to be less unwieldy and franker than on-the-record full group discussions could be. All but Paul were women. All were white. They were smoking and talking. He was listening.

They had been working at this hospital for most of their working lives and told stories of various fellow workers and people in management. The conversation moved from joking with a fellow worker to the deterioration of cleaning services since it had been outsourced to what was happening in the negotiations. Would management impose their last contract offer? That was not acceptable to members. Were members obliged to work under those terms to which they had not agreed? Wouldn't that be a lockout? If they were locked out, would they get unemployment benefits? If they didn't, could they make it through the coming winter?

Some said they had freezers full of food from their gardens. Some said their home furnaces' fuel tanks were full for the winter. One said she had no husband and thus no household support to fall back on. During this discussion, Paul learned two things:

- These women had given their working lives to this hospital; and
- From their perspective, the management of this hospital had no compunction about literally pulling the plug on their lives.

They had been sitting around the table for hours with the negotiating team. The woman in charge of the kitchen saw to it that the anthropologist got fed during one of the many breaks. In the end, management announced that they would impose their last offer, but the negotiator filed requests for information that stalled the negotiations.

Paul left that evening with the conviction that he was witnessing class warfare. The loans that sustained the hospital had been acquired through the good offices of a local politician, a politician who was not returning or receiving phone calls from his constituents, much less the representatives of their union.

and is put in the hands of remote management elites who know neither the people nor the area. The unit of decision making is no longer the locale, the community, but the globe-spanning corporation. Labor is an abstraction, a line item in the corporate budget.

When Paul was riding with Teamsters, he heard British Petroleum negotiators provide Chicago truck drivers the corporate bottom line for labor for transportation. That, they argued, was the bedrock of the negotiations. All else followed from that single abstraction. Teamsters could take it as benefits or as wages, but that was a finite figure from "corporate." It came down from corporate headquarters and could not be changed without permission. To British Petroleum, the truck drivers that Teamsters knew as fellow workers were part of a complex equation for producing profit.

That formula for producing profit starts with capital and ends with profit, as we explained in Chapter 5. In between is a market that organizes anonymous transactions among multiple buyers and sellers who neither know one another nor care about or for one another. To care for another would undermine the power to bargain. Labor is the only commodity that can transform others from whatever they are into what corporations can sell for money—commodities—on the same market to produce profits.

As we've said before, anthropology differs from political science and other social sciences because it is comparative as well as holistic and ethnographic. Holism means that we look for connections of everything to everything else. We don't see economic systems without also seeing the political systems that define access to resources. Ethnographic means that we like to see how things really are on the ground. We study unions ethnographically so we can see what actually happens in them rather than base our understandings on abstractions or theories that come from our imaginations. Being comparative, anthropologists put any example that we are trying to understand in a context of what we know of all other social systems ancient and modern.

So, in modern systems, the people who control capital control access to resources. The people who control nothing but their own labor and have to sell it to make a living do what the capitalist class tells them to do. That's the kind of system we have in the United States.

Is there an alternative? Yes, but it requires that people who sell their labor organize themselves to control their own labor for their own benefit. That's what unions are supposed to do. That's also what cooperatives attempt to do.

None of this can happen unless people understand the realities of their own social, political, and economic systems. That's what moves anthropology beyond the confines of classrooms and libraries and makes it relevant to everyday life. We understand political, social, and economic systems as they are.

Once you understand how these things work, you can begin to change them. You can't just wish it so. Understanding why your car isn't running won't fix it. You must do the work of repairing it and get your hands dirty. Fixing a democracy requires that every citizen understand clearly and then organize and act on their understandings while always guarding against thought control, as we explained in Chapter 8. For instance, some abstract and complex theorizing tells us that there are four kinds of capital—**natural, social, cultural,** and **economic**. Economic capital is the kind that corporations convert into profit. The capitalist class controls that. Ordinary people don't have that.

But we have other kinds of capital. We have social relations that can be valuable. Your parents can get you into Yale. Your uncle can get you a job, or your teacher can write you a letter of recommendation. The friends of your friends can help you when you need it. People who have more social relations have more social capital, and to be a human being, even to be a primate of any kind, or a wolf or an elephant or a wild horse, you have to have some social relations, some social capital.

Cultural capital is everything you know that might be of use to you in making a living. You know how to farm? That's a form of cultural capital. You have some friends who farm? That's social capital. But you can't convert any of that into a hill of beans unless you have access to some economic capital to buy machines, seed, and get access to some land. In this scheme, the land would be natural capital. Natural capital refers to natural resources, like coal and iron ore, and isn't worth anything without the knowledge of what to do with it and the technology to do it.

What's wrong with this scheme? It suggests that everyone has access to some forms of capital. You have no friends? Maybe you know a lot. You don't know anything? Maybe you have lots of friends who can help. And there's the third kind of capital, economic capital, that a few people have and most don't. But that's just one form of capital. So this thinking goes that people can convert knowledge, skill, and social relations into profit in much the same way as corporations convert capital into profits.

This neglects the fundamental reality that to convert capital into profit, corporations use the labor of people. That same relationship defines what capital really is—no metaphors here: real capital is built into the way our economic system works. It defines two classes: people with access to capital and people without access to capital. No amount of religious belief, no amount of sociological theorizing, no amount of economic hypothesizing can change that reality. And all the talk of social, cultural, and other kinds of capital distracts our attention from the realities of our class system, distorts it, makes it invisible.

That's why it's disappointing to see a whole land cooperating in their own thought control by calling themselves middle class and believing that there is no ruling class. That's why it's disappointing to see working people voting against themselves because they hate liberals.

But that's what anthropologists are here for, to bust myths. The Occupy movement at least made room for the discussion of class and class war in the United States for the first time in nearly a century.

Curtis White wrote a book called *The Middle Mind: Why Americans Don't Think for Themselves*. At the beginning of this book, we said we couldn't do anthropology without some form of relativism, but we warned against extreme relativism. That's what White is talking about. Good advice here is "keep an open mind, but don't let your brain fall out." Descriptive and ethical relativism—not judging other people—are necessary for anthropology.

Preamble to the IWW Constitution (1908)

The working class and the employing class have nothing in common. There can be no peace so long as hunger and want are found among millions of the working people and the few, who make up the employing class, have all the good things of life.

Between these two classes a struggle must go on until the workers of the world organize as a class, take possession of the means of production, abolish the wage system, and live in harmony with the Earth.

We find that the centering of the management of industries into fewer and fewer hands makes the trade unions unable to cope with the ever growing power of the employing class. The trade unions foster a state of affairs which allows one set of workers to be pitted against another set of workers in the same industry, thereby helping defeat one another in wage wars. Moreover, the trade unions aid the employing class to mislead the workers into the belief that the working class have interests in common with their employers.

These conditions can be changed and the interest of the working class upheld only by an organization formed in such a way that all its members in any one industry, or in all industries if necessary, cease work whenever a strike or lockout is on in any department thereof, thus making an injury to one an injury to all.

Instead of the conservative motto, "A fair day's wage for a fair day's work," we must inscribe on our banner the revolutionary watchword, "Abolition of the wage system."

It is the historic mission of the working class to do away with capitalism. The army of production must be organized, not only for everyday struggle with capitalists, but also to carry on production when capitalism shall have been overthrown. By organizing industrially we are forming the structure of the new society within the shell of the old.

But epistemological relativism—saying that everything is the same as everything else, that we can't make judgments about what is better and what is worse—makes us into morons because that means we can no longer think. We can just swap opinions and say they're all good. They're not.

If everything is equally good, if all systems of ideas are equally good, then we can't make any political judgments. We can't decide what is good for our country and what's bad for it . . . or for ourselves or the ones we love. Are we willing to say that it's OK to benefit from the misery of others? If everything is equal, then slavery is OK. Or fascism.

So although we need to be relativistic to understand others, we also need to keep our faculties of judgment strong and active so we can know the difference between bullshit and brilliance, between fascism and democracy, between a good economic program and a bad one, and, White says, between a good work of literature and a bad one. But to do that requires that we be able to "read" the works critically, to sort out and understand their messages, and we must be willing to judge them. That's why White is against the "it's all good" approach of some of the cultural studies folks.

When we lose track of those questions, we lose our ability to judge things on their own merits because we no longer understand what counts as meritorious. We don't follow arguments. We talk about how we feel rather than what we think. If all positions are equally good, we can allow creationism or intelligent design in our schools along with evolution. If all positions are good, we must believe the people who say there is no global warming as much as ones who warn against it. And those who say there was no Holocaust along with those whose relatives died in it. Or those who believe slavery is OK as well as those who don't.

It's about promising individual freedom and making choice impossible. No matter what you do, it's the same thing. Go stand in front of a soap counter at a store. Read the labels. Lots of different brands. Freedom of choice. Or cereal. Read the ingredients. Some kid cereal will be some kind of grain product plus sugar. So you want to be healthy and you get some Nature's Path Organic Optimum Power Breakfast. No kidding. Ingredients are organic wheat bran and guess what? Sugar? No, not sugar. It's "organic evaporated cane juice." Cereal or soap—they're all made of the same stuff, making picking one impossible. You can choose whatever courses you want, as long as they fulfill the requirements. Cars give us freedom to travel. We all get cars, and we're jammed up on big highways breathing our own exhaust fumes.

As citizens of the entertainment state, we see everything and are responsible for nothing. We are passive bystanders, like people watching a movie while the media bring wars in distant lands into our houses. We don't feel the burning napalm; we are not responsible for those who do. That's some other place. If we don't like it; if it doesn't entertain us sufficiently, we can change the channel and watch Australian rules football. But our movies and television programs are here. White suggests analyzing them critically, asking questions about what they are telling us—"reading" them, as he says. But this requires that we do something more than simply consume them and judge them on the basis of whether we "like" them. It's not just a matter of opinions.

This is all about a giant entertainment industry that keeps us occupied and amused and arguing about what we like and what we don't while we are not understanding the signals or messages we get or seeing the realities of the political and economic structures that we participate in. So we don't even think about class. We don't talk about the ruling class and the working class. It's impolite. It sounds "socialist." We don't like that. It makes us feel uneasy. Somebody might think that we're . . . liberals.

Class is the most important issue for anthropology. We can't understand anything else without understanding class and how it works. No longer is there refuge for people outside a global system of information, culture, commerce, capital, labor, and feeling, all of which mutually affect the others. We'll discuss the global system in the next chapter, but class determines all of those things that make it work.

According to the economists Emmanuel Saez and Gabriel Zucman (2014), in 2013, the richest one-tenth of 1 percent of the U.S. owned 22 percent of the wealth and were one hundred times richer than the poorest 90 percent of Americans, who had 23 percent of the wealth. Saez and his colleagues predict the disappearance of the American middle class by 2030 if nothing changes.

THE YEAR OF THE GREAT REDISTRIBUTION

Robert Reich
University of California, Berkeley
Blog post, January 4, 2014

One of the worst epithets that can be leveled at a politician these days is to call him a "redistributionist." Yet 2013 marked one of the biggest redistributions in recent American history. It was a redistribution upward, from average working people to the owners of America.

The stock market ended 2013 at an all-time high—giving stockholders their biggest annual gain in almost two decades. Most Americans didn't share in those gains, however, because most people haven't been able to save enough to invest in the stock market. More than two-thirds of Americans live from paycheck to paycheck.

Even if you include the value of IRA's, most shares of stock are owned by the very wealthy. The richest 1 percent of Americans owns 35 percent of the value of American-owned shares. The richest 10 percent owns over 80 percent. So in the bull market of 2013, America's rich hit the jackpot.

What does this have to do with redistribution? . . . stock prices track corporate profits. . . . And 2013 was a banner year for profits.

Where did those profits come from? Here's where redistribution comes in. American corporations didn't make most of their money from increased sales (although their foreign sales did increase). They made their big bucks mostly by reducing their costs—especially their biggest single cost: wages.

They push wages down because most workers no longer have any bargaining power when it comes to determining pay. The continuing high rate of unemployment—including a record number of long-term jobless, and a large number who have given up looking for work altogether—has allowed employers to set the terms.

For years, the bargaining power of American workers has also been eroding due to ever-more efficient means of outsourcing abroad, new computer software that can replace almost any routine job, and an ongoing shift of full-time to part-time and contract work. And unions have been decimated. . . .

All this helps explain why corporate profits have been increasing throughout this recovery (they grew over 18 percent in 2013 alone) while wages have been dropping. Corporate earnings now represent the largest share of the gross domestic product—and wages the smallest share of GDP—than at any time since records have been kept.

Hence, the Great Redistribution. . . . government sets the rules of the game. Federal and state budgets have been cut, for example—thereby reducing overall demand and keeping unemployment higher than otherwise. Congress has repeatedly rejected tax incentives designed to encourage more hiring. States have adopted "right-to-work" laws that undercut unions. And . . . the tax system is rigged in favor of the owners of wealth, and against people whose income comes from wages. Wealth is taxed at a lower rate than labor. . . .

America has been redistributing upward for some time—after all, "trickle-down" economics turned out to be trickle up—but we outdid ourselves in 2013. At a time of record inequality and decreasing mobility, America conducted a Great Redistribution upward.

The figures change from one year to the next, but since 1970, even with the Great Recession, wealth has been increasingly concentrating at the top, poverty increasingly at the bottom, and fewer and fewer people in the middle. Now think about the whole world. A tiny minority of people own most of the wealth and control most of the resources. You could type their names on one piece of paper.

The rest of us? We work for them. You and us and everyone else whose name is not on the list, whether we live in the homeland in Africa or one of the places our ancestors walked, sailed, or flew to in more recent times. Your dad owns his own business? Where does he buy his supplies? Who sets that price? Your mom is a consultant? She provides a service and makes a living, but who makes the profit off her labor? Everyone who's not on that sheet of paper has interests in common. It doesn't matter whether we live in Iraq or Israel or Iceland or Alabama, what gender or color or sexual orientation we are, or how educated we are. Like doctors and lawyers, lots of professors think they are members of some middle class, but certainly not the working class. But they *are* members of the working class because they don't own the means of production—their university, the medical system, the legal system. We are all in the same boat. And it's not the same boat the folks running the show are in.

Some folks were against World War I for just this reason. They said, "Why would a working person from England want to kill a working person in Germany? You folks are not enemies. You have common interests. Your enemies aren't in different countries." Their slogan was "A bayonet is a weapon with a working man at both ends." So is a bomb and so is a missile. The guy dropping a bomb or driving a Hummer through Iraq has more in common with the people he's trying to kill than he has with the people who sent him to Iraq to kill them. And way back behind whoever the guy in the Hummer may shoot at, invisible to the media, are some very rich Saudi Arabian, Pakistani, or Qatari businessmen.

If you've been reading or listening to all of the back-and-forth braying between liberals and conservatives, book after book, one radio talk show and TV program after another of "I'm right and you're wrong. Nyah!" this may sound like a political statement. We don't have any interest in the liberal–conservative debate. But we do have an interest in understanding our own conditions and the human condition clearly. And sometimes that requires us to speak bluntly.

When Jay Gould said he could hire half of the working class to kill the other half of the working class, he was speaking of guns in the hands of Pinkertons he hired. The contemporary approach, as Barbara Ehrenreich puts it in her book on the middle class, *Fear of Falling*, is for the employing class to hire half of the working class to *manage* the other half of the working class. Anthropologists are part of that structure. We too eagerly join with sociologists to speak of "SES," socioeconomic status, or to assert that in the United States there is no class, only status.

What happened to the working class that was so clearly visible to the Industrial Workers of the World that they could unambiguously state in the preamble to their constitution that there are but two classes—the employing class and the working class—and that they have nothing in common? Jay Gould furnished part of the answer. He and the employing class hired the guns and killed a lot of working people until the others got the message. The American Cultural Revolution finished the job with an ideology of a classless America and the idea that wealth comes from wealth, not from surplus labor.

Consider the alternatives for class consciousness. One is discussion. And what your mom told you is right: "Sticks and stones may break my bones, but words can never hurt me." Or anybody else. So what you say doesn't matter. But what happens when people do what the Industrial Workers of the World thought they should do and organize? What happens when they get angry and get together and figure out where their real enemies are? Sometimes they start shooting. But reasonable people don't do that. Reasonable people know what happens to people who do. So reasonable people sit around and talk, until talking just isn't enough.

When the rage of impotence moves people in the United States to arms, they are met with sure and swift and overwhelming violence from any one of a number of U.S. government agencies from Alcohol, Firearms, and Tobacco to the Coast Guard to the National Guard or a local Special Weapons and Tactics Team likely trained, if not armed, by the Department of Defense or the Federal Bureau of Investigation. It seems almost every agency of government has its own goon squad. For those agencies that do not maintain their own means of violence, there is the all-purpose Department of Homeland Security. The examples are all too frequent in the news from Ruby Ridge to Waco to Wounded Knee to the latest worker gone postal or whacko with a gun, taking as many others as possible with him to the next life. This force and the fear of it keep our "choices" limited. In every local area where people joined the Occupy movement, the troops were called out to clear them away.

James Scott (1985), a political scientist, observed that Indonesian peasants are not fooled by ruling-class mind control, but they also know from hard-won experience that head-on resistance only results in tragedy. It may be that every generation in every land must pay a price in blood to learn that lesson, but what the Indonesian peasants taught the Yale scholar remains universally true.

Sometimes people form new religions and revitalization movements and think they are invulnerable or that if they sacrifice their lives they will enter heaven. The safer alternative is to remain within the law and try to organize for common purposes. Some countries, such as the Scandinavian ones, demand it. But even this element of corporatist states is weakening under the hammer of global economics as manufacturing moves its well-paying jobs to the cheap labor markets of the third world to achieve greater profits for shareholders, save on their tax bill, undercut the tax base, and threaten the social contract that has underwritten class cooperation on mutually agreed terms.

Other lands, such as the United States, pass laws so the employing class can systematically destroy whatever gains the working class may threaten to make through organizing. Companies and the government hire academics to make the sham complete by proclaiming learnedly that there is no ruling class, that the markets control everything. So corporations endow universities and think tanks and buy professors to tell us that there is no class, that money begets money according to natural law and that hard work pays off. We all participate in the delusion, believing that as workers and consumers we have some agency in that market.

In the previous chapter, we discussed meritocratic individualism. Katherine Newman has documented the negative effects of the idea that you get what you deserve and deserve what you get. It works fine as long as you have a job, but when you lose it, it can't be anyone's fault but your own. When you've spent your whole work life preaching this and telling others that you're giving them what they deserve, it must be true for yourself as well.

We have a friend who is an anthropologist. He has a brother-in-law who worked for a big corporation. His job was to go around the country firing people as the corporation moved its manufacturing to other countries. He did this with the certainty that he was good at his work and deserved his good salary. Then, after he had fired everyone, the corporation fired him. He never saw it coming. That's how blind people can be.

The ideology of meritocratic individualism disguises the structure of classes. It says that everything is the fault of or the responsibility of individuals. If you do your part, you will enjoy the rewards. This is a good way to get people, like our friend's brother-in-law, to act against their own interests. And when they get screwed, they blame themselves. That's a pretty neat trick.

In contrast, Newman argues that working-class people understand that some things are way beyond their control. If they get laid off or fired, they know that it's not their fault. They know that it's because of a corporate restructuring or downsizing or something structural, so they don't take it so personally.

We found Newman's ideas persuasive, so while we were working with unions in Chicago, we decided to see whether we could find any evidence that working-class people think more structurally. We did a survey and asked people what they thought the most important thing for success is. These were union stewards and activists. They were Polish, Hispanic, black, white, men, and women. They said that innate talent or ability was the most important thing. This is right out of Newman's meritocratic individualism. "The most able people are rewarded."

Next they put hard work. "I worked for everything I have."

Everyone agreed that the structural features of race and gender were least important. Hispanics thought race was more important than gender, blacks thought the two were about equal, and whites and Poles thought gender was more important. This suggests that even working-class people buy into the ideology of meritocratic individualism.

Paul looked at a union bargaining unit in Chicago that's made up of lawyers, paralegals, and support staff. He reasoned that lawyers would be more middle class in their outlook, whereas working-class support staff would be more structural and paralegals would be somewhere in between. He was dead wrong.

Most support staff and paralegals said that people who get higher salaries deserve them. Most attorneys did not agree. Support staff and paralegals thought hard work was the main reason for higher salaries and talent and education were less responsible. Luck and networks they thought to be unimportant. But attorneys thought networks were most important and put work and talent after education. So the attorneys were showing the structural way of thinking, and the paralegals and staff were showing a meritocratic individualist way of thinking.

These were some strange attorneys, however. They worked for a legal aid foundation doing poverty law—helping poor people out with evictions, cases that involved getting their kids back from child welfare, and such matters. Paul's interviews with the lawyers showed that they were ideologically motivated—they wanted to do good and thought their law practice was a way to do that. They were paid much less than they could get in private practice.

So Paul did the same thing with some private practice attorneys in another large Midwestern city. There's a joke about a lawyer and some other folks who are shipwrecked and hanging onto life preservers trying to get to a small island. Sharks are circling them, but they go to the lawyer and nudge him ashore. Some of the others ask the lawyer why the sharks helped him and nobody else. She said, "Professional courtesy." Anyway, the private-practice lawyers put hard work right at the top. They worked hard for everything they have. You bet! Then comes talent. And they're bright, too. Education comes in third; luck, fourth; and last, their networks.

We couldn't find any evidence that working people think more structurally than the people the ruling class hires to manage them. They've taken on the ideology of meritocratic individualism, at least some important aspects of it.

So, if everyone agrees that individual merit gets us where we are and the lack of it keeps us back, isn't it true? Isn't that what the American dream is built on? Isn't that what our immigrant ancestors believed in and lived out? Not really. How do we know that? Because we can test it and measure it. We can look at the data and see that black folks as a group don't get as far ahead as white ones. We can measure the work women and men do at the same job and identify the one variable that causes one group to get paid less than the other. Yes, there are exceptions, and it is these exceptions—and our media's ability to magnify them—on which the American ideology of meritocratic individualism relies. It's a myth, albeit a powerful one.

In Chapter 7, we explained how Doukas (2003) argues that a great cultural revolution occurred in the United States about beginning of the twentieth century when the trusts reorganized themselves as corporations. They did a lot of the same kinds of ruthless things that they do today, but they didn't have any way to justify their antisocial actions. So they began to peddle the idea that all wealth comes from wealth. Capital makes money, according to natural laws of economics. That's when they bought the professors and endowed the think tanks and invented a whole "science" of economics. One economist who objected to the process, Scott Nearing, was fired and then in frustration dropped out of the whole academic system and went back to the land as an early "new homesteader." The Nobel Prize economist Joseph Stiglitz calls this reorientation of economics "market fundamentalism," equating it with a religion because facts can't change the minds of people who believe these things. The economist Michael Yates also calls economics a religion rather than a science.

Before the cultural revolution, Doukas suggests, most Americans held to the gospel of work—that labor creates all value—as we discussed earlier in this book. Despite the national-level cultural revolution, lots of people still hold to the gospel of work, and this may be the reason people identify success with hard work.

Paul and Dimitra Doukas got together to compare notes and figured out, as far as they could tell, that the gospel of wealth isn't as strong as they thought it might be, that the ideology of meritocratic individualism is well established, but that some working people still adhere to a gospel of work. We can't sort these things out by talking about them or by making more theories about them. The only way we can sort them out is by doing more ethnography to find out just how people think and why.

If you're not a white male, you're probably wondering where race and gender come into this story. As we said earlier, the concept of race was invented to naturalize and justify using slaves to make fortunes for their owners. But the anthropologist Karen Brodkin shows us that Africans, Europeans, Mexicans, and Asians were each treated as members of inferior races when capital recruited them into the labor force. This making of racial distinctions depended on and still depends on residential and workplace segregation, so people don't mix. This facilitated the degradation of work as what unskilled people do—the mass production work of inferior people. The making of race and the making of class are two views, two sides of the same process. Brodkin says that the manufactured cultural code of the United States takes white people as the real Americans with agency. Male and female nonwhite people are savage "hands" that do the work. They are dangerous aliens inside the country. The white managerial middle class as well as the ruling class depend on the work they do. Want to drive this point home to your pals? Rent or borrow from the library the satirical movie *A Day without a Mexican*.

Social movements make a difference. Some blacks enter the managerial middle class and government. A black man became president. Some women gain high corporate and government positions. A woman came close to becoming president and may yet make it. Brodkin's main point, however, is that concepts of race and gender are based on Julian Steward's cultural core, how people organize to produce things.

There is no Nasrudin story in this chapter. But there is one about a follower who gave a Sufi master five hundred pieces of gold.

The Sufi said, "Do you have more money than this?"

"Yes," the disciple says.

"Do you want more?" asks the Sufi.

"Yes," says the follower.

"Then keep the five hundred pieces of gold because you need it more than I do. I have nothing and don't need anything. You have a lot and want even more."

Discussion Questions

- What is the difference between the working class that you've read about here and the middle class as you understand it?
- How does the mainstream notion of the middle class benefit the highest levels of the ruling class? How does it keep working people from changing a system that is inherently unfair to them?
- Find examples of working-class role models in the media—movies, cartoon strips, television shows, and so on. What do they have in common? Was it hard to find them? If so, why?
- Look up the article by Emanuel Sasz and Gabriel Zuchman at the website voxeu. What is the basis for their conclusions that wealth differences in the U.S. are exploding?
- Find the record of major contributors in any recent election by going to Followthemoney.org or Opensecrets.org. What difference is there between who gave to the Democrats, Republicans, Greens, and Libertarians? What similarities are there? Why do you think this is so? If you're having trouble figuring out what political action committees are and who belongs to which ones, why do you think that's so?
- What class do you belong to? Why?
- If you're not already there, do you think that hard work will make you a member of the ruling class?
- If you belong to a fraternity or sorority, did you join it for the networks it would give you once you graduate? Do you expect to be networking with members of the ruling class?
- Name some members of the ruling class. If you can't, why do you think that is so?
- Someone once said that there are two ways to gain great wealth: steal it and inherit it. What did this person mean?

Suggested Reading

Brodkin, Karen. *Caring by the Hour: Women, Work and Organizing at Duke Medical Center.* Urbana: University of Illinois Press, 1988.

de Zengotita, Thomas. *Mediated: How the Media Shapes Your World and the Way You Live in It.* New York: Bloomsbury, 2005.

Doukas, Dimitra. *Worked Over: The Corporate Sabotage of an American Community.* Ithaca, NY: Cornell University Press, 2003.

Durrenberger, E. Paul, and Dimitra Doukas. "Gospel of Wealth, Gospel of Work: Hegemony in the U.S. Working Class." *American Anthropologist* Vol. 110, No. 2 (2008): 214–224.

Ehrenreich, Barbara. *Bait and Switch: The (Futile) Pursuit of the American Dream.* New York: Metropolitan Books, 2005.

Ehrenreich, Barbara. *Fear of Falling: The Inner Life of the Middle Class.* New York. Perennial, 1990.

Ehrenreich, Barbara. *Nickel and Dimed: On (Not) Getting by in America.* New York: Metropolitan Books, 2001.

Fink, Deborah. *Cutting into the Meatpacking Line: Workers and Change in the Rural Midwest.* Chapel Hill: University of North Carolina Press, 1998.

Klein, Naomi. "How Science Is Telling Us All to Revolt." *The New Statesman*, October 29, 2013.

Lind, Michael. "Tea Party: Rich, Elite, Right-Wing Tradition." *Salon*, October 22, 2013.

Newman, Katherine. *No Shame in My Game: The Working Poor in the Inner City.* New York: Knopf, 1999.

Saez, Emmanuel and Gabriel Zuchman 2014 "Exploding Wealth Inequality in the United States. Center for Economic Policy Research. Vox 28 October, 2014 at the website http://www.voxeu.org/

Williams, Brett. *Debt for Sale: A Social History of the Credit Trap.* Philadelphia: University of Pennsylvania Press, 2004.

Commercial agriculture is big business, and it uses big vehicles! *Photo by Suzan Erem.*

12

Back to the Land

In this chapter, we use a couple of examples to bring together some of the themes we've talked about before. We discussed commercial production and how it's different from household production, how states work, political economy and culture, and how classes work. The most basic thing anyone does besides reproducing people is producing food. Anthropologists figure out where the food in any society comes from and who controls it.

Here we're going to talk about what happens when you try to introduce commercial agriculture into places where people are producing their own food, how the idea of doing that developed in American agriculture colleges, "ag colleges," what the ag colleges are about, how they promote industrial agriculture, where the Farm Bureau came from and how it opposes farmers, and some of the ways the Soviet Union responded to democracy the same way the United States did. So, if it seems complex, that's because it really is. But it's not so complex that we can't understand it.

The goal of industrial agriculture isn't to produce food any more than the goal of the American health-care system is to produce health or health care; it's to produce money, profit that all commercial enterprises seek to maximize. As we discussed in Chapter 5, the goal of household production is to produce what the people of the household need. If they are on the land as farmers or peasants, that usually means that they produce most of their own food. They may produce something else to get some money. Lisu produce opium and get money. The point is that they produce the commodity to get money to buy what they need, rather than to put it back into production as capital.

In World War II the Japanese wanted to deprive the British of the productive capacity of India, a colony that was sending Great Britain war material from the beginning, when the United States was still neutral and not helping Britain with the war at all. The Japanese invaded Thailand and Burma, built air strips and roads, and started a push toward India.

It was during this time that the British anthropologist Edmond R. Leach was working with tribal guerillas—freedom fighters or terrorists, depending on how you look at it—in Burma. His experiences in the Kachin Hills were the basis of the book we've mentioned before, *Political Systems of Highland Burma*. The British and French both promised their colonies that if they helped with the war, they could have independence after the war.

After the war, the British and French reneged on their promises of independence. That's what got the long war in Vietnam started. Finally, the Vietnamese threw out the French, only to have to face the Americans. But they finally threw the United States out as well and got their independence after about thirty years of constant warfare. In India, Gandhi started his nonviolent independence movement, and the British gave Burma independence when they figured out the Burmese were ready and able to fight for it.

Meanwhile, after World War II, Americans were wondering where global poverty was coming from. Some thought that people in poor countries were just uneducated—if Americans taught them enough of the right things, they'd create booming economies like the United States had. These analysts hadn't figured out that the process of development in some countries drives the underdevelopment of other countries. One of the problems of taking your own myths to be true is that when you try to fix something, you get it wrong. If you think the drive shaft of your car is cooling it, you're going to put the thermostat in a really stupid place, and it's not going to do you any good.

The folks who had experience educating poor rural people were extension agents at America's ag colleges—like Penn State, Iowa State, Auburn, and the University of Illinois. So the U.S. government got these ag experts involved in creating programs to promote development in the third world.

We've seen that household production is limited—it doesn't grow. We've also seen how capitalist or commercial production does grow. The point was to promote growth, so the aggies thought they'd do the same thing they'd been trying to do in the United States. They wanted to convince folks to exchange their household production for commercial production. These American ag experts helped develop markets and credit for farmers.

Suppose you were in Thailand and didn't have enough land to feed your family, but your uncle had more than he needed. It would serve both of you well if you would work some of his land and give him part of the crop in exchange for using it. You got the rice you needed; he got some extra rice. Or maybe a landowner didn't use the rice fields during the time between harvesting one crop and planting a new crop of rice. Maybe that landowner would let you use some land to grow vegetables that you could sell in the market.

When larger landowners got capital and began to produce market crops, they had no reason to let you use their land for anything. They could produce tomatoes or tobacco to sell. The more land they had, the more crops they could grow and the more money they could make. That was the name of the game. But they needed labor, so they'd hire you and pay you the amount that you needed to get by another day—your daily rice. This was the minimum definition of necessary value that we discussed in Chapter 7.

Now suppose someone gets sick or dies or one of the kids wants to go to school. You need some money, so you sell your small parcel of land to your uncle. His holdings increase and yours decrease. As this process happens, more people have access to no land. As values change from community values or family values to commercial values, wealthy people feel less and less obliged to their communities and make less land available to others.

As more people have no access to land, they are available for wage work, and the more people who are available, the lower the wages. There's less emphasis on food crops, more rural poor people, and less food. That means higher infant mortality rates, greater rates of starvation and disease, and more migration to cities. Because every contribution to the family is important, poor people have more kids, and the process intensifies.

Lucien Hanks described this process in his book *Rice and Man*. Figure 12-1 shows what the process looks like in our system's terms.

There is more capital in play; more people are producing more commercial crops like tomatoes and tobacco. Both of these contribute to increasing the country's gross domestic product, an economist's measure of prosperity. People are selling products to people in other countries, so the balance of trade is better—our country is exporting more than it was and getting more money. So all of the measures that economists look at are improving. Later, we're going to show how this approach to development can devastate a country's economy and be damaging to the people who live there, while at the same time making them available to multinational firms as cheap labor.

As the process continues, there are more poor people, disease, and general misery. Fewer people can take care of themselves or their families, but it

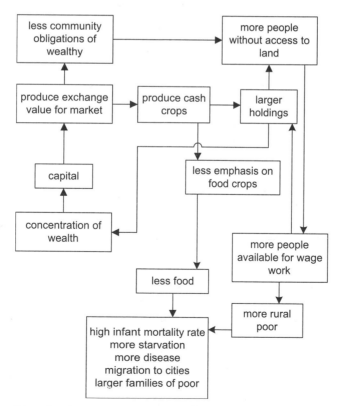

Figure 12-1 How development works.

looks good to economists, who never get out of their offices. It's the kind of thing anthropologists see wherever we do fieldwork. From where anthropologists stand, it's hard to believe that education could solve the problem.

Why did anybody think such a system would do anyone any good? Because it's what people did in the United States. In 1861, Congress passed the Morrill Act to support agricultural colleges with grants of land. The colleges were supposed to help farmers by developing agricultural sciences and teaching farmers better methods. In 1914, Congress passed the Smith–Lever Act to fund systems of agricultural experiment stations and extension agents to get the knowledge to the farmers. Here you see the relationships among law, political economy, and culture that we discussed in Chapter 10.

You might know how to grow corn, hay, oats, horses, cattle, and pigs. The question for the agricultural economists was how to organize all of these into one system so that you had enough oats to feed the horses, enough horses to plow and harvest the corn, enough corn to feed the cattle and pigs, enough cattle for the milk you needed to sell for income, and enough pigs for the meat and income you needed. Farm management developed as part of agricultural economics to answer these questions. So, early in the twentieth century there was an institutional system—agricultural colleges and experiment stations—to support detailed studies of farm management.

The goal of the ag colleges was to increase production and productivity—to increase the amount of agricultural products per unit of labor and land—to raise efficiency. Between the end of the Civil War in 1865 and 1890, a farm depression occurred, and farm prices fell steadily. One reason for the fall of prices was overproduction. Farm production increased 53 percent between 1870 and 1880, mostly because people were developing new farms in the Midwest and West. During the same time, the population increased 26 percent. The increased per capita food consumption and exports were not sufficient to absorb the increase in farm production, so prices fell. This began the problem of the farm surplus.

One result was grassroots populism. Populist organizations such as the Grange attempted to regulate the railroads and to establish marketing, processing, manufacturing, and purchasing cooperatives. Many cities and towns in the United States have local food cooperatives, consumer cooperatives in which consumers band together to buy food so that they can control the food available and so that corporations do not profit from their purchases. Another kind of cooperative is based on production rather than consumption, worker cooperatives, in which workers organize to run their own company, whether it is to produce appliances, bicycles, bread, or buildings. Robert Marshall is an anthropologist who has studied cooperatives in Japan. We will hear from him a little later.

In the United States in the 1930s, farmers realized that they could not benefit just by increasing efficiency. If they increased production, they were hurting themselves by flooding the market with cheap products and lowering the price. You might produce 100 bushels of corn and get $100. Increased efficiency might get you 150 bushels of corn, but since everyone is doing the same thing, the price falls, and you might get $90 for your whole crop. You still have to pay the same debts plus whatever debts you incurred for the costs of increasing productivity—maybe buying fertilizer or new equipment or pesticides.

Populists had the idea that if enough farmers banded together, they could influence the market by acting as one group. They could hold their corn off the market until they got the price they wanted. They could organize to make their own machines and buy, transport, and distribute other things they needed, such as clothing and farming supplies and tools.

The cooperatives were large groups of households. Each household was operating as a household production unit, but working together, they had the force of a large industrial unit. Other enterprises such as railroads, processing companies, and retailers like Sears, Roebuck and Co. were organized as commercial firms. The initial success of the cooperatives scared the firms. If the cooperatives were successful, the firms would be out of business. This was one of the reasons for the corporate cultural revolution in the United States that we discussed in Chapter 8. Here we are going to see how it worked in rural areas.

About 35 percent of the wholesale prices went to farmers, but 65 percent went to railroads, elevators that stored the grain, and banks. The railroads, banks, and Sears, Roebuck and Co. got together and created an organization that was supposed to look like a democratic farmers' organization but would really operate against the interests of farmers. If this sounds like a big conspiracy, it's because it was. They organized the Farm Bureau as a propaganda machine against the cooperative and populist movements.

The Smith–Lever Act connected the Farm Bureau to the extension service. The county agents from the extension service had to deal with groups of locally organized farmers to provide them with the new knowledge from the ag colleges to increase efficiency and improve farm profits. The Farm Bureau's role was to organize the local groups of farmers. And it was logical that the county agent would also be the leader of the Farm Bureau.

Farmers started losing their farms. This has been going on for so long that ag economists have names for the process. One is called the "treadmill." You increase productivity, but so does everyone else. The price per unit decreases, and your income remains the same or decreases. You are on a treadmill. More productivity, less income per unit, steady or less total income. This is a self-intensifying loop. As such, it's unsustainable, and you lose your farm.

You get caught on the treadmill, you can't make the payment on the farm, and it gets foreclosed for the debt you owe the bank for the loan that allowed you to increase productivity in the first place—the note to buy the machinery or chemicals you needed, unless you started out a little bit ahead. Then you buy the farms that other farmers are selling. This is "cannibalism" because some farms grow at the expense of all the others.

The rates of farm ownership decreased as more and more farmers lost their farms to banks. The rates of tenancy increased, and farmers began to worry about becoming a peasant class of tenant farmers working for banks.

Farmers looked down on working people in cities who, they thought, lived the squalid lives of urban workers. There was something degrading about having so many people in one place, something decadent about cities. Farmers didn't live on wages and didn't like the idea of it. They knew that wages made a person subservient to a boss. On a farm you can see the results of your own work in a way that wage workers never can—even if someone else takes it all away from you.

As more and more farmers lost their land and tenancy rates increased, farmers began to feel like peasants. Farmers weren't peasants and didn't want to be. Their self-image, with the guidance of the Farm Bureau and the Extension Agency, shifted to being businessmen. The Farm Bureau tried to convince people that farmers, railroads, elevator companies that stored grain, processors, and suppliers were all alike, that they were all in the same boat, that they were all businesses, like shrimpers. And as happened to shrimpers, these interests developed cultural codes that hurt farmers.

The ag colleges wanted to figure out how to most efficiently organize the complex components of farm production, and they also used this business model as a starting point. They assumed that all farming worked just like any other commercial enterprise—like a railroad company. A business is a business, and their job was to translate good business practices to farmers.

The populist movements of the nineteenth century failed. But early in the twentieth century, they rose again for the same reasons. One group was the Farmer's Educational and Cooperative Society of America. This group had learned the lessons of cooperatives and decided to try it again. Antitrust laws had been used against some cooperatives, as happened to the shrimpers' union, but an act of Congress in 1922 exempted cooperatives from antitrust legislation, so that couldn't happen again.

The Farm Bureau was already in place, and the ag colleges were preaching the gospels of the farmer as businessman and increased productivity.

As the population increased before World War I, farm prices recovered, and the farm situation looked pretty good for a while. As the situation improved, the populist movement declined. After the war, prices began to decline because of oversupply. Again populists proposed cooperatives. The ag colleges kept preaching higher productivity rather than organizing farmers for their own interests.

The agricultural economists who were actually keeping records and doing the ethnography of farm management made meticulous descriptions of the farms of that time, just as Chayanov had done in Russia. And, like Chayanov, they found that the farms they were studying did not fit the models they were supposed to. One of these researchers from Iowa State wrote in the late 1920s that the way they were doing the studies was fictitious because there weren't any profits. But, he said, he had to compute fictitious profits anyway. Over half of the farmers were making "negative profits."

Businesses can't stay in business in that situation. Farmers could. Farmers could keep going by cutting back their expenses somewhere. There's always somewhere to cut. They could put off repairing the barn so that they wouldn't need to buy the building materials. But after a few years, the barn would be in worse shape and finally beyond all repair. They could cut expenses by not sending the kids to school, not buying new clothing, and growing more of their own food in household gardens.

Another study of the same period showed that if a farm kept milk cows, it did better than farms that did not. A third study showed that farmers could not sell milk for what it cost them to produce it. No business can be better off if it sells commodities for less than they cost to produce. How could that be?

It worked for farmers because the milk money gave the family some cash income throughout the year that they could use for things like sending the kids to school and building materials to repair the barn. And although the investigators attributed prices to the fodder, hay, and grain farmers fed their milk cows, this didn't actually cost the farmers any cash. So, although the calculations showed greater cost of inputs than outputs, that's not how the farmers thought about it. What the ag economists actually doing the ethnography found was the same as Chayanov had found in Russia. They were seeing household economies, not businesses, in action.

But none of these findings, based on meticulous empirical research, could break through the assumptions of agricultural economics, for instance, that they had to attribute costs to food for the milk cows and money values for the farmer's labor. Their cultural codes were that strong. But cultural codes are so strong that sometimes even reality can't break them down.

When we have this kind of situation, when the data cannot affect the assumptions, we have one of two things. It could be a religion, but there aren't any superhuman agents involved here. Or it could be an ideology that is driving a policy. Remember, ideology is the selective use of ideas from the cultural code to support one group of people. Here, it was a matter of ideology and policy to support businesses.

We talked about A. V. Chayanov when we discussed household production. A short review of material from Chapter 5 is in order here.

Remember, there are two ways to organize production:

- Household production centered on use values; and
- Commercial production centered on exchange values.

Remember also that there are four preconditions for commercial production:

- Everything is a commodity;
- There is labor available to hire for wages, commodity labor;
- It's possible to expand labor time beyond necessary labor; and
- There's no interference in the cycle of production where people use money to buy commodities to turn into other commodities to sell for the original amount of money and some more that we call profit—the dynamic of capitalism.

And remember that there can be household production units even in complex capitalist systems.

The cow war

The ag colleges kept supporting the Farm Bureau and gave their propaganda the badge of scientific respectability. Despite what they said, they didn't care about farmers at all. Maybe individuals did care, but this is like really nice people getting caught up in racist institutions and inadvertently supporting racism. It's not about the individuals; it's about the power of an organization controlled by a handful of interests driving the resources in the direction of those interests, often under the guise of another name.

In the 1920s and 1930s, more and more farmers were losing their land. If you had milk cows and chickens, you could sell the milk and eggs to get a little money to keep the family going, even if the banks took all of your farm income from crops and fattening livestock for meat. So the milk cows and chickens were important elements of the organization of farms, even if they did not contribute much to the total income.

During that time, it turned out that many cows in Iowa were infected with tuberculosis, and their milk was spreading the deadly disease. The state said it would test all the cows, kill the infected ones, and reimburse the farmers who lost cattle at the rate of two-thirds the value of the cow. The problem was that it took six to nine months to get reimbursed. If you lost your cows, you had nothing to keep your family going in the meantime.

In 1929, a group of farmers sued the agriculture department of Iowa, talked to the governor, and made a mass appeal to the legislature in Des Moines and nothing happened. In 1931, when the veterinarians came to Cedar County in eastern Iowa to test the cattle, the farmers intimidated them. The governor called out the National Guard and declared martial law. Today, it's hard to imagine eastern Iowa, home of law-abiding farmers, being under martial law.

The authorities arrested and tried the organizers of the cooperatives of the Farmers Educational and Cooperative Society. The prosecution had to move the trial to another county because they couldn't get a "fair" trial in Cedar County, where everyone was a member of the Farmer's Union. They moved the trial to Scott County, where most people were members of the rival Farm Bureau. Court records show that all of the members of the jury that convicted the leaders were also members of the Farm Bureau. Quite a coincidence.

The Farm Bureau was saying cooperative people were Bolsheviks, Communists, and radicals, all really bad words at that time. That period was like the later McCarthy witch hunts for Communists. Businesses were trying to discredit any opposition to them and tried to get all of their opponents arrested or deported as Communists.

Eventually, the Farmers Union members were pardoned. But the damage was done. To this day, the Farm Bureau enjoys a membership in the hundreds of thousands, whereas the Farmers Union struggles to reach a thousand.

Capitalist production was developing in Russia, but slowly. For one thing, there was a lot of interference in the process by the czarist government. In Russia, capitalists faced the same problems others in Europe had faced earlier—lack of free commodity labor, as in the Shan village Paul studied. There was no well-developed working class that would create the revolutionary conditions Marx and Lenin wrote about. There were lots of peasants and rural farmers.

The revolution happened in the name of industrial workers, but most people weren't industrial workers, and the city people who had been active in the revolution didn't know anything about rural people. The same thing happened in China, and in the next chapter we'll show you how that is working out. But back to 1918.

Europe was in the middle of World War I. The new government in the Soviet Union made a separate treaty with the Germans and quit fighting. There was no way the Germans wanted to fight in Russia, and the new Soviet government was still trying to get organized. But the British wanted the Germans to have to fight in Russia so that they'd have to throw all of their people, food, and equipment to the east and not against the British, French, and Americans. Besides, they had no use for the Communists.

The British asked the Americans to help them with an expeditionary force to go into Russia from ports on the Arctic Sea and try to get the Germans' attention in the east. They didn't get far before the war ended on November 11. But they left all of their guns, ammunition, trucks and other supplies there for the White (czarist) Army to use against the Communist Reds. The Europeans and Americans didn't trust Lenin and his Communists. They didn't much trust the czarist White Army, either. But they knew they couldn't lose if the country was torn apart by a civil war.

Americans often wonder why the former USSR would have borne them any malice or would have been paranoid about the United States having atomic weapons. From the Soviet point of view, the English and Americans had invaded Russia to help the czarists overthrow the new government. Just for comparison, imagine what would have happened if France and Germany had invaded the United States when Roosevelt instituted the New Deal. Maybe they would leave soon, but not before they heavily armed a force of Republicans who wanted nothing more than to undo the New Deal. Not a pretty picture.

There were other problems in the Soviet Union. One was that a lot of people took the ideas that they heard about during the Soviet revolution seriously. The "soviet" part of "soviet union" means something like a self-governing democratic group, something like a cooperative. So people organized free soviets of people who worked at the same place. They organized their own production and began to exchange their goods with other soviets.

This was a problem because it made fighting the civil war and recovering from World War I difficult. There was no centralized planning to connect the different parts of the economy. Railroad workers and sailors in the Red Navy organized themselves into free soviets. To deal with that, Lenin sent Trotsky to Kronstadt, the headquarters of the navy, to shoot them all. That was the end of the free soviet idea.

But food was getting tight. Peasants were not cooperating with the revolution. City people had to go to the countryside to try to buy food or get it from relatives.

We can understand this from the point of view of household production units. There's a revolution on behalf of urban workers. One of their demands is cheap food. Food prices are low. If prices are low, that's the same as decreasing productivity for farmers. If you are selling crops, money is the thing you are trying to produce. So if you could sell grain for $2 a bushel and now you can get $1, your productivity has been cut in half. With food prices so low, it wasn't worth the effort for peasants to produce any more than they needed for themselves. If you cut productivity in household production units, the production decreases, as we explained in Chapter 5. That's what happened, just as Chayanov said. So there's less food available in the system.

There were two ideas about what to do about this problem. Chayanov suggested that differences in levels of production and income were the result of different needs of different households. Households with more consumers need more income or food, so they produce more. Marxist theory told Lenin and the Marxists that capitalism was an inevitable development in the countryside. (Theory was as much a religion for them as it is for American economists.) So they believed that if one farm produced more, it was more capitalist.

Chayanov argued that the best way to increase production was to let the peasants get something out of it by empowering them to organize cooperatives. Each person would own his own farm. They would control the co-ops for their own advantage and demand and get reasonable prices for their products. Then they would increase production and there would be more food for people in the cities. Everyone would benefit.

The Marxists thought the best thing to do was nothing. Let capitalism develop and encourage it by providing easy credit and agricultural extension, just like the system that the United States exported to poor countries that we discussed at the beginning of this chapter. When capitalists had concentrated all of the means of production into a few hands, the government would take it over and turn it over to collectives to create socialist agriculture.

Lenin died and Stalin came to power, and the food situation got worse. Stalin thought, like the American ag economists, that farming was like any other industrial process—best done on large farms or factories in the field. The government would own the farms just as it owned factories. There wouldn't be any farmers, just industrial workers producing food.

Stalin knew that if he started this program where peasants were already farming, they would revolt. The last thing he needed was another civil war. So he went to Siberia to develop the new industrial agriculture with modern equipment—tractors, trucks, railroads, harvesters. But he didn't have any farmers to work for him, so he rounded up peasants and forced them to work on the new collective farms.

But Chayanov was still arguing for cooperatives. Stalin called him a counterrevolutionary, arrested him, and had him shot in 1931. Stalin was just as successful in destroying cooperatives in the Soviet Union as the capitalists he hated were in the United States.

Stalin had one more problem. He couldn't find anybody who knew how to run one of his factories in the field. Who in the whole world had been thinking about these things—concentrating land, efficiency of farming, industrial methods, advanced technology, crop breeding, and how to organize all of these into industrial farming? American agricultural economists.

They had been writing about it for years. But industrial farming hadn't developed yet in the United States. Family farming was still hanging on. Some of these ag scientists were about to despair because the realities were so different from their neat theories. They didn't want to give up their ideology of serving business, so they concluded that farmers were backward and stupid. Therefore, when Stalin asked whether they'd like a shot at doing what they'd been talking about, they jumped at the chance, and Stalin got his new industrial farm managers from Iowa State University and other ag schools.

These guys wrote home, and *Wallace's Farmer*, a farm magazine, published a lot of the letters. These aggies were eager to be at the front lines of agricultural development, to put their futuristic ideas into practice. They got to Siberia and faced a surly bunch of drafted peasants, whose language they couldn't understand or speak, and an economic and political system they didn't know. Where's the lumberyard? Where does a guy get bailing wire? Where does a farmer get a tractor?

The aggies tried to help Stalin set up his collective farms because Stalin's image was like their vision of what a farm ought to be. And while the reactionary Farm Bureau was branding cooperativists as Bolsheviks and putting them in jail in the United States, Stalin was calling folks with the same ideas counterrevolutionaries and killing them. Neither socialism nor capitalism could tolerate the cooperative movement. And the guys the Farm Bureau liked in the United States were helping Joe Stalin set up his Communist farms in the USSR.

Since those days in the 1930s, family farms have just about disappeared from the American scene. American agriculture is now pretty much what those aggies of the 1930s were thinking about—factories in the field. The policy they have been promoting for more than a hundred years has finally been borne out. Someone once quipped that capitalism has achieved for agriculture in the United States what Communism never quite did in the Soviet Union—truly centralized industrial agriculture.

Now, instead of working for farmers, the ag colleges work for corporations to help them develop genetically modified organisms (GMOs) and try to get the idea of industrial control of the planet's food accepted as a scientific inevitability.

We don't know who first chipped stone to make tools, who first put stirrups, harnesses, or bits on horses, or who started breeding plants and animals. But in 1859 in the first chapter of *The Origin of Species*, Darwin wrote about breeders who produce the characteristics they desire in new generations of plants and animals. Well before Europeans arrived, Native Americans in what is now Mexico were developing corn by this method. Nature operates in the same way, Darwin argued. Those individuals who share a characteristic that helps them to survive and breed, or one that breeders select, will perpetuate and increase the characteristics that facilitated their persistence. This he called **natural selection**. He thought of it as the same process of selection that plant and animal breeders use, but accomplished by natural rather than human means.

He didn't know anything about genetics. Since that time, we have learned about the means by which characteristics are inherited and we've even learned how to intervene in the process to add desirable traits to plants by directly manipulating their genetic structures. Today, most corn, soybeans, and cotton produced in the United States are from such genetically engineered crops or GMOs. Genetic engineering is not the same kind of process as selective breeding. Selective breeding uses natural process to achieve a human goal. But genetic engineering uses techniques of microbiology and biochemistry to actually move genetic material from one organism to another. So, when champions of GMO claim that it's nothing new, because farmers have always tried to improve their crops, it's a lie.

One modification is to include in the genetics of the plant a substance that will kill common insect pests. In short, the plant has its own pesticide so farmers don't need to apply it via spraying. GMOs that inhibit pests are regulated as pesticides. Critics suggest that insecticides don't do humans any good and may damage us as much as they damage the insects they target. Another use is to add desirable characteristics to a crop such as grafting the vitamin A–producing capacity of carrots into rice to produce "golden rice." A third use is to add characteristics useful to the industrial production of fuels or pharmaceuticals. The most common use of GMOs is for crops to withstand the application of herbicides to kill weeds.

Thus, an herbicide that is frequently used in the Midwest is Monsanto's Roundup. Monsanto has also produced a GMO corn that is not affected by Roundup called Roundup-ready corn. (Note the genius in the marketing: What if it were called "Roundup-resistant corn"? That's what it is, after all, but then Roundup would be something that a natural food like corn needed to resist, hence the "ready," which sounds so, you know, ready to go, ready for action, ready for the good stuff to get applied to it.) So, a farmer can plant the GMO corn and then spray Roundup on the fields and not hurt the corn. American law requires that each GMO crop be studied and approved by the relevant government agencies including the Department of Agriculture, the Food and Drug Administration, and the Environmental Protection Agency.

This process is supposed to guarantee that the GMO will not do environmental damage, for instance, by becoming a noxious weed if it escapes farm fields, is not damaging to health if people eat it, and is safe to grow and produce. Critics argue that these processes have not been sufficiently rigorous or vigilant. If the process is a neutral scientific one, there would be no need for the biotech industry to spend more than $547 million in campaign funds and lobbying to ease regulatory oversight, to promote approval of new products, and to prevent the labeling of GMO products. If there were nothing wrong with GMOs, the industry would not oppose labeling foods that contain

Rigging food systems

The processes and laws that regulate GMOs in the United States were established before genetic engineering developed and cannot be directly responsive to it. You see, the Food and Drug Administration determines what information corporations must provide on food labels. Since the regulatory process does not see any difference between GMO and other foods, the Food and Drug Administration does not require that labels indicate whether products contain GMO ingredients, but there is nothing to prohibit them from doing so. None of them do. In a 2010 survey Consumers Union conducted, 95 percent of U.S. consumers favor mandatory labeling of meat and milk from GMO animals, and in 2013 a *New York Times* poll found that 93 percent of respondents favored mandatory labeling of GMO food.

Many fear that the influence of biotech corporations within the agencies of government is too great to ever get federal agencies to mandate GMO labeling. They have instead gone to state governments, and by 2013 legislation had been introduced in half the states of the United States but only passed in Connecticut and Maine. However, the bills both contain clauses stating they will not go into effect until the states surrounding them pass similar laws. Ballot initiatives in California and Washington failed in the face of massive industry resistance. In 2014, Vermont passed such a law and a coalition of the Grocery Manufacturers Association, the Snack Food Association, the International Dairy Foods Association, and the National Association of Manufacturers immediately challenged it in federal court. Vermont's attorney general requested the suit be thrown out because Vermont has every right to require GMO foods be labeled if they are sold in Vermont. In 2014, a ballot initiative in Oregon to require GMO labeling was the most expensive initiative ever in that state. Again, if GMO food is not harmful, one wonders why the industry spends so much money on political struggles to prevent labeling. And if GMO is so beneficial, one wonders why the industries using the technology don't tout it on their labels as part of their marketing campaigns.

---

them. But they have mounted a huge propaganda campaign to defend GMOs as natural and inevitable.

Food safety is one concern. Another is weeds. If people regularly use powerful herbicides it changes the environment of the weeds. No herbicide kills all weeds. It's the same problem with antibiotics. Any organisms that survive the antibiotic or the herbicide will be the founder of the next generation of weeds or microbes. And that next generation will be resistant to the herbicide or antibiotic. That's how natural selection and plant breeding work, although here it is neither natural nor intended, but superweeds are a by-product of the massive use of herbicide resistant crops paired with herbicides.

GMO foods are protected by copyright. That means only the corporation that produced the food can sell it and that it can specify the conditions of its use. Thus, if it sells seed to a farmer who grows and sells a crop, fine. But if a buyer uses the seed for research, that's an unauthorized use and therefore against the law. This has precluded any independent testing of claims of the safety of GMO foods. Only government laboratories are exempt from this rule and corporate influence in U.S. government agencies is so strong that this is not a threat.

European Union law requires the use of the precautionary principle, the idea that if there is no scientific consensus, the person or corporation suggesting approval of something must prove that it does no harm. In the United States, law allows the public use of such a thing unless someone can prove that it *does* do harm. Thus, in the United States, to ban GMOs, opponents would have to prove that they are harmful. Although they have adduced much evidence, there is no scientific proof, in part because of corporate interference with the normal operation of scientific research. In the European Union, corporations have not been able to prove that most GMOs do no harm so they are not allowed.

We want to return to the cooperative movement for a moment. Anthropology is comparative, so let's look at a couple of other examples of agriculture.

First, we'll look at Guatemala, where Catholic liberation theologists organized cooperatives and unions. In the late 1960s, a big destructive earthquake took place. The government called for foreign aid to help. By the time the government organized, the cooperatives and unions already had the situation under control through their grassroots organizations. That threatened the government.

Remember Chapter 8 about how states work? Now we're going to see an example. If these popular and democratic organizations could deal with the massive devastation of the earthquake, what could they do if they decided they wanted to change the government? The government began a program to discourage such organizations. The major element of this program was to kill the leaders of any organizations so that nobody would want such a job. That was the beginning of the terror and civil war that racked Guatemala for years.

There is one other place where people tried organizations like free soviets. That was in the Spanish province of Catalonia during the Civil War. The Spanish people had a parliamentary democracy and elected a parliament and government. The leader of the army in Morocco, who represented the ruling class, didn't like the idea, so he brought his Moorish league into Spain to overthrow the elected government. The "loyalists," or people who supported the elected government, fought against this army. Lots of people joined the fight—Communists, Socialists, liberals, capitalists, anarchists. All got together to protect the republic.

This was 1936, just as National Socialism, the Nazis, were getting ugly in Germany and the Fascists in Italy. The Nazis and Fascists helped this general, Franco. The only help the loyalists could get was from the Soviet Union. Since the Russian Communists hated the German fascists, and since the Germans were helping Franco, the Russians helped the Spanish loyalists.

During this time, the anarchists of Catalonia set up free soviets. But the Communists didn't like them any more in Spain than they did in the Soviet Union. So the Communists shot all the anarchists. George Orwell was there and wrote about it in his book *Homage to Catalonia*.

WORKER COOPS

Robert Marshall
Western Washington University

Some workers own and manage their own businesses democratically by voting—one-person, one-vote. Each worker owns one share of the business. Democratic control presents a genuine alternative to capitalist firms in all parts of the economy, but especially in the service sector where startup costs are relatively low.

People start worker cooperatives all around the world. In the US, Europe and South America workers have bought the business from their previous employer who can no longer make a profit or would like to retire. The largest worker cooperative I ever worked with is in Japan and has several thousand members. They started as an independent laborers union in the 1970s and gradually evolved into a worker cooperative in the 1980s as they began to contract construction projects directly.

Spain and Italy have large worker cooperatives in manufacturing and engineering, but these are rare in the US and worker cooperatives are not yet abundant anywhere. Cooperation solves many problems for employees who typically have no voice in management, no share in the profits their work creates, and no job security. However, worker cooperatives still have problems that become clear when we ask why, if they are so good for workers, are there not more of them everywhere.

Worker cooperatives face the same kinds of problems other businesses do such as how to make good decisions, how to make sure everyone is pulling their own weight, how to do the best job they can. But in one area, worker cooperatives and conventional businesses are dramatically different. Some debate whether employees of capitalist firms are exploited because they do not receive the full value their work creates, or whether they are paid fairly through the workings of the market for their labor.

Conventional capitalist businesses use money they don't pay their employees, called retained earnings (surplus value), to grow bigger and to reward owners and managers. The more workers a well-run business hires, the larger and more profitable it will be for its owners, so they see growth as a goal. Worker cooperatives do not buy their workers' labor; they divide the difference between their costs and their income among all workers. Adding another worker will not add any income to any other worker's paycheck so there is no reason to grow—why grow if it brings new headaches?

But once they have gotten started, worker cooperatives almost never fail. They know their businesses well, and they rarely take risks that would require them to go into debt. The only serious problem facing established worker cooperatives is how to return a worker's share in the business when retirement comes. Worker cooperatives need to be big enough that returning a worker's share will not harm the business. One attractive feature of worker cooperatives, then, is that they work best with a workforce of good size evenly spread over all ages of workers.

But it was in the Basque country of Spain where the most successful Co-operative movement was established by a Catholic priest named José María Arizmendiarrieta in the town of Mondragón. The priest educated young people in Catholic social thinking and, in 1943, established a technical college in the civil war–devastated town. He established a credit union and a cooperative university that formed the basis for the foundation of other cooperatives. The movement was successful in regenerating the area with a self-contained economy and then spread to become international. Although they offer an alternative to capitalism, they are embedded in a capitalist system and, from some points of view, operate as a large firm might, even though managed by workers.

So the ruling class really does not appreciate it when people of the working class organize democratic groups for their own interests, unions, or cooperatives. It doesn't matter whether it's in the capitalist United States or the Communist Soviet Union or Spain or Guatemala. The ruling class has no use for democracy. How long will Spain, as a member of the European Union, tolerate the Mondragon cooperative system?

One day four kids came up to Nasrudin with a bag of walnuts and asked him to divide the walnuts evenly. He asked them whether they wanted the walnuts divided God's way or the human way.

"God's way," the kids all said.

So Nasrudin opened the bag and gave two handfuls to one kid, one handful to another, two walnuts to the third, and nothing to the last kid.

"What kind of division is this?" the kids asked.

"It's God's way," Nasrudin answered. "God gives some people much, some people little, and some people nothing at all. If you'd asked for the human way, I'd have given you equal amounts."

Discussion Questions
- Compare the treadmill farmers get on with the kind of treadmill that credit card debt can cause. What do they have in common? What is it about agriculture that makes it different?
- Discuss how the Farm Bureau's propaganda to and about farmers is similar to or different from the ideology of meritocratic individualism.
- When farmers, shrimpers, and many other kinds of "independent" workers organize collectively, they can be charged under the Sherman Anti-Trust Act. Find out more about the creation of that act and the criminals it targeted. How are they different from the family farmers or fishermen of today?
- What are the social, economic, and cultural ramifications of corporate agriculture? What are the benefits and costs of the vertical integration (where one company might own everything from the pig to the grocery store) of agriculture?
- If religion is always justifying governments, why are there Catholic priests organizing cooperatives and other democratic organizations in Guatemala and Spain?

- If governments are so anti-co-operative, how can some cities have food co-ops?
- What do you think Nasrudin meant when he said that giving the kids equal shares of walnuts was the human way of dividing them?

Suggested Reading

Bookchin, Murray. *The Spanish Anarchists: The Heroic Years 1868–1936*. New York: Harper, 1978.

Kern, Robert. *Red Years—Black Years: A Political History of Spanish Anarchism 1911–1937*. Philadelphia: Institute for the Study of Human Issues, 1978.

Mintz, Jerome R. *The Anarchists of Casas Viejas*. Bloomington: University of Indiana Press, 1994.

Orwell, George. *Homage to Catalonia*. New York: Harcourt, 1980. (Free at http://www.george-orwell.org/Homage_to_Catalonia/index.html/.)

Container ships move consumer goods across the globe. This port in South Carolina is one of the busiest in the United States. *Photo by E. Paul Durrenberger.*

13

Global Processes, Local Systems

In the previous chapter, we saw how importing commercial agriculture can break up local economic systems and create the preconditions for capitalism that we discussed in Chapter 5. Because there are many people with no access to livelihood, they become available as wage workers. The people without access to resources become a critical resource for corporations and an important labor pool for the global economy. In the next chapter, we're going to show how this works out for the individuals who get those jobs.

Let's review some logic. Some people say, "Isn't it better for poor people in the third world to have a low-paying job in a factory than to have no job at all?" Remember that the answer depends on the question. We think this is the wrong question. We think the question should be "Why do these folks need to look for a job?" Remember we can only understand other people if we keep open minds and do not judge them. But if we take cultural relativism to the extreme, as we discussed before, everything is equal, and we can't make any judgments about ethics, morals, or politics. Yet, as people, we believe some things are better than others.

We live in state systems that administer societies built on inequality. When we see that the people who work the hardest don't reap the greatest benefits, the inequalities of class and race and gender demand that we make ethical and political judgments.

How can anthropology help with this? First, it can help us to see things as they really are, to see the inequalities and the systems behind them. We cannot do that unless we can see past the fog of the state and corporate-sponsored spin doctors and mind controllers. Second, anthropology's comparative method can give us ideas about how things *could* be different in any given system. We see egalitarian societies with equal access to resources and can conclude that we could use those principles for organizing even global social orders—that every person deserves one share of our planet just by being here. No more, no less. That's one way to make the political and ethical judgments—to favor anything that moves in that direction and oppose anything that does not.

What kind of system has the world become with speed-of-light communications, computer tracking of people and things, container shipping, and computer-controlled robotics?

Because people can communicate so quickly and accurately and because of container shipping, corporations can put their factories anywhere local governments will let them. Wal-Mart keeps its shelves full of stuff from China. As we'll show you in the next chapter, anthropologists doing fieldwork all over the world see people going to work in factories where they used to see people working in their fields. You're probably wearing clothes from those factories.

One basis for anthropology is ethnography. We like to get up close and understand people as individuals. That means that sometimes we get so involved with the trees that we don't see the forest. Sometimes it takes a whole group of anthropologists working in different locations to see the patterns. Richard Apostle and others got together to see what kinds of patterns they could see in the changing fishing industries they were studying in Atlantic Canada and Scandinavia (and then wrote *Community, State and Market on the North Atlantic Rim: Challenges to Modernity in the Fisheries*).

They wanted to see whether fishers (that's the nongendered term anthropologists use for fishermen and fisherwomen) and fish-processing plants in all of these places were responding to the global economy in the same way. This work can help us understand other aspects of the global economy. They divide the world into three dimensions.

The first is community, where people know each other and they have complex relationships and overlapping identities. So you may be someone's boss and coach the soccer team her daughter plays for. You may both belong to the parent–teacher organization at the school and see each other at band concerts that your kids are in. And you may be neighbors. We can think of a community as networks of social relationships in which the people treat each other pretty equally.

The second dimension is the state, where relationships are hierarchic, formal, and bureaucratic, as we discussed in Chapter 8 on states. Relationships here are one-dimensional, professional, and involve authority. A county health department is charged to enforce regulations about sewage disposal and water use. Generations of experience have gone into making the regulations. Everyone in the county may be their relatives but they still enforce the regulations. Because the dog catcher is your neighbor doesn't mean she won't catch your dog.

The third dimension is the market, where there is competition, economic efficiency, and rationality. Nobody cares who you are; the only thing they need to know is how much you're willing to pay for what or how much you're willing to take for what. It doesn't matter if someone is a relative or from your town or a stranger from halfway around the world. It's impersonal. People are there for just one of two things: to buy or to sell. So it's one-dimensional. The relationships are fleeting and impersonal and lack any inherent value— you don't know or care about the other person just because you sold or bought something. Think eBay or Amazon.com. You're out to get the best deal for yourself and the rest of the world be damned.

Community, state, and market. Aztecs had all of these things. But the market was not important compared with the state. With globalization, the market expands and the state contracts. Some people think that states will become so unimportant that they won't have much role in the future. This is reasonable when you think about economic systems. But it's not so reasonable if you remember that markets can't exist without states to enforce the laws and rules that markets depend on.

If you take out all the links that make a system work, then there's no way you can control it. It would be like driving a car where the accelerator, brake pedal, and gear shift lever didn't connect to anything. When corporations become so big that they straddle many different states, the policy of any one state doesn't make any difference to the whole economic system because the system isn't inside the state, and the connections are somewhere beyond the confines of a single state.

The connections may be inside a corporation that buys ore from one place, ships it to refineries in another, and then ships aluminum to other countries where people make it into various products. This is the example that George Beckford discussed in *Persistent Poverty: Underdevelopment in Plantation Economies of the Third World*. Suppose you had a car that you thought was a regular car. It had always worked before. First, the steering goes out and the car won't respond to the steering wheel. And then the accelerator goes out, and then the brakes, and then the transmission. If you have any sense, you jumped out of the car when the steering went out. Problem is, people can't jump out of their countries. Just as trying to drive a car like that might make a person crazy if you thought it ought to actually work, if you didn't know it was all screwed up, trying to make policy in a country whose economy has been disarticulated makes for crazy politics.

On the other hand, Joseph Stiglitz points out that markets aren't just there naturally like mountains, the sea, and air. A state system creates the policies that actively establish and maintain markets. When the Soviet Union collapsed, there weren't any market mechanisms. There, markets didn't just erupt out of nothing to replace the centralized economic system. The "market fundamentalists," as Stiglitz calls economists who think the market is natural, were puzzled when markets didn't automatically come into being to solve all problems. But markets couldn't come out of nothing without all kinds of law about contracts, real estate, patents, ownership of ideas, ownership of things, banking, and ways to enforce these laws. That requires the machinery of a state. No state, no market. No market-friendly policies, no market. The funny thing is that in this void, something a lot like Icelandic chieftains moved in—the Russian Mafia—and to the extent it could enforce the rules, it ruled the market that had begun to develop.

If the market expands to connect more and more people, some states may become less influential, but others become more influential. If there's a market, there's a state. But relative to states, the market is far bigger than it was for the Aztecs.

These fisheries folks also showed that it was the policies of the different states that made the differences in how things worked out in Canada and Scandinavia. There are some surprising results. Norway is a centralized **welfare state** or **corporatist state**, and Canada is a **federal system**, so you might think that things in Canada would be a lot more decentralized than in Norway. But that's not what happens. Canadian fishers aren't organized—they can't get together for anything—so power in the fisheries is centralized in the Ministry of Fisheries. But in Norway, with its mandatory union structure, people have the means to speak for their interests so power is decentralized. It's decentralized, paradoxically, because the state requires the structures that work that way.

What both countries share is a welfare program for corporations. Fisheries corporations have sufficient clout that they can get politicians to rescue them when they get into trouble. That's again a matter of policy, politics, and states. There is another area where the market works—finances. People don't just trade *things* on markets; they also trade money and stocks. These financial markets are strange because what they trade isn't real—it's a bunch of cultural fictions that exist only because people agree that they exist. We've all seen what happens when some people stop believing that the fictions are real. In 2009, what banks once held as assets became "toxic assets" that nobody wanted because they couldn't figure out what they were worth. Something you can't sell isn't a commodity; it has no value at all if you can't use it, and nobody can figure out a use for a subprime mortgage or even a bundle of them.

Suppose that we all agree that what's really going on in the world is that the Norse gods are fighting it out with the Greek gods. We could bet on outcomes. Thor versus Dionysus. Both of them were heavy drinkers, but we'd bet on Thor. We could have a market in god futures—what we think the gods are doing. As long as everyone agreed on the premise, it would work. That's like money. It's all a fiction. It isn't real. Money is just paper with some fiber in it so it'll survive the washing machine, but hand someone a $100 bill instead of a $1 bill for a tip and you'll know the difference. That's only because you both agree that the paper, the fiber, and the number of zeros actually mean something.

That's why economists like Stiglitz make a distinction between finance and substantive economies. The substantive economy is the way things get made and circulated—the kind of thing that economic anthropologists usually talk about. Finance is the money-magic part of it, and it may have nothing to do with the substantive part. During the Great Depression of the 1930s, as many as a quarter of Americans were out of work, and everyone was worried. There were no fewer factories. There were no fewer people to buy things. The substantive economy didn't change a bit. But the failure of the money magic was enough to bring down the whole system. That's what was going on in mid-2009 when the entire United States fell into the Great Recession.

In 1944, the United Nations sponsored an international conference at Bretton Woods, New Hampshire. It was toward the end of World War II, and Europe had been devastated by the fighting. The conference was meant to get the financial side of things started again. The idea was to help even enemies like the Germans and Japanese avoid any more depressions and other conditions that start wars. By then, some economists had figured out that government policies can make a difference in markets and did not believe in the religion of markets regulating themselves.

THE MAGICAL WORLDVIEW OF CAPITALISTS

Paul Trawick
Idaho State University

In the global south there is a closed system worldview concurrent with the laws of thermodynamics whereas the north shares a magical worldview based on the magic of money and a fantasy of an expandable open system.

My comparative studies show that people sustainably regulate water management systems by conceding to one another equitable rights to use water and equal power to say who gets what. They know that if one person takes more there is less for everyone else. Because the system is closed it benefits everyone if everyone conserves water. Archaeology shows that these systems can endure and benefit people for centuries. The closed system worldview supposes that raw materials and fossil fuels are not inputs from outside the system, but a fixed endowment of natural wealth, like irrigation water, that humans should rightly hold in common because we cannot create it. It makes us, as consumers of cheap labor and scarce natural resources, responsible for the costs of producing wealth, and impels us to level those costs by limiting our numbers and our appetite for energy and stuff.

Capitalism promotes the fantasy that natural resources and energy are inexhaustible and clever engineering can solve all problems, so we can expand production forever. Markets regulate all problems. Money fuels markets and money represents debt. A loan is a promise to repay it and more and cost banks nothing except their risk while guaranteeing future income. Bankers lend that same money again and again, multiplying it and driving governments' printing of cash. If everyone paid their debts, there would be no money in circulation. A lot of effort goes into managing money in the financial sector and this magic diverts attention away from the raw materials, energy, and labor people expend to pay interest. So, while it is virtual and magical, the use of money has concrete consequences. The idea that markets regulate economies conceals the origins of wealth and denies any responsibility for negative consequences such as climate change and global poverty. People can create wealth out of nothing—like the software code for a new app—so accumulating it has no costs or limits and we don't need to hold each other accountable for what we do with it. Rather than the reciprocal and egalitarian morality of irrigators, capitalism developed a morality that justifies the misery of many for the benefit of few.

The only way to make the world more stable and sustainable is to make it less unequal by redistributing accumulated surplus wealth. Irrigators teach us that a different "invisible hand" must regulate our economies: a spirit of generosity and self-restraint that is timeless, quintessentially human, reciprocal and obligatory, having its origin in the closed and limited nature of the world to which we all belong and must all learn to share.

People of the global North have benefitted from the illusion of an open system at the expense of people in the South. As the ones who suffer most from that process, the people of the South have begun to organize populist political movements to revive a closed system worldview and the morality and that politics that go with it.

This group set up the International Bank for Reconstruction and Development, which we now know as the World Bank, to get the development process started. To ensure economic stability, they set up the International Monetary Fund (IMF). A British economist named John Maynard Keynes was there.

Keynes thought that depressions got started when people didn't have enough money to buy things. Without money, they couldn't create demand for the goods that corporations hire workers to make. The solution is to get money into the hands of the people. There are two ways to do this. One is to cut taxes. But it doesn't work to cut taxes for rich people; they already have plenty of money. The goal is to make a big difference in how much money ordinary people have. The second way is to increase government spending. If the government builds roads and airports and schools and parks, it hires workers who get wages that they can spend to increase demand.

The way this worked out in the United States in the early twenty-first century was that when the newly elected Democratic president, Barack Obama, proposed spending money on government projects that would hire people so they could earn money to spend, the Republicans did everything they could to stop him. They were the same ones who caused the problem by not wanting any regulations on finance, but they didn't want any new solutions to it, either. Their only solution was the same solution that had gotten us into the mess in the first place: cut taxes for their rich friends and contribute to a self-intensifying system of concentrating the wealth in fewer and fewer hands while more and more people have nothing. They didn't dare speak up against more regulation. There's a time and a place for everything and even these people could see the harm that deregulation had done . . . chiefly to themselves. But the plan went through and everywhere people started going to work on roads and bridges to repair the damage of decades of neglect.

The IMF's job was to keep an eye on the economies of the world and, when one of them began to slump, help that country create more demand. The IMF would lend the country money so that the country could cut taxes or increase its spending. The idea behind the IMF was that countries would cooperate to solve economic problems in the same way they cooperate in the United Nations to solve political problems. Everyone in the world who pays taxes supports the IMF, but we don't get to vote. The major developed countries have the most power, and the United States has veto power. The creators of the IMF realized that sometimes governments need to do what markets can't.

But then the 1980s brought a big change. That's when Ronald Reagan and Margaret Thatcher were sponsoring the ideology that markets are natural forces, the ideology that justifies corporations, as we saw in Chapter 8, neoliberalism. Iceland was not exempt. Icelanders elected their own neoliberal governments that supported market solutions to everything, including fisheries management and the ITQs that we discussed in Chapter 10. In Chapter 14 we'll see how that worked out, but suffice it to say here that they destroyed the economy of the country, impoverished everyone, and left as it all crashed down on everyone else's heads in 2008.

The poor countries of the world were often in such dire straits that they couldn't refuse an IMF loan, no matter how bizarre the terms. We'll see in the next chapter that that can have a negative impact on the lives of working people, just as the Great Depression did in the United States.

At about the same time as the neoliberal market fundamentalists came into power in the early 1980s, there was what Stiglitz calls a purge in the World Bank. Until then, its leaders had been dedicated to eradicating world poverty. In 1981, Reagan put the market fundamentalists in charge. Instead of asking how to help governments solve economic problems, their religion of economics taught them that governments were the problem because they might meddle in the market. They believed that free markets could solve every problem.

The IMF was supposed to deal with crises, but now the third world was in continuous crisis. Crisis was normal. The World Bank started making what it called "structural adjustment loans" instead of providing money for building projects. But it could only do so if the IMF approved, and the IMF imposed its own conditions.

The IMF was supposed to do the money magic for the whole world and deal with things like a country's rate of inflation, interest rates, balance of payments, and borrowing. The World Bank was supposed to take care of more substantive things like what the government spent money on. Since all of these substantive things could affect the money magic, the IMF thought that everything in the country was its responsibility to regulate. To the market fundamentalists, all countries were the same. The kind of difference we just discussed between Canada and Norway wouldn't even be on their radar.

Both of these Bretton Woods institutions are run by the developed countries: the United Kingdom, Italy, France, Canada, Japan, Germany, and the United States. These are known as the G-7. If they add Russia, that makes the G-8.

Stiglitz (2002) says, "A half century after its founding, it is clear that the IMF has failed in its mission. It has not done what it was supposed to—provide funds for countries facing an economic downturn, to enable the country to restore itself to close to full employment" (p. 15). And the G-8's religion of market fundamentalism is no better than a G-string for covering up their failures. They've made matters worse. The ideas behind these policies are called the Washington Consensus, which, Stiglitz says, is a consensus of the IMF, the World Bank, and the U.S. Treasury Department about which policies are good policies.

There was a self-intensifying loop in the process of the Depression. Countries closed down on themselves and didn't want to do anything to help other countries. To deal with that problem, the Bretton Woods conference also suggested a World Trade Organization to encourage the free flow of goods and services. It didn't get started for another fifty years, in 1995, and it doesn't make the rules of trade, but gives countries a way to negotiate them among themselves.

Stiglitz's big contribution is to point out that all things are not equal. Different countries have different conditions at different times. Sometimes tariffs can be useful. The question is "Useful to whom?" For instance, we discussed the American tariff on sugar that just keeps the price up so that ADM can sell its corn sweeteners. It also helps the Cubans who ran away from

Castro and set up new plantations in Florida's Everglades to make money by producing sugar while they destroy that state's environment.

Sometimes it's not good to put a country's money into the international system of money magic, especially if the country doesn't have the institutions to manage it. It can cause the kind of separation from finance and substantive economy that happened in the Great Depression. Stiglitz (2003) sums it up this way: "The result for many people has been poverty and for many countries social and political chaos" (p. 18).

Stiglitz says point blank that commercial and financial interests of the wealthiest nations control the Bretton Woods institutions for their own interests. (Remember, this guy's an economist. He used to *work* for them. He's done the ethnography, whether he called it that or not.) So multinational corporations are pulling the levers of the world economy. Trade ministers control the World Trade Organization and speak for their country's trade interests to keep as many subsidies and trade protections as possible to help them. That raises the price of goods to consumers in the country, but that's not the issue. The issue is how to protect those corporations. Nobody asked you whether you were in favor of the sugar tariff.

Finance ministers control the IMF. They are close to financial firms and see the world through the eyes of the money shamans. This is like asking an Inca priest what he thinks of the Sun God. They impose controls on government spending and cut subsidies in other countries so that prices go up for poor people. They cut health-care programs because it's bad for governments to spend money. They tell other countries not to pay for education. And nobody gets to vote on any of this. As we will see later, this makes the IMF responsible for the Ebola outbreak of 2014.

Sometimes working people and poor people get pushed to the wall and riot. That's the social chaos part. Or the dearth of health-care facilities may result in a pandemic disease that threatens a whole continent. But economists would be the first to say that it's not personal. We say it should be personal. It affects persons.

Stiglitz sees a parallel between the development of the U.S. economy and the world economy. In the nineteenth century, the United States spread west. The government helped the railroads and telegraph systems with lots of huge subsidies, and the costs of transportation and communication decreased. Local markets and companies became national. But the government set minimum wages and working conditions and regulated interstate commerce. The government developed and supported the ag colleges and other programs to encourage agriculture that we discussed in Chapter 12. The government even gave people land so that a lot of people had a chance to farm. World War II required centralized planning and coordination and that cemented many of these national-level processes and removed them from locales. That was the end of diversified farming in Iowa, for instance. During the war, committees decided which regions were best suited to which crops and developed policies to move farmers toward specialized crops, what we now call monocropping.

EVO MORALES AND THE NEW BOLIVIA

Charles McKelvey
Presbyterian College, Clinton, South Carolina, and University of
Havana, Cuba
His blog is *The View from the South: Commentaries on world events from the Third World perspective*

After conquering the Inca Empire in the sixteenth century, the Spanish imposed systems of forced labor to supply raw materials integral to the development of the world-economy: first silver, then tin, and then natural gas and petroleum. In the mountains of South America, Bolivia's peripheral function in the world-economy has co-existed with autonomous indigenous communities, agricultural societies with communal forms of land ownership. But as the world-economy expanded, it has increasingly consumed indigenous land and autonomy.

During the twentieth century, Bolivian mine workers, peasants, and factory workers formed a popular movement that resulted in a government developmentalist program from 1930 to 1985. Forged through an alliance between the popular sectors and the national industrial elite, it makes some concessions to popular demands and provides some protection for national industry, without threatening the interests of foreign corporations.

Beginning in the 1970s, the world-economy entered a global crisis, because it could no longer expand by conquering and incorporating new lands and peoples. The global elite responded with the neoliberal project and structural adjustment policies, eliminating governmental protections of national industries and currencies and of the needs of the popular sectors.

In Bolivia, this began in 1985 and stimulated a revitalization of the popular movements, with mass mobilizations protesting specific neoliberal measures. Indigenous organizations were dynamic in the revitalized movement of the 1990s, reflecting the fact that 61% of the population self-identifies as indigenous. In the period 2000–2006, the popular movement intensified with mass mobilizations, road blockings, general strikes, work stoppages, and hunger strikes that created generalized chaos. New political parties were formed, including the Movement toward Socialism (MAS), a federation of social movement organizations and unions, founded in 1995. Its principal leader was Evo Morales, an indigenous coca farmer who had been born and raised in a poor town in the Bolivian high plains and who emerged as a leader in the coca farmers' union. Morales and MAS won the presidential elections of 2005.

The government of Morales has sought to put into practice an alternative economic model based on control of natural resources and the establishment of national sovereignty. It has attempted to break with a political–economic system in which the national elite along with transnational corporations, international finance agencies and the United States are the principal political actors in the country. It has followed a vision of autonomous development tied to the demands of a popular movement composed of indigenous organizations, peasant organizations, unions of workers in the petroleum and gas industries, professionals, and small and medium sized businesses.

Evo Morales and the new Bolivia *continued*

In 2009, the people of Bolivia approved a new Constitution, developed in a Constitutional Assembly with ample popular participation. Evo Morales was re-elected president under the new Constitution in 2009 and 2014, with substantial majorities.

Evo Morales expresses a perspective on global affairs that is typical of leaders and movements of the Third World. He affirms the need to live in harmony with Mother Earth; the social and economic rights of all persons, including the rights of access to water, electricity, telecommunication, nutrition, education and health services; and the right of the nations of the Third World to true sovereignty, including control of their natural resources.

The difference is that now, when transportation and communication costs are falling and drawing the world closer together, there is no world government to manage things. There's the IMF, the World Bank, and the World Trade Organization, and neither you nor anyone else gets to vote on who runs them. Democracy?

How could a bunch of highly educated economists with PhD's screw up the world's economy? By looking after the interests of corporations and the ruling class instead of the people of the planet. The year 2009 is proof. OK, let's try a little relativism here. Suppose an Inca priest told you that the world would cease functioning if you didn't do what you were told. You'd better believe him because you want your world to continue functioning and you're not about to test that by questioning the veracity of an Inca priest. There was a death penalty for that, a strong incentive to believe. The point is that the Inca priest doesn't have to be right any more than these money shamans do. Remember, in hindsight, the Maya kings who kept building temples were wrong. It's the nature of hindsight that you never have it in the middle of a process, only after it's finished its course.

"But they have to be accountable," you might say. "If finance people make mistakes, the market punishes them."

You'd *wish* you were punished like that. We'd all say, "Punish me some more." CEOs from BankAmerica, Citicorp, JPMorgan, Bankers Trust, and the First National Bank of Chicago all made bad loans in Asia. The JPMorgan guy got his remuneration cut by nearly 6 percent, all the way down to $3 million a year. Some guys have to live a *whole year* on that. How do they manage? But it turned out not to be all that bad for the poor guy because of other perks he got that made the total package nearly $9 million. So he probably didn't have to max out his credit card. The other guys were punished for their bad behavior with *increases* in remuneration from 8 to 48 percent from around $500,000 a year up to more than $12 million a year. Not bad for a shaman . . . who gets it wrong. And even when these same guys were begging for government handouts, they continued to get their lavish bonuses. They were impervious to failure, mistakes, and natural selection. These guys who hate

WALL STREET

Karen Ho
University of Minnesota
Author of *Liquidated: An Ethnography of Wall Street*. 2009, Duke University Press.

Whereas steady production (whether in factories, farms, or stable corporate institutions) used to be sources of jobs and wealth in the United States, since the re-regulation of banking in the 1980s, more profit occurs in the financial sector where those who already have money invested in the stock and bond markets (and those who advise and manage this money) claim not only a larger share of the pie, but use their influence to shape how corporations, savings, and many other kinds of institutions act.

As advocates and advisors to stock and bond markets, Wall Street investment banking institutions have transferred billions of dollars in savings, retirement funds, and mortgage loans *away from* traditional banks, corporations, and lending institutions and *into* financial markets. The more money that goes into financial markets, the more empowered and influential financial advisors, actors, and institutions have become. Three decades of such maneuverings have changed the priorities and policies of the entire American cultural economy away from retirement and employment premised on long-term corporations answerable to a social contract.

By studying the powerful, anthropologists can gain access to the values, practices, and models that shaped this cultural transformation. All change is historically contingent, culturally specific, and constructed through particular ideologies, practices, values, and embodiments. Instead of approaching Wall Street's empowerment as an inevitable result of capitalism, my employment and two years of ethnographic research on Wall Street shows how the contemporary landscape came to be culturally constituted.

Since the 1980s, Wall Street investment banks have singularly recruited from a handful of elite universities in the United States, in part to bolster and codify an aura of pinnacle status and a "culture of smartness." Despite their youth, inexperience, and highly unsustainable and speculative practices, these amply resourced, highly networked and pedigreed workers are valued as "the smartest," and tautologically framed as proper experts and advisors to the global financial markets precisely because they belong to institutions already branded by the larger world as "smart."

These financial actors (bankers, investment managers, private equity managers) undergo intense socialization on Wall Street where they are thrown into a highly insecure environment of intense financial deal-making that becomes a further sign of their "smartness" and superiority. Faced with the expiration of their own jobs yet simultaneously empowered, these financiers understand their constant insecurity as testing and developing their mettle, and are often unsympathetic to the plight of most workers.

Financiers' compensation is premised on bonuses for the number of transactions and they are rewarded even if their deals implode. In this highly volatile environment

Wall Street *continued*

of privilege and insecurity, investment bankers learn to relentlessly push short-term transactions intended to boost stock prices. Financiers internalize as challenges and sources of empowerment their understandings of what it takes to be successful in the new economy, to act simultaneously with the market that they have had a strong hand in constructing. Their elite networks, privileged class backgrounds, and high compensations allow them to weather crises. This local cultural model leads to continual crises, volatility, and inequality, but also helps to explain how Wall Street actors came to understand themselves, at least for a moment, as "masters of the universe."

welfare were using government welfare for their banks to pay their own outsized bonuses—maybe the only people on the planet who get paid for screwing up big time.

How do they get away with it? The easy way, if you can manage it, is to control the government so you can make the rules, or rather, be sure there are no rules. With no effective regulation of the financial system, in the late twentieth and early twenty-first centuries, Bernard Madoff was able to bilk his investors out of billions of dollars. He pleaded guilty to the charges against him, but because of the plea deal, he didn't have to reveal what happened to the money or who was in it with him. Madoff is in jail and the feds seized his $11 million mansion in Florida and his fleet of pleasure boats. That's the price you pay when the law is enforced. Still, he and his family had a mighty nice life for an awfully long time. And some still do.

Why are people willing to accept that this kind of thing can happen?

See whether you recognize any of these names:

> Heritage Foundation
> American Enterprise Institute
> Brookings Institution
> CATO Institute
> Institution for International Economics

If you listen to NPR or any other news, you'll hear them mentioned for their study or comment about something that's in the news. These are some of the thought controllers we talked about in Chapter 8. The combined budgets exceed several hundred million dollars in any given year. The same guys sit on their boards, and the same firms contribute money to them. These are the guys that run the corporations and want you to think that that's the only way to do things.

Early in the 2009 session of the U.S. Congress, legislation called the Employee Free Choice Act was introduced in the Senate and the House. In the previous session it passed the House but failed in the still Republican-controlled Senate. Under current U.S. labor law, if you want a union, you have to ask your boss if he'll deal with the union you select if you get a majority of your fellow workers to sign up. He can say yes, and some do.

Meltdown

For eight solid years, those who believed that corporations rather than government should control things took control of Washington, D.C., and relaxed the regulations on financial companies so they could pretty much do whatever they wanted. They found out they could trick people into borrowing money using their houses for collateral. It didn't matter if you had a way to pay it back, like a decent job with a regular income. The person who got you to sign on the dotted line got a commission. And the company she worked for got a commission. All the way up the line.

Each mortgage was supposed to represent a flow of money—and it would if each person could meet the monthly payments. So the mortgage was a resource, like a cow that gives milk. So you could put a bunch of mortgages together and sell them like a herd of cattle. Then people could buy and trade shares of these "financial instruments," as they were called.

But many of the loans had built-in time-bombs. After a few months, the interest rate would jump and the monthly payment would skyrocket. Now what looked like a loan you could pay off became one you couldn't pay—not on the wages you made, not if you wanted to buy food or gas, not if you wanted to buy the medicines your family needed. And surely not if you lost your job. So whoever held your mortgage—remember it may have been sold two or three times by now—could repossess your house and throw you out.

That's what subprime lending was all about. It would be bad enough for you to be thrown out of your home, but now the investors were afraid because they weren't sure about what resource they had invested in. What would happen if everyone stopped paying these new, higher monthly payments? The investment would be worthless. Streets were lined with rows of empty, repossessed houses. So what had seemed like sound investments turned to bad ones as more and more people defaulted. That led to a crisis with a number of banks and other lending agencies. They began to cry that capitalism couldn't work without them, they were "too big to fail." They were probably right. So various governments around the world stepped in to save them.

This is almost funny, when you think about it. Here are a bunch of robber capitalists trying to steal from working people. When their scheme backfires, they come crying to the government they never believed in and say, "Capitalism can't work without us, save us to save the system." And these same fat-cat failures are still drawing down their multimillion dollar compensation packages and bonuses, only with government money now, claiming it's the only way to keep "good people" in the industry. So much for the market punishing failures. But the funny part of it is that when this all came down, some people suggested that the government should actually buy stock in the banks. The people behind the scheme were the ones who had wanted the market to regulate everything without any government interference. Now the same people were begging for government interference. But the government purchasing stock in banks is the same as nationalizing the banks. Socialism! So, it seems, only a socialist system could keep a capitalist system going. Well, we think that's funny. It wasn't until August 2009 that Congress took the first moves to limit how much money financial robber barons could pay themselves for their great services to society.

The mortgages and packages of mortgages and other such financial instruments were fictions.

For instance, in 2014 Volkswagen, accustomed to dealing with German unions, agreed to allow United Auto Workers to organize a union in its new plant in Tennessee. Southern Republican lawmakers united to threaten to withhold future benefits and subsidies to any future foreign companies wishing to locate in the union-free South if workers voted in favor of the union. That would terminate any hope of jobs for working people, so these Republicans argued that if workers voted for a union, there would be no hope for future jobs. So the union lost that vote by a narrow margin.

Americans reading this book might ask why any company would want a union. Volkswagen wanted one so it could set up work councils like they have in Germany, arenas where management and workers can get together to improve the operation of the factory because managers have no idea what goes on during the production process and workers have no power to make any difference, but together they can improve the process. Some American firms have tried a kind of faux version of this, but never allowed workers any real decision making power.

But most U.S. companies are not like Volkswagen and do not agree to allow a union. That means you're going to have to fight for your union. When you have 30 percent of the employees signed up, you can file for an election, and the National Labor Relations Board will set a date and supervise the election. Between the announcement of the election and the time of the election, the boss will probably hire a "management consulting firm" to advise how much of the law he can break and how much he has to obey. Then he'll declare war on you and the union and probably fire you and the people you've been talking to. It's against the law, but it takes a long time to enforce the law. The boss knows that it'll scare the rest of the workers and he'll only have to pay you back pay if you finally do win your case in three years or so, the time it usually takes. He'll call in workers one by one, pull their personnel folders, look in them, and then look up at the worker and say, "I'm really worried about your future with this company. I'm worried about the people you talk to . . ." That's not considered a threat under the law, but tell that to someone to whom it's happened. So you're likely to lose the election.

The Employee Free Choice Act would tell the boss that he must negotiate with the union when a majority of workers sign up. If a majority show that they want a union by signing a card, they can have one without the election. Under this law Volkswagen workers in Tennessee would have a union. This is called "card check recognition," or recognition of a union by means of checking the cards people have signed. The law just takes the control of the process out of the boss's hands and puts it into the workers' hands. And it mandates that the boss must negotiate a contract within ninety days; if that fails, he must go to mediation; if that fails in thirty days, it must go to arbitration. In other words, the boss can't stall negotiating forever as he can under the present law.

So the National Manufacturers' Association and their state branches and the Chamber of Commerce and their local and state affiliates budgeted $200 million to fight this legislation. They mounted a nationwide big-lie campaign in which they misrepresented every dimension of this legislation. Why would anyone believe it?

In State College, Pennsylvania, the local NPR (National Public Radio) affiliate radio station broadcasted a news item right after the legislation was introduced. A Republican senator from Pennsylvania, Arlen Specter, was bucking the GOP leadership and supporting the stimulus legislation to fund building projects.

> *Arlen Specter cast what he calls his most difficult vote ever, nearly 30 years into his Senate career. That would be last month's "yes" on the $787 billion economic stimulus bill. It's a vote that made him the only Republican facing reelection next year to support it. Now, with GOP anger still simmering, Specter is under pressure to buck the party again and support "card check" legislation. That bill would make it easier for workers to form unions.* Opponents of the measure say that the bill would eliminate secret ballots when it comes to voting for or against unionizing, forcing workers to sign a card in public—instead of vote in private thereby opening the door to intimidation and coercion. *It's only the latest tight spot for the 79-year-old Republican senator. Specter says he is in meetings every day about the card check bill. But he's not revealing to anybody which way he is leaning.*

That's 154 words. The part in italics is 41 words, or 27 percent of the piece. And that part is wrong. Paul contacted the announcer who responded with this:

> *Nearly all of the story was directly from the AP [Associated Press], which described the bill simply by saying, "That bill would make it easier for workers to form unions." I am aware that there is considerable opposition to the bill, and wanted to outline, in one sentence, the major objection to it. The line summarizing that opposition is from the Web site of the U.S. Chamber of Commerce, which is one of the major organizations which stand in opposition to the bill.*

So, this guy takes an uncritical stance and winds up repeating part of the big lie the Chamber of Commerce is putting out. The next day, the local chamber issued its news release and there was the whole big lie again. So imagine this happening at radio stations and in newspapers all over the country because a professional spin doctor at the Chamber of Commerce is doing a good job. Most people hear the news and begin to think of the Employee Free Choice Act as some kind of thing that takes away peoples' right to vote. The right to vote is important, so they're against the legislation.

This was in 2009. In 2015 it was still not law and was nowhere close to becoming one. So, the big lie works. This one little example of hegemony shows how corporations manage mind control.

Corporations want you to be a good consumer and shut up about people who don't have health insurance and work two jobs and are still living under the poverty line. They want you to think that markets make that happen or people's bad choices make it happen. They want you to be more worried about whether abortions are murder or about your right to have a gun or about terrorists within our borders than you are about what *they* are doing. That's a lot of money, a lot of talent, and a lot of contacts that they contribute to making all of us think that what's happening in front of our eyes isn't really happening. They cover up the mistakes. They say that's the way it's supposed to be, the way it has to be. And we're not just talking about the Internet, radio, newspapers, and television. Many of these organizations and corporations have inroads into our public schools. From the time you enter first grade, you're getting lessons about how to follow orders, color within the lines, work hard and you'll get ahead, and more, as we discussed in the guide to students at the beginning of this book. In a lot of ways, we're living in what the movie *The Matrix* described.

Remember that's the same way the corporate cultural revolution came about. It worked then; it's working now. These are institutions that remove the feedback loops between reality and their actions.

Here we have a system that's as dangerous as one that's self-intensifying— one with no feedback loops from reality. It's as if we took that diagram from Chapter 3 (shown here as Figure 13-1)—and took out the loops to and from "reality." Replace "culture" with "genetics." If we acted that way as a species, we'd be as dead as a bunch of dodos by now. Adaptation means there is some kind of feedback between genetic changes and what happens next based on the realities the species faces. No species can survive the way the IMF does.

How does any of this affect us? More than we think.

Wal-Mart is one of the corporations driving this kind of process around the planet, as we saw in Chapter 12. It operates lots of factories in China. Communism in the Soviet Union gave us Stalin, and in China it gives us Wal-Mart. Now Wal-Mart is integrating the parts in between the factories in China and the Wal-Mart where you shop. It has its own container ships that go to the west coast of the United States. It's opened its own container facility at the Port of Houston, in Texas, but has to wait for the widening of the Panama Canal to receive the really big ships. It has its own trucks and drivers. And it is fanatically antiunion.

These are the things that worry Ken Riley, the president of Charleston, South Carolina's longshoremen's union, International Longshoremen's Association Local 1422. Ken and his fellow workers are probably the best-paid black people in South Carolina, the state with the lowest union membership in the country. South Carolina advertises itself that way like the third world country we mentioned earlier . . . they aren't going to have any unions, except maybe the longshoremen, who have been there and been organized longer than the forces that would destroy them. They belong to a union that controls the docks all the way up and down the East Coast. Because other organized longshoremen control the docks on the West Coast, in Korea, South America and in Europe. And the moment they relinquish control, it all goes down the drain.

What's the answer? Ken thinks the answer is for all the transportation workers and unions—the teamsters, the longshoremen, the airline workers, everyone—to get together and make a stronger union.

Globalization close up

Let's see how this looks close up. Your government gets caught up in a structural adjustment program and must pay back loans. It must cut spending, so the schools and clinics close and your kids don't have a school to go to. The department of agriculture stops all of its programs to help farmers, so there aren't any subsidies to keep the price of food down. Therefore, you must pay more for food. You have no access to land, so you can't grow anything, so you look for a job in a factory, and maybe you think that you're lucky to get one that pays enough for you to feed your family one day at a time. You feel so lucky that you don't complain when your supervisor rapes you in the back of the factory during the break. At least you didn't get pregnant; that would get you fired.

The government thinks you're lucky, too. It had to work hard to get that factory here. In fact, it had to tell the corporation that it wouldn't enforce any environmental regulations and would send the police or the army to help the corporation if you and your fellow workers tried to organize a union.

After a while, the water you've been getting from a stream or canal gets a funny color, odor, and taste to it. You first noticed it shortly after the factory started up. One of your kids is wheezing all the time with asthma, but you can't take her to a clinic because there isn't one. That one wheezes herself to death in your arms one night. Your skin is always itchy now. Maybe it has something to do with the water you bathe in. Another kid lives a few years and dies of cancer. Your husband can't find any work, but you keep working. When people talk to you about a union, you remember the people the death squads have killed and ask them to leave you alone.

Your breathing is labored now, and you remember that your mom died coughing up blood with what the nurse at the clinic called TB. One night you start coughing and can't stop. Your husband holds your head in his lap and strokes your hair and the lesions on your skin. You open your eyes for one more look, and the coughing takes over. You can't even tell him that you loved him; you can't thank him for the years with the kids. You feel your lungs turning inside out as you cough your last. You are twenty-eight.

You've made countless pairs of shoes, stitched countless shirts, woven untold numbers of sweaters, made plastic things you couldn't identify, because that was your job. That was what you could do for your species. You did it the best way you knew how.

Grim? You bet. But that's what many anthropologists see around the world. That's globalization from the other end of the telescope.

And you don't have to go far to see it. American students might want to spend some time just across their southern border, in Ciudad de Juarez, just across from El Paso, Texas. For Americans who live farther north, try South Carolina, Mississippi, Alabama, where the United States has imported third-world conditions. Europeans can cross the Mediterranean to Libya or any country in Africa or Asia or Latin America.

That's a good plan as long as the government allows it. But in 1999, a Danish shipping company decided to hire a stevedore—the guy who arranges everything at the docks—who was using nonunion labor. The Local 1422 guys picketed whenever one of the Danish ships came to port.

Figure 13-1 Our cultures tell us how to act and our actions change things.

In South Carolina, it's not just a labor thing. It's also a race thing. That same year, the NAACP declared a boycott on South Carolina until the state government agreed to remove the Confederate flag from the statehouse where it had been flying since . . . the Civil War? No—since 1961 when the federal government made its first civil rights laws. It's not about heritage; it's about racism and oppression.

Many anthropologists see that racism is a way to keep working-class people of all races so angry at each other that they don't recognize their enemies in the ruling class. So racism is about class.

One of the Danish company's ships arrived in Charleston and waited offshore until more than six hundred cops showed up, and marched up and down the street just down from the union hall, not far from where the Danish ship was docked. They barricaded streets downtown to keep people away from the docks. The show was meant to intimidate the longshoremen into no longer protesting the nonunion stevedore.

Ken told his guys to let them come. The state was using a lot of money to bring these cops and their helicopters, patrol boats, and dogs to Charleston. The men would not picket. They would not confront. That was a good plan. And it worked until late the night of January 19 when. . . .

Here you get different stories, and it doesn't really matter who threw the first blow. What matters is that the police had been provoking a confrontation by their massive presence, and they got one. That started a twenty-month-long battle between the longshoremen and the attorney general. The legislature got into the act and passed laws that were even more antiunion. Ken and the longshoremen have learned that if they give an inch, the ruling class will take a mile. We tell the whole story in our book, *On the Global Waterfront*.

The Charleston longshoremen are as much part of the global system as the third world workers in the factories that make the goods in the containers these men and women (there are a few) load and unload every day.

So how did that system get started? By the 1960s, American corporations were facing competition from other countries. They could either become more efficient, as we explained in Chapter 5—that is, use less labor to produce their products—or find some other way to reduce costs. Many focused on a sustained attack on organized labor that started about the same time as the changes in the Bretton Woods institutions, with Ronald Reagan. They thought that if they could bust unions, they would reduce their labor costs and not have to increase productivity.

They also started exporting jobs to third world countries that offered plentiful low-cost female workers for the labor-intensive manufacturing processes, such as making clothes, shoes, toys, and electronics. European countries still had tariffs in place to protect their industries and they had inexpensive migrant labor coming in from North Africa, Ireland, and the Mediterranean. Japanese corporations revamped their manufacturing methods and increased their productivity with robotics. They also made use of low-cost labor in Taiwan, South Korea, Thailand, and Malaysia.

Some countries tried to become self-sufficient by producing the products that they needed at home and avoiding imports. Remember, this is called import substitution, substituting your own products for imports, as we explained in a previous chapter. In Latin America, industrial workers organized into unions to demand a share of the fruits of the industrial system, a share of the surplus value they created. They joined with growing urban middle classes and rural migrants who were coming into cities because they had no other way to make a living. From these coalitions came populist political movements.

These movements and the unions made these countries unattractive to corporations that were looking for places to put factories that would assemble imported components to make a product for export. Corporations like GM wanted a labor force that did not expect or could not demand an increasing share of the surplus value they created. Hong Kong, Taiwan, Singapore, and South Korea were authoritarian states that controlled their middle classes and their workers, often with military help from the United States. In helping these governments, the United States was helping corporations get what they needed—cheap and controllable labor. But there was a side-effect. In supporting those corporations, the United States was supporting dictators and discouraging democracy. This is one reason the rest of the world does not see the United States as supporting democracy, but discouraging it.

The policies of different states created different environments. Latin American countries weren't so attractive to corporations; Asian countries were more attractive. The difference was how much they would repress any opposition. We've seen what happens to some small local economies when multinational corporations shift the emphasis from the country itself to the corporation and destroy the links in the economic system in the country.

In Chapter 5, we saw the upward spiral of capitalist economic systems. But there's a downside. As they enlarge productive capacity, they produce more than they can sell, so they look for new markets and reduce costs of production. That leads them to look for new markets and sell their factories, where they are required to pay higher wages, fire their middle management (like our friend's brother-in-law in Chapter 11), try to make full-time jobs into temporary or part-time jobs, and contract out some of the jobs.

The corporations paid lower wages, and that meant less demand because working people had less money in their pockets. As corporations moved factories and fired white-collar workers, there were fewer jobs and more people looking to social programs for help. With lower wages, the tax money wasn't coming in to support the social programs, and all of this can result in social and political problems.

We can illustrate these relationships with one of our systems diagrams, the mother of all diagrams (Figure 13-2). So get ready—we'll walk you through it.

There's one big self-intensifying loop in this diagram. From "surplus supply" to "pressure to reduce costs" to "cut labor costs" to the four boxes that are ways of cutting labor costs, from selling factories to firing middle management to making permanent jobs temporary and part-time to contracting jobs out—all of these mean fewer jobs, which is another way of saying more unemployment. That means less wages enter the economic system, so people have less money to spend, so there's less demand for goods, and that means that there's more stuff to sell than there are people with money to buy it.

Every loop through that cycle makes the problem of surplus supply greater, which leads to looking for new markets and relocating to different countries with policies that don't make corporations control pollution, that don't make them pay taxes, that provide markets for their stuff, and that offer to control labor supplies and not allow unions.

At the same time, fewer people are getting wages, and fewer wages in the economy means more people will need public health care, more people will be more annoyed because they can't support their families, and social and political problems will emerge. That is, people will do things that the ruling class sees as "problems." If there's a democracy, one of those things is to vote for populist candidates, as we discussed earlier. The pressure on corporations to reduce costs also ties into a series of other variables that the second diagram shows. As there is increased productivity, there is less profit per unit of stuff and, finally, less profit overall. That means corporations borrow capital and must pay interest, and paying interest means less profit. This is a self-intensifying loop, so the process gets faster and faster over time. And less profit means there's pressure to reduce costs. That's where we came in.

There's another process at work as well, what we might call the "politics of production." The state doesn't have anything to do with it, but it's a reorganization of corporations away from the business of producing things to producing wealth. As corporations borrow capital, the power in them shifts from management to finance people. And that means the money shamans take over. And that applies even more pressure to reduce costs. Americans saw this process at work early in 2009 as unemployment rates rose to historic levels.

An alternative to dealing with the causes of the social problems these processes bring is to deal with consequences by closing the lid down tight with repressive police power like George W. Bush tried to with his PATRIOT Act and like tin-horn dictators around the world do, often with U.S. support. Who benefits from the fear of terrorism and the subsequent repression? Not you. You're less safe because of these moves because they drive more and more people around the world into the arms of the revitalization movements and others who organize terrorists.

The speed-of-light communication systems allow for global financial markets. As larger productive capacity makes for greater productivity, there is less surplus value per unit produced, which means less profit. That situation increases the pressure to reduce costs we just talked about, and it leads corporations to borrow capital or get it on the stock market. But enlarging productivity means that corporations need more capital. So the reduction of profit per unit and the greater productive capacity lead corporations to the stock market or to markets to borrow money. That means they have to pay interest, and that reduces profits and makes for greater pressure to reduce costs. When finance becomes more important than production, the magic of money is more important than the realities of production. With their talk of realism and bottom lines, the money shamans take over corporations. Then the companies are not driven by what they produce and how they produce it, but by their finances. When that happens, if there is no regulation, they can make up their own numbers as Enron execs did, build a house of cards like Lehman Brothers did, or just lie like Bernie Madoff did.

As corporations spread their manufacturing around the planet, they isolate the process from any local or regional fluctuations; they remove

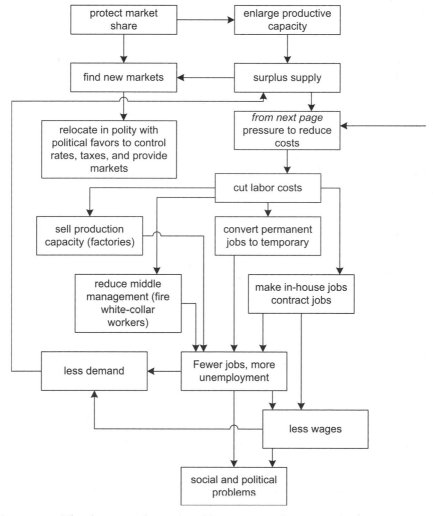

Figure 13-2 The downward spiral and how money shamans take over.

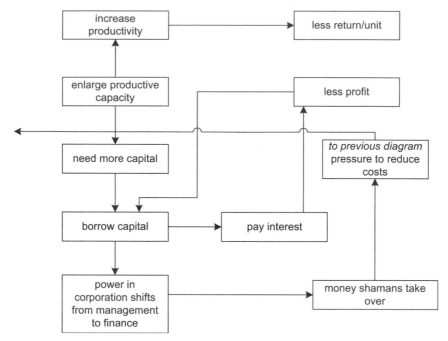

Figure 13-2 *(continued)*

themselves from any local systems and become their own system—just as Wal-Mart is doing. If there is a revolution in Burma, for instance, the corporation can move its factory to Sri Lanka or Israel or Mexico. Or, when the money shamans are in control, they can get out of production altogether and just contract it out to locals in different places. Take a look at the labels in your clothing. The stuff from any one famous brand is likely to be from several different continents. That's because they contract out the production, often to sweatshops in those other countries, always to the lowest bidder, thus fueling a race to the bottom to see what country can be most competitive by having the fewest environmental rules, financial rules, safety rules, or labor unions.

Now the corporate economic systems straddle a number of different places and states and are part of none. All the links are inside the corporation.

We've also seen that interest rates, inflation, government borrowing, balances of trade, and prices of goods are all related. Governments can try to control these variables by policies and institutional arrangements to control interest rates, expenditures for social programs, and taxes. But at the same time, states lose control of their own territorially based economic systems as the links of the systems are all inside corporations or "trade agreements" and not in states or other polities.

Add to this that the IMF controls the conditions for loans, and many governments have little influence on what happens in their own countries. Those states that can impose conditions on other states gain in power.

Some of the consequences of these processes are that some governments become irrelevant to their economic systems. That makes their political processes irrelevant—it doesn't matter how the leaders are selected because they can't do anything. The local economic systems everywhere are unlinked, disarticulated. As that happens more and more, people are driven to look for jobs for their subsistence, and it becomes less and less possible to make a living in a household economy. As poor people flood into cities from the country, there is more unemployment and a widening gap between the rich and the poor, a gap we see in the United States when we think of the difference between CEOs and burger flippers or when we look at income statistics over time.

Some countries, like the Scandinavian ones, have an idea that the government is supposed to help people. This idea that governments are to help people is called a **social contract**. Think of Social Security in the United States. If you work, you pay into it. It's not a pot of money that the government invests. What you pay is used to pay people who can't make a living because they're retired or injured or for some other reason. You pay your part to support those people, and you should be able to bet on everyone else paying their part to support you if you need it. That's called a *social contract*. You do your part, and everyone else does their part, and the government sets up the system and makes sure it runs fairly. This is the redistribution we discussed in Chapter 5.

As we wrote the first edition of this book, in 2005, Americans were talking seriously about changing that system, about doing away with the social contract. Instead of each person who works paying some of the way for those who can't, as in our Social Security system, the idea was that every person should set aside some money to put in the stock market. That called on everyone to bet their futures on the magic of money. Nobody would benefit, except the companies that would buy and sell stocks—and they are the ones that were big supporters of this move and the president who espoused it, the Republican George W. Bush. But it was based on another big lie, that the social security system was not working well.

From a few years down the historic road, it's clearer what was going on, but the debate was serious and had long-term consequences as the Bush administration actually succeeded in contracting out a number of government functions. So although fewer people worked for the government, the cost of government increased. Why? Because those in power gave the contracts to their friends, adding a layer of profit onto what was a government function. That's where the term "crony capitalism" comes from. Yes, the same people who say government costs too much also say the private sector can do the same job cheaper and better. Well, when everyone's stock market accounts crashed in 2008, people stopped talking about privatizing Social Security. But the whole idea came out of those corporate think tanks we mentioned earlier.

Let's go back to the IMF. When states stop funding schools and healthcare systems because the IMF demands structural adjustments, they are breaking the social contract they have with their people. People respond with populist political movements, as we discussed in Chapter 12, sometimes with revolutions. In Latin America, leftist and socialist parties have come to power, and a generation of charismatic leaders, such as Hugo Chávez and Nicolás Maduro in Venezuela, Rafael Correa of Ecuador, and Evo Morales in Bolivia arose.

One response may be localism and identity movements—people no longer take their identity from their country but from a smaller place, and they participate in identity politics. We get white separatist movements and Confederate flag movements. There's even a group called Christian Exodus that's urging its followers to move to South Carolina because it's so backward they hope to take over its politics, drop out of the United States, and invite everyone who doesn't agree with them or who is a different color to leave.

South Carolina was a good place to do this because it is backward. As the whole American economy slid into recession, South Carolina had the highest unemployment rate in the country, but proudly, also the lowest rate of union membership—and still does. Those two statistics are related. It is also near the bottom for every other measure of health and welfare that anyone has ever made. Its governor, Mark Sanford, also proudly announced he would not accept the stimulus package money available in early 2009 because of the strings attached: he would have to increase unemployment benefits and didn't believe Washington, D.C., should dictate that to a state. Eventually, he signed the papers to receive most of the money. Then he disappeared from his wife, family and supporters for a romp with his girlfriend. That ended his governorship, but, unbelievably, he made a comeback and got elected to Congress in 2013.

Finally, money magic is no longer even connected with production processes. People can talk about the bottom line of a company that doesn't even produce anything. Finance is no longer linked to the substantive economy and becomes its own sphere of magic. That makes for strange and unpredictable movements in global finance markets.

Two economic anthropologists, Monica Lindh de Montoya and Miguel Montoya, compared Sweden and Venezuela. Sweden's wealth is from manufacturing; Venezuela's is from oil. The Swedish government gets its revenues from taxes; Venezuela gets it from the world oil market.

If a corporation moves a factory from Sweden to the third world for cheap labor, it hurts the chances of Swedish workers to get jobs and hurts the Swedish economy. That means less tax income for the state. But what threatens Venezuela is dips in the world price of oil. Sweden maintains its social services and the social contract, but Venezuela has had to get loans and become a victim of the IMF.

There's no upheaval in Sweden. But in 1999 Venezuelans elected a populist president, Hugo Chavez. In Sweden, people can save some money and use it to invest in stocks. In Venezuela, people can't get ahead enough to think of buying stock. In Sweden, corporations must let people know everything they're doing. It's called transparency. People can see what companies are doing. In Venezuela, there are no such laws. Half the people in Sweden invest, but only 5 percent of Venezuelans do.

When Volvo threatened to move from Sweden, the stockholders got together to stop them. In Venezuela, that wouldn't have been possible.

THIS IS WHAT DEMOCRACY LOOKS LIKE

Caroline S. Conzelman
University of Colorado at Boulder

"Power concedes nothing without a demand."

—*Frederick Douglass*

Shortly after I began my ethnographic research in Bolivia in 2003, President Gonzalo Sánchez de Lozada (nicknamed Goni) secretly contracted with a private foreign corporation to extract and export natural gas. Infuriated, a group of Aymara people started a protest to reject Goni's deal and demand a national dialogue. For 500 years, they reasoned, this Andean region had been exploited for its raw materials—silver during the Spanish colonial era, oil in the early 1900s, and tin during WWII—primarily via forced labor under authoritarian governments, with the spectacular profits accruing to the wealthy few and very little reinvested to benefit indigenous peoples and their communities. Many people wanted both the energy and the profits from the gas reserves to be used for the development of Bolivia, so they got organized and spoke out.

The president—one of the original architects of Bolivia's neoliberal agenda to privatize industry and promote exports—rejected the call for dialogue. As more people blocked streets, Goni directed the military to restore order. Hundreds of protesters were injured and dozens killed. Soon tens of thousands of people around the country were marching and occupying government buildings demanding Goni's resignation. He finally stepped down and fled to the United States.

The U.S. Embassy stood by the Bolivian ruler, claiming that the protesters were anti-democratic because they were disrupting the economy and interfering with the electoral system. In this neoliberal view of democracy the only way to change leaders is through formal elections, and protest is not legitimate because it creates disorder. This ideology also associates democracy with an exclusively capitalist economy, so any perceived threat to the global hegemony of "free trade" is considered a subversion of democratic principles—and therefore a legitimate military target.

However, the protesters in the Gas War claimed that they were the true practitioners of democracy. To them, the right to peacefully assemble in public spaces, influence the design of their nation's economy, and demand transparency, accountability, and dialogue is what democracy is all about. As I would learn during my fieldwork with Aymara coca farmers, this grassroots democracy has deep roots in Andean communal life and the ancient cultural values of reciprocity, political and economic equality, and consensus.

The indigenous protesters called attention to their history of marginalization, exploitation, and oppression under 300 years of colonialism, 150 years of elite republicanism and capitalism, and 40 years of U.S.-backed military dictatorships and neoliberal austerity. Indigenous people weren't even considered citizens until the 1952 Revolution overthrew the old oligarchy. They have always challenged systematic injustices using diverse methods of individual and collective agency in the public sphere. In 2005, a broad coalition of social movements inspired a "democratic revolution" that resulted in the election of Evo Morales, Bolivia's first indigenous president, and the promotion of "Andean socialism."

This is what democracy looks like *continued*

Democracy is both system and process. It is meaning and practice. It springs from culture and place. It respects particular histories and dreams of the future. It can take many different forms and cannot be imposed from the outside without violence and the denial of the right to self-determination. Some assume that political science is the only way to study democracy, but anthropologists know that ethnography provides a more accurate portrayal of what this profound, complex, and ancient idea actually looks like on the ground.

In Sweden, people think about the social contract, and the country has a tradition of investing only in companies that treat their workers and the environment well. Nothing like that exists in Venezuela.

But Hugo Chavez paid off all of Venezuela's debts to the World Bank in 2007, five years early, and cut all relationships with the bank and the IMF. He moved Venezuela toward a more meaningful social contract with its people with a universally available program of health care, improved education, and other such social programs. In 2013, Hugo Chavez died. It was ironic to see some of the people who objected to Venezuela's nationalization of many parts of its economy begging the United States to nationalize its failed banking and automobile industries.

The market has spread all over the planet, and some states have become less important, whereas others have become more important. The spread of the market is not inevitable, natural, or an autonomous process. It's a consequence of state policies. But all states are not equal. The only ones that count are the G-8, and the most powerful of those is the United States.

That's a reason for Americans to feel proud, right? It could be, if Americans used that power to do what we discussed at the beginning of this chapter—to provide one share of this planet for every person on it. To the extent that their policies do not do that, Americans must be ashamed, not proud. And that's why in the beginning of the book we said that the impression that the United States is doing almost everything wrong is largely correct.

The states that establish the rules of globalization serve the interests of corporations. In serving the interests of corporations, these states are unable to serve the interests of their citizens by protecting their environments or ensuring their economic welfare. They break the social contract. In democratic states, those in which citizens elect governments, this causes tensions. There is a tension between the interests of corporations and the interests of the people. We saw this emerge in the United States in the Democratic victories at the polls in the 2006 election and even more in the 2008 election. But it is well to remember that although the Democrats won the election and President Obama enjoyed unprecedented popularity ratings well into his first year, the victory was not a great landslide. And most Americans never vote. In the midterm election of 2014 Americans returned Republicans to a majority in both houses of the U.S. Congress, just as after their meltdown, the Icelanders reelected the parties that caused it.

We see the same tensions playing out in the process of globalization as people gather from around the world to protest wherever international bodies meet to discuss policies of world trade. If we want to understand these movements and their manifestations from protest to suicide attacks, we must understand the systems that give rise to them.

Nasrudin would go to the market and buy ten eggs for one coin each and then sell ten eggs for the same amount he paid for each single egg. People said, "What kind of trading is this?"

Nasrudin said, "Look at the other traders. And look at me. I don't cheat anyone, and I am surrounded by customers who like me. What could be more satisfying than that?"

Discussion Questions

- Exporting industrial production—what happens when firms have factories all over the globe making different components of products they sell? What are the political and economic causes and consequences? What are the relevant systems?
- Exporting industrial agriculture—what happens to rural economies and communities when industrial production replaces household production?
- Check the zoning ordinances in your hometown, or a nearby city, on the Web. Do those rules apply to all companies and corporations? What's a variance? Who gets them?
- Some laws are local, some state, and some federal. What kind of laws do we have for international corporations? What happens if there aren't any?
- Do you know anyone who works for Wal-Mart, McDonald's, Burger King, or Subway? If you do, talk to them. Ask about their wages, benefits, and working conditions. Tell your classmates how it feels to work there. Can you think of any reasons a person might say it was a good job?
- Check on the Web to pick one community or state and see what it did with the 2009 stimulus package money it received. How much of that ended up in the pockets of working people and how much of it ended up as profit to private sector investors? If you can't tell, why can't you? How does it compare to programs you know about from the New Deal? What has changed since then to make a difference?

Suggested Reading

Beckford, George L. *Persistent Poverty: Underdevelopment in Plantation Economies of the Third World*. New York: Oxford University Press, 1972. (Reissued Kingston: University of West Indies Press, 2000.)

Greider, William. *One World Ready or Not: The Manic Logic of Global Capitalism*. New York: Simon & Schuster, 1998.

Lewellen, Ted. *The Anthropology of Globalization: Cultural Anthropology Enters the 21st Century*. Westport, CT: Bergin & Garvey, 2002.

Who decides how much the shrimp boats harvest? *Photo by E. Paul Durrenberger.*

14

Connecting the People to the System

Did you ever wonder who made your T-shirts, blue jeans, cellphones, tablets, computers, shoes, cars, and other commodities that keep the American and other consumer economies going? When we talked about low-wage factory work fueling the global system, it was just an abstraction. When we talked about young women doing most of the work, it was another abstraction. But anthropologists like to know those people personally.

In the previous chapter, you saw how the global system operates, but you didn't see any people in those systems. It's all just arrows and boxes. Ethnography—the details of closely observed daily lives—is one leg of the stool that also depends for its balance on comparison and holism. We try to understand whole systems of relationships and then to place them in comparative perspective to draw inferences about the human condition.

But what happens when the stories are not located in any particular place? What do we do when we realize that the causal factors are located at great distance from the places where we do ethnography? What do we do when we find out that no matter how detailed our observations of daily life, no matter how moving our accounts or accurate our methodologies, all of our work is missing the major causes, and we are just describing consequences?

The system, the relations, the holism, the dynamics of the realities escape our worm's-eye view of ethnography. So what was once anthropology's great strength—our ability to describe and understand daily life as people live it—becomes one of our great weaknesses as we attempt to understand the reasons, the forces, the determinants of daily life anywhere on the planet. We move with the people. This is and has been our great contribution. We check the assumptions of the great thinkers as we see people living their lives.

Ride with a former International Brotherhood of Electrical Workers union rep as he drives through Chicago pointing out abandoned factory buildings saying, "This plant used to be ours. Gone to Mexico. And this one." Go with Paul to the docks of Biloxi in the late 1980s, before Hurricane Katrina destroyed it, just before the gambling boats arrived, to hear the shrimpers talking about the threat of imports, the threat of foreign pond-raised shrimp, the problem of too many boats chasing too few shrimp, as they called it.

If he just looked at the statistics and worked on the assumptions of economics, Paul would see a tragedy of the commons. Remember, that's what economists call it when everyone has free access to a resource like a common pasture and puts as many sheep or cows on the common ground as they can because they have nothing to lose, and if they don't, someone else will. Then, according to economists, pretty soon the commons is overgrazed and useless to anyone. This is usually a story they tell to persuade people that everything should be private property. Lots of ethnography shows that in reality people aren't that stupid. But what if the people directly using the commons aren't the ones making the decisions?

Paul found that the Biloxi shrimpers themselves didn't make any of the important decisions. To focus on the shrimpers left out the processors who did make the important decisions.. As long as Paul focused on the docks or the boats or even the fishing industry, he could only have vague intuitions about the nature of the important systems and how they were affecting the shrimpers.

So he read what a couple of sociologists, Alessandro Bonanno and Douglas Constance, chronicled of the rise and fall of tuna canneries in California. The joining of nylon nets with power blocks to pull them with engines in 1957 revolutionized the tuna-fishing industry. American tuna operations expanded their operations from Mexico to Chile. Postwar reconstruction legislation gave the Japanese a distant-water fishing fleet to supply American canneries on American Samoa. As labor costs escalated in the 1970s, the Japanese made use of lower-cost labor and capital from Taiwan, Korea, and Malaysia. Meanwhile, the fleets of Taiwan and Korea expanded and offered competition.

In some areas, porpoises swim with tuna, so purse seiners set their nets on schools of porpoises to catch the tuna but in the process kill the porpoises. The response to the killing of porpoises led to the passage of the U.S. Marine Mammal Protection Act of 1972, which set a quota on tuna to control porpoise killing.

Fishers invested in larger boats to maximize their share of the quota before it was filled, so tuna boats grew larger. The American fleet was excluded from its usual tuna grounds in the 1970s when many nations adopted the increasingly common two-hundred-mile exclusive economic zones and reserved these waters for their own nationals. At the same time, Latin American countries developed national tuna fisheries, which increased competition for tuna and markets. American fishers began to exploit the western Pacific until the newly emerging nations in the Pacific Islands claimed their exclusive two-hundred-mile economic zones.

During the same decade, processors purchased purse-seining boats to integrate vertically to ensure constant supply for their canneries in California and to meet the growing U.S. demand. In the 1980s, the world tuna fleet caught more tuna than the market could absorb, beef and poultry prices were low, and there was an economic recession. In the United States, a major market for world tuna, sales declined.

Costs of fuel, labor, and finance increased, and many U.S. tuna producers left the market. Because the U.S. dollar was strong relative to other currencies, producers of other lands were better able than U.S. producers to withstand the cost–price squeeze. Because of this imbalance in currency values, their costs were less if they were in pesos rather than U.S. dollars. This led to a redistribution of tuna fishing and started the restructuring of the world industry. All but one continental U.S. tuna cannery closed. The same ten multinational corporations catch, process, and trade tuna. As interest rates and the carrying costs of boats increased, vertically integrated corporations sold their tuna boats to shift the risk to operators. They then imported foreign-caught or processed tuna on the world spot market and expanded into shipping to supply their plants.

Causes of these shifts include the exclusive economic zones, fluctuations of exchange rates, the world recession, the corporate responses of seeking lower wages and production costs, local policies to attract industry, international financial moves, tax policies, interest rates, and new processing and shipping technologies.

Anthropologists can't see any of these processes with ethnography. If we stay on the docks of Biloxi with Paul, we couldn't see any of the factors that determine the lives of the people who live there.

When Paul's students read Bonanno and Constance's book, they complained that they read through the first half of the book before they ever got to any ethnography, and even then it was pretty thin. It was all theory and tables and accounting stuff. How was that anthropology? To be fair, it was sociology.

Just before that they had read Mary Beth Mills's ethnography of Thai factory women. Mills discussed the consolidation of the Thai state and its incorporation of the Lao people in the Northeast, but she didn't explain where the factories came from or why they are in Thailand or how they affected the Thai economy. In her ethnography, students saw the workers, but not the system that puts a factory there in the first place. One place those factories came from is the restructuring of the tuna industry.

Here's how that worked: the Thai Board of Trade favors export-oriented firms to generate foreign currency to help with the balance of trade—the kind of money magic the IMF likes. That makes Thailand a favorable locale for tuna-canning factories. The fourth largest company in Australia has seven tuna-processing plants in Thailand. A subsidiary in San Diego purchases frozen tuna on the world market to import to the Thai factories. The same subsidiary distributes Thai tuna products in the United States.

Most of the labor cost of processing tuna is from slicing off the meat. Processors therefore remove the meat where labor is cheap, freeze it, and ship it to plants in U.S. territory, such as American Samoa or Puerto Rico, where it can be canned and sold as a product of the United States. U.S. processors have met foreign competition by relying on the world market for tuna meat rather than catching the fish with their own boats, and they can send it to Thailand for even cheaper processing. In 1990, twenty-two tuna canneries were operating in Thailand.

By 1987, 35 percent of American tuna was imported from Thailand, forcing U.S. processors to move offshore and close their mainland canneries because of high operating costs. They couldn't withstand the foreign competition as the amount of imported tuna tripled, and U.S. companies began to put their labels on imported canned products.

Where is the ethnography? We can't see these processes ethnographically. If we follow the daily lives of factory workers as Mills did or of fishers as Paul did, we lose sight of the causal variables, the factors that determine the conditions of their lives. We study dependent variables and ignore independent variables.

But to concentrate on those systems takes us far away from the docks and the boats, the coffeehouses and bars where ethnographers feel more comfortable hanging out with shrimpers and workers. It takes us to corporate reports and archives, to tables of numbers and abstractions that we can't see. It takes us to those nowhere lands where there are no people, the systems that somehow exist in another dimension created by the cultural imagination, places like corporations and nations and agencies. When we find people to talk to, they will be wearing stockings, high-heeled shoes, neckties, jackets. Many anthropologists, accustomed to moving with working people, farmers, and peasants, feel uneasy moving with these "suits."

So we keep doing ethnography. We keep on checking our ideas with what we can observe in everyday life. That's what Josiah McC. Heyman did in his study of the U.S.–Mexico border region. His meticulously detailed history of the region is based on understanding the dynamics of households while they tried to make their livings under the changing conditions of the border as mines came and went and as people were moved around according to the needs of capital for labor. See the sidebar for just part of the complex story that he tells in his book, *Life and Labor on the Border.*

In Heyman's ethnography we see the direct consequences of money magic and the global system for the everyday lives of working people. And it hasn't been good. So if jobs are leaving the United States to go to Mexico and it's not doing the Mexicans any good, who is benefiting? Capital. Corporations and banks.

But that's not the end of the story. These factories are owned by companies from all over the world: Malaysia, the Philippines, China, Mexico, the United States, Spain, Japan, Taiwan, and Korea. In 1998, Mexico hiked the minimum wage 14 percent, but the price of goods had gone up 18.6 percent. Workers were still losing out. In 1987, it took eight hours and forty-seven minutes of wage labor at minimum wage to earn enough to buy the $54 basic subsistence "basket" of goods for two people for a week. In 1998, it took thirty-four hours. That's nearly four times more time for the same money. In terms of household economies, that means the productivity of labor was about one-quarter of what it had been. And this is just for a couple, not for any kids or older people. In 1998, the Mexican government removed its subsidy for tortillas so that their price doubled.

Back to money magic. Between 1998 and 2002, dollars went down relative to pesos. That means that pesos gained some value relative to dollars: more dollars per peso. But the dollar strengthened relative to the money of

The Move to Mexico

In 1965, Mexico established the legal framework for large export factories or maquiladoras with its Border Industrialization Program. This was like the Thai or the Chinese government enticing industry. The program established a zone with special privileges for foreign companies. They wouldn't have to pay tariffs on imports, many of them paid no taxes, and foreigners could own land in the zone. The first factory came to Agua Prieta, just across the border from Douglas, Arizona, in 1967. By 1986, there were twenty-six of them. Most of the workers in the factories, as in China, Thailand, and Indonesia, are young women. They can provide their families with a regular paycheck.

Young men seek to establish broad networks of relationships that will guarantee them a choice of various alternatives in the future. The short-term cost of this flexible income strategy is that they may be out of work at any given time but their contacts give them more opportunities for the future. The women deal with this unpredictability by being steadily employed in the factories, even if they don't pay good wages. The young women coordinate their work with the older women of the households, who do most of the domestic work. In the early 1970s, the workers spent much of their income, about 40 percent of it, in Arizona, but this depended on a stable exchange rate between pesos and dollars.

Then, in 1982, Mexico suffered an economic crisis brought on by many of the forces discussed in the previous chapter. By 1987, the peso was worth one-hundredth of its 1982 value in dollars. Suddenly it was if their dollar had become worth a penny when they tried to buy things in the United States.

Mexico has a huge foreign debt and cannot repay the principal. It struggles just to pay interest. That means it must increase exports so that they are more than imports—that is, improve their balance of payments to raise money to pay interest. The border factories contribute to increasing the exports to improve the balance of payments, so they're important to the money shamans of Mexico. There are plenty of other places with cheap labor competing for factories. The Mexican government had to reduce the real wages of workers to compete with the Caribbean and East Asia in a race to the bottom.

By one calculation, in 1986, the real wages of Mexican workers were just over half, 60 percent, of what it was in 1982; by another, they were just under half, at 45 percent. That's drastic either way you figure it. The 1982 minimum wage was $74.64 per week. In 1986, it was $23 per week. That's less than $5 per day. To boost exports, factory sound trucks drove through neighborhoods advertising for workers. Because people were worse off, they worked more to try to keep even. Households started sending younger children to work in the factories.

International capital created conditions in Mexico to coerce them into supplying cheap labor via crippling loans on which Mexico must pay interest. This is a way to recruit labor into the factories like the enclosures in England did. It's another way to give people no alternative but factory work.

The minimum wage is so low and household needs are so great that factory managers can manipulate and control their young women workers by even small bonuses, awards for overtime, and other privileges.

The Move to Mexico *continued*

The official or corporatist unions in Mexico are part of the government. They don't have much to do with the workers. Since low wages are part of the government's policy, the official unions don't challenge it. The devaluation of the peso destroyed the cross-border way of life. The policy of strong exports and low wages meant lives of factory drudgery for many, and such things as building or owning a house and education for kids are not possible to attain.

the Philippines, Sri Lanka, Singapore, Malaysia, and Thailand. That meant that the same dollar could buy more in those lands at the same time it bought less in Mexico. So the dollars capital paid for labor in Mexico went up in Mexico and down in Asia. Since 2002, the dollar has increased again against pesos. That lowered the cost of business in Mexico. This is the kind of thing international financiers keep an eye on.

In 1994, the North American Free Trade Agreement (NAFTA) set up new rules for clothing and textiles. The special breaks in tariffs that Mexico got under NAFTA let it replace China as the largest supplier of cloth and clothing to the United States. But then in 2000, the United States gave the same breaks to the Caribbean, Central America, and China. In 2001, when China joined the World Trade Organization, the United States gave China other breaks, and China and the Caribbean became the leading suppliers of clothing and cloth to the United States. The question is whether Mexico can drive down living standards and wages even more to keep up its exports to pay the interest on its debts. Each move in this international game of finance and manufacturing, each change of rules and regulations, means a worse life for workers all over the world.

Many of these plants use toxic chemicals, including heavy metals, solvents, and acids. There are no adequate systems of water treatment to control environmental pollution. Letting you work in a poisonous factory that's polluting your air and water so that you can get by until the next day is no favor. Most maquiladora workers are women between sixteen and twenty-eight. It is not only their health at stake but also that of their kids.

This system plays out in different ways in different countries. Sometimes the women work in factories and bring a paycheck home to help out, as in Mexico and Indonesia. Other times, they leave home and move to where the factories are. There, like the earliest industrial workers in the United States in the age of water power, they live in dormitories or crowded urban rooms, as in China and Thailand.

Here's the important lesson. It's one that economists don't understand: the working people of the world don't have any important decisions to make in this system. Nothing they can do or say or decide or think has anything to do with how it operates. How does a decision to buy one less tortilla because the price doubled affect the laws of NAFTA or the interest that Mexico owes or the fact that their government feels they actually have to pay the interest on such monstrous loans? As long as it's business as usual, working people cannot do anything. To exercise any agency, people must be able to imagine different systems. Then they join the Zapatistas. But that's a different part of Mexico, way south in Chiapas.

When the international banking community demanded a restructuring of the Mexican economy to better pay interest on the loans, the government cut off subsidies to peasants for fertilizers and chemicals and removed price supports for crops. The government wanted to obliterate traditional peasants and replace them with industrial agriculture, as we discussed earlier with regard to Russia and the United States. They wanted them to produce export crops and improve the balance of payments. They wanted to see the communal lands of peasant communities privately owned. These changes went through in 1992.

On January 1, 1994, the first day of NAFTA, the Zapatista Army of National Liberation seized towns in eastern and central Chiapas and proclaimed a revolution. Today the revolution continues. Chiapas is full of anthropologists who know the people and the area up close and personal. They've done and are doing the ethnography. We can't tell the story here, but you can read it in the books by June Nash and George Collier and Elizabeth Lowery Quaratiello. So extreme conditions make for extreme responses. But there is some sense of agency.

Mills describes how schools and government programs impose nationalism, Thai ethnic identity, and language in the Lao areas of northeastern Thailand. New roads allowed rural people to develop new economic relations with distant markets and moved peasants toward producing cash crops for commodities, as we discussed in Chapter 12. Young women from these peasant households do not go to Bangkok and work in factories because they need to support their families. They do it in response to images of modernity from Thai elites in mass media, bureaucracies, and schools. The wages the young women send home do make contributions to poor households, but they're most important to prosperous households that have enough land to make good livings. Here's why: the young women yearn for the modern consuming lifestyle and adventure in the big city, but they must balance that against their sense of duty. Working in Bangkok goes against the ideal of feminine restraint and virginal purity, but the contributions to the households show they are dutiful daughters supporting their families at home so that they can pay the expenses of farming, educating younger siblings, building new houses, and making donations to the Buddhist temples. These show their morality, whereas televisions and refrigerators they buy for their parents show their modernity.

But low-wage workers in Bangkok can't live the high life of urban adventure or consumption. The girls use most of their wages for food and crowded living quarters. They have running water, electricity, markets, and some entertainment, but they must put up with pollution, noise, congestion, crowding, isolation, insecurity, and unhealthy and oppressive working conditions.

Managers try to use traditional patron–client roles to control women, but the women don't accept it. However, any slight protest they may make is quickly disciplined. The Thai government has a history of violence against any demonstrations and labor organizing.

It's hard enough for single women, but if they're married and have kids, they have that many more mouths to feed. They get out of their houses and away from their parents, but they don't have any relatives to help them when they need it. If women manage to get a little education, their opportunities in the rural villages are limited. About the only possibility is to go home, get married, raise kids, and become an agricultural worker. Whether they stay in the city or return to the village, these women accommodate rather than challenge economic and political structures. Images of modernity emphasize the goals of individual fulfillment and self-expression and shift the women's attention away from their oppressive conditions that limit their opportunities to actually be the modern people they imagine they might be. The villages raise the kids to provide the factory labor when they grow up and offer a place to return home to when they're used up by the time they're thirty. In this way the villages subsidize the low wages the firms pay their workers.

The political situation in Thailand is complex. In 2001 the people elected a populist prime minister who instituted many programs to benefit poor and rural people, but an alliance of the ruling class sponsored a coup d'etat in 2006 to depose him. In 2010, his supporters organized mass demonstrations in Bangkok to force the government to hold new elections. A military crackdown killed eighty and wounded more than two thousand people. In 2010 there were further demonstrations and another crackdown with consequent killings and injuries. After a sniper killed a protest leader while reporters were interviewing him, the demonstrations intensified and the crackdown spread throughout the country. Demonstrations continued through 2014 when the military staged a coup and declared martial law. It's difficult to penetrate through the details of who did what to whom to get to the underlying dynamics of these events, so we will just mention them and let you use what you have learned here to figure that out, but our guess is that it has to do, as it does in other countries, with the conflict between the owners of capital and the workers of the country.

In Indonesia, Diane Wolf learned about households whose daughters work in factories. Although some anthropologists talk about "household strategies" or plans, in fact, people in poor Indonesian households make decisions experimentally as they go along. They do not have strategies. They don't enjoy the luxury of being able to plan into the future. There may be household coping mechanisms or household practices, but no strategies or planning.

Unlike in Thailand, in Indonesia there is a relationship between the resources available to households and the likelihood that their daughters will work in factories. However, Wolf shows that whereas households of factory workers are poor in land, women from the poorest families with many dependents do not work in factories because others in the household need them

Chinese factory girls

Hong Kong anthropologist Pun Ngai worked in a factory that made navigational components for German cars. Hong Kong people owned the electronics factory that was located in an industrial village of the Shenzhen special economic zone in Guangdong Province.

Pun Ngai tells us that young rural Chinese women are leaving their villages to work in special industrial zones where the Communist government has allowed and even encouraged international capitalists to build factories like the maquiladora factories in Mexico to feed the insatiable markets for products. The young Chinese women are caught up in three different systems that sometimes work together and sometimes work against each other:

- The socialist state, with strict restrictions on where people can live;
- Global capitalist production with its continual need for disciplined labor and ever-increasing consumption; and
- The patriarchal Chinese family system, with its oppression of women.

Pun Ngai chronicles women's struggles to form and live their identities; discover the range of choice, how much agency they actually have, among the different pushes and pulls of these systems; and maintain their senses of self in the face of often absurd circumstances that the larger systems determine.

After its revolution in China made in the name of the urban working class, the Chinese Communist Party made the workers or proletarians (*gongren*) a privileged class. These proletarians were workers, neither male nor female, but the status of worker was out of reach of the vast rural peasantry.

This working class wasn't so much real as it was something necessary for Mao's Communist ideology. But Deng Xiaoping started neoliberal reforms, and his kind of Communism imported global factories and denounced any practices or ideologies that might get in the way. One thing that would surely get in the way of these factories would be anything like class struggle. After all, the Communist state is collaborating with global capitalism.

But a product of the factories is a *real* working class. This working class isn't just something people invented because it fit an ideology. In fact, the state would really rather that nobody noticed they were in the working class. So, in China, as the economic system changed and created a real working class, the state began to deny that there is any working class. The Communist Party that was supposed to be the leaders of the working class now invites businessmen, managers, and capitalists to join up and be comrades.

Most of the new workers are rural women who get temporary changes of their residency status so they can live in the growing manufacturing centers. The Chinese term *dagong* means "working for the boss" or "selling labor," and it means that you're selling your labor. If Mao's revolution was meant to free working people, those working people are now selling labor to capitalists with the blessings of the Communist state. The Chinese word *mei* means "younger sister," but it also means a young and

---

Chinese factory girls *continued*

unmarried woman. Chinese put the two words together to get *dagongmei*, which means something like "factory girl."

The male counterpart is *dagongzai*. Industrial commodity labor is highly gendered, and the young women are constantly reminded formally and informally that their roles and their work are the roles and work of young women.

These women work long hours at exhausting jobs and live in crowded dormitories because they want to consume the stuff of modernity—they want to be modern women with fashionable clothes and makeup and hair. This consumer desire changes the disciplined and obedient factory girls into shameless sexual women who are seductive and liberated enough to release the lust of the consumer who always wants to buy more stuff. Their desire to be like city dwellers drives dagongmei fantasies of consumption that their wages cannot support. In fact, they are rural women—they walk and talk and act like rural women. No amount of makeup or new clothes can change that. In trying to live up to images of womanly beauty and disguise their rural origins, they just reinforce their class and gender differences.

In Mao's China, everyone was a comrade, neither male nor female, neither high nor low. Reform China replaces the classless, sexless comrade with sexualized consumers and producers in highly gendered workplaces. People seek identity in consumption. The more they try to move themselves away from rural poverty and become modern women, the greater their desire to consume, and the harder they work to get the money to buy the goods. Here is another self-intensifying loop. The more stuff they buy, the more they emphasize their original identity as rural women.

Chinese patriarchy worked as well with Chinese socialism as it does with capitalism. Urban men don't want these working girls as wives. At about the age of twenty-five, most women factory workers return to their villages to be married into the patriarchal households they were trying to escape.

---

for the daily work of maintaining the household or to take care of children. Corporations have "conveniently" located their factories in rural areas.

The Indonesian factory workers continue to live in their own households with their fathers and mothers and siblings. They don't have to move to the big city and live in cramped rooms like the Thai factory workers. They don't escape the control of their parents, but since they make major contributions to their households, their position in the household changes, and they have a lot more influence than they would if they didn't work.

There is no escape for the Arab women who work in Israeli factories. The anthropologist Israel Drori's ethnography shows how managers use cultural understandings to control women and make them subservient. They expand the local forms of patriarchy beyond the homes into their work lives to manage the women who produce clothing for the international market. He shows the cynical use of knowledge not to understand people or help them, but to subordinate them on the job.

Drori documents the daily lives of Druze and Arab seamstresses and supervisors in the Galilee region of northern Israel as they fell in love and were torn from their lovers; as they anticipated establishing their own households; as they got married and were raped by husbands; as they worked day in and day out to bring income into their male-dominated households.

Israeli managers acted like fathers and brothers to control women as Arab men control daughters and sisters. These roles expressed closeness within relationships of unequal power. Women gained some autonomy through their work, but the work just put patriarchy in another form in the factory; it didn't let the women escape it.

Drori shows the seamstresses negotiating the shared culture of work in these plants by the way they give meaning to their work, negotiate with management, and attempt to redefine concepts of gender, rights, obligations, and autonomy in terms of familiar family values that bridge their home lives and their work lives. By relating to management as patriarchs, workers use the moral feelings and behavior they know from home. But this use of home-like relationships at work contributes to complex, self-contradictory, interlocking activities that can lead to conflict. The reconstruction of patriarchal relationships in the plants creates an organizational culture of control that maintains hierarchal relationships at work.

Management must create a work culture of shared meaning that derives from both local homes and their managerial responsibilities. If the managers want to use the women's labor, they must do it in terms that are acceptable to the workers' male family and community members and keep the production lines running in the factories.

Drori had to make some hard choices of his own. To make room for his vivid ethnographic treatment of the lives of workers and managers in complex situations, he had to sacrifice discussing larger issues, such as the enduring violence of the area, the subjugation of peoples and their resistance and fight against it, and the struggle of labor to organize a collective voice through unions. Although most organized labor in Israel belongs to the General Labor Union, the ethnography shows that such a structure is ineffective, perhaps counterproductive, for representing the interests of Arab and Druze women in the Israeli garment industry.

Seamstresses are not subservient, quiet, apathetic, or fatalistic but passionate, active, and determined to seize opportunities to better their lives when they arise. The problem is that such opportunities never arise. All of the passion, activity, noisiness, agency, and determination of these women comes to nothing without institutional structures that could make these women effective at changing rather than adapting to their situations.

One more example. We've mentioned Iceland and the neoliberal governments that wanted to break the social contract and put everything on a market basis and how that initiated the ITQs or individual transferable quotas. That meant making the fish in the sea private property rather than an open-access resource that everyone could use. These policies turned out to be important keys to the economic meltdown of the country because these were just the first steps in a series of neoliberal policies that destroyed the country's economy and its government and has threatened the independence of the nation.

It's ironic that the Icelandic economist Ragnar Arnason wrote about the great benefits of the ITQ system in glowing terms in the *Electronic Journal of Sustainable Development* in 2008 as Iceland teetered on the brink of collapse. Remember what we said about economists being optimists with no feet on the ground or any idea of reality? This is an excellent example. Arnason compared fishery resources to oil with the important difference that fish stocks are renewable so the profits from them are sustainable. But, he argued, because of inappropriate institutional structures, especially because people often treat fish as a common pool resource instead of private property, there is too much fishing capital, the price of fish goes up, and the quality of the environment goes down. This is just another case of the economists' misunderstanding of what they call the tragedy of the commons.

There is no profit in the system and governments lose money if they subsidize unprofitable fisheries just to supply food or to keep people employed according to the social contract. He argued that because the problem is made by policy, there is a policy solution—to define harvesting rights and allow only those who own them to fish—something like ITQs.

The benefits are increased efficiency because of less effort (fewer people fishing), less capital (fewer boats), higher quality fish, larger stocks of fish, and better coordination between the supply of fish and market demand. All fisheries problems solved by the wisdom of an economist! And the virtues of private property. Remember, economists base their whole discipline on the idea of private property and their chief duty is to make corporations and capitalism seem natural and inevitable.

An important economic outcome, our Icelandic economist continues, is that the quotas themselves come to have value; a market for them develops where people can buy, sell, and trade the quotas. Now the right to fish is a commodity akin to an oil lease—permission to take oil from a place. So in Iceland, companies formed to own quotas. The companies' stock was then traded on the stock market. So we go from fish to the right to catch fish to a share in a company's ownership of rights to catch fish. This is the beginning of what the novelist Einar Már Gudmundsson calls a web of deceit.

The value of the quotas depends on how much profit people expect them to yield. They're like shares of a company that pays dividends. This lets people put a money value on the whole Icelandic fishery. As more and more species were included in the ITQ system, the total value of the fishery increased to between $3.5 billion and $4.5 billion. By 2002, ITQ values came to equal more than 40 percent of the annual gross domestic product of the country. The relative proportion declined after that because other sectors of the economy grew rapidly, chiefly the magical ones—financial firms and banks that ran on the value of the ITQs.

The important point is not just what part of the economy the quotas represent. Arnason (2008 p. 38) says, "The crucial point is that these ITQ values represent new wealth that did not exist before." These were marketable assets. Wealth created from nothing.

You just can't beat that! This is a way to create wealth without the bother of doing any work, by just announcing a policy! But that's not all. You can use this wealth as the basis for raising financial capital, and that's what happened in Iceland. People sold their quotas and moved their winnings—their capital—into other sectors of the economy. The new capital went into the financial sector. Other things that helped were other privatizations and reductions of corporate taxes. Banks and investment companies expanded as government regulations were dropped and banks were privately run rather than government operated.

Some people like Gísli Pálsson, Agnar Helgason, and Einar Eythórsson pointed to the dangers of ITQs—increasing concentration of wealth, decreasing involvement with fishing by those who controlled the fishery, and decreasing adherence to the idea that fish processing should benefit local communities. But economists would not see those as dangers. As stock companies formed, the owners of the quotas knew nothing about fishing. Crewmen lost income and struck in 1994, 1995, and 1998 until a new share system was negotiated.

We have said before that Iceland has a system that is designed on the basis of a social contract to look after people—to guarantee jobs, housing, health care, education, and retirement. But this depends on seeing these things as rights, not as commodities. So as the idea of replacing rights with commodities began in fisheries, there were contradictions with the law. Various court cases have failed to reconcile these contradictions of the ITQ system in Iceland.

The Icelandic constitution grants equal employment rights to all citizens, and the Fisheries Management Act of 1990 defines fish resources as public property; therefore, it must be unlawful to deny a person a quota just because he didn't own a boat at the time the ITQ system was started. On the other hand, the rights had been permanently given away, so the whole system must be unconstitutional. But the Icelandic supreme court has also found that the permanent allocation of ITQs is constitutional because the quotas are private property.

But Eythórsson said that the ITQs are the basis for the economic strength of companies with large quota holdings and have contributed to the profits of those companies. Another consequence of ITQs has been a change in the way fisheries policy is determined. Instead of negotiations between all of the component organizations and owners—crew, skippers, owners—meeting in an assembly with people from the Department of Fisheries, each representing their own interests as we discussed for Scandinavian fishers in Chapter 13, these varied interests were replaced by two committees of politicians, lawyers, and economists . . . but no one who knows anything about fisheries— fishers, skippers, or boat owners.

Eythórsson asks how it is possible for a system that lacks consensus and that a majority of people oppose to be established and maintained. He suggests that it is because some decisions are irreversible and that most organizations and individuals have at one time or another been co-opted during the decision-making process. If any group is sufficiently organized to raise hell, it can negotiate something that will keep them happy, but keep the system going. Then they have some stake in the future of the system itself and are less likely to object to anything

But after the ITQs in the fisheries, everything became fodder for the neoliberal formula of the market: the telephone system, the energy system, and finally, in 2000, the government-run banks were privatized.

The journalists Nigel Holmes and Megan McCardle chronicled the decline from there. The bankers had good political connections and were able to get the regulations lifted. The banks borrowed heavily from foreign lenders and depositors.

Although Americans are great ones for buying on credit, Icelanders took the idea one step further. If wealth is free, anyone can get in on it. You might think it's a bit over the top that Americans spent about 140 percent of their income, but Icelanders took that up to 213 percent per household. The average household "wealth" grew by about half. Note that that wealth is not real. It's not tons of fish or piles of yams but fictitious financial "objects" like stocks, all of which was built on money borrowed from foreign sources by banks that weren't regulated.

As debt grew, so did interest rates in Iceland. Banks advertised high interest rates in Great Britain and a lot of British people deposited money with them to cash in on the easy money. Among the depositors were many municipalities and other agencies of local governments looking for some safe place to park some cash for a while and maybe relieve their burden on taxpayers—such as police departments. These deposits came to a total of $1.3 billion.

With only small capital reserves, the Icelandic banks began lending money and grew quickly—on paper. But without any regulations, they didn't limit their lending to the amount of money they had—they borrowed more. But with small cash reserves, they couldn't pay the money back. But there was no law or rule against that, so they kept doing it.

Then they financed investment firms that started buying stocks across Europe with borrowed funds. So you could buy stock in a company that just bought other stocks. The stock market rose at an average of 44 percent per year from 2001 to 2007. That's what economists call the creation of wealth. It's what reality-oriented people call a bubble that's got to burst.

As Icelandic interest rates increased, Icelanders borrowed foreign money—euros, dollars, francs—from foreign banks because they had lower interest rates. Icelanders with foreign loans had to pay back francs, dollars, or euros, and Icelanders' salaries and wages were being paid in their own krona. This would work as long as krona were strong relative to other currencies, but the payments on these loans were only cheap as long as krona were strong relative to other currencies. However, if you can create wealth out of nothing, there is no limit. Not even the sky.

Then came the beginning of the financial crisis in the United States. This had little to do with anything that happened in Iceland except that foreigners began to notice that the banks in Iceland were deeply in debt, that they had no cash reserves to repay the money they had borrowed, and that their debts were so big relative to the government and the whole Icelandic economy that there was no way the government could bail out the banks. The three largest banks owed ten times the whole country's gross domestic product—as much as all of Iceland could produce in ten years.

Then lenders stopped lending to Icelandic banks and the international money shamans began to bet against the Icelandic economy. Beginning in 2008, the krona crashed and by October it had fallen 43 percent relative to dollars, which were also crashing against other currencies. In 2005, a dollar would buy about 60 krona; by the end of 2008 it would buy about 125 krona. That went up to about 148 in 2009. From the point of view of Icelanders, their money had lost more than half its value relative to dollars. It would be like all of your money being divided in half, the same thing that happened to Mexican workers when their pesos were devalued.

Virtually everything but fish, lamb, and milk is imported into Iceland, so the price of virtually all foods, gas, clothing, beer, wine, and other commodities depends on the exchange rate of krona. The higher the value of krona, the lower the price of food; the lower the value of krona, the higher the price of commodities. So almost overnight, almost everything in Iceland doubled in price.

Icelanders had to pay off their own personal debts in foreign currencies using worthless krona. What looked like a good deal when krona were strong suddenly became an unbearable burden when the currency crashed. Now it took everything you had each month to pay your debts and you had to pay twice what you had been paying to buy what you needed for your family.

Imagine what it feels like to wake up one morning and everything costs twice as much as it did yesterday. You've borrowed twice your income but now you must pay back four times your income because your salary just got cut in half by the crash of your national currency. So much for any sense of security that those constitutional guarantees might have given you. For the first time, Icelanders felt the kind of massive insecurity that Americans learn to live with from the time we're born.

Meanwhile, the bandit financiers, those Viking capitalists, were lording it over the whole world, jetsetting from one house to another, living high on the hog and bragging about it.

Nobody on the world market would buy krona because they were worthless, so it ceased to operate as an international currency. The government shut down the stock market and nationalized the banks. The United Kingdom invoked antiterrorism laws to freeze Iceland's assets in British banks because so many of their citizens and agencies had deposited money in Icelandic banks to get the high rates of interest. Holmes and McCardle draw the moral that the massive borrowing and debt is the culprit and that international regulators should focus on that process.

The Icelandic government searched the world for a large loan to bail it out. They finally had to accept a loan of $2 billion from the IMF, but that put them in the same situation as the underdeveloped countries we've been discussing. Now the sense of insecurity was heightened because everyone in

Iceland knew how the IMF works, how it carves away social programs and commoditizes everything.

As we've repeated throughout the book, the economic system is connected to the political system. Icelanders started mass protests outside the Parliament building in Reykjavík. These became mass riots until the government resigned late in January 2009.

Iceland has a system of proportional representation, so that if you win 10 percent of the votes, your party gets 10 percent of the seats in Parliament. It's not a winner-take-all, two-party system. There are usually five or so parties, and new parties come and go, but a couple of parties have been around a long time: the Independence Party, which is conservative, and the Social Democrats, more liberal. If one party wins a majority of votes, they get to name the prime minister, but that's never happened in Iceland, so the party with the most votes must try to form a coalition with some other party to make a majority.

The president is separately elected and is a largely ritual office of promoting all things Icelandic to foreigners and regulating the political process inside Iceland by announcing which parties won how much of the vote and calling on the representative of the largest block of seats in Parliament to form a government. The president also signs legislation from the Parliament and has a kind of theoretical veto power that is rarely exercised.

In October 2008, the Independence Party held twenty-five of the sixty-three seats in Parliament and had formed a coalition with the Social Democrats. But the rest of Parliament and the demonstrations forced the neoliberal prime minister to call a new election in May 2009 and then to resign. Then the president called on the head of the Social Democrats to form a coalition with the Left-Green movement until the election. She, in turn, appointed the social affairs minister to be interim prime minister.

In Iceland, when the people found out that the neoliberals were wrong, they changed the government. But they'd all paid a high price to learn that economists are fools and the neoliberals were wrong. Most had lost whatever they thought they had. And they faced the prospect of becoming another underdeveloped country in debt to the IMF.

The Icelandic novelist Einar Már Gudmundsson (2009) says that the neoliberal concept of the market is religious. "This is up to the market," or "We'll let the market decide that." Replace the word "market" with the word "God" and you can immediately see the religious content of this ideology. "The invisible hand becomes the Will of God, irrespective of how people feel about God." The entrepreneurial Vikings who had engineered the bubble were only offering sacrifices to the market. A new class of the superwealthy came into existence in Iceland and reduced the middle class to paupers. "All sense of values was thrown out of kilter. Ordinary vocations, like that of teaching, were considered déclassé. No one took the bus anymore. Everyone jumped into a new car, even cars people didn't own but bought on installment, from the tires upwards." The people who ran the privatized banks thought their accomplishments were so worthy that they, like their American counterparts, awarded themselves huge salaries and bonuses. The president of the country trotted around the planet in the company of these superrich, superfashionable people. The Independence Party paved the way for these guys, but the Social Democrats didn't oppose the process.

Gudmundsson roots the process in postmodern relativity that preaches the irrelevance of politics, reality, and history. Thus, neoliberals can have free rein in politics and commerce as well as the media where they put on airs on talk shows and youth come to worship financial snobbery. Gudmundsson says:

> As a consequence we are not only dealing with a financial depression which is rattling the homes of this country and all the foundations of society, but a profound spiritual depression which makes it even more difficult to face the financial one, or to be more precise, the ruling class will get off scot-free and the people will be left in the clutches of the IMF, which, given its record, will demand even further privatization and that the welfare system be demolished even more thoroughly than is already the case.

We can quote from an e-mail Gísli sent Paul in answer to some of these questions: "Issues such as responsibility and belonging were pushed to the sidelines, money and shares dominating the discourse. That discourse, I suspect, is now giving way to a more sensible discourse on sociality. It will be difficult to find the right track. And for the time being the fishing system is intact, despite the fact that it started the craze and everything else is up in the air."

In July 2009 Parliament narrowly passed a bill to seek admission into the European Union. In the past, Icelanders had not wanted to give up their collective fishing rights to the European Union, but now they are private property, so few people have any stake in them any more.

In 2013 there was another election in Iceland, this time with the lowest voter turnout since its independence from Denmark in 1944, 81.4 percent, which would be considered high in the United States. The conservative Independence Party won the highest number of votes with 26 percent, with the Progressive Party close behind with 24 percent and the Social Democrats with 13 percent. Instead of the usual five parties, fifteen participated. After the election, the Independence and Progressive Parties formed a coalition government as together they held a majority of seats in Parliament. Both parties oppose joining the European Union, so Iceland is once again debating its place in Europe. The matter will likely be resolved by a referendum. But perhaps the most interesting point about the election is that the voters returned the party responsible for the meltdown to power.

This is the world you live in. The cell phones, computers, garments, and HDTVs produced in these factories across the globe connect all of us in a political economy like we've never experienced in the history of humankind.

There is so much to learn, so much to understand of this new global system. The challenge is to never lose sight of the people.

We wrote this book to give you the tools to understand your world. We think we did pretty well to discuss money magic, the unreality of finance versus real substantive economies, the religious nature of economics and the role of government and corporations. We're empiricists and don't indulge in prophecy, but we think that with these ideas, anyone can understand much of what is happening in the world today as it happens.

Discussion Questions

- Without getting too personal about it, everyone read a clothing label from your own or someone else's clothing. Make a list of the countries your and your classmates' clothing comes from. What do these countries all have in common?
- See if you can find out whether any of the countries on your list are involved in an IMF "structural readjustment" program.
- What kind of choices do you think the people who made your clothing had? In other words, do you think they really like working in those factories?
- If not, why do you think they are working there? What difference does this make to you? Should it make a difference? Why or why not?
- The next time you go clothes shopping, try to find clothes made in America. What do you think happened when clothing manufacturing moved out of this country? What kinds of jobs did people get after they lost their union textile or other manufacturing jobs?
- Pick a sector of the economy and find out what the average wage and benefits are for those jobs. Then figure out how that compares (adjusted for inflation) with the average wage and benefits of the same sector jobs in 1970. What does the difference do for families who want to buy a home? Let one parent stay at home to raise the children? Put their children through college? Retire early?
- What kind of questions would you ask politicians who promise to bring jobs to your community?

Suggested Reading

Collier, George A., with Elizabeth Lowery Quaratiello. *Basta! Land and the Zapatista Rebellion in Chiapas.* Chicago: Food First Books, 1999.

Drori, Israel. *The Seam Line: Arab Workers and Jewish Managers in the Israeli Textile Industry.* Stanford, CA: Stanford University Press, 2000.

Eythórsson, Einar. "A Decade of ITQ-Management in Icelandic Fisheries: Consolidation without Consensus." *Marine Policy* Vol. 24, No. 6 (2000): 483–492.

Guomundsson, Einar Már. "Letter from Iceland: A War Cry from the North." *Counterpunch* (February 23, 2009). http://www.counterpunch.org/einar 02232009.html/.

Heyman, Josiah McC. *Life and Labor on the Border: Working People of Northeastern Sonora, Mexico, 1886–1986.* Tucson: University of Arizona Press, 1991.

Holmes, Nigel, and Megan McCardle. "Iceland's Meltdown: An Economic Morality Play in 10 Acts." *The Atlantic* (December 2008).

Mills, Mary Beth. *Thai Women in the Global Labor Force: Consuming Desires, Contested Selves.* New Brunswick, NJ: Rutgers University Press, 1999.

Ngai, Pun. *Made in China: Women Factory Workers in a Global Workplace.* Durham, NC: Duke University Press, 2005.

Kathleen Reedy, a human terrain team social scientist and resident of Red Lion, Pennsylvania, listens as Afghan women tell her about the challenges they face on a daily basis during a women's shura at Jaji Maidan. The shura was the first women's shura held in the area to discuss women's business opportunities. The meeting helped initiate dialogue between the women of Jaji Maidan and their government. *Photo by U.S. Army Spc. Tobey White.*

15

Anthropology Goes to Work

In addition to biological anthropology, archaeology, linguistics, and socio-cultural anthropology, many recognize a fifth field of applied anthropology, the use of anthropological understandings in a wide swath of settings from medical to military to solve problems. In this chapter, we're going to bring a bunch of other people's voices in so you can hear what kind of jobs and work there are out there for anthropologists. You'll want to read all the sidebars, especially the first one, where you'll hear that not all anthropologists agree with every direction the field should or does go into.

When Paul lived in the Lisu village in Thailand, the wife of one of the shamans got very sick, and after trying everything he could think of, the shaman took her to a hospital in the lowlands in Chiangmai. When he returned he told the story of being in the hospital and how, to move from one place to another, people would go into a small room and wait for it to move. The door would open and if you were in the place you wanted to be, you got out, but if not, you waited for the room to move again. People didn't believe him until Paul verified that there were such rooms in the hospital. U Beh, another villager, had also taken his wife to the hospital. He told a more tragic story. He took her there because her leg was swollen, but the lowlanders removed her leg. When he learned that, he waved his machete at them and shouted, "How can she work in our fields with no leg?" They threw him out and, thinking nobody wanted his wife, they injected her with a drug to kill her and disposed of her body. When he calmed down and went back for his wife, they told him she had died and her body had vanished.

Now imagine you're Hmong highlander from Laos of the same period and you've fled to Minneapolis because you helped the American CIA with their secret war against lowlanders there, and now the Americans have left and you know what the lowlanders will do to you and your family if they catch you. But Minneapolis? How do you manage this? The cold, the city, the strange people. And you wind up in a hospital. It's like something in a strange science fiction movie. You can't make out what anyone is saying, why they're so excited and rushing around, so you're scared to death.

If you're Hmong, that means your soul is going to just leave. Your body is still there, caught in the nightmare, but the soul has fled. The journalist Anne Fadiman wrote the moving story of Hmong encounters with the medical system in California in her book, *The Spirit Catches You and You Fall Down: A Hmong Child, Her American Doctors, and the Collision of Two Cultures.*

ANTHROPOLOGIST HEAL THYSELF

Grant McCracken
Freelance anthropologist
Author: *Culturematic.* Harvard Business Review Press, 2012.

In the old days, clients would call and ask, "What's the solution?" Now, they ask, "OK, like, what's the problem?" For a relatively brief period in the 20th century we created an anthropology that was a powerful way of figuring out what the problem is. We had formidable powers of pattern recognition. We were good at working with messy data, multiple and shifting interpretive frames, respondents who struggle to say what they mean, and clients for whom the world was now so changeable and "hard to think" that even simple acts of decision-making were perilous.

I used anthropology to solve problems for the Ford Foundation on the vanishing middle of American politics, Oprah Winfrey on the way Americans make homes, Netflix on how and why people watch TV, to name three.

I am not an academic. I write half the year and consult half the year so I can fund my own anthropology. It takes some time to get this model up and running but it can be a good way to be an anthropologist. It's an alternative to the academy. I have used it to publish 11 books and write a blog of some 1.5 million words. But I don't see many anthropologists using this approach and this is itself an anthropological puzzle. The world is filled with people eager for our way of figuring out problems and solutions. Governments, institutions and other disciplines keep banging at the door. Why have we not stepped up?

Part of the problem is that some anthropologists have turned into world renouncers. They have turned the field into a study of the moral, political and epistemological reasons why they can't do anthropology in the real world. And when some dare apply anthropology this way, the accusations fly. I'm told I've used anthropology for profit, not for good, as though these were mutually exclusive. After 30 years of doing this, every senior academic anthropologist has more money in the bank than I do. I've used my ill-gotten gains to fund my anthropology.

The supposition here is that unless one cleaves to the moral, political and epistemological sensitivities of the academy, one mustn't *have* any moral, political and epistemological sensitivities. Removing anthropology from usefulness is not without its moral and political costs. I don't ever see these factored in. The world is a turbulent, perilous place. Anthropologists can help. To refuse to help is problematical. Let's go a little farther. To remove oneself from usefulness is immoral.

I look back on my discipline in its academic form and frankly I am embarrassed by what I see. There is a shocking narrowness of opinion. The field has created and insisted on a gravitational field that discourages differences of opinion. The field likes to think of itself as maximally cosmopolitan. But in point of fact it proves little, smug and ill informed. One case in point: many anthropologists talk about American culture in a manner that is shot through with stereotype and falsehoods. If they were talk about any other culture this way, they would be bounced from the discipline.

The world is eager for anthropological advice. Those who are prepared to answer this call will have to engage in a D-I-Y retrofit. Anthropologist heal thyself.

Back to Minneapolis. The doctors don't know what to do with this strange person who has a bunch of people hanging out in the lobby speaking the unknown tongue until a psychiatrist who has worked in Laos and knows the language and a lot of anthropology lets them know that one of those folks in the lobby is a shaman who can call missing souls and start the healing process. No amount of medical science can do a thing until they do that. So, the doctors let the shaman call your soul.

Joseph Westermeyer was able to bridge the two radically different cultures so the doctors could begin to treat Hmong refugees when they had health problems. Medical anthropology does this kind of thing . . . not only translate so doctors and patients can understand one another, but also teach the medical staff about different emic systems and how they can affect people's health.

Anthropologists have proven so useful in medical practice that there is a whole subdiscipline of medical anthropology to deal with these issues and many applied anthropologists work in this field. Anthropologists want to understand what people do. That means we have to *know* what they do . . . really do, not what they say they do. That's what ethnography is about.

Health-care providers may be puzzled by the spread of HIV/AIDS among injection drug users. They may see drug use as a moral deficiency or a character weakness of individuals and not want to do anything that might promote drug use . . . like provide free sterile needles. Anthropologists knew, from their ethnography of successful needle-exchange programs around the world, that if people could suspend their judgment of drug users and get over the idea that providing clean needles is aiding and abetting drug use, they could slow the rate of spread of AIDS. But if they clung to their judgments, they could do nothing.

In his book, *Drugging the Poor: Legal and Illegal Drugs and Social Inequality,* Merrill Singer pointed out the relationship of class to drug use. All drugs are commodities, whether a drug corporation makes them or drug cartels import them. The distinctions between legal and illegal drugs simply reinforce the position of the drug users in the class system. He suggests that poor people use drugs to medicate themselves to dull the pressures of being poor. Here is where mind control comes in. If we see illegal drug use as the cause of the deterioration of urban centers, according to the usual American stereotype, and blame the drug users, we fail to see the role of class inequality as a source of misery and a cause of drug use, so we don't have to understand it, much less change it. In that sense, blaming drug users acts as a distraction from the real problem.

James W. Carey is an anthropologist who works for the federal Centers for Disease Control and Prevention (CDC) in the Division of HIV/AIDS Prevention. The CDC first hired anthropologists in the late 1980s to help with HIV prevention and other sexually transmitted infections. Anthropologists do basic research and develop interventions, as well as contribute to public health education programs, laboratory activities, and administrative jobs. The CDC may employ anthropologists as full-time employees, contract with

MEDICAL ANTHROPOLOGY

Mark Nichter
University of Arizona

One of anthropology's fastest growing sub disciplines, medical anthropology studies the social and cultural dimensions of health whether they be 1) upstream and seen as precursors of illness or a means of preventing illness/promoting health, 2) midstream involving the divination, diagnosis, and classification of illness and states of vulnerability and "at riskness," or 3) downstream and involved with curing disease or managing illness, coping with pain and suffering, or regaining health and well-being. Medical anthropology has four large, and many small branches. Here I can give only a few examples.

Cultural/medical anthropologists study local perceptions of bodily processes, illness, and its treatment to understand values, norms, power relations, ways of expressing agency and dissent, and moral identity. They focus on how people explain illness as an expression of the politics of responsibility, and local interpretations of sickness as signs of larger disorders within the household or community, environment, society or local cosmology. And they study all healing systems as ethnomedical phenomena reflecting pervasive cultural ideologies ranging from hydraulic (block and flow) and mechanical, to ecological and non-linear system models of health and healthy social relations.

Applied medical anthropologists focus on solving practical problems such as what influences how people seek out healthcare where there are many alternatives, who makes the decisions, and how decisions are related to predisposing, enabling and health service related factors as well as real world contingencies. They conduct research on cultural responses to child survival and infectious disease programs, adverse changes in diet, misuse of pharmaceuticals and increased use of tobacco and to help formulate policies for culturally sensitive health interventions, monitor interventions to help correct policies not achieving their goals, and assist in evaluating outcomes and longer term impacts.

Critical medical anthropologists focus on social and societal determinants of health and health disparities within and between populations. They draw attention to structural factors that render populations vulnerable, create risky environments that expose people to synergistic problems like poverty, drug use, violence, prostitution and HIV, and that contribute to the maldistribution of resources and illness in a population. In addition, they study the biopolitics of poor health, and ways victims of poor health are blamed for their problems by representing them as unhygienic citizens and sources of disease and contagion. Other critical medical anthropologists study the political ecology of disease: factors leading to health systems weakening and the ways climate change, environmental destruction and ecological disruption affect interspecies health leading to the (re)emergence of diseases that can be passed from animals to humans such as avian flu, ebola, rabies and Lyme disease.

Biocultural medical anthropologists embrace both applied and critical medical anthropological agendas while maintaining a core interest in evolutionary biology. They investigate the human life cycle and the short and long term health consequences of

Medical anthropology *continued*

differential access to resources, biological trade-offs required for survival, and expo-
sure to stressors ranging from water or food scarcity to poverty, forms of oppression,
fear and uncertainty, psychosocial stress related to one's relative social position, and
feelings of entitlement and worthiness or unworthiness.

My own work covers all four branches: global response to emerging pandemic diseases; the shift from treating global health as a humanitarian to a biosecurity issue;
"one health"—an agenda that attends to the link between animal and human health;
interventions that address pneumonia—the biggest killer of children in less developed
countries, and tobacco use—the biggest preventable risk factor to adult mortality; the
biopolitics of health policy and health systems; and the growing importance of self
care and complementary medicine in an era marked by neoliberal ideology.

them for specific jobs, or hire them as student interns or postdoctoral fellows.
In 1994 and 1995 there were approximately nineteen anthropologists working with the CDC; by 2014 that number had expanded to at least seventy-
four. Of these, twenty-eight had PhDs; twenty-three had MAs and another
twenty-three had BA degrees in anthropology. CDC anthropologists frequently have additional degrees in other fields. For example, in 2014, at least
thirty anthropologists had Masters of Public Health degrees (seventeen of
the BAs, sixteen of the MAs, and seventeen of the PhDs). Many anthropologists (sixteen) still work in HIV/AIDS prevention in the United States, half
that many in international HIV/AIDS programs, and fewer in Occupational
Safety and Health, Diabetes, Environmental Health, and numerous other offices at the agency that address both infectious and noninfectious diseases.
Occasionally, CDC anthropologists assist with the agency's response to
public health emergencies, such as the 2014 ebola outbreak in West Africa.

Carey's advice to students interested in working with the CDC or with
other public health organizations is to be skilled in collaborative multidisciplinary teamwork. He says the days of lone anthropologists working by
themselves are gone. For students interested in applied anthropology careers
outside of academic settings, Carey recommends studying significant public
health issues and research problems. Students also should master multidisciplinary literature in that field and be skilled in written and oral communication across disciplines. Another key skill includes being able to write clear
and scientifically rigorous reports and research proposals. Anthropologists
may have important insights, but if they cannot communicate their ideas and
research findings to others outside of anthropology, they will not successfully help solve public health problems in the United States or in other
countries.

Small-scale ethnographic work may not always be the best approach.
Because the challenges are diverse and require the use of different kinds of
research. Many CDC researchers use a wide array of theories and methods

drawn from numerous disciplines. Anthropology students interested in applied public health careers also should learn as much as possible about epidemiology and consider getting additional training, such as through an MPH program, as a means to augment their anthropology degree. Nearly all of Carey's research projects on public health at the CDC have involved large multidisciplinary teams and used mixtures of ethnographic, epidemiologic, and statistical methods.

Anthropologists' research and theoretical understandings are only useful when they are translated into practical and effective interventions that health-care workers can use. Carey emphasizes communication and focusing on practical solutions for public health problems. Many ideas and observations may be interesting. But it also is essential for anthropologists working in public health to explain how their findings can be used to help improve public health programs.

The medical anthropologist Paul Farmer is the founder of Partners in Health. He said, "the idea that some lives matter less is the root of all that's wrong with the world." That's another way of saying what we said at the beginning of this book, that every person on our planet deserves one share of it, no more and no less. Farmer may be best known from his work in Haiti and the book, *Mountains beyond Mountains: The Quest of Dr. Paul Farmer, a Man Who Would Cure the World*, by writer Tracy Kidder.

Farmer pointed out that the received wisdom about ebola is that it infects health-care workers and kills most people it infects. The 1976 epidemic started in a mission hospital in the Congo where nurses reused needles and did not wear gowns, masks, or gloves because they didn't have them. Nor did the nurses or their patients have access to modern medical care. The way to treat the shock that occurs when there isn't enough blood for the heart to pump it through the body is to rehydrate by drinking fluids or using intravenous fluids. Any emergency room in the United States or Europe can offer this kind of care and can put patients in isolation wards.

But in those areas where ebola was most prevalent in the 2014 epidemic, doctors and nurses were scarce. In Liberia there were fewer than 50 doctors working in the public health system to treat more than 4 million people, most of whom live in rural areas. There was one doctor per 100,000 people. (By comparison, there were 240 doctors per 100,000 people in the United States and 670 per 100,000 in Cuba.) There were also few hospitals in Liberia and no protective equipment such as gowns, gloves, masks, and face shields.

"In Liberia there isn't the staff, the stuff or the space to stop infections transmitted through bodily fluids," Farmer wrote in 2014. Ebola also spreads to those who treat the dead. It was so prevalent that throughout West African countries it was doubling every few days, with the worst still to come. The level of fear and stigma was even greater than normal for a pandemic disease, although its effects were still small by comparison with the death toll of AIDS, tuberculosis, and malaria, which was around 6 million per year across Africa.

The problem, Farmer suggested, is not that we don't understand ebola—we do—or that it is especially strong. Most people who are promptly

ELIZABETH K. BRIODY

CulturalKeys

Co-author (with Gary Ferraro) of *The Cultural Dimension of Global Business.*
2012, Pearson.

I have been a researcher and consultant for most of my career—first at General Motors R&D and now at my own firm, Cultural Keys LLC. I love what I do. I get to know and work with different kinds of people and I have the opportunity to help organizations improve their effectiveness.

Let me tell you about one recent example. Administrators from a large hospital in the southern U.S. wanted to change their culture to interact with and respond better to their needs. They needed to improve patient satisfaction scores because under the Affordable Care Act government reimbursement is at risk if both patient satisfaction and clinical scores are not high. This hospital hired me to help them.

Administrators required employees to receive training in a communication technique known as AIDET to use with patients. AIDET emphasizes five aspects of staff–patient communication:

A = Acknowledge the patient (e.g., smile, make eye contact)
I = Introduce yourself to the patient
D = Indicate the duration (e.g., of tests, discharge process)
E = Explain (e.g., initial diagnosis) and ask if there are any questions
T = Thank the patient.

Those in dietary and housekeeping services adopted the technique and used it to improve their interactions with patients and do their work in a way that patients found pleasant, caring, and helpful.

Opposition mounted against AIDET in other departments, some quite vocal: "Not applicable to my job duties," or "Just another stupid customer service program . . ." The reaction from nursing was mixed but largely negative; many felt that introductions and thank yous were inappropriate because nurses and patient care assistants interact with the same patients several times during their shifts.

Here's where the ethnography comes in. I saw that many staff were intent on getting their tasks done (e.g., taking a patient's blood pressure, getting a patient discharged) as quickly as possible. It was clear that people were focused on the *task* and directed little attention to patients. Patients typically interpreted this task intensity approach as brusque, unkind, or worse.

Yet, many other staff members spent time with patients, answered their questions, talked with them about their concerns, and did what they could to make them comfortable. Staff members were understanding and proactive, seeking and implementing solutions to care for their patients. Patients highly valued this *empathetic engagement* approach, just as they had valued AIDET. However, empathetic engagement went beyond AIDET because it encouraged two-way communication.

My analysis showed that staff used AIDET only when they initiated the interaction—because they needed to clean a patient's room or pick up a food tray. They used

Medical anthropology *continued*

empathetic engagement when patients initiated the interaction. When I figured this out, I saw why nursing, in particular, had largely rejected AIDET—because AIDET was not designed to engage patients in their own care while empathetic engagement was.

So I focused my recommendations on reinforcing the value of both AIDET and empathetic engagement. In addition, I recommended training and coaching for those task-intensive staff with little patient rapport. Identifying and explaining the emerging cultural patterns and the satisfaction of creating, testing, and implementing interventions to improve an organization's effectiveness make my job interesting, fun, and rewarding. (For more information on this case, see my article in the *Journal of Business Anthropology*, 3(2):216–237, Fall 2014.)

---

diagnosed and get supportive care such as fluids, electrolyte replacement, and blood transfusions survive. But in 2014 Africa hospitals and clinics were closed and trade networks collapsed. Ebola, says Farmer, is a symptom of a weak health-care system.

Grotesque and growing disparities in access to care in a global political economy caused the epidemic. Nothing else. Trying to treat ebola patients in a weak health-care system just helps to transmit it by infecting the staff. You can read Paul Farmer's Ebola Diary in the *London Review of Books* of October 2014, pages 38–39, which you can access online.

Or maybe you've just come across a mass burial in Chile. In 1973 during the Nixon administration, the U.S. Central Intelligence Agency sponsored a coup to oust and murder the democratically elected socialist president, Salvador Allende. General Pinochet's CIA-backed military junta took over the government and replaced years of democracy with a brutal dictatorship that lasted seventeen years. Their closest advisors were neoliberal economists from the University of Chicago and their followers. Naomi Klein documents this in her book, *The Shock Doctrine*. The generals murdered and persecuted Allende's supporters. Security forces caused thousands of people to disappear. Their families and friends are still looking for them, trying to understand what happened to them.

A similar military junta seized control of Argentina in 1976. The Argentine military learned their techniques from the American School of the Americas and French veterans of their war in Algeria. The Argentine military also murdered thousands of their own citizens.

Chile joined Argentina, Uruguay, Paraguay, Bolivia, and Brazil in Operation Condor as part of a U.S. supported Cold War effort to eliminate any Communist influence and to destroy any opposition to the dictatorships. The total numbers are not available, but some sixty thousand people were killed. Forensic anthropologists have had a major and ongoing task of identifying the victims of these murders.

Forensic anthropologists in the United States are employed to identify remains of American military personnel who have been killed in combat. They can also verify child abuse by analyzing the characteristic skeletal indicators of systematic and repeated assaults. By then it's too late to help the child, but the evidence they uncover may help put the abuser away. One forensic anthropologist, Kathy Reichs, uses her experience and knowledge of forensic anthropology as background for her crime novels that feature the fictional Temperance Brennan, dramatized in the television series, *Bones*.

When the National Marine Fisheries Service was given the task of managing the commercial fisheries within the two-hundred-mile coastal limit Congress established in 1976, their charge was to manage the fisheries so there would be the greatest yield of fish that was sustainable over the long term. The director reasoned that that meant managing people because "fish don't listen to you," he said. He therefore started hiring anthropologists.

Today, social sciences are part of the National Marine Fisheries Service to help the agency in its stewardship of fisheries resources, and anthropologists are there finding out what the people in the system think and do, doing the ethnography. Paul served for several years on the Southeast Atlantic Regional Fisheries Council and attended their meetings a couple of times a year. There was another anthropologist on the council and an anthropologist on the staff. Even so, anthropology did not usually prevail, but it was well represented in discussions.

Ethnographers have shown that effective fisheries management is close to the people it affects and involves them. Co-management entails building institutions and creating structural conditions that promote and encourage local communities to manage their own resources and their own development. The goals are the same as those of political and economic democracy and result in resilient and sustainable systems. Our ethnography shows that management for adaptability and long-term system viability is local and not generalizable, that it's practical, and that it can be implemented.

Why don't we see it everywhere? What's the barrier? One of them is the bureaucratic structures of economists and fisheries biologists who privilege their abstractions over ethnographic realities.

As a member of the Scientific and Statistical Committee of the South Atlantic Fisheries Management Council, Paul observed these abstractions in action as well-intended people gathered to work out what the best scientific knowledge was and how to use it in fisheries management. He had reviewed proposals and seen the requests for proposals that generate the research that produces the knowledge. The problem was that few of them were doing anything that could possibly result in sustainable co-management.

Imagine a bunch of well-intended medieval European priests discussing how many epicycles and retrograde motions a planet traces as it completes its orbit, along with the sun, around the earth. They compare observations, discuss methodologies and models, and agree on what the best available science is. Give them a proposal to study planetary motion around the sun and you're a whack job who just doesn't get it.

So when the anthropologist who was on the staff of the Council left for another job and the Council decided to replace her with an economist,

FISHY ANTHROPOLOGY
Patricia Clay
NOAA/NMFS

I have worked for 20+ years as an anthropologist for the National Marine Fisheries Service (NMFS-pronounced "nymphs"), the federal agency that regulates marine fishing in federal waters to the 200 mile limit. There's a headquarters in Washington, D.C. and five regional offices and six overlapping science centers that administer policy and do research. As a regulatory agency, we attract the ire of both fishermen and environmental NGOs. In fact, one informal measure of whether or not we are balancing the interests of the fish and the fishermen is whether we are sued by both sides over a given regulation!

When I first was hired, I was the only social scientist in a regional office who was not an economist but there was one sociologist at headquarters who understood anthropology and anthropologists pretty well. NMFS had decided they needed some scientists who understood why fishermen acted and re-acted the way they did, since you can only influence the people that catch fish, not the fish. I took the job and continue to enjoy it because I can research almost anything important to fishing and fisheries regulations, but especially because I can be the voice of often under-represented groups within the management process.

When I joined NMFS, there was a tendency to talk of "fishermen" as a monolithic bloc rather than a diverse set of individuals with overlapping alliances based on port, gear type, target species, and membership in fishermen's associations, cooperatives, or allocative groups (e.g., those with individual transferable quotas—ITQs—or other catch shares). Explaining the importance of these social institutions and networks is one way I help to influence policy.

Further, we lacked good sociocultural data. Over the years, and as an additional eleven full-time sociocultural employees (7 anthropologists) and various contractors have been hired across all NMFS regions, the situation has slowly improved. As we have acquired quantitative (e.g., surveys) and qualitative (e.g., oral histories) data, we have been able to establish our credibility. It was a long fought battle to establish that our discussions of likely impacts were based on expert knowledge rather than just stories, anecdotes.

One case study involves the Northeast groundfish fishery. Groundfish are bottom dwelling fish, including cod, haddock, pollock, and many flounders. In 2010, a cooperative-like catch share system called "Sectors" was created. NMFS social scientists in the Northeast knew this could have both positive and negative social and economic impacts for fishermen. So the sociocultural and economic staff created a set of indicators to track and analyze changes. Stated goals of the Sectors, included: lessening overfishing, controlling fleet capacity, achieving economic efficiency, and encouraging diversity [undefined] within the fishery. Initial indicator results showed more control over landings levels, fewer vessels (lowering fleet capacity), proportionately fewer smaller vessels (lessening diversity of boat sizes), and higher revenues to vessels remaining in the fishery (increasing economic efficiency). These results, especially the levels of consolidation and the loss of smaller vessels, became a focus of public debate and formed one basis for follow-up efforts to tweak the program. Here was social science (including anthropology) in action in the real world. These are the moments I feel proudest of what I do.

GATHERING INTEL
Kathi Kitner

August, 2005: "You want to intern at Intel? I'll get back to you." A PhD student had emailed me asking for help as I was the mentor coordinator for the National Association for Practicing Anthropologists (NAPA).

I went back to sorting fishery licenses by species caught, trying to add another indicator to a definition of community that we social scientists had been developing for the U.S. east coast. For over a decade I had worked with the National Marine Fisheries Service[1], where politics stymied efforts to do useful ethnographic research to guide policy. I tried to refocus on my work.

But the student's question kept bothering me. I spun from one computer monitor to another and Googled "anthropologist + Intel Corporation," and zipped off an email to a colleague on the west coast who might know.

March, 2006: I'd been at Intel two weeks. My head was spinning as I stood at the ferry landing in Xiamen, Fujian Province wondering how the hell to get a boat to Gulangyu. But I find a couple of teenagers eager to practice their English, and they kindly help me buy a ticket and a beer and I am off, thinking about what it really means to work as an anthropologist at Intel. Five of us—Intel and Nokia designers and anthropologists—spent the next 10 days studying one street in Xiamen—interviewing shopkeepers, street peddlers and apartment dwellers about their lives and histories, and the rhythms, flows and poetry of an ancient street in a southern Chinese city to understand how new technologies collide and collude in a country voraciously devouring the future. Does a mobile phone that allows a recent female immigrant to talk to her distant family affect how she experiences the city, the streets, her home? What shifts in her life, what is immutable? What other types of technology might she use or avoid? What might she be doing in five or ten years?

These kinds of questions guide me through China, Chile, Canada, Mexico, Brazil, India, England, Indonesia, Kenya, Bangladesh, Uganda, Tanzania, and South Africa as I explore the intersections of culture and communications technology.

Intel employs anthropologists because we ask things that engineers don't.

I have recently been exploring the new Internet-connected world that can tell us about the world and the world around us. How does the hidden become visible? Where do we find escape? Privacy? What are the dark sides? How is this always-connected world different for a small business versus a university sorority house?

That Ph.D student? She interned at Intel, defended her dissertation, got a university teaching job, was unhappy, and then came to Intel full time. No longer excavating ancient cultures in Asia, she is instead leading a team of technologists, designers and human factors engineers to probe new usages of handheld technologies and has found her place in the material cultures of the present.

---

[1]While not employed directly with the NMFS, I was employed in the federal policy making structure of the National Fishery Management Councils, of which there are five currently.

Paul could no longer even remotely support such a system and he resigned his seat on the committee.

As he wrote his letter of resignation, it occurred to him that whatever stock assessments are put before the Council as the best *available* knowledge, it is never the best *possible* knowledge because the Council isn't asking the questions or funding the research that could produce it. To be the best possible knowledge, the Council would ask for, support, and fund research on co-management, sustainable systems, and ethnography. In the review process they wouldn't ask biologists or economists to evaluate proposals from anthropologists.

There are anthropologists in other government agencies such as the Agency for International Development, the Park Service, and the military.

And some anthropologists work with the 99 percent to help them find their voice. David Graeber, for instance, is an anthropologist who was active in organizing the Occupy Wall Street movement in 2011. It is that movement we have to thank for bringing the severe economic inequities of the United States and the rest of the world into focus so that class warfare gained the attention of the news media and became a political focal point in the United States. Class warfare is the war of the 1 percent against the 99 percent. Because of the Occupy movement, those disparities are in the news and have become the focus of some political rhetoric. That's a mark of success.

In understanding AIDS and ebola, the stakes are great and global, but not impossible. But those stakes make others pale by comparison. What if every person on the planet had one share of it? Don't you think most of the health-care problems would fall into place? But as long as the World Bank is sponsoring structural readjustment programs that make poor countries decrease their already inadequate health-care systems, don't you think such problems will increase? But anthropologists also make contributions in areas of less consequence. If corporations are part of the cause of the unequal distribution of wealth across the planet and of the political maladies of modern democracies and other political systems, they are surely the predominant institutional form on the planet. So, just as some anthropologists work for states, some work for corporations.

One, Adidas, was making running shoes and trying to expand its market. They were making gear to appeal to people training for specific sports. They knew that people bought gear to gain a competitive advantage. But as a business, they knew they could only hurt themselves if they worked from that unproven assumption. So, Adidas hired a Danish firm named ReD Associates to help. ReD trained Adidas designers in ethnography and then sent them to spend a day with customers—to run and do yoga with them to see how they used the gear—to do the ethnography. One of their anthropologists sent cameras to dozens of customers and asked them to take pictures of something that made them work out. Thirty women responded. Twenty-five of them sent pictures of a little black dress. They weren't training to be good at sports. And it got Adidas and ReD an article by in the August 24, 2013, edition of *The Economist* and improved Adidas's market share.

GETTING BUSY

Ken Anderson
Intel

We settled into a back table of side street café in Heihe Northern China to talk with a Chinese merchant who lives there and takes Chinese goods into Russia to sell and trade. We met her in a public park but she thought the three foreigners (two Intel anthropologists and a cultural guide) were drawing too much attention. She apologized for being so busy that it had been hard to find a time to meet and went on to talk about the difficulties of being away for months and the demands of being home after a long absence.

What were we doing there? A year earlier on another project I noticed that busyness was a part of conversations with people from Shanghai to London to Portland. But what did "busyness" mean?

Historical time studies from China, UK, and USA showed that people had more free time now than in the 1960s so why were they claiming to be busy? Clearly, something cultural was going on. Heihe was one site in our research plan to study "busyness" and people's conceptions of time that would affect ideas of "busy."

Before Heihe, we spoke with bike messengers in London (time in minutes), beach goers in Salvador de Bahia (time in hours), border traders in Suifenhe (time in months) and freelancing creatives in San Francisco (time in weeks). After leaving China we would go on to research single moms in Chicago (time in days) and commuters in New York and Los Angeles (time in hours). A multi-sited comparative approach highlights what is unique to a location and what is general.

Our team at Intel can't be expert in all the places we go so we partner with anthropologists who have recently done ethnographic research in the area to be cultural guides to help establish rapport and provide knowledge about local culture. For our short-term studies cultural guides are as important as good translators so I can to ask good questions, discover patterns, and use anthropological theories to translate the research into corporate action.

Findings of interest to anthropologists like how busyness had become an indicator for being middle class in America, part of the new China or modern in Brazil didn't matter to Intel. What mattered was how peoples' lives had become a series of interruptions, giving the constant feeling of busyness. The border crosser, for example, received three phone calls and eight text messages during two hours in the café. At home, a 30-minute accounting task took over an hour with parent and kid interruptions. We described this phenomenon as social hyperthreading, borrowing engineering language to facilitate corporate understanding.

This ethnographic research combined with market research, engineering development and lab testing, led to the launch of Intel's turbo. For decades Intel had been designing around continuous maximum processor use of two hours. Our research demonstrated virtually no one could spend two uninterrupted hours on anything. Optimal processors required instant but not sustained power.

> Getting Busy *continued*
>
> Being part of corporate conversations means being able to translate field research and anthropological theory into everyday business action with marketers and engineers. Ethnographic research was fundamental in establishing three divisions of Intel around health, education and home computing products, as well as the launch of the Corporate Strategy Office, Galileo and Edison products in 2014. Making sense of people's worlds has made social science a routine part of Intel's strategy and innovation.

A young woman named Erin Holland graduated from Penn State with a BA degree in anthropology. She was working with a marketing firm in Pittsburgh and her employers wanted to hire more anthropology graduates. Paul went to Pittsburgh to visit her and talk with her bosses, who agreed to let Erin work with him to develop a course on business anthropology.

Paul wanted to check with the people who hire anthropologists to see what skills they needed. So in 2007 he went the Ethnographic Praxis in Industry Conference (EPIC) to ask them.

They told him PhDs were too set in their ways. People didn't need to go to graduate school and learn literary theory or how to make things inexplicably nuanced. They wanted people who could think like anthropologists. And they wanted people who could work:

- On schedules,
- With teams,
- And make themselves intelligible to their bosses—

skills that are well beyond the reach of many PhDs.

So Erin and Paul developed a syllabus to do those things. First it outlined things you have learned in this book on the nature of anthropology: that its objective is to use a holistic view and comparative studies along with ethnography to describe how sociocultural systems work and how they got that way. Anthropology describes social structure, the groups people form and the relations among them and social organization, the way people use their social structures and, through using them, change them, as well as culture, patterns of thought that people learn by growing up in a particular time and place. Finally, a system is a set of elements related in such a way that if one changes, the others change, and applied anthropology is developing and using these kinds of analyses and insights for real-world purposes in business and other organizations.

In the syllabus for that class, Paul went on to list characteristics he had learned from EPIC—that people who hire anthropologists want BAs with anthropology degrees who can:

- Think like anthropologists—thus you should know some theoretical background and some examples;

- Deal with RFPs (Requests for Proposals) When an organization needs some specific task done—design a product, explore a market segment, develop new services or products—they write a request for a proposal saying what they want done. You should be able to prepare a proposal for the project. The organization then evaluates all the proposals and selects one agency, like ReD, to do the work. The response to the RFP is the way the agency gets the work;
- Work within time constraints;
- Work in teams;
- Collaborate with clients;
- Make and present arguments;
- Present proposals;
- Identify the problem to solve;
- Provide unique and deep insights;
- Do their own research project instead of following some established path;
- Get information and communicate that process: "How did you get there? Can you do it again?" Someone who can walk someone else through the process;
- Translate rigor and method to the client;
- Be flexible—always have a plan B to go to;
- Deal with time deadlines—how much information can you get in that time? It may not be ideal, but something to get us to a better level than we are now;
- Get experience and information within time constraints. This is not an academic world; and
- Has professional skills.

Undergraduates would have to learn how to think like anthropologists in other courses; this one was just for technique.

The specific objectives of the course were:

1. To learn how to think like an anthropologist.
2. To learn how anthropologists do ethnography.
3. To learn how to critically assess ethnographic work.
4. To learn techniques of observation, interviewing, photography, video production, and presentation.

There were readings from the growing literature on business and design anthropology but few from the literature of traditional applied anthropology. To emphasize learning by doing, Paul assigned students randomly to groups and gave each group a client to work with: a local alternative newspaper, a student organization, the Department of Anthropology, and others. The first task of each group was to figure out how they could help their client. Paul emphasized that they didn't have to agree with or like the clients, but they did have to work with them and figure out how to help them.

REAL ANTHROPOLOGY

Erin Holland
Applied anthropologist

Six days on the ground. Could I get enough information, the right information, and the depth an ethnographer needs? I had barely a week to make a solid report. Six days, six community clinics, sometimes six hour drives through the desert.

I am often in situations of limited resources but unlimited expectations. Four days in Shanghai to pull together a deep understanding of what moves the mobile phone market, or three days in Chicago cooking with couples to understand the role of convenience in their meal planning is not what my academic colleagues would consider to be ethnographic fieldwork.

And here I was with a team of architects and designers in the U.A.E., charged with redesigning community ambulatory clinics in villages across the Emirate. As the ethnographer, my job was to discover the emotional and cultural experience of the patient and translate those findings for our architectural design team. Each day, we drove to remote towns far from the shining capital to interview elders, community leaders, clinic directors, doctors, nurses and staff and observe them with patients. We photographed waiting rooms, timed interactions, and asked patients and community members to participate in written surveys and hands-on workshops.

On day three the team's engineer suggested that the best way to make everyone happy was to build each clinic exactly the same so the design could be replicated and costs lowered. His response to the challenge of the diverse needs we observed was to force the people and the culture to adapt to his structure, rather than design the structure to meet the needs of the people. After all, the West is the model of medicine and wouldn't these villagers be pleased to have that in the form of a very efficiently designed clinic?

I knew that the more efficient design would leave these clinics with challenges for years to come. I gathered my colleagues into an exam room and asked them to wait—a patient would be coming soon to meet with the doctor and we were invited to observe. The four of us waited ten minutes before the patient arrived for his exam. Along with him were his wife, his teenaged children, his younger brother and his wife's cousin.

Eleven of us crowded into this room, designed slightly larger than the Western standard, and watched. Shoulder to shoulder my team began to sweat and fidget to find a comfortable way to stand. Here, care is a community effort and the facility needed to support this belief. One hour of participant observation shifted my colleague's perception and his design approach, and brought to life a meaningful contrast to the way the West treats its sick and sickness. Our limited resources and ethnographic approach yielded a lasting insight that held value beyond any architectural budget.

Over the past ten years my job title has ranged from Research Analyst, Brand Planner, Ethnographer, and Strategic Consultant. In each case, anthropology's tools and theories provided a framework from which I have approached problems in a variety of disparate industries. The constant is a focus on understanding culture—the patterned means of expressing knowledge, identity, status and connections. Untangle these patterns and systems of belief and behavior and the possibility for solving problems and creation is boundless.

From the EPIC meetings, Paul developed a list of organizations that employ anthropologists and worked out tentative agreements to accept students from the course as summer interns. That way, students could take the next step and learn by working at a real job.

From the peaceful operation of corporations to the U.S. occupation of Iraq and Afghanistan is a large leap. But another field for applied anthropology is in those occupations. This was hotly debated both in the military and in the academy. Some argue that the best way to help local civilians and the military in these occupations is to be there when the interactions occur, on the ground, with the American military.

In Sal al-Din Province of Iraq, the United States had been paying a civilian security force that was called Sons of Iraq. Early in 2009 they were supposed to be placed under the Iraqi government. But not all of them would be on the payroll. The government of Iraq didn't trust the locals and allowed only 20 percent of Security Forces to come from them. What would the rest—the 80 percent—do? There were no jobs except perhaps with the insurgents. The Human Terrain Systems group that the anthropologist Christopher King was with interviewed 503 such individuals anonymously. Seven of them said they'd likely somehow align with the insurgents. When a brigade intelligence office asked King to identify the 7, he refused because he'd promised anonymity and because although they'd expressed certain attitudes, they hadn't outright said they'd join the insurgents. The brigade commander respected this decision and valued the report.

In 2007, the executive board of the largest professional association of anthropologists in the United States, the American Anthropological Association issued a statement disapproving of Human Terrain Systems. The association named a commission to investigate the matter and they also condemned the program and officially turned against it.

Many would agree that the wars in Iraq and Afghanistan were part of a larger program of American corporate control of oil resources. That's what we felt and that's why we opposed the war from the beginning in 2003. We were at a meeting of the Society for Applied Anthropology in Portland, Oregon. When we heard the war had started, we joined the demonstrations against the war in the park. And we were active in the Peace Center in State College, Pennsylvania, where we lived at that time. Paul tells the story of being thrown in jail because of his opposition to the Vietnam War in 1972 in his memoir, *At the Foot of the Mountain*.

You don't have to approve of a foreign policy or a war to think that anthropologists could help both the military and the people of the place or to think that your colleagues are using their professional skills in a constructive way if they work with the military. It might not be a job you'd like to take on, but that doesn't give you the right to dictate that they should not. To give the question more context, ask which does the most harm, the military or the development programs that disarticulate economies, drive rural people into poverty, increase infant mortality and create wave after wave of urban poor to fuel the labor demands of international capital. Or the World Bank. Or any

ANTHROPOLOGY AT WAR

Kathleen Reedy
Rand Corporation

The morning wasn't that hot, but after walking several miles of mountain trails at 10,000 feet in 50 lbs. of body armor I arrived at the Afghan village sweaty, hungry and grumpy. As we took off some of our gear, about a dozen older men showed up and greeted everyone individually. Not surprisingly, as a woman in civilian clothes, I was a hit. Tea and snacks arrived, and we sat talking in small groups. I had hoped to ask about the impacts of a recent flood, but the man I was talking with instead asked belligerently, "In ten years, how many factories have you Americans built?" In response, I asked how old he was. "About fifty," he said eyeing me. "Then, how many factories have *you* built in fifty years?" The room went silent. The American soldiers looked on in horror. The man I'd been speaking to guffawed, gave me a nod of acknowledgement and proceeded to answer all my questions about flooding with good cheer.

The thing about being an anthropologist in a war zone is that, while you may not get to do full-on ethnography, you can still use your observation skills.

The holistic understanding through emic and etic views I learned about in Anth 101 has given me a way to understand the dynamics of oppression and see the effects of political and economic domination: starvation, human trafficking, war. My etic perspective allows me to understand that normal American life is tied into the same system that leaves others living in squalor. The emic perspective I've gained from moving with those people has given me deep sympathy for them.

For me, that translates into an obligation to apply that knowledge to make the world better. When I had the opportunity to join an organization that embedded social scientists with military units in Iraq and Afghanistan to help bring a faster end to the wars, I signed up, despite the academic backlash. While worrying about falling down a mountain and making a fool of myself in front of soldiers was terrifying, being blacklisted by my own discipline for doing engaged anthropology in a manner the establishment condemned was worse. Despite academia's concerns, I did not want to become a part of a killing machine—I just thought I had a better chance to make changes from inside the system.

The military was working with the State Department and the US Agency for International Development to shift the focus from killing enemies to developing economic and political environments that reduced people's desire or need to turn to violence. Not surprisingly, most soldiers weren't very good at these tasks, but that was where I could help.

It was intimidating, though, to stand in front of a brigade commander and a room full of his officers and tell them that everything they were doing was wrong. "People aren't afraid of Al Qaeda or worried about security. They're worried about corruption, and they're afraid of their government." That commander looked at me for a long moment then asked what I thought we should do about it. It was even more intimidating when he listened to me and said, "Make it happen."

There aren't many jobs where a young woman can tell a senior person he is wrong, make a recommendation, and have him take the advice.

I can't measure the impact of my efforts but I know that I changed the way that some commanders thought and acted. For me, that's enough for a start.

ACTION ANTHROPOLOGY AND COMMUNITY GARDENS

Barbara J. Dilly
Creighton University

In the 1970s, when students in America demanded relevance from their educations, Sol Tax from the University of Chicago drew them into community activism with both the intellectual rigor that anthropology demands and the political passion it engenders. When I became a professor at Creighton University in Omaha, Nebraska I was full of fire to help people change the world. It was going to start in my classroom, right in the middle of America where we have a lot of problems with agriculture!

But something had changed since the 1970s. Students didn't want to change the world but to find personal meaning and purpose. But those can be the same thing. My qualitative field research methods class seemed like the perfect place to help students learn collaboratively with community partners who shared a common problem: "Where do we find healthy locally-grown food?" Creighton students have to buy their food on campus from one industrial food system source. There is plenty of it, but it's not fresh. Residents in the surrounding low income neighborhood live in a food desert created by the same industrial food system as well as the American class system. So in 2013, I defined a research question that would engage the problem that both groups shared: "How can Creighton University further community partnerships with Gifford Park residents that will promote healthy local food production, distribution, and consumption in and around Omaha?

People in Omaha's low income neighborhoods were already converting vacant lots to community gardens. Creighton University owned a vacant lot in Gifford Park, a low income neighborhood. So, I charged the students to get to know the neighborhood, build rapport, and find out what local residents needed. Through these relationships, we eventually worked with a group of Bhutanese refugees seeking to integrate into the neighborhood without losing their cultural identities. Creighton provided garden space and water. Students participated in community activities celebrating cultural diversity and learned from the refugees about their resilience to solve their problems of cultural survival as they adapted to their new neighborhood.

Students learned action anthropology by doing it. They learned what they could do and how Creighton University could provide resources to support cultural survival for refugee populations. They became community partners in the quest for more sources of fresh vegetables in their neighborhood, and in the process learned about the larger food insecurity that results from problems within industrial agriculture. Refugee gardening revealed more research questions regarding diversity of healthy food needs for low income residents. This provided opportunities for students to give greater voice to the diverse cultural interests of multiple community groups seeking city-wide policies that support community gardens as grass-roots economic development strategies. And the project is engaging students in the problems of American agriculture. Through action anthropology, the community garden project is relevant to society, the university and it is giving students meaning and purpose!

corporation you care to mention. And those who work at universities in any capacity are equally complicit in their measured reproduction of these systems as they prepare working class students to assume their managerial roles. And in such judgements where do we find the relativity that is supposed to be the hallmark of anthropology?

Occupation or no, food is at the base of all social orders and anthropologists have long been concerned with understanding how societies feed themselves. In response to the industrialization of agriculture we discussed in Chapter 12, a local food movement has arisen across the United States and in many other countries. Some of this has been inspired by the international slow food movement, some by the organic movement of the Rodale Institute, some by the expectation that our world oil supply is running out, and some by a simple wish for self-reliance.

Scott and Helen Nearing, who we mentioned in Chapter 11, among the best known of the back-to-the-landers, published their book, *Living the Good Life: How to Live Sanely and Simply in a Troubled World*, in 1954. It was a chronicle of their move back to the land in the 1930s. With a PhD in economics from the University of Pennsylvania in 1909, Nearing was an academic but he was fired from his position at the University of Pennsylvania for his radical views. *The Good Life* was a Bible for people who, like Nearing, wanted to withdraw from what they saw as a corrupt system and live by their own efforts. There were many others before and after to follow this path. An earlier "new pioneer" was Paul Corey, Iowa author who went to upstate New York to homestead. He wrote a manual, *Buy an Acre*, for what he saw as a wave of people who would follow, after the end of the Second War. "When World War II is over," he wrote in 1944 (p. vii), "the country around our cities for a radius of from fifty to one hundred miles become the New Frontier of America. Ten million tiny homesteads will spring up. . . ." Instead, the suburbs sprawled from the cities spawning highways and fast-food shops as we discussed in the introduction.

Instead of people producing their own food on their small plots, agriculture industrialized and threatened the food of the world and by the end of the twentieth century more people were participating in local food production and distribution via Community Supported Agriculture, farmers' markets, and other means of distributing locally grown foods to local communities. Organizations like the Pennsylvania Association for Sustainable Agriculture began in 1992 to support local sustainable food production and distribution. About the same time (1990), the Midwest Organic and Sustainable Education Service was organized. There are many other such organizations around the United States and the world.

Anthropologists are especially concerned with understanding the culture cores of the societies they study and live in. It didn't take long for anthropologists to participate in the ethnography of these movements around the world, and some began to follow the Nearings and Coreys back to the land themselves to provide alternatives to what they saw as corrupt and corrupting academic, government, and corporate employment.

Edward M. Maclin, for instance, moved to his grandparents' Tennessee dairy farm in 2009 along with his wife and daughter. Maclin was working on a dissertation about the World Wildlife Fund's efforts at conservation in the Arctic while the climate is radically changing, especially in the Arctic. Unlike Malinowski, isolated on his Pacific island to pursue ethnography, Maclin was straddling the worlds of the American Mid-South and the Arctic as well as the worlds of the farm and the academy. A 2012 article in the *New York Times* about the political scientist James Scott, whose work we have mentioned in this book, had said that being a farmer had made him a better scholar, although there were complex cross currents. Inspired by the *Times* article, in 2013 Maclin pulled together a group of anthropologists who had at least one foot planted on farms for a session to discuss such questions at a meeting of the American Anthropological Association.

We were there and contributed a piece on our work at Draco Hill in Eastern Iowa. By then, some, like Alice Brooke Wilson of the University of North Carolina, Chapel Hill, had grown up surrounded by alternative agriculture. This provided a series of views on alternative agriculture. We heard others at a session of the Society for Applied Anthropology in 2014.

Suffice it to say that contemporary anthropologists are struggling to understand this movement as it inserts itself into the nooks and crannies of the American food system. Some are participating in it to make a living, others as ethnographers, and still others as an alternative to academic/corporate/government employment.

So applied anthropology covers the waterfront from work with the Occupy Wall Street Movement to the military in Iraq; from tech corporations to hospitals and marketing firms, although there's no consensus about the ethics of applying our knowledge to the everyday world of events. If there were such a consensus, we are sure there would be at least several cogent minority reports. Some say the university is the only proper place for anthropology. But let's review the role of universities in our global system. Their role is to make that system seem reasonable, natural, and inevitable so that you don't question it. Universities are designed to train you to take a place in that system so that you can do your part. But that makes universities an indispensable part of that same system.

The rise of the Chicago School of economists led by Milton Freidman and the formulation of their doctrine of neoliberalism that has caused untold misery and suffering around the world came out of the American university system, part of the cultural revolution in the United States that led to events in Argentina, Chile, and Russia that we discussed earlier. No one seems responsible for the misery; it's just a natural consequence of the natural working of a natural economic system, Neoliberals tell us, to provide themselves and their followers a screen of respectability and innocence.

An old labor union song says, "Without our brain and muscle not a single wheel can turn." Lots of people have to do their parts to make any system work. Today in the United States, whether it's the universities or the corporations or the military, it's all the same system. If we didn't participate, it couldn't work. And, with your university education, you're preparing to join that system in some capacity.

Today, whether it's the universities or the corporations or the military, it's all the same system. If we didn't participate, it couldn't work. If you serve one part of it, you serve all of it. A stock broker once asked Paul what he thought of social investment funds, mutual funds that invest in what they take to be progressive corporations with good social and environmental policies. Paul replied that once you've decided to put your money on Wall Street, you'd already made the ethical decision. The rest was just nit picking. That's one reason why, inspired by the Slow Money movement, Paul pulled a lot of his retirement savings out of Wall Street and put it into local food and farm endeavors.

It's not up to us to tell you whether it's ethically correct to serve a university, a corporation or a branch of the military. It's up to you to think about what you've read here, to read more from the list of readings we offer below, to discuss it with others, and to make up your own minds. What we can tell you is that any way you go, you will find some good anthropologists to keep you company.

Discussion Questions

- In Cuba there are 670 doctors per 100,000 patients compared to the United States' 240. That's almost three times as many. So why do you think Americans think socialized medicine is such a bad thing?
- Discuss arguments for and against anthropologists serving with the military. How is that different from anthropologists working with corporations? How is it different from anthropologists working with other agencies of the government? With universities?
- Why do you think anthropologists would shun colleagues who work with the military? Or corporations? Or universities?
- Why is ethnography the key to all aspects of applied anthropology? Discuss examples from the sidebars. How is ethnography different than surveys or focus groups used by marketing companies?
- Why do you think Intel hires anthropologists? Why does the CDC? The military?

Suggested Reading

Colborn, Lisa L., Susan Abbott-Jamieson, and Patricia M. Clay. "Anthropological Applications in the Management of Federally Managed Fisheries: Context, Institutional History and Prospectus." *Human Organization* Vol. 65, No. 3 (2006): 231–239.

Corey, Paul. *Buy an Acre: America's Second Front.* New York: The Dial Press, 1944.

Durrenberger, E. Paul, and Tom King, editors. *State and Community in Fisheries Management: Power, Policy, and Practice.* Westport, CT: Bergin & Garvey, 2000.

Durrenberger, Paul. *American Fieldnotes: Collected Essays of an Existentialist Anthropologist.* Amazon, 2014.

Ervin, Alexander M. *Applied Anthropology: Tools and Perspectives for Contemporary Practice*. 2d ed. Boston: Pearson/Allyn & Bacon.

Fadiman, Anne. *The Spirit Catches You and You Fall Down: A Hmong Child, Her American Doctors, and the Collision of Two Cultures*. New York. Farrar, Straus and Giroux, 1997.

Forte, Maximillian C. "The Human Terrain System and Anthropology: A Review of Ongoing Public Debates." *American Anthropologist* Vol. 113, No. 1 (2011): 149–153.

King, Christopher. "Managing Ethical Conflict on a Human Terrain Team." *Anthropology News* Vol. 50, No. 6 (2009): 16.

Klein, Naomi. *The Shock Doctrine: The Rise of Disaster Capitalism*. New York: Picador, 2007.

Nearing, Scott and Helen. *Living the Good Life: How to Live Sanely and Simply in a Troubled World*. New York: Schocken, 1973 (originally published in 1954).

Stiglitz, Joseph. *Globalization and Its Discontents*. New York: Norton, 2003.

Westermeyer, Joseph. *Poppies, Pipes and People: Opium and Its Use in Laos*. Berkeley: University of California Press, 1983.

Where do we go from here? *Photo by E. Paul Durrenberger.*

16

The End is Near

You've met some of the characters—they are mostly nameless; they are the people. You won't know them by their celebrity in the news, but you may remember them by the name of the group they belong to—Icelandic fishers, Gulf Coast shrimpers, American janitors—or the part of the world where they live—Trobriand Islands, Truk, Burma, Chicago, Thailand. You know some of the plot, some of the stage directions. It's a story based on the work of many anthropologists over many years.

There are questions of ethics and values—things like ethnocentrism and sexism and racism. There are questions about where you stand. Anthropologists usually stand with the people whose stories we tell, not with the kings or presidents or priests or rulers or philosophers. Sometimes that makes us uncomfortable in the universities where we teach. Ask your instructor about that. But we do more than tell the stories; we try to understand why the stories are the way they are—the structures the people are living in and how they got to be that way.

We have seen that all things human are interconnected. Anthropology is holistic. There's a lot of complexity, but it's not so complex that you can't understand it. You just have to use your brain and the analytical skills you have learned and not be fooled by appearances.

Tom Robbins is a novelist, not an anthropologist. The Chink, one of the characters in his book *Even Cowgirls Get the Blues* (and yes, that's his name, politically incorrect although it may be—that's in fact part of the author's point because the character is Japanese), says, "Life isn't simple; it's overwhelmingly complex. The love of simplicity is an escapist drug, like alcohol. It's an antilife attitude. . . . Death is simple but life is rich. I embrace that richness, the more complicated the better" (Robbins, 1977, p. 256). Anthropologists often end books like this with stirring words. We think that's a great custom, so we're going to borrow some stirring words for you.

Charles Hockett (1973) talked about state systems. He called them civil society, meaning societies with cities. This is what he said about three-quarters of the way through the Twentieth Century:

> Not only cities but most aspects of the civil pattern have ceased to have any survival value. Minor tinkering will get us nowhere. Obviously we cannot return to tribalism. We need something totally new—something at the moment unimaginable.

> *Man's task in the twenty-first century is not to kid around with limited political, economic, or religious loyalties. No institution—no family, no city, no church, no nation, no international organization—deserves our respect and support except insofar as it functions to promote the welfare of the entire human species. Man's task in the twentieth century is to disassemble the juggernaut [of civil society] itself, before it shakes to pieces and in the process destroys the precious chrysalis within. That is our only hope.*
>
> *Can we do this?*
>
> *Certainly we cannot if we continue to rely on the sorts of political leaders the nations of the world have chosen in recent decades—men with the breadth of perspective and imagination of a bunch of prunes. But it is not clear that other leaders could do any better. Despite our enormous collective ingenuity, it is possible that our problems now exceed our capacities. (Hockett, 1973, p. 670)*

What do you call something that rings more true now than when it was written in 1973? Prophetic, maybe.

Anthropology lets us see the juggernaut. All the corporate think tanks and company-paid professors can't hide that. We go behind the simple answers of the thought controllers. We have seen the juggernaut too many times. Nowadays, we see it in Afghanistan, Iraq, and Syria; before we saw it in El Salvador, Guatemala, Nicaragua, the Spanish Civil War, Burma, Vietnam. Can we disassemble it?

Listen to Marvin Harris writing in 1971:

> *If anthropology has any suggestion to those seeking to participate in the creation of novel varieties of personal and cultural life, it is that to change the world one must first understand it. The importance of this advice varies directly with the odds against the desired personal or sociocultural innovation. When the odds are drastically against a hoped-for outcome, ignorance of the causal factors at work amounts to moral duplicity. In this sense, the study of humanity has the force of a moral obligation; all who are interested in the survival and well being of Homo sapiens must find in it a common purpose. (p. 596)*

That's what anthropology does. That's what it is for. We have given you some of the tools of the trade. We've shown you how you can see through, behind, and into political and economic systems and the cultures that go with them. Today, it's obvious that all people live in a global system. The hunters of the Amazon use shotguns and sell game. Ecotourists are everywhere. You can get to any place on the planet in a day or two. Even the remnant groups that most closely resemble foragers are parts of larger systems. The fallout from Iceland adopting the ITQ system can affect a British municipality. Subprime loans and business cheating in the United States can lead to a global financial crisis. When the money shamans begin to question their own gods as they sit in their skyscrapers in the most modern of cities, people in factories and villages around the world are in economic peril.

To understand the global system, we can't rely on the worm's-eye view of ethnography. You can't do classical ethnography where there are no communities—where the people you are trying to understand don't live in one single place but all over the place: shrimpers in Mississippi, for instance, or Teamsters in Chicago or longshore workers in Charleston.

So how do we do the ethnography of globalization? We're going to have to count on your collective ingenuity and creativity to do it. You have the foundation. You have strong shoulders of those who came before you to stand on. But you're the ones who are going to have to do the job.

We told you at the beginning that we'd tell you what anthropology knows. Human systems keep changing, and our knowledge of them changes with them.

We know what economists do: they tell us that their religion is reality because it supports the capitalist system. In this they are very human, just like the Inca priests preaching that the god kings were natural and necessary.

There are many different kinds of sociologists, and we can't go into that here, but one thing they do is take the polls and surveys and tell us how people are reacting to or dealing with the system to provide information to the people in charge so they can keep the system going, suggesting an occasional tweak here or there. Some of them do other things, much as we're advocating here. Check out Sudhir Alladi Venkatesh (2008), for example. He wrote *Gang Leader for a Day* and quickly learned the difference between what his sociology profs were telling him and what ethnography had to say when he started hanging around gang members on the streets of Chicago.

Many psychologists and therapists support the system, too. They have the tough work of helping individuals struggling with the constant contradictions of the system and trying not to go crazy or get totally depressed when they do everything they're supposed to do and it doesn't work out the way it's supposed to. Psychologists and therapists try to convince folks to fix themselves rather than to mess with the system. The system is too big. It's quixotic to think about fixing that. Get used to it. And if you can't, maybe we can find some drugs that'll help.

Some anthropologists do most of the above, too. Some work for corporations to help them make money. Some work for governments or the World Bank to figure out how to convince people to accept programs that are going to hurt them. Some work for marketers to figure out how to get people to buy more stuff they don't need. Anthropologists can make a lot of money doing that kind of work, by the way, and we don't disparage it.

But some anthropologists help us to see things as they are—help us to see behind and beyond the mind-fog of state and media mind control to understand how our political economies and cultures work. That vision can make you feel crazy, unmoored, as though you've just been freed from the Matrix. In showing us those realities, these anthropologists provide alternatives to the system. To be fair we hasten to add that many sociologists, a few economists, and some psychologists also do that. And you don't have to be a scientist to see clearly. Many journalists, novelists, filmmakers, songwriters, and poets do that even better than we do, especially getting the word out about what they've discovered.

Anthropologists aren't free of the kind of magic that economists use, either. To be an anthropologist, you pretty much have to go to graduate school and get a magic piece of paper called a PhD. Universities are one of the last holdouts of medievalism. You're experiencing your own brand of it.

You get a PhD, and that gives you the tools, some of the vision, and lets you see parts of the system at work. You can use the skills you've learned to tell other people the vision of anthropology—the vision of a single species and how we got to be the way we are and why it's important to make a fair world and not to settle for an unfair one. You can tell people what happens to unsustainable systems. That's what archaeologists do.

People may say, "You don't understand—it's very complicated." Economists and their students will say, "But that's the way the market works." They'll say, "Actually, in reality, . . ." and so on. But some will hear. Some will listen.

You'll have to get used to being pretty much invisible and having lots of people not paying you much attention. That's OK. They have other things to worry about. If you want to make a difference, if you want to help move toward a more fair system, anthropology is one thing to do. There are others. You may become a novelist or a journalist, a sociologist, or even (gasp) an economist, and you can still use what you've learned here.

The more you understand things clearly, the more choices you have. Understanding also brings responsibility. The greater your understanding, the greater your responsibility to the rest of the species. Shamans may be nuts, but they put that talent to work in the service of their people.

The better your understanding, the more choices you have. One of those choices is the ethical and political choice we mentioned earlier. Whenever it's up to you, be sure that what you do and say moves in the direction of everyone on the planet having one share. Not more and not less. It doesn't matter where you are. You may be a restaurant worker, a computer specialist, a sales "associate," a community organizer, or a businessperson. You will have that choice at times. The important thing is to recognize when it's yours and use it well.

You know the heroes of fiction—people like Zorro, Xena the warrior princess, Wonder Woman, Batman, Don Quixote, Captain America. They all held justice close to their hearts as all of us learn to when we are kids. We are supposed to outgrow the stories of heroes like these when we give up on justice, when we grow up, that is, and accept that we live in an unjust world. These heroes all live in streamlined worlds where everything goes their way and they can overcome any obstacle the bad guys throw at them.

Except Don Quixote. He's nuts. He thinks he's living in a different time or a different reality than the rest of the people, but he never despairs in his quest for justice.

The English-speaking world has picked up on the crazy part of his character, and the word *quixotic* means "at least impractical and bumbling, perhaps humorous, maybe nuts." To call someone quixotic is negative—a bad thing to be. Our friends who speak Spanish and Portuguese, however, tell us those folks pick up on the noble part of it and say it's positive—a good thing to be.

Different writers could make any of the legendary heroes of fiction into bumbling idiots disconnected from the realities of life. Since Cervantes, other writers have told stories of quixotic characters. One is in the 1971 movie *They Might Be Giants*. George C. Scott plays Justin Playfair, a judge who may think he's Sherlock Holmes. He wears the clothes and talks the talk. Joanne Woodward plays Dr. Mildred Watson, a shrink trying to figure out whether he's crazy. When she tells him that she's Dr. Watson, he responds with Sherlock Holmes's trademark slogan, "the game's afoot," and he drags her along on a crazy but somehow saner-than-it-looks adventure through New York.

At one point, she says, "You're just like Don Quixote. You think that everything is always something else."

"Well, he had a point," Playfair answers. "Of course, he carried it a bit too far. He thought that every windmill was a giant. That's insane. But, thinking that they might be, well. . . . All the best minds used to think the world was flat. But what if it isn't? It might be round. And bread mold might be medicine. If we never looked at things and thought of what might be, why, we'd all still be out there in the tall grass with the apes."

We know you didn't sign up for a course in comparative literature, but we want to end the book with something hopeful, something that lets you know that you have some choices to make. One of those choices is to keep on saying, "They might be giants" and keep on checking even if it makes you feel out of step, out of balance.

It's OK to be a little unbalanced. Anyone looking behind the curtain of his or her culture is going to feel uncomfortable and unbalanced. Most of our cultures these days tell us to accept unfairness. We're telling you that you don't have to. We're telling you that for the good of our species, none of us *should* accept it.

We once had the pleasure of hearing the author John Nichols speak. He's the guy who wrote *The Milagro Beanfield War* and other books that we've enjoyed reading because they help us see things clearly. This is what he said:

> You eat right, you exercise, and you still die. Everyone dies, but the point is to enjoy life. The sun goes nova and the history of the planet and the sun is a blink of an eye in time. It's equal to the life of a mosquito. In the final analysis everything is hopeless.
>
> Capitalism and so on. Any hope? You just keep on struggling.

If we keep telling you how the world sucks, there's not much place for hope. So we're saying, yeah, the world sucks, but make it a better place. Keep struggling. It's funny that to find so many heroes we have to go to fiction or myth. But we don't always have to resort to fiction. We can point to real-life heroes like Ken Riley or Emma Goldman or Eleanor Roosevelt or Martin Luther

King Jr. or Gandhi. Some people see Barack Obama as a present-day hero, and certainly his rise from working-class kid from a single-parent home to the first black president of the United States has been heroic. But he would be the first to tell you not to count on any heroes coming along, that to change things requires us all to get together and work together. But we also know that to make people heroes is only to tell part of their stories. They were just ordinary people forced to do extraordinary things. You can look inside yourself to that part of you that knows that it should be a fair world and discover the extraordinary things you will do.

You've learned why the world isn't fair and how it got that way. We're telling you now that it's up to you to make a difference. Most of us live in societies where we can still vote. A lot of Americans are pissed off with the one-party system we have to endure, the Republocrats, but we can still participate in one of its branches and try to get better nominees for offices. What would happen if everyone in the United States voted for their own interests? For the fair thing? It has happened once or twice in American history. During the Great Depression, for example, when the Republocrat bosses were shaking in their boots because it looked like there might be a revolution in the streets, they put up Franklin Delano Roosevelt with his New Deal. But the powers that be have been dismantling the New Deal ever since, hoping we'd all be too busy being good consumers or just trying to stay afloat to notice.

Could Americans do it again? Could we rock the boat enough to make them play fair for a while? This is a question that shook apart the United Farm Workers in the 1980s and shook apart the whole labor movement in the summer of 2005. Shall we use our time and resources on politics and trying to get good folks elected? Or do we organize our power in the workplaces by getting more people into unions and working for their own interests directly at work and not even play the corporation political game of who buys which politician? And it's harder than it's ever been with corporate control of our media limiting the choices we hear and see every day and the Internet causing a silo effect of what news we get and where we get it from. It will be up to your generation to tackle the ethnographic challenges the Internet presents.

Ultimately, to change the status quo requires one thing: organizing. If you'd like to learn more about organizing, go to the Web site for the Organizing Institute of the American Federation of Labor–Congress of Industrial Organizations (AFL-CIO). You can sign up anywhere in the country. You can go to a seminar for a couple of days to learn what organizers do in the labor movement. If you like what you see and they like what they see, you can learn more and then get a job with a union. It'll pay wages and have benefits.

If unions don't trip your trigger, there are many other social action organizations, from social justice to environmental to peace and more, where you can train as an organizer. One well-respected community organizer training opportunity is the Industrial Areas Foundation, which you can read more about at http://www.industrialareasfoundation.org/. It's not a job for family people, as Suzan can tell you. She's done it. But it gets you in touch with people. It's all there. You experience everything from crushing defeat to

WHAT DOES ANTHROPOLOGY HAVE TO SAY ABOUT SOCIAL MEDIA AND ACTIVISM?

John Postill
RMIT University
Melbourne
Author of *Freedom Technologists and Political Change in an Age of Protest.* Forthcoming. See http://rmit.academia.edu/JohnPostill/

21 November 2014

In the Spring of 2011 I took a short break from anthropological fieldwork among internet activists in Barcelona (Catalonia, Spain) to visit friends and family in Madrid, where I was raised. In a bar near the centre, over cold beers and tapas, I was introduced to a group of middle-aged, mid-tech bookish people. When they learned I was living in Barcelona, the unavoidable subject of Catalonia's national aspirations, which most Madrileños adamantly oppose, was raised.

Thankfully the subject soon changed to my research. Although I tried my best to explain what I was doing, I felt I was not getting through. When I reported, for instance, about the marches calling for "Real democracy now!" to be held across Spain that coming 15 May, I only got blank stares. The same happened when I explained how organisers were heavy users of social media, or when I talked about the close link between the planned marches and earlier online protests to defend the rights of internet users.

There was one exception: a man in his early 50s with an IT background did "get" what I was talking about. He had followed events closely via social media and knew about the #15M demonstrations and their internet activism roots. This man spoke my language. Not the language of Madrid's mainstream media, but rather the language of Spain's (including Catalonia's) online activism scene.

Then it struck me. For the past nine months I had been so fully immersed in the world of internet activism that my take on current affairs was coming from a small corner of Spain's media landscape. More importantly, so was that of my research participants. We were all living in what I call a "viral reality," the hybrid making and sharing of news by media professionals and amateurs via social media.

This experience got me thinking about the need for a more anthropological, i.e. more holistic, understanding of present-day media, one in which we question the assumption that "new" media are replacing "old" media. As a number of media scholars have argued, instead of replacement we have the co-existence and uneven mixing of countless media formats. The challenge for activists and academics alike is how to grasp this dynamic, rapidly changing complexity.

What can the anthropology of media offer towards this collaborative effort? First, we can offer first-hand experiences of immersion in small media worlds followed by unexpected "aha" moments of realising their inescapable specificity, like the one I had in Madrid. Second, we can "follow" hybrid media actors such as Spain's Ada Colau or Malaysia's Jeff Ooi, both activists turned politicians who have learned how to work across media platforms to reach new publics. Third, anthropologists have studied

What does anthropology have to say about social media and activism? *continued*

dynamic political systems for many decades in places as diverse as Highland Burma, urban Zambia and rural Mexico. We now need to connect this rich tradition to the study of digitally mediated political conflict instead of jumping on the latest bandwagon. Finally, we most definitely need to get politically involved. As Spain's 15M (indignados) protesters are wont to say, this is only the beginning. There is far more techno-political change in the making than mainstream news of the rise and fall of protest movements from Wall Street to Hong Kong would suggest.

exhilarating victory. You'll work your ass off. You'll learn more than you ever thought you could. And you'll be doing good work. No matter what, you'll walk away with the skills to change the way things are, and you'll carry with you the insights you've learned from anthropology to help guide your way. Another way you can get a start is by signing up with Americorps and seeing some faces of our land you haven't seen before. Or you can go overseas with the Peace Corps.

A former head of the Chicago Coalition for the Homeless was talking to Suzan one day. He was exasperated with a new batch of organizers he had hired. They had gone out to the homeless shelters, as organizers are supposed to do in their first few weeks, and had come back to him complaining about the treatment of the homeless people at these shelters. The food wasn't good. The bedding wasn't comfortable. The places weren't safe. He told Suzan he looked at those organizers and said, "Our job is not to make the homeless shelters better. Our job is to get rid of the need for homeless shelters."

At Penn State the fraternities and sororities needed some reason to exist beyond the usual partying. Some genius hit on the idea of putting together something that everyone loves or has to say they love—kids—with something everyone hates—cancer. Kids with cancer. Beat that for a cause. Raise money for them and you have the reason for being. So they put together an organization to produce a dance marathon every year and raise several millions of dollars to help the families of kids with cancer. That's a great thing to do. (Of course Penn State takes a huge chunk of that for "overhead.") Now think of what they could accomplish if they changed the mission just a little and started thinking about why there are any kids with cancer that need help. That doesn't happen in societies with good health-care systems. It doesn't happen in Sweden or Iceland or Canada. What would happen if these students put all of that energy behind getting the same kind of health-care system for our kids and addressing the root causes of many health problems in the environment?

Answers depend on the questions. The question is not "Isn't a factory job for pennies a day a better alternative for third world people than no job at all?" The question is "Should anyone have to work in a factory? Should anyone have to work for pennies a day?" or "Should some people get access to all the land and others get thrown off the land and forced into factories or the streets?"

What do you have to do with those distant people dispossessed of their land who have to work in miserable factory jobs? There may be a chapter of United Students against Sweatshops on your campus. You can see what they're about at http://www.studentsagainstsweatshops.org/. If you have a chapter, you can go to a meeting and see what people at your university or college are doing from the consumer side of things. If there's not a chapter, you can start one. You can ask your anthropology instructor to sponsor the group or help you out. She's probably seen some of those sweatshops and knows some of the workers.

This is the kind of view anthropology can give you. This is the difference you can make. We all face situations where we can do one thing or another. We know the right thing to do, and we also know that it's not the thing that pays off best or the thing that we're "supposed" to do. We're telling you it's OK: do the right thing. Do the fair thing.

So in part, we're appealing to the Zorro, the Wonder Woman, the Xena, and the Superman in all of you. We're appealing to the Don Quixote in you, too. But we're saying be sure to check whether those really are giants. Use all of your knowledge and skill to find out what's really going on. Don't break your lances on windmills, but be willing to see those windmills in a new way. And be willing to call them giants if that's what they turn out to be.

The problem with hero stories is that one hero always comes to save the day for a group of people. The people in those stories never think they could organize themselves and work together to solve the problem themselves. They don't know the strength of their own numbers and their own intelligence. They wait around to be saved. They look for a hero and sure enough, in the stories, the hero comes and saves the day.

Many of Paul's former students never waited for their heroes. Instead, they let their inner heroes out. They have become union organizers and community organizers. They spend their lives bringing people together to make their living and working conditions better. Some have gone on to become religious leaders as their way of improving their communities. Suzan and Paul spend their time these days improving the health of a former farm and teaching young people who come through how to do the same, learning as much as they teach! If you'd like to join them, check the Worldwide Opportunities in Organic Farming, https://wwoofusa.org/ , and get in touch.

And they are organizing a statewide group to protect farmland to be used for growing healthy food, making it more affordable to the next generation of farmers. Other former students have become social workers and marketing professionals, artists and writers. The stories they tell are laced with how their anthropological background has helped them understand the world around them and the people in it. Still others have followed Paul into academia and become professors.

The work of these people is infused with compassion that leads them forward, with an understanding that we are all inexorably connected and that no one person's way of making sense of that world is the only right one. They understand the larger systems in which they live. They know that even if they know the nicest people, those people are part of a cruel and unjust system that serves a few at the cost of the many and that each day they can do one thing to change that equation.

The Chink in *Cowgirls* has a reputation for being a prophet or holy man. Sometimes people make pilgrimages to see him. He always refuses to see them because he refuses to be anyone's prophet. He says that by turning them away, he's setting them free before they become disciples. He says:

> *All a person can do in this life is to gather about him his integrity, his imagination and his individuality—and with these ever with him, out front and in sharp focus, leap into the dance of experience.*
> *"Be your own master!*
> *"Be your own Jesus!*
> *"Be your own flying saucer! Rescue yourself.*
> *"Be your own valentine! Free the heart!" (Robbins, 1977, p. 260)*

So we say don't wait for some hero to show up. And don't wait to be famous either. We don't know who made the first tool. We don't know who walked first on two feet or planted the first crop. They're the ones who started it all. Everyone since then is just a footnote. Einstein? He's nothing compared to that first chopping tool. Attila the Hun? Genghis Khan? Alexander the Great? Who figured out a person could ride a horse? It's better if you're remembered by the group you belong to or the place you live. But organize that group so it can move the world.

Knowing you can make a difference, any difference, will give you hope, strength, and purpose.

That's what it is to be human.

Suggested Reading
Robbins, Tom. *Even Cowgirls Get the Blues.* New York: Bantam, 1977.

Glossary

Acephalous: without a head. A term British anthropologists used to describe egalitarian societies.

Adaptive: biologically speaking, a feature that lets more offspring survive and grow up to reproduce; culturally speaking, a feature that promotes the survival and well-being of most of the people in the system so it can continue.

Agency: the ability to make real choices. Agency depends on the choices systems make available as well as your position and power in the system. More power means more choices. But no matter where you are in any system, you have some choices.

Applied anthropology: the use of analyses and insights that anthropologists develop to solve practical problems for industry, government, social movements, or the military.

Archaeology: the field of anthropology that concentrates on gathering and interpreting material evidence we can use to understand the histories of our cultures. The nature of the evidence demands certain techniques, for instance, of excavation, but archaeologists are asking and helping to answer the same questions about cultural processes that cultural anthropologists are asking and answering, so there's a lot of interchange between archaeology and sociocultural anthropology. Many see them as the same thing but using different sources of evidence.

Aspiration: the puff of breath after a consonant: for example, after the *p* in *pit*.

We use a superscript *h* to represent this sound.

Asymmetrical redistribution: redistributive exchange in which the center people do not give away everything received, but keep some of it to support themselves, their relatives, or specialists. See **redistribution; rank.**

Balanced reciprocity: People give exactly as much as they receive and receive exactly as much as they give.

Biological anthropology: the field of anthropology that focuses on the history of our species, how we came to be the kinds of animals we are, and the role of culture in the process—questions about our biological nature and its relationship to culture.

Blaming the victim: when people blame destructive or malicious acts by others on the person on the receiving end. For instance, "If you didn't want to get injured, you shouldn't have gone to Iraq."

Capital: the money that buys the things someone needs to produce exchange values, to produce commodities to sell on markets to get the capital back plus some profit.

Capitalist system: system of production to produce **exchange value** and extract **profit** that is organized by markets.

Classes: groups of people in a political economy defined by their differential access to resources in a stratified system. See **stratification; political economy; state.**

Cline: what is created when all the points of the same elevation are connected. By extension, the line we create whenever we connect all of the dots in a diagram that are the same—for instance, barometric pressure on a weather map. It shows the distribution of a single value for a variable.

Commodity: something that people can buy and sell on a market.

Comparative: noticing and explaining similarities and differences among many different systems.

Core: the rock left in one's hand after breaking off a flake with a hammerstone to make a pebble tool.

Corporatist state: See **welfare state**.

Cross cousins: the children of ego's parent's siblings of the opposite sexes: father's sister's kids and mother's brother's kids.

Cultural adaptation: the way people solve problems. The solutions don't always work in the long run. The solutions may cause new problems or make old ones worse.

Cultural capital: a misleading metaphor for everything you know that might be of use to you in making a living. This is a misleading metaphor meant to convince people that everyone has some capital and that if you're not rich, it's because you haven't used your capital well. See the definition of *capital*. See also **blaming the victim**; **meritocratic individualism**; **deficit theory**. We say that cultural capital is not capital. It's knowledge.

Cultural codes: emic categories and the way people use them to make sense of their worlds and decide what to do.

Culture core: the social, political, and religious patterns most closely connected to the way people get their livings, central aspects of the culture.

Cultural ecology: an approach in anthropology that emphasizes that although all of the elements of a culture are interrelated, the parts that have most to do with the way people make

their livings, the cultural core, are the most important and determine the rest.

Cultural relativity: suspending judgments and opinions and being open to understanding other ways of life. We don't ask whether something is good or bad; we ask how the people understand and use it.

Deficit theory: the theory that if a particular group of people don't do something well, then something is wrong with those people. Often used to justify racism. Akin to **blaming the victim**. "You're experiencing this problem because something's wrong with you."

Dependent variable: a variable that hangs on, or depends on, other variables in the system. It is the thing we want to explain. The other values of the other variables determine the value of the dependent variable.

Descriptive relativism: suspending your natural ethnocentrism so that you can describe another culture from the point of view of the people in it.

Drudgery: how much a person doesn't want to work anymore. The drudgery of labor depends on how important it is to produce whatever the people are working to produce.

Ecology: the total web of relationships among life forms in an area.

Economic capital: that which corporations convert into profit using labor. See **capital**.

Economic system: the relationships of consumption, production, and exchange so that if one changes, the others also change.

Egalitarian: a political form in which there are as many positions of prestige as people capable of filling them. All have equal access to resources. See **acephelous**. Associated with reciprocal exchanges.

Emic: the differences that make a difference inside the culture or language. Those features of the world or sounds that cultures or languages define and recognize.

Epistemological relativity: the idea that all ways of knowing things are equally true.

Epistemology: how we know things. Different cultures define different ways of knowing things. A set of assumptions that governs what and how we think and how we see the world and act within it. Cultures are epistemologies.

Ethical relativism: the idea that there are no absolute values of good and bad; ethical judgments depend on the culture.

Ethnocentric: displaying **ethnocentrism**.

Ethnocentrism: thinking that your way of doing things is either the only way or the best way. The opposite of **cultural relativity**.

Ethnographic: basing our ideas of how any given system works on detailed local description and observation. Being with the people we want to understand and seeing things from their point of view.

Ethnography: living with a people and observing everything they do and say. See **ethnographic**.

Etic: all the differences that anyone outside the system can see. People inside the system may not see it the same way, but if we only valued the inside views, we could never compare different systems. The etic stance lets us stand outside any culture to understand them all.

Exchange value: value determined by the amount of labor it takes to produce something. How much you can get for something if you trade it for another thing.

Exponential: every time the value of something is increased on the horizontal axis, the value on the vertical axis gets bigger by doubling or by squaring or by *multiplying* by some value instead of by always *adding* the same amount. So the bigger it gets, the faster it gets bigger.

Federal system: a group of groups in which each member group recognizes a central authority. For instance, each state in the United States recognizes the authority of the U.S. government. But each state retains certain powers and rights.

Feuds: fights between groups of people who are usually related, often started out of vengeance.

Fieldwork: living with the people. See **ethnography**.

Firms: production units of **capitalist systems**.

Free labor: people who are available to work for wages because they have no alternatives, such as household production, or are not caught up in alternative systems of production, such as slavery.

General reciprocity: giving to or helping others without any specific expectation of return, but with a general expectation that others will help you or give to you when you need it.

Hegemony: when one country rules or controls others. A term often used by anthropologists for when one group has control over another, especially by controlling the way they think. For instance, some say that the rulers have hegemony over the cultural codes of the ruled because the rulers shape the way people think in schools, media, and religious institutions.

Holism: seeing things as connected. Instead of looking at religion, literature, politics, economics, or history as separate spheres of life, anthropologists see them as connected.

Household production: production units based on the balance of need and drudgery.

Ideologies: almost a synonym for **cultural codes** when they are used for political ends. When ideologies are political—conservatism, liberalism—the people select parts of their cultural code to support one political position.

Import substitution: substituting your own products for imports.

Incest prohibition: a prohibition on having sex with certain relatives.

Independent variable: the variable that causes or has something to do with the dependent variable. A change in the value of an independent variable causes a change in dependent variables.

Individual transferable quotas (ITQs): quotas based on the history of a fisher's catch in the past that can be bought or sold.

Interdependent variables: when an increase or decrease in the value of one variable creates an increase or decrease in another and the second variable, the interdependent one, passes it on to a third.

Kindreds: the group of all relatives within a certain genealogical distance who are related by any link at all—for instance, all first cousins.

Lineages: a group of people all related to a common ancestor through either the link with women or the link with men.

Linguistic anthropology: the field of anthropology that studies the nature of language and how it is related to the rest of culture.

Loop: following a series of arrows in a system brings you back to the starting point.

Marginal utility: the usefulness of the next thing compared with the one before.

Market exchange: exchanging things in terms of exchange value. Usually involves money.

Markets: places where things are exchanged; the exchange of things according to **exchange values**.

Matrilineal lineages: a group of people descended from the same ancestor through women.

Matrilocal (also uxorilocal): residing with the wife's people.

Meritocratic individualism: the belief that we are separate individuals who think for ourselves and that we get rewarded according to our individual merit.

Mind control: See **thought control**.

Nationalism: when a nation claims to be the best one.

Natural capital: a misleading metaphor for natural resources, like coal and iron ore, that someone has access to. This is a metaphor used to make people think that natural resources are really a kind of capital. Compare with the definition of *capital.*

Natural selection: the process by which those characteristics that allow individuals to have more offspring become more widely spread in the population (selected for) and those that allow individuals to have fewer offspring become rarer (selected against). See **adaptive**.

Necessary labor: the amount of labor to produce necessary value, the value necessary to reproduce the same amount of labor.

Necessary value: the amount of value that necessary labor produces. Capitalist firms pay this amount as wages so that workers can continue to work and reproduce labor.

Negative utility: a metaphor based on the idea of utility as usefulness. Negative usefulness would be something damaging.

Neoconservatives: people who believe in an ideology that advocates a global market policed and controlled by American arms for American objectives.

Neolocal: residing in a different place from the family of either mate.

Parallel cousins: the children of the parent's siblings of the same sex: father's brothers and mother's sister's kids.

Patrilineal lineages: a group of people of the same ancestor linked through the men.

Patrilocal (also virilocal): residing with the husband's people.

Phoneme: each distinct sound that any human language understands as different from other sounds. Different languages recognize different sounds.

Each language uses between thirteen and forty of them.

Phonemic: as of or pertaining to phonemes. A phonemic system is the set of sounds the native speakers actually hear and distinguish as distinct.

Phonetics: all the sounds people can actually make. People put different phonetic sounds together to make single phonemes, like *t*s and *t*h and *p* and *p*h in English.

Political economy: the interacting economic and political systems.

Polymorphic: of many forms.

Price: largely but not exclusively determined by value. May be higher or lower depending on such factors as fashion.

Profit: surplus value that the owners of capital appropriate and may put back into production or into political action or consumption.

Qualitative: something that cannot be counted, quantified; for example, how good the smell of baking bread is when you smell it on an evening walk in the fall.

Quantitative: something that can be counted; for example, the number of molecules of bread you must inhale before you can detect the smell of baking bread.

Rank: a political form in which there is equal access to resources but fewer positions of prestige than people capable of filling them. Associated with redistributive exchange.

Reciprocity: giving as much as you get, at least in the long run. There's usually a time delay between the giving and the getting.

Redistribution: based on reciprocity, but instead of people giving things directly to each other, giving things to some central person, who then redistributes them to the people who need them.

Redistributive system: a system of exchange based on redistribution.

Regulating mechanism: a part of the system that keeps the values of variables within certain limits.

Reliability: the notion that everybody else who checks the same thing will get the same results.

Residence rule: a pattern of where newly married couples live.

Revitalization movements: arise to quickly reorient peoples' cultural codes when their experiences do not match their expectations, often when foreigners have taken control, as in colonial situations, usually involving a prophet and a vision.

Ruling class: that class in a stratified political economy that has access to resources. See **classes; political economy; stratification; state**.

Science: the epistemology that we never accept anything as really true, just as what we *think* we know until we find out differently by checking it over and over again against what we can observe. Science is based on **reliability** and **validity** as well as the assumptions that we base theories on. When valid and reliable observations don't match theories, we change the theories.

Self-help: if someone has done you harm, you harm that person back. See **feuds**. This may mean not harming the same individual but harming his or her kinship group, village, or other social group.

Self-intensifying loop: See **loop**. In a system without a regulating mechanism, each trip through the loop makes the values of the variables get greater. See also **exponential**.

Shaman: a person spirits can possess.

Social capital: a misleading metaphor for the people someone knows who can help when needed. The idea is that social relations can help people. But the metaphor is misleading because it's meant to convince us that we all have some kind of capital even if we don't because we all have some social relations that can be useful to us. See **capital; blaming the victim; meritocratic individualism; deficit theory**.

Social contract: the idea that people support their governments when the governments actually help the people.

Sociocultural anthropology: the field of anthropology that studies how contemporary cultures and societies work and how they got this way.

State: the institutional structures in stratified political economies that enforce and ensure unequal access to resources. Based on force or **thought control** or both. See **stratification; hegemony; ruling class; subordinate classes**.

Stratification: a political economy in which there is unequal access to resources. See **state**.

Structure: how things are put together with other similar things. Grammatical structure is how elements of language relate to each other so we can connect sounds to meanings. Kinship structure is how different kinds of kin-based groups are organized. Political structure is how different aspects of political systems are organized (see **federal system; welfare state**). Economic structure is how parts of economic systems are put together. As a general term, it means how things are organized. See **agency**. Agency is our own sense of control and ability to decide. Structure is outside our immediate control, although we can change it with concerted effort.

Subordinate classes: those classes in stratified political economies that do not have access to resources. See **stratification; classes; political economy; state**.

Surplus labor: the amount of labor people do after they've produced the value necessary for them to work another day and reproduce. To get people to do it, you must have a system that doesn't allow them any other alternatives, often based on force.

Surplus value: the extra value that **surplus labor** produces, the source of **profit** in capitalist systems.

Sustainable: a system that does not have a **self-intensifying loop** and can continue in operation indefinitely.

Swidden: slash-and-burn fields.

System: a set of elements connected such that if you change one of them, you change the others.

Thought control: ruling-class control of cultural codes to make people think their political economy is natural and inevitable, ordained by gods or history as the only possible political economy and to make people think they have little or no agency to use in changing the system. See **classes; ruling class; subordinate classes; state; hegemony; agency; structure**.

Use value: the value of things because of the need they fill.

Validity: means that you're really measuring what you think you are measuring.

Variable: something that can be more or less; it varies.

Wages: the amount that firms pay people for working. It must equal the amount of value it takes to continue to work and reproduce labor (see **necessary value**). Historically, people do not work for wages unless there are no alternatives. In return for allowing the people who get necessary value for wages for their work to work, firms expect workers to produce more than that amount (see **surplus value**), which is the source of profits.

Welfare state (also corporatist state): a government in which businesses, labor, professionals with technical knowledge and experience, and government officials all negotiate together to make policies that benefit everyone. For instance, farmers, agribusinesses, the department of agriculture, and the people who elected officials appoint in a ministry of agriculture would all negotiate together to make agricultural policy. Everyone has a voice through such organizations. The usual examples are Sweden and other Scandinavian countries.

References

Apostle, Richard A., Gene Barrett, Peter Holm, Svein Jentoft, Leigh Mazany, Knut Mikalsen, and Bonnie McCay
1998 *Community, State, and Market on the North Atlantic Rim: Challenges to Modernity in the Fisheries.* Toronto: University of Toronto Press.

Arnason, Ragnar
2008 "Iceland's ITQ System Creates New Wealth." *The Electronic Journal of Sustainable Development* Vol. 1, No. 2: 35–41.

Bakan, Joel
2004 *The Corporation: The Pathological Pursuit of Profit and Power.* New York: Free Press.

Beckford, George L.
1972 *Persistent Poverty: Underdevelopment in Plantation Economies of the Third World.* New York: Oxford University Press. (Reissued 2000, Kingston: University of West Indies Press.)

Bell, Kirsten
2005 "Genital Cutting and Western Discourses on Sexuality." *Medical Anthropology Quarterly* Vol. 19, No. 2: 125–148.

Bennett, Matthew R., John W. K. Harris, Brian G. Richmond, David R. Braun, Emma Mbua, Purity Kiura, Daniel Olago, Mzalendo Kibunjia, Christine Omuombo, Anna K. Behrensmeyer, David Huddart, and Silvia Gonzalez
2009 "Early Hominin Foot Morphology Based on 1.5-Million-Year-Old Footprints from Ileret, Kenya." *Science* Vol. 323, No. 5918 (February 27): 1197–1201.

Bigelow, Gordon

2005 "Let There Be Markets." *Harper's Magazine* Vol. 310, No. 1860 (May): 33–38.

Bonanno, Alessandro, and Douglas Constance
1996 *Caught in the Net: The Global Tuna Industry, Environmentalism, and the State.* Lawrence: University Press of Kansas.

Brodkin, Karen
1988 *Caring by the Hour: Women, Work and Organizing at Duke Medical Center.* Urbana: University of Illinois Press.
2000 "Global Capitalism: What's Race Got to Do with It?" *American Ethnologist* Vol. 27, No. 2: 237–256.

Chayanov, A. V.
1986 *The Theory of Peasant Economy.* Madison: University of Wisconsin Press.

Collier, George A., with Elizabeth Lowery Quaratiello
1994 *Basta! Land and the Zapatista Rebellion in Chiapas.* Oakland, CA: Food First Books.

Conklin, H. C.
1954 *The Relation of Hanunóo Culture to the Plant World.* Doctoral dissertation, Yale University, New Haven, CT.
1957 *Hanunóo Agriculture. A Report on an Integral System of Shifting Cultivation in the Philippines.* Rome, Food and Agricultural Organization of the United Nations.

Drori, Israel
2000 *The Seam Line: Arab Workers and Jewish Managers in the Israeli Textile Industry.* Stanford, CA: Stanford University Press.

Doukas, Dimitra

2003 *Worked Over: The Corporate Sabotage of an American Community.* Ithaca, NY: Cornell University Press.

Durrenberger, E. Paul
1989 *Lisu Religion.* DeKalb: Northern Illinois University Center for Southeast Asian Studies.
1992 *The Dynamics of Medieval Iceland: Political Economy and Literature.* Iowa City: University of Iowa Press.

Durrenberger, E. Paul, and Dimitra Doukas
2008 "Gospel of Wealth, Gospel of Work: Counterhegemony in the U.S. Working Class." *American Anthropologist* Vol. 110, No. 2: 214–224.

Durrenberger, E. Paul, and Suzan Erem
2005 *Class Acts: An Anthropology of Service Workers and Their Union.* Boulder, CO: Paradigm.

Ehrenreich, Barbara
1990 *Fear of Falling: The Inner Life of the Middle Class.* New York: Perennial.
2001 *Nickel and Dimed: On (Not) Getting by in America.* New York: Metropolitan Books.
2005 *Bait and Switch: The (Futile) Pursuit of the American Dream.* New York: Metropolitan Books.

Ekvall, Robert
1968 *Fields on the Hoof: Nexus of Tibetan Nomadic Pastoralism.* New York: Holt, Rinehart & Winston.

Elliston, Deborah A.
1995 "Erotic Anthropology: 'Ritualized Homosexuality' in Melanesia and Beyond." *American Ethnologist* Vol. 22, No. 4: 848–867.

Emihovich, Catherine
2005 "Fire and Ice: Activist Ethnography in the Culture of Power." *Anthropology and Education Quarterly* Vol. 36, No. 4: 305–314.

Erem, Suzan
2001 *Labor Pains: Inside America's New Union Movement.* New York: Monthly Review Press.

Evans-Pritchard, E. E.
1949 *The Sanusi of Cyrenaica.* Oxford: Clarendon Press.

Fink, Deborah
1998 *Cutting into the Meatpacking Line: Workers and Change in the Rural Midwest.* Chapel Hill: University of North Carolina Press.

Frank, Thomas
2004 *What's the Matter with Kansas? How Conservatives Won the Heart of America.* New York: Metropolitan Books.

Galbraith, John Kenneth
1992 *The Culture of Contentment.* Boston: Houghton Mifflin.

Goldschmidt, Walter
2006 *The Bridge to Humanity: How Affect Hunger Trumps the Selfish Gene.* New York: Oxford University Press.

Goodenough, Ward H.
1956 "Residence Rules." *Southwestern Journal of Anthropology* Vol. 12, No. 1: 22–37.

Guðmundsson, Einar Már
2009 *A War Cry from the North. Counter Punch.* February 23, 2009. http://www.counterpunch.org/2009/02/23/

Hanks, Lucien
1972 *Rice and Man: Agricultural Ecology in Southeast Asia.* Chicago: Aldine–Atherton.

Harris, Marvin
1971 *Culture, Man, and Nature: An Introduction to General Anthropology.* New York: Crowell.
1974 *Cows, Pigs, Wars, and Witches: The Riddles of Culture.* New York: Random House.

Henry, Jules
1963 *Culture against Man.* New York: Random House.

Heyman, Josiah McC.
1991 *Life and Labor on the Border: Working People of Northeastern Sonora, Mexico, 1886–1986.* Tucson: University of Arizona Press.

Hockett, Charles
1973 *Man's Place in Nature.* New York: McGraw–Hill.

Holmes, Nigel, and Megan McCardle
2008 "Iceland's Meltdown: An Economic Morality Play in 10 Acts." *The Atlantic* (December).

Jablonski, Nina G.
2008 *Skin: A Natural History*. Berkeley: University of California Press.

Jolly, Alison
1972 *The Evolution of Primate Behavior*. New York: Macmillan.

Lapham, Lewis H.
2004 "Tentacles of Rage: The Republican Propaganda Mill, a Brief History." *Harper's* 309 (September).

Lave, Jean
1988 *Cognition in Practice: Mind, Mathematics and Culture in Everyday Life*. New York: Cambridge University Press.

Leach, Edmund
1954 *Political Systems of Highland Burma*. Boston: Beacon.

Lewis, I. M.
2003 *Ecstatic Religion: A Study of Shamanism and Spirit Possession*. 3d ed. New York: Routledge.

Lewis, Michael
2009 "Wall Street on the Tundra." *Vanity Fair* (April): 140–147.

Lowie, Robert H.
1948 *Primitive Religion*. New York: Liveright.

Malinowski, Bronisław
1922 *Argonauts of the Western Pacific: An Account of Native Enterprise and Adventure in the Archipelagoes of Melanesian New Guinea*. Long Grove, IL: Waveland Press (reprinted).

Mead, Margaret
1950 *Sex and Temperament in Three Primitive Societies*. New York: Mentor.

Mills, Mary Beth
1999 *Thai Women in the Global Labor Force: Consuming Desires, Contested Selves*. New Brunswick, NJ: Rutgers University Press.

Montoya, Miguel
2002 "Emerging Markets, Globalization, and the Small Investor: The Case of Venezuela." In *Economic Development: An Anthropological Approach*, edited by J. H. Cohen and N. Dannhaeuser. Walnut Creek, CA: AltaMira. Pages 265–289.

Montoya, Monica Lindh de

2002 "Looking into the Future: Anthropology and Financial Markets." In *Economic Development: An Anthropological Approach*, edited by J. H. Cohen and N. Dannhaeuser. Walnut Creek, CA: AltaMira. Pages 241–264.

Nash, June
2001 *Mayan Visions: The Quest for Autonomy in an Age of Globalization*. New York: Routledge.

Newman, Katherine
1993 *Declining Fortunes: The Withering of the American Dream*. New York: Basic Books.

1999 *No Shame in My Game: The Working Poor in the Inner City*. New York: Knopf.

Ngai, Pun
2005 *Made in China: Women Factory Workers in a Global Workplace*. Durham, NC: Duke University Press.

Nichols, John
1974 *The Milagro Beanfield War*. New York: Holt, Rinehart & Winston.

Orwell, George
1952 *Homage to Catalonia*. New York: Harcourt, Brace. (Originally published in 1938 by Secker & Warburg, London.)

Pálsson, Gísli
1989 "Language and Society: The Ethnolinguistics of Icelanders." In *The Anthropology of Iceland* edited by E. Paul Durrenberger and Gísli Pálsson. Iowa City: University of Iowa Press. Pages 121–139.

Rappaport, Roy
1967 *Pigs for the Ancestors: Ritual in the Ecology of a New Guinea People*. New Haven, CT: Yale University Press.

Reed, Adolph
2001 *Class Notes: Posing as Politics and Other Thoughts on the American Scene*. New York: New Press.

Richardson, Miles
1975 "Anthropologist—The Myth Teller." *American Ethnologist* Vol. 2, No. 3: 517–533.

Robbins, Tom

1977 *Even Cowgirls Get the Blues. New York: Bantam.*

Saez, Emmanuel, and Gabriel Zuchman
2014 "Exploding Wealth Inequality in the United States." Center for Economic Policy Research. *Vox* 28 October 2014. http://www.voxeu.org/

Sahlins, Marshall
1968 "Culture and Environment: The Study of Cultural Ecology." In *Theory in Anthropology: A Sourcebook*, edited by Robert A. Manners and David Kaplan. Chicago, Aldine. Pages 367–373.
1989 *Social Stratification in Polynesia.* American Ethnological Society Monographs No. 29. Brooklyn: AMS Press.

Schlosser, Eric
2002 *Fast Food Nation: The Dark Side of the All-American Meal.* New York: Harper.

Scott, James
1985 *Weapons of the Weak: Everyday Forms of Peasant Resistance.* New Haven, CT: Yale University Press.

Spiro, Melford
1966 "Religion: Problems of Definition and Explanation." In *Anthropological Approaches to the Study of Religion* edited by Michael Banton. New York: Tavistock. Pages 85–126.
1991 *Anthropological Other or Burmese Brother? Studies in Cultural Analysis.* Somerset, NJ: Transaction.
1996 *Burmese Supernaturalism.* New Brunswick, NJ: Transaction. (This is a reissue of the expanded edition published in 1978 by the Institute for the Study of Human Issues, which was based on the original 1967 edition from Prentice Hall.)

Steward, Julian
1955 *Theory of Culture Change: The Methodology of Multilinear Evolution.* Urbana: University of Illinois Press.

Stiglitz, Joseph
2002 *Globalization and Its Discontents.* New York: Norton.

Stout, Dietrich
2008 "Technology and Human Brain Evolution." *General Anthropology* Vol. 15, No. 2 (Fall): 1–5.

Tattersall, Ian
2004 "Innovation in Human Evolution." In *The Epic of Evolution: Science and Religion in Dialogue*, edited by James B. Miller. Upper Saddle River, NJ: Pearson. Pages 91–98.

Venkatesh, Sudhir Alladi
2008 *Gang Leader for a Day.* New York: Penguin Press.

Wallace, Anthony
1956 "Revitalization Movements." *American Anthropologist* Vol. 58, No. 2: 264–281.

White, Curtis
2004 *The Middle Mind: Why Americans Don't Think for Themselves.* New York: Harper.

Williams, Brett
2004 *Debt for Sale: A Social History of the Credit Trap.* Philadelphia: University of Pennsylvania Press.

Wolf, Diane
1992 *Factory Daughters: Gender, Household Dynamics, and Rural Industrialization in Java.* Berkeley: University of California Press.

Wolf, Eric
1951 "The Social Organization of Mecca and the Origins of Islam." *Journal of Anthropological Research* Vol. 7, No. 4: 329–356.

Yates, Michael D.
2003 *Naming the System: Inequality and Work in the Global Economy.* New York: Monthly Review Press.

Zinn, Howard
2003 *A People's History of the United States: 1492–Present.* New York: Harper Collins.

Sources for Nasrudin and Sufi Stories

Ornstein, Robert
1968 *The Way of the Sufi.* London: Jonathan Cape.
1972 *The Psychology of Consciousness.* San Francisco: Freeman.
1973 *The Subtleties of the Inimitable Mulla Nasrudin.* London: Jonathan Cape.
1977 *Pleasantries of the Incredible Mulla Nasrudin.* Therford, Norfolk, UK: Lowe & Brydone.

Index